Cardiovascular and Coronary Artery Imaging

Cardiovascular and Coronary Artery Imaging

Volume 1

Edited by

AYMAN S. EL-BAZ
University of Louisville, Louisville, KY, United States;
University of Louisville at AlAlamein International
University (UofL-AIU), New Alamein City, Egypt

JASJIT S. SURI
AtheroPoint, Roseville, CA, United States

ELSEVIER

ACADEMIC PRESS
An imprint of Elsevier

Academic Press is an imprint of Elsevier
125 London Wall, London EC2Y 5AS, United Kingdom
525 B Street, Suite 1650, San Diego, CA 92101, United States
50 Hampshire Street, 5th Floor, Cambridge, MA 02139, United States
The Boulevard, Langford Lane, Kidlington, Oxford OX5 1GB, United Kingdom

Notices
Knowledge and best practice in this field are constantly changing. As new research and experience broaden our understanding, changes in research methods, professional practices, or medical treatment may become necessary.

Practitioners and researchers must always rely on their own experience and knowledge in evaluating and using any information, methods, compounds, or experiments described herein. In using such information or methods they should be mindful of their own safety and the safety of others, including parties for whom they have a professional responsibility.

To the fullest extent of the law, neither the Publisher nor the authors, contributors, or editors, assume any liability for any injury and/or damage to persons or property as a matter of products liability, negligence or otherwise, or from any use or operation of any methods, products, instructions, or ideas contained in the material herein.

British Library Cataloguing-in-Publication Data
A catalogue record for this book is available from the British Library

Library of Congress Cataloging-in-Publication Data
A catalog record for this book is available from the Library of Congress

ISBN: 978-0-12-822706-0

For Information on all Academic Press publications
visit our website at https://www.elsevier.com/books-and-journals

Publisher: Mara Conner
Acquisitions Editor: Tim Pitts
Editorial Project Manager: Mariana L. Kuhl
Production Project Manager: Surya Narayanan Jayachandran
Cover Designer: Mark Rogers

Typeset by MPS Limited, Chennai, India

Contents

2.   Technique of cardiac magnetic resonance imaging   33

Ahmed Abdel Khalek Abdel Razek, Dalia Fahmy and Germeen Albair Ashmalla

3.   The role of automated 12-lead ECG interpretation in the diagnosis and risk stratification of cardiovascular disease   45

Salah S. Al-Zaiti, Ziad Faramand, Khaled Rjoob, Dewar Finlay and Raymond Bond

8.   CT angiography of anomalous pulmonary veins   **181**

Ahmed Abdel Khalek Abdel Razek, Maha Elmansy, Mahmoud Abd El-Latif
and Hala Al-Marsafawy

12. Heart disease prediction using convolutional neural network   **245**

Ajay Sharma, Tarun Pal and Varun Jaiswal

List of contributors

Ahmed Abdel Khalek Abdel Razek
Department of Diagnostic Radiology, Faculty of Medicine, Mansoura University, Mansoura, Egypt

Olusola Adekoya
Department of Internal Medicine, Kettering Health, Kettering, OH, United States

Lakshmi Alagarsamy
Department of Physics, Mannar Thirumalai Naicker College, Pasumalai, Madurai, India

Hala Al-Marsafawy
Pediatric Cardiology Unit, Pediatrics Department, Faculty of Medicine, Mansoura University, Mansoura, Egypt

Salah S. Al-Zaiti
Departments of Acute and Tertiary Care Nursing, Emergency Medicine, and Cardiology, University of Pittsburgh, Pittsburgh, PA, United States

Chris Anthony
Section of Cardiovascular Imaging, Robert and Suzanne Tomsich Department of Cardiovascular Medicine, Sydell and Arnold Miller Family Heart, Vascular and Thoracic Institute, Cleveland Clinic, Cleveland, OH, Unites States

Germeen Albair Ashmalla
Department of Diagnostic Radiology, Faculty of Medicine, Mansoura University, Mansoura, Egypt

Mina M. Benjamin
Department of Cardiology, Loyola University Medical Center, Maywood, IL, United States

Raymond Bond
Faculty of Computing, Engineering and Built Environment, Ulster University, Coleraine, United Kingdom

Jit Brahmbhatt
Department of Cardiology, SBKS Medical College & Research Center, Piparia, India

Song Ding
Department of Cardiology, Ren Ji Hospital, School of Medicine, Shanghai Jiao Tong University, Shanghai, China

Mahmoud Abd El-Latif
Mansoura University Hospital, Mansoura, Egypt

Maha Elmansy
Department of Diagnostic Radiology, Faculty of Medicine, Mansoura University, Mansoura, Egypt

Dalia Fahmy
Department of Diagnostic Radiology, Faculty of Medicine, Mansoura University, Mansoura, Egypt

Ziad Faramand
University of Pittsburgh Medical Center (UPMC), Pittsburgh, PA, United States

Dewar Finlay
Faculty of Computing, Engineering and Built Environment, Ulster University, Coleraine, United Kingdom

Zachary Gilbert
Department of Internal Medicine, Kettering Health, Kettering, OH, United States

Varun Jaiswal
National Centre for Disease Control (NCDC), New Delhi, India; Department of Food and Nutrition, College of Bio-Nano Technology, Gachon University, Seongnam, South Korea

Mingxin Jin
Biomedical Engineering School, Shanghai Jiao Tong University, Shanghai, China

Rosaria Jordan
Wright State University, Dayton, OH, United States

Mateusz Krysiński
Silesian Center for Heart Diseases, Zabrze, Poland

Małgorzata Krysińska
Silesian Center for Heart Diseases, Zabrze, Poland

Langeswaran Kulanthaivel
Cancer Genetics & Molecular Biology Laboratory, Department of Bioinformatics, Science Campus, Alagappa University, Karaikudi, India

Paul C. Kuo
Department of Surgery, Morsani College of Medicine, University of South Florida, Tampa, FL, United States

Juan Linares
Department of Cardiovascular Disease, Kettering Health, Kettering, OH, United States; Wright State University, Dayton, OH, United States

Zeeshan Mansuri
Department of Cardiology, SBKS Medical College & Research Center, Piparia, India

Tarun Pal
Department of Biotechnology (Bioinformatics), Vignan's Foundation for Science, Technology and Research, Guntur, India

Binjie Qin
Biomedical Engineering School, Shanghai Jiao Tong University, Shanghai, China

Mark G. Rabbat
Department of Cardiology, Loyola University Medical Center, Maywood, IL, United States

Sangeetha Rajaram
Department of Physics, Mannar Thirumalai Naicker College, Pasumalai, Madurai, India

Sangeetha Ramanathan
Department of Physics, Madurai Kamaraj University, Madurai, India

Reza Reyaldeen
Section of Cardiovascular Imaging, Robert and Suzanne Tomsich Department of
Cardiovascular Medicine, Sydell and Arnold Miller Family Heart, Vascular and Thoracic
Institute, Cleveland Clinic, Cleveland, OH, Unites States

Khaled Rjoob
Faculty of Computing, Engineering and Built Environment, Ulster University, Coleraine,
United Kingdom

Michael P. Rogers
Department of Surgery, Morsani College of Medicine, University of South Florida, Tampa,
FL, United States

Brian Schwartz
Department of Cardiovascular Disease, Kettering Health, Kettering, OH, United States;
Wright State University, Dayton, OH, United States

Marco Shaker
Department of Cardiology, Loyola University Medical Center, Maywood, IL, United States

Ajay Sharma
Department of Biotechnology and Bioinformatics, Jaypee University of Information
Technology (JUIT), Solan, India; Department of Computer Science, Shoolini University,
Solan, India

Roopesh Singhal
Department of Cardiology, SBKS Medical College & Research Center, Piparia, India

Ryan Stuart
Department of Internal Medicine, Kettering Health, Kettering, OH, United States

Gowtham Kumar Subbaraj
Faculty of Allied Health Sciences, Chettinad Academy of Research and Education,
Kelambakkam, India

Ewaryst Tkacz
Faculty of Biomedical Engineering, Department of Biosensors and Processing of Biomedical
Signals, Silesian University of Technology, Zabrze, Poland

Damian Valencia
Department of Cardiovascular Disease, Kettering Health, Kettering, OH, United States;
Wright State University, Dayton, OH, United States

Oscar Valencia
Department of Biochemistry, Loyola University, Chicago, IL, United States

Sindhu Varghese
Faculty of Allied Health Sciences, Chettinad Academy of Research and Education,
Kelambakkam, India

Bo Xu
Section of Cardiovascular Imaging, Robert and Suzanne Tomsich Department of
Cardiovascular Medicine, Sydell and Arnold Miller Family Heart, Vascular and Thoracic
Institute, Cleveland Clinic, Cleveland, OH, Unites States

CHAPTER 1

Advanced coronary artery imaging: optical coherence tomography

Damian Valencia[1,2], Juan Linares[1,2], Zachary Gilbert[3], Ryan Stuart[3], Olusola Adekoya[3], Oscar Valencia[4], Rosaria Jordan[2] and Brian Schwartz[1,2]

[1]Department of Cardiovascular Disease, Kettering Health, Kettering, OH, United States
[2]Wright State University, Dayton, OH, United States
[3]Department of Internal Medicine, Kettering Health, Kettering, OH, United States
[4]Department of Biochemistry, Loyola University, Chicago, IL, United States

1.1 Introduction

Optical coherence tomography (OCT) is a low radiation imaging technique that uses nondestructive low-coherence light, typically near-infrared, to capture submicrometer resolution images within optically scattering material or biological tissues.

First presented in 1990, in vivo imaging with OCT was not achieved until 1993, primarily used by ophthalmologists to detail the retina [1]. Endoscopic use was later employed in 1997, closely followed by its regular application in cardiology in the early 2000s. Most recently, OCT has been employed in clinical practice by interventional cardiologists to obtain high-resolution images of coronary arteries. OCT has since revolutionized intracoronary imaging, upturning intravascular ultrasound (IVUS), and producing images up to 10 times higher in resolution [2,3].

At present, well-powered trials have consistently demonstrated no difference between invasive and noninvasive strategies for the management of stable coronary artery disease. New technologies aiming at enhancing the understanding of coronary plaques and their appropriate management are urgently needed. OCT has emerged as a novel tool for imaging complex vessel anatomy, plaque identification, and for planning percutaneous coronary interventions (PCIs) [4–6]. This chapter will review the mechanisms, technical aspects, clinical applications, safety, and complications pertaining to OCT.

1.2 Basic principles of light

1.2.1 Backscatter

In context to the principles of OCT, backscatter (or backscattering) refers to the reflection of light waves through a sample (coronary walls, plaques, thrombus, and stents) and back toward the OCT probe [7]. Simply put, backscatter can be thought of as the reflectivity within a penetrable sample.

Cardiovascular and Coronary Artery Imaging
DOI: https://doi.org/10.1016/B978-0-12-822706-0.00001-9

1.2.2 Attenuation

In addition to understanding backscatter, the concept of light attenuation is also critical to OCT image interpretation. Attenuation is the gradual loss of flux, specifically light intensity through a medium. The intensity of light at a specific depth can be calculated using Beer's Law, also known as the Beer–Lambert–Bouguer Law, detailed below (Eq. 1.1). This is possible through the correlation of light absorbance and sample concentration [8].

$$A = \varepsilon \ell c$$

Eq. 1.1: Beer–Lambert–Bouguer Law (Beer's Law). A is the absorbance, ε is the molar attenuation coefficient, ℓ is the optical path length, and c is the concentration of the attenuating species.

1.3 Mechanism and technical modalities of OCT

As an optical analog to IVUS, OCT employs monochromatic, low coherence, near-infrared light (wavelength of 1250–1350 nm) to penetrate biological tissues to a depth of 1–2 mm. The OCT probe then rotates (frequency of 100 revolutions/s), allowing for the acquisition of 50,000 data points in axial lines per second [9]. A Michelson interferometer (Fig. 1.1) is used to reflect light using a series of mirrors and through the tissue sample. OCT can be performed using two separate interferometer techniques, time domain and frequency domain [10]. Detection is achieved through broadband interference and partial coherence between each wave within the coherence length. Significant differences between IVUS and first-generation time-domain OCT (TD-OCT) are detailed in Table 1.1.

1.3.1 Time domain

In TD-OCT, the path length of light to the reference arm is varied to calibrated distances throughout time. The change to the reference path length allows for partially coherent light beam detection at differing tissue depths while staying within the coherence length [11] (Fig. 1.2). This process creates known, detectable, echo delays. Both the reference and sample signal are then combined in a fiber coupler, followed by detection by a photodetector.

The interference of the two partially coherent light signals can be expressed in reference to the light source intensity (I), seen below (Eq. 1.2).

$$I = k_1 I_S + k_2 I_S + 2\sqrt{(k_1 I_S \cdot k_2 I_S)} \cdot \mathrm{Re}[\gamma(\tau)]$$

Eq. 1.2: Interference of two partially coherent light signals expressed in reference to light source intensity (I). $k_1 + k_2 < 1$ represents the interferometer beam splitting ratio, $\gamma(\tau)$ is the complex degree of coherence, and τ is the time delay.

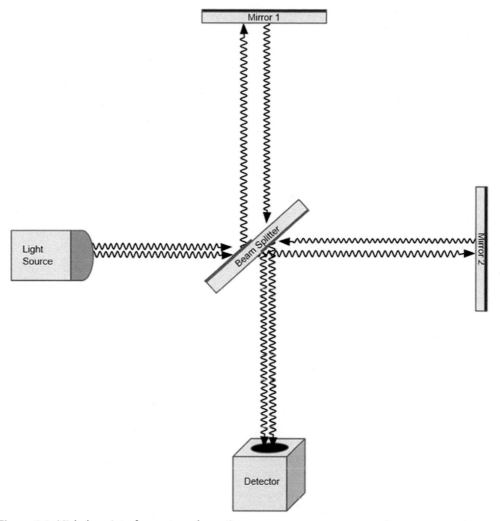

Figure 1.1 Michelson interferometer schematic.

Table 1.1 Comparison of IVUS and first-generation time-domain OCT.

Specifications	IVUS	First-generation OCT
Axial resolution (μm)	100–150	10–20
Lateral resolution (μm)	150–300	25–40
Frame rate (fps)	30	15–20
Pullback speed (mm/s)	0.5–2.0	0.5–2.0
Scan diameter (mm)	8–10	6.8
Tissue penetration (mm)	4–8	1–2
Balloon occlusion	Not Necessary	Highly recommended

IVUS, Intravascular ultrasound; OCT, optical coherence tomography.

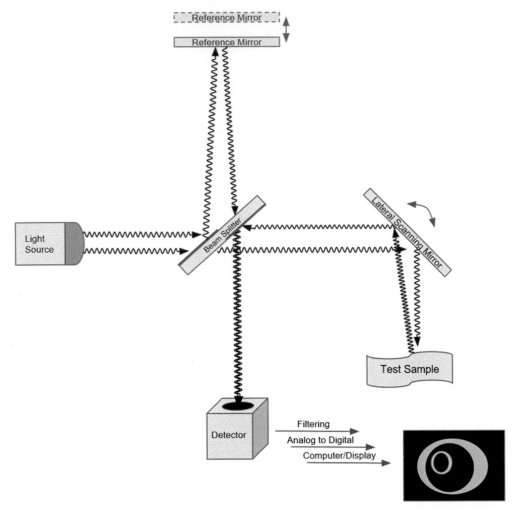

Figure 1.2 Time-domain OCT schematic. *OCT,* Optical coherence tomography.

Coherence gating relies on the principle of interpretable light wave interference, constructive or destructive, within the coherence length. Coherence is represented as a Gaussian function, seen below, where the enveloping function is amplitude modulated by an optical carrier [12]. The peak of this Gaussian enclosure represents the point location of each structure that is imaged. Signal strength (amplitude) is varied with respect to surface reflectivity (Eq. 1.3).

$$\gamma(r) = \exp\left[-\left(\frac{\pi\Delta\upsilon\tau}{2\sqrt{\ln 2}}\right)^2\right] \cdot \exp\left(-j2\pi\upsilon_0\pi\right)$$

Eq. 1.3: Coherence is represented as a Gaussian function, where the enveloping function is amplitude modulated by an optical carrier. $\Delta \nu$ represents the spectral width (of the light source) in the optical frequency domain and $\nu(0)$ is the center optical frequency of the source.

Translation of one arm within the interferometer results in a Doppler-shifted optical carrier, as well as depth scanning [13]. The Doppler-shifted optical carrier has a frequency that can be expressed in terms of frequency, detailed below (Eq. 1.4).

$$f_{\text{Dopp}} = \frac{2 \cdot v_0 \cdot v_s}{c}$$

Eq. 1.4: Doppler-shifted optical carrier frequency expressed in terms of frequency. $\nu(0)$ is the central optical frequency of the source, $v(s)$ is the scanning velocity of the path length variation, and c is the speed of light.

The axial resolution of OCT is equivalent to the coherence length of the light source. The lateral resolution can be described as a function of the optics, defined below (Eq. 1.5).

$$l_c = \frac{2\ln2}{\pi} \cdot \frac{\lambda_0^2}{\Delta\lambda}$$

$$\approx 0.44 \cdot \frac{\lambda_0^2}{\Delta\lambda}$$

Eq. 1.5: Lateral resolution as a function of the central wavelength and light source width. $\lambda(0)$ is the central wavelength and $\Delta\lambda$ is the spectral width of the light source.

First-generation coronary TD-OCT systems employed both an imaging wire and occlusion balloon, as transient occlusion of blood flow to the tissue sample was required using this method due to blood refraction artifact [14]. A flushing fluid, typically lactated ringers or normal saline, was used to substitute blood within the coronary artery at the imaging site [15]. Setup for this technique often required a high degree of clinical skill and experience. Patients can experience acute coronary syndrome (ACS) symptoms and EKG changes throughout normal saline flushing. The average duration of vascular obstruction during TD-OCT is 48.3 ± 14.7 seconds [15]. When comparing the safety of the first-generation TD-OCT to IVUS, no significant risk was appreciated. In addition to the increased image quality of coronary lumen borders, the OCT catheters are smaller and can cross narrow lesions. Later-generation TD-OCT systems use low-molecular-weight dextran, or contrast, passed through a guide to displace blood, removing the need for an occlusion balloon, and allowing less experienced operators to perform imaging [2,15].

1.3.2 Frequency domain

In frequency-domain OCT (FD-OCT), also known as Fourier-domain OCT, swept-source OCT (SS-OCT), or optical frequency-domain OCT, light wave interference is

Table 1.2 Comparison of TD-OCT and FD-OCT.

Specifications	M3 (TD-OCT)	C7-XR (FD-OCT)
Axial resolution (μm)	15—20	12—15
Lateral resolution (μm)	39	19
Frame rate (fps)	20	100
Lines/frame	240	500
Pullback speed (m/s)	0.5—2.0	10—25
Scan diameter (FOV) (mm)	6.8	10
Tissue penetration (mm)	1—2	1—2
Balloon occlusion	Highly recommended	Optional

TD-OCT, Time-domain OCT; FD-OCT, frequency-domain OCT.

achieved through spectrally separated detectors, either time encoded or spatially encoded, and variable frequency light sources. In contrast to TD-OCT, interferometric measurements are recorded as a function of optical wavelength and time. A tunable light source (sweep range of 1250—1370 nm) is used with a fixed reference mirror [2]. This change allowed for decreased scanning time with comparable image quality [16]. Reduced scanning times also decrease the risk for microvascular ischemia during flushing if performed. Significant differences between TD-OCT and FD-OCT are detailed in Table 1.2.

1.3.3 Spatially encoded

Spatially encoded frequency-domain OCT, also referred to as spectral-domain OCT or Fourier-domain OCT, utilizes dispersive elements to distribute differing optical frequencies and extract spectral information via a stripe line-array charge-coupled device (CCD) or complementary metal-oxide semiconductor (CMOS) sensor [17]. This method allows for full depth imaging on a single exposure (Fig. 1.3).

1.3.4 Time encoded

In time-encoded frequency-domain OCT, also referred to as SS-OCT, the optical spectrum is filtered in successive frequencies, then reconstituted prior to Fourier transformation. This technique allows for small instantaneous bandwidths at high frequencies (up to 200 kHz) [18].

1.4 Scanning techniques

An interferogram is obtained as the light scattered within a sample is recombined, detailing information throughout the z-axis [19]. To obtain a multidimensional image, the light source must be panned if the sample is fixed. A linear scan will produce a two-dimensional

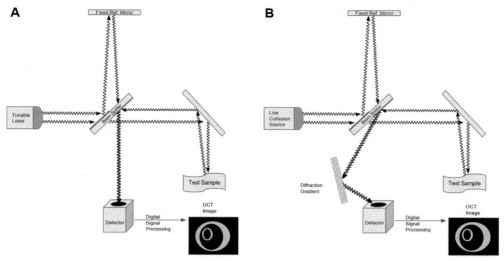

Figure 1.3 Spectral discrimination OCT schematics. (A) Spectral discrimination by swept-source OCT. (B) Spectral discrimination by Fourier-domain OCT. *OCT*, Optical coherence tomography.

image corresponding to a tissue cross-section (x–z axes), as opposed to an area scan that can produce three-dimensional (3D) images (x–y–z axes).

1.4.1 Single point scanning

Single point scanning, also known as line-field confocal or flying-spot TD-OCT, combines a series of lateral scans (A scans) to produce real-time images (B scans). This method relies on coherence gating through an axially scanning reference arm and movement of the sample for two-dimensional lateral scanning [20].

1.4.2 Parallel scanning

Parallel or full-field TD-OCT eliminates the need for sample movement by using a charge coupled device (CCD) to capture full-field illumination [21]. 3D images can be generated with a stepping reference mirror coupled with the CCD or using a two-dimensional smart detector array with a complementary metal oxide semiconductor (CMOS).

1.5 Pullback

The OCT docking system operates an automated pullback method for probe retraction within the catheter. A rapid pullback is required to reduce bias introduced by cardiac movement [22]. Previously, it was needed to occlude the artery during pullback for imaging acquisition [23]. Current models of OCT use a contrast medium, thereby reducing the risk of further cardiac ischemia and lethal arrhythmias [22,24]. Contrast injection can be automated or performed manually. There are two distinct pullback strategies by which OCT can operate, survey mode and high resolution (hi-res) mode [25]. Although high-resolution mode can increase frame density to 10 frames/mm, compared to only 5 frames/mm in survey mode, the frame rate is similar between modalities (180 frames/s). Hi-res mode achieves this by utilizing slower pullback speeds, 18 mm/s instead of 36 mm/s, and decreased pullback lengths, 54 mm compared to 75 mm. This difference allows for a significant increase in image capture, 540 frames in hi-res mode compared to only 375 frames in survey mode.

1.6 Image interpretation

1.6.1 Basic image orientation and interpretation

Coronary images are most often displayed in a radial cross-sectional view [26]. This image will always contain the imaging catheter and guidewire shadow frequently referred to as a comet tail because of its appearance. The vessel wall surrounds the image, with the blood-cleared lumen in the center. If desired, L-mode can be used to visualize the vessel in a longitudinal view [25]. The longitudinal view is sometimes referred to as an ant farm because of its cavernous-like offshoots (Fig. 1.4).

1.6.2 Image interpretation and normal coronary anatomy

Prior to detailing the image qualities of various plaques within the coronary arteries, one must be able to identify normal anatomy [29]. Current-generation OCT is high resolution (10–15 µm) and can distinguish between the three vascular tissue planes

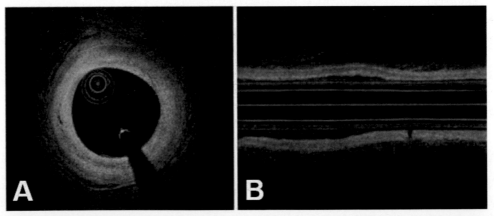

Figure 1.4 Normal coronary anatomy and positioning of the OCT catheter. (A) M-mode (axial view). (B) L-mode (longitudinal view) [27,28]. *OCT*, Optical coherence tomography.

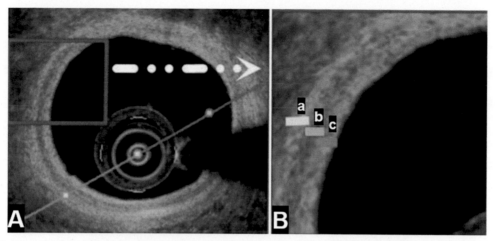

Figure 1.5 Coronary artery with visible vessel intimal layers. (A) OCT image depicting three distinct layers of the lumenal wall (box). (B) Heterogeneous tunica adventitia (a), low backscattering tunica media (b), and high backscattering thin tunica intima (c) [31]. *OCT,* Optical coherence tomography.

(tunica intima, tunica media, and tunica adventitia) [30]. Typically, the intimal layer is high backscattering, as opposed to the tunica media, which is low backscattering. The adventitial layer is heterogeneous and easily distinguished from the other two planes (Fig. 1.5).

1.6.3 Coronary plaque and thrombus characterization

Distinguishing between plaque types and thrombus composition is possible using current OCT systems [32]. Plaque composition can be revealed through the analysis of image homogeneity, reflectivity, and lesion margins [33]. The same principles apply to thrombus identification [1].

1.6.3.1 Fibrous plaques

Fibrous plaques produce homogeneous high signal (high backscatter) regions that are low attenuation [34] (Fig. 1.6).

1.6.3.2 Calcified plaques

Calcified plaques produce sharply demarcated borders, although similar to lipid–rich plaques have regions of low signal [35]. The plaques often appear to be heterogeneous with low backscatter and low attenuation and may be described as "islands" within the lumen. Calcium may present as a nodular plaque, superficial, or deep deposit (Figs. 1.6 and 1.7).

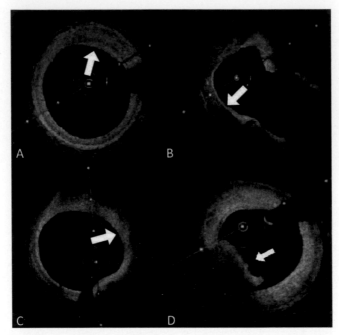

Figure 1.6 Various coronary plaque morphologies. (A) Homogenous high signal fibrous plaque (arrow). (B) Sharply delineated borders with low signal calcified plaque (arrow). (C) Poorly delineated borders with high attenuation and low signal lipid-rich plaque (arrow). (D) High-backscattering red thrombus within the vessel lumen (arrow) [31].

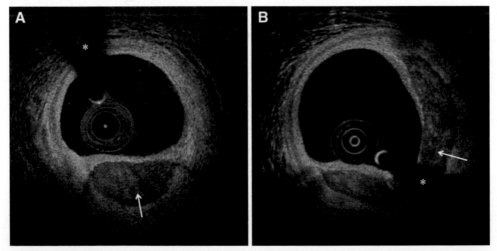

Figure 1.7 Calcified plaques. (A) Heterogeneous calcified plaque (arrow). (B) Large circumferential calcified plaque (arrow). (*) signifies the OCT catheter shadow [36].

1.6.3.3 Lipid-laden plaques

Plaques that are rich in lipids produce a high attenuation, poorly delineated region of low signal (low backscatter) [37]. They often appear to be homogenous and are described as "shadows" or "murky water" (Figs. 1.6 and 1.8).

1.6.3.4 Red thrombus

Primarily composed of red blood cells and fibrin, red thrombi appear as high backscattering (at the leading edge) and high attenuation (beyond the leading edge) protrusions within the vessel lumen [39] (Figs. 1.6 and 1.9).

1.6.3.5 White thrombus

White thrombi are platelet-rich lesions; they appear to be homogenous with high backscattering throughout with low attenuation [39,40] (Fig. 1.10).

1.6.4 Imaging coronary stents

Intracoronary metallic stents appear similar to the OCT catheter, with high backscatter at the leading edge of each strut and a trailing shadow [41]. Neointimal growth may occur, which can alter the stents' appearance [42] (Fig. 1.11).

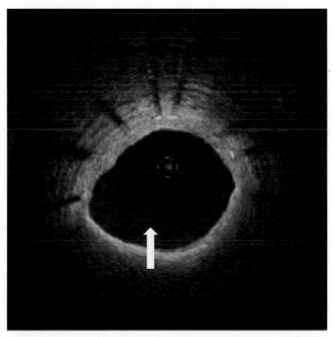

Figure 1.8 Lipid-laden plaque within the vessel lumen (arrow) [38].

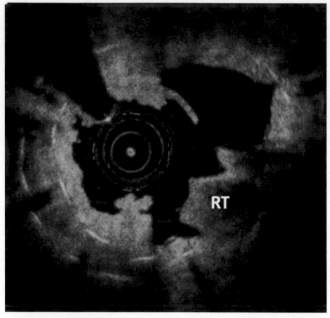

Figure 1.9 Red thrombus (labeled RT) [22].

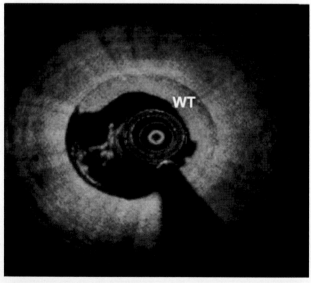

Figure 1.10 White thrombus (labeled WT) [31].

Figure 1.11 Intracoronary metallic stent with stent strut shadow artifact [43].

1.7 Image artifact

As with any other technology, having a general understanding of image artifact is very important to avoid misinterpreting findings. Table 1.3 summarizes some types of arti-facts and potential solutions described in the medical literature [8,62].

1.7.1 Inadequate blood purging

Residual blood within the vessel at the time of image acquisition may cause light attenuation, which in certain circumstances, can be misclassified as thrombus or other intravascular lesions. Typically, blood density after purging is low and does not impair the identification of the vessel lumen or area measurements. If blood is present during imaging, it will appear as a signal-rich region within the lumen. The high-intensity signal from within the lumen can cause significant shadowing, causing decreased lumen wall intensity [63]. Additionally, high scattering red blood cells may cloud the appearance of stent struts, creating other distortions [merry-go-round (MGR), bloom-ing, ghost strut] discussed below (Fig. 1.12).

1.7.2 Saturation artifact

Saturation aberrations typically appear as a result of high-intensity signals which exceed the dynamic range of the data acquisition device [64]. This results in the appearance of a bright line (or lines) for the A-scan in an image. Depending on the artifactual fre-quencies, the artifact line can extend radially to the edge of the OCT image. In these cases, the line may begin to broaden at its periphery. Highly specular surfaces, for

Table 1.3 OCT artifacts and mitigation techniques [44–62].

Guidewire shadow	Computational and artificial intelligence methods
	• A technique that combines Expectation-Maximization (EM) and Graph-Cuts (GC), and postprocessing refinements using a convex hull approach to eliminate the guidewire shadow artifact [45]. • Dynamic programming method used for artifact correction [46]. • A computational method using a combination of discrete wavelet packet frame (DWPF) and an adapted version of the Otsu threshold to ascertain lumen segmentation [47]. • Multistep automatic lumen contour detection methodology using Otsu binarization and intensity curves, lumen contour position correction, and image reconstruction and contour extraction [48]. • ARC-OCT image processing methodology that relies on the transformation of OCT images according to reflectivity and absorption of the tissue and local regression using weighted linear least squares and a polynomial model to achieve artifact correction [49]. • Automatic distance regularized level set-based segmentation algorithm [50]. • Morphological corrosion operation, region removal, and orientation comparison are used to remove the catheter and guidewire altogether. By implementing this method, the catheter and guidewire can be removed completely regardless of position and shape irregularity [51].
	Physical removal, adjustments, and novel guidewires
	• Guidewire shadow may be reduced by detaching the guidewire from the imaging catheter, that is, moving the guidewire close to the vessel wall, or by exchanging it for a smaller diameter wire, or by removing the guidewire. Furthermore, shadows from guidewires with a sparse spring coil are smaller than their actual diameters [52]. • Placing the catheter in the least eccentric position will avoid OCT underestimation of length and overestimation of diameter [53]. • Specialized guidewire, which had a small diameter and lacked the dipping polymer structure, produced fewer shadow artifacts than its generally used counterparts [54].

(Continued)

Table 1.3 (Continued)

	• Physical removal of the guidewire may be performed in research grounds [44]. • Physical removal of the catheter has also been implemented in clinical settings [55].
Ghost lines	Ghost lines or rings are processed separately and removed via a rapid algorithm that detects circular objects based on Hough transform [56].
Concentric diplopia	Catheter reshaping to its original configuration eliminates this artifact [44].
Residual blood	• An automatic level set-based segmentation algorithm is used to eliminate noise and blood artifact [50]. • A method that employs image enhancement, median filtering, binarization, and morphological closing to reduce speckle noise, and minimize the effect of blood artifacts [51]. • Adjusting flushing settings and re-flushing catheter before obtaining a new image. If there are concerns about contrast use, consider using alternate solutions such as Dextran [44].
Gas bubbles	• Adequately preflushing catheter will avoid this artifact [44].
Artifacts related to catheter location and movement, and NURD	• A single beam motion-tracking scheme is used to reconstruct a longitudinal map of the coronary artery. Motion distortion compensation is performed by tracking the relative longitudinal velocities of a catheter employing a single beam [57]. • Commercial systems for image stabilization and NURD compensation using a global rotational block matching-type technique. Computerized mathematical models using dynamic time warping, finding a continuous path through a cost matrix that measures the similarity between regions of two frames being aligned [58]. • Research method using a technology named "Heartbeat OCT" combines a fast Fourier domain mode-locked laser, rapid pullback, and a micromotor actuated catheter, eliminates NURD and motion artifact [59]. • Investigational method using 4D magnetic particle imaging-guided catheter tracking corrects for motion artifact due to catheter bending and heartbeat [60].
Sew-up or seam artifact	• Faster acquisition rate and higher pullback speed [61].

(Continued)

Table 1.3 (Continued)

Obliquity and eccentricity	• Automatic lumen segmentation technique based on wavelet transform and mathematical morphology [47].
Blooming artifact	• Adjusting flushing parameters, including the use of a viscous fluid flush medium to adequately clear blood from the lumen, reduces the blooming artifact [62].

OCT, Optical coherence tomography.

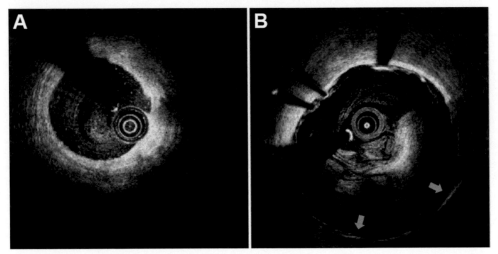

Figure 1.12 (A) Retained luminal blood in a coronary artery during OCT imaging. (B) Retained blood within a stented superficial femoral artery. Stent struts are also visualized with merry-go-round artifact (arrows) in the periphery [62]. *OCT,* Optical coherence tomography.

example, stent struts, are usually identified as the cause of such artifacts, although guidewires, microcalcifications, and cholesterol crystals can be implicated (Fig. 1.13).

1.7.3 Nonuniform rotational distortion

Any variation in the angular velocity of the mono–fiber optical catheter can result in image distortion [65]. Nonuniform rotational distortion (NURD) is typically the result of imperfections of the torque wire or catheter sheath crimping, causing impairment of smooth rotation of the optical catheter. Tortuous vasculature can also impair optical catheter rotation, causing similar distortions [66]. NURD's typically appear as image blurring or smearing in the lateral direction (Fig. 1.14). Due to smaller probes used in OCT, this type of image aberration is seen less often compared to IVUS.

Figure 1.13 Image saturation artifact secondary to stent struts can be seen as tangential lines radiating outward (arrows) [62].

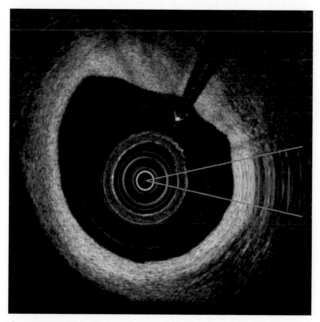

Figure 1.14 Nonuniform rotational distortion can be seen between the two lines [62].

1.7.4 Sew-up artifact (seam artifact)

In cases of rapid wire movement or vessel motion, light data may become misaligned during image formation, which may appear as lumen wall discontinuity [64]. As stated, these artifacts typically appear as gradients along the lateral direction at the lumen wall but can also appear within the vessel (Fig. 1.15).

1.7.5 Fold-over artifact

Fold-over artifacts are a byproduct of modern OCT systems (FD-OCT). When imaging large vessels or branching arteries, the lumen or structure borders often fall outside the field of view [64,67]. Signal aliasing, sometimes referred to as phase wrapping, occurs along the Fourier transformation, producing an image that appears to fold back onto itself in an inverted reflection. When this distortion is present, vessel geometry and dimensions cannot be accurately assessed (Fig. 1.16).

1.7.6 Bubble artifact

Small gas bubbles sometimes form within the silicon lubricant between the sheath and revolving fiber-optic catheter in TD-OCT. Due to the considerable variation in the refractive index between the lubricant and the bubbles, high backscattering signals with associated shadowing will be produced. This, in effect, reduces the signal

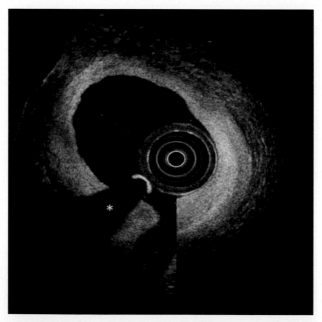

Figure 1.15 Sew-up or seam artifact can be appreciated at the 6 o'clock position as a discontinuous luminal border. (*) signifies the guidewire shadow [62].

intensity of the vessel wall [68]. This artifact can easily be identified when a distinct region of brightness is noted within the catheter (Fig. 1.17). Bubbles are often introduced when the imaging catheter is placed without correct preflushing.

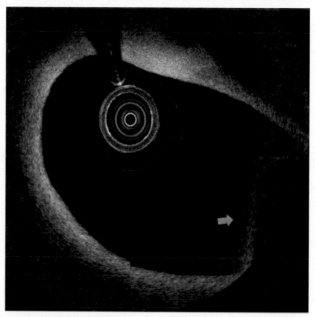

Figure 1.16 Fold-over artifact (arrow) [62].

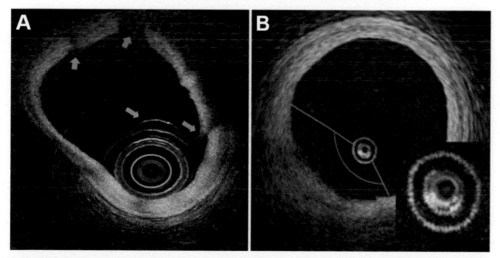

Figure 1.17 (A) A luminal bubble can be seen adherent to the catheter (center arrow), with an associated bubble shadow (arrow to right) causing surrounding tissue distortion (top two arrows). (B) A bubble can be seen inside the catheter (inset) [62].

1.7.7 Tangential light drop-out

During certain circumstances, the OCT catheter may be positioned against an arterial wall causing light to be emitted nearly parallel to the luminal surface. This positioning can cause an appearance of attenuation in the absence of light penetration [68] (Fig. 1.18). This artifact may be confused for a thin-capped fibroatheroma, accumulated macrophages, a lipid collection, or even a necrotic core. Therefore it is essential to interpret images that are obtained nearly parallel to the OCT light beam with caution and consideration for an artifact phenomenon.

1.7.8 Merry-go-round artifact

The Merry-go-round (MGR) artifact is a result of increased distance between the A-lines, larger beam spot diameter in far field, or residual blood attenuation, all leading to reduced lateral resolution. It appears as an elongation of the stent strut arc length laterally [69]. During 3D imaging, MDR artifact can create the appearance of additional struts that do not exist, termed ghost struts (Fig. 1.19).

1.7.9 Blooming artifact

Stent struts are highly reflective and can cause high-signal density at the surface, causing axial stretching of the stent strut, also referred to as blooming [61]. The increased strut reflection thickness is termed blooming thickness. This effect can be compounded by residual blood artifact (Fig. 1.20).

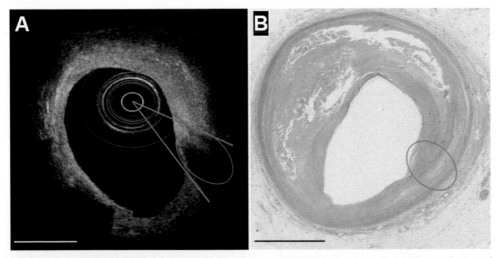

Figure 1.18 (A) Tangential light dropout can be seen between the lines (circled), producing the appearance of coronary pathology. (B) A histologic, hematoxylin and eosin-stained slide depicts the location of tangential light drop-out (circled). No necrotic core is visualized on histology [62].

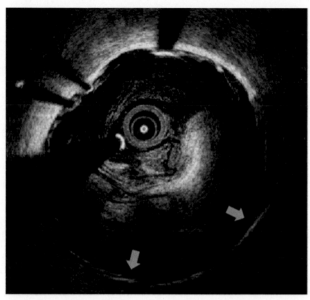

Figure 1.19 Stented vessel with luminal blood artifact. The stent struts can be seen with MGR artifact (arrows) [62]. *MGR*, Merry-go-round.

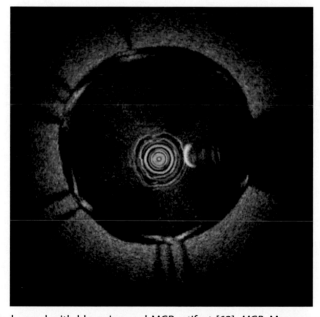

Figure 1.20 Stented vessel with blooming and MGR artifact [62]. *MGR*, Merry-go-round.

1.8 Clinical applications

OCT enables physicians to overcome the limitations of coronary angiography, providing precise data about coronary anatomy and plaque characteristics, which are valuable in risk stratification and treatment options [4].

1.8.1 Plaque analysis

Recognition and awareness of plaque composition is important because plaque histopathologic features may alter treatment options and clinical outcomes. It has been estimated that thin cap fibroatheromas (TCFA) are responsible for greater than 80% of vulnerable plaque rupture resulting in ACS. TCFAs are defined as lipid-rich coronary plaques (lipid arc with any plaque in ≥ 2 quadrants) with a thin fibrous covering less than 65 μm at its thinnest segment [32,70]. Other high-risk lesions include plaque erosions and calcified nodules. Early identification of plaque characteristics is necessary to improve clinical outcomes. Current generation high-resolution OCT can identify TCFAs at an early stage, detecting caps less than 100 μm [71]. In addition to earlier detection, OCT can more precisely characterize plaques compared to other imaging modalities, including IVUS [72]. Comparisons between OCT and IVUS imaging can be seen below (Fig. 1.21).

1.8.2 Diagnostic imaging: stable coronary artery disease

Although fractional flow reserve (FFR) remains the gold standard for estimating the pathophysiologic effects of a coronary lesion, imaging modalities such as IVUS and OCT can aid in plaque characterization for more accurate risk stratification and intervention planning [74]. Some current-generation OCT models allow for automated volumetric lumen segmentation, eliminating reader error and variability between operators, previously present with IVUS [75].

1.8.3 Interventional imaging: acute coronary syndrome

When compared to coronary angioscopy, intravascular OCT has a 100% sensitivity for detecting intraluminal thrombus, compared to the 33% sensitivity of IVUS. As such, intravascular OCT has been deemed the gold standard for the detection of fibrous plaque rupture [76]. Published literature has also detailed intravascular OCT as a reliable method for the detection of non-CAD-related ACS, including coronary artery dissection, which may reduce unnecessary stenting [77,78].

1.8.4 Postintervention imaging

Although IVUS has been viewed as the imaging modality of choice for coronary stent evaluation, it is still somewhat limited by its low resolution in evaluating neointimal hyperplasia (NIH) [79]. Some studies have shown OCT to have increased diagnostic accuracy for the detection of in-stent lesions, specifically lesions which occupy <30%

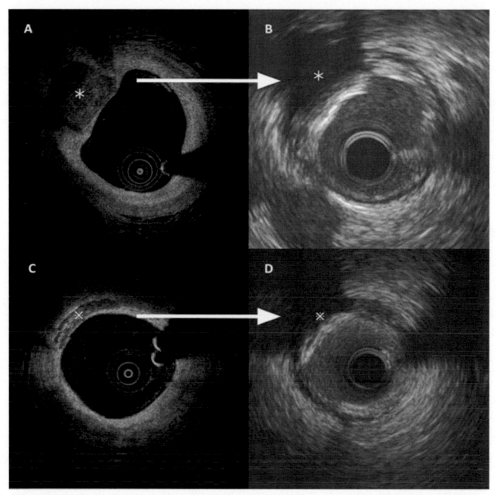

Figure 1.21 OCT and IVUS images of thin and thick calcium plaques. (A) Thick calcium plaque marked by (*), visualized by OCT. (B) Thick calcium plaque marked by (*), visualized by IVUS. (C) Thin calcium plaque marked by (x), visualized by OCT. (D) Thin calcium plaque marked by (x), visualized by IVUS [73]. *OCT*, Optical coherence tomography; *IVUS*, intravascular ultrasound.

of the stent area [43]. Modern generation OCT systems have also shown improved detection of incomplete stent apposition, as well as detection of uncovered struts, compared to IVUS. Incomplete stent apposition is defined as a separation between the stent strut and the arterial intimal wall, not including cases of jailed coronary branches, which have evidence of blood flow [80,81].

Malapposition is any distance between the strut and the lumen that is greater than the strut thickness plus the axial resolution of the OCT system in use [82]. It has been well documented that the distance between the intimal wall and strut in some malapposed stents decreases with time due to NIH. Although this has been documented, one must not rely on NIH for stent placement. It is still crucial that interventionalists maximize positive outcomes with adequate stent placement.

Longitudinal stent deformation (LSD) is a feared complication of PCI, as it has been associated with in-stent restenosis (ISR). Although LSD can be difficult to identify on angiography, it is easily detected by OCT [83]. During repeat intervention for ISR, OCT provides high-quality images to ensure complete apposition during balloon inflation [84].

1.9 Safety and complications

Contemporary OCT is relatively safe, only using 5—8 mW of applied energy, which allows for minimal risk of functional or structural electric injury to biologic tissues. Previously, risk of ischemia during luminal blood displacement was possible. Modern systems are capable of rapid flushing and imaging, greatly reducing this risk [85]. Similar to other coronary angiographic procedures, there is a risk of contrast-induced nephropathy, coronary dissection, coronary spasm, and arrhythmia, although these risks are not specific to OCT. Access site injury, hematoma, bleeding, and thrombosis are also risks, although again are not specific to OCT imaging. Major risks include myocardial infarction, major embolization, and death and occur <1%.

1.10 Innovations of OCT

Throughout the recent past, many iterations of OCT have been developed and employed in clinical practice. Below, we have detailed the most pertinent OCT systems (since 2009) with specific mention of crucial differences. Currently, two types of catheters can be used for OCT systems: the Dragonfly Intravascular Imaging Catheter and the Dragonfly Duo OCT Imaging Catheter [22].

1.10.1 C7-XR system

In 2009 the OCT pioneer, LightLab Imaging Inc., was granted approval by the United States Food and Drug Administration for its C7-XR System in addition to their C7 Dragonfly Imaging Catheter. Although already used in numerous countries throughout Europe and Asia, this was the first approval for OCT in advancing coronary angiography in the United States. The C7-XR Imaging System was the first FD-OCT System capable of quick high-resolution (15 μm) images in under 3 seconds (100 fps) [86]. This system also offers nonocclusive imaging capabilities, a step up from previous generations of OCT imaging. This breakthrough technology has since allowed clinicians to more accurately assess intracoronary luminal abnormalities, occlusions and optimize therapeutic options [87].

1.10.2 ILUMIEN system

Additional advancements in OCT were achieved with the release of the ILUMIEN System. This system can measure FFR by using radio waves from the proximally placed aortic pressure transducer and a distally aligned intracoronary pressure transducer. Using a combination of the functional aspects of FFR and anatomical aspects of OCT, clinicians are able to accurately detail the extent of coronary artery disease, improving overall PCI outcomes [4,88]. The ability to seamlessly switch between FFR and OCT was also introduced with this system.

1.10.3 ILUMIEN OPTIS system

Similar to the ILUMIEN System, the ILUMIEN Optis System integrates both OCT with FFR technology, although it also offers live 3D imaging with automated measurement software [89,90] (Fig. 1.22). The finer resolution obtained with the ILUMIEN Optis System allows for improved microscopic visualization of coronary disease. This system incorporates the Dragonfly Duo Imaging Catheter; this catheter allows for improved catheterization speeds by reducing pullback time. The ILUMIEN Optis System is also equipped with PressureWire Aeris technology, which can provide measurements of pressure differences in coronary blood flow.

1.10.4 OPTIS integrated system

The current OPTIS Integrated System is able to provide vessel image coregistration in addition to a tableside controller. The controller allows the clinician to review images on the catheterization lab monitor without breaking the sterile field. Live-feed

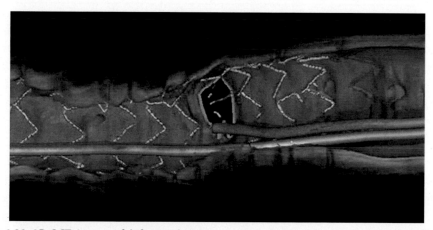

Figure 1.22 3D-OCT image of bifurcated coronary artery lesion with stent strut detection. The guidewire can be seen within the vessel lumen [39].

coregistration allows the clinician to view the OCT image alongside angiography [91]. Automated measurement technology, as was provided in prior systems, is also available [92].

1.10.5 OPTIS mobile system

The OPTIS Mobile System provides the same capabilities as the OPTIS Integrated System but has the added benefit of being mobile [93]. This system continues to feature OCT and angiography coregistration coupled with FFR. The tableside controller continues to be a standard feature. The mobile aspect allows hospitals and clinicians to work in multiple catheterization labs without changing equipment, allowing for broader clinical applications.

1.11 Clinical trials

1.11.1 ILUMIEN I trial

At the time of publication, the ILUMIEN I trial was the largest nonrandomized, prospective observational study of its kind to determine the effects of pre- and postprocedure OCT on operator decision-making and clinical outcomes in patients undergoing PCI for unstable angina, stable angina, or non-ST elevation myocardial infarction (NSTEMI). The study results were profound, finding that OCT altered operator decision-making in 66% of cases, with 98% of patients achieving a favorable clinical outcome [4].

1.11.2 ILUMIEN II Trial

The ILUMIEN II trial then evaluated measurement accuracy between OCT and IVUS, specifically the degree of stent expansion within a coronary artery. The degree of stent expansion was defined as the stent area divided by the average of the proximal/distal lumen areas. Data regarding minimal stent area achieved after PCI were obtained from the ILUMIEN I and ADAPT-DES trials [4,94]. The study found no significant difference between OCT- and IVUS-guided stent expansion (72.8% vs 70.6%, with a $P = .29$) [95]. When comparing major tissue protrusion, stent edge dissection, intramural hematoma, and stent malapposition, there was no difference between OCT- and IVUS-guided interventions [95].

1.11.3 ILUMIEN III Trial

The ILUMIEN III trial compared OCT, IVUS, and angiography-guided PCI minimum stent area. The final average minimum stent areas for OCT, IVUS, and angiography were 5.79 [2], 5.89 [2], and 5.49 mm [2], respectively [96]. These findings suggested that OCT-guided PCI is not inferior to IVUS-guided intervention. Major adverse cardiac events were 4% with OCT, 1% with IVUS, and 1% with angiography [96].

1.11.4 ILUMIEN IV Trial

At the time of publication, the ILUMIEN IV trial, which is comparing OCT and angiography-guided PCI postintervention lumen area and diameter, is currently in progress [97]. The study was started on March 26, 2018, and is estimated to be completed by July 31, 2022. This is the first large-scale, globalized, prospective, double-blinded, randomized study in which researchers are assessing final stent dimensions with OCT imaging after angiography-guided and OCT-guided intervention. The trial has enrolled approximately 3650 patients in 125 medical centers across Europe, Asia, and North America.

References

[1] Fujimoto J, Pitris C, Boppart S, Brezinski M. Optical coherence tomography: an emerging technology for biomedical imaging and optical biopsy. Neoplasia 2000;2(1−2):9−25. Available from: https://doi.org/10.1038/sj.neo.7900071.

[2] Terashima M, Kaneda H, Suzuki T. The role of optical coherence tomography in coronary intervention. Korean J Intern Med 2012;27(1):1. Available from: https://doi.org/10.3904/kjim.2012.27.1.1.

[3] Pinilla Echeverri N, Sibbald M, Sheth T. Usefulness of imaging techniques in the assessment of coronary disease − optic coherence tomography. Rev Colomb Cardiol 2019;26:198−204. Available from: https://doi.org/10.1016/j.rccar.2019.04.010.

[4] Wijns W, Shite J, Jones M, et al. Optical coherence tomography imaging during percutaneous coronary intervention impacts physician decision-making: ILUMIEN I study. Eur Heart J 2015;36 (47):3346−55. Available from: https://doi.org/10.1093/eurheartj/ehv367.

[5] International Study of Comparative Health Effectiveness With Medical and Invasive Approaches - American College of Cardiology, <https://www.acc.org/latest-in-cardiology/clinical-trials/2019/11/15/17/27/ischemia>; 2019 [Accessed 16.02.20].

[6] Sedlis S, Hartigan P, Teo K, et al. Effect of PCI on long-term survival in patients with stable ischemic heart disease. N Engl J Med 2015;373(20):1937−46. Available from: https://doi.org/10.1056/NEJMoa1505532.

[7] Nguyen V, Faber D, Van der Pol E, Van Leeuwen T, Kalkman J. Dependent and multiple scattering in transmission and backscattering optical coherence tomography. Opt Express 2013;21 (24):29145. Available from: https://doi.org/10.1364/OE.21.029145.

[8] Furukawa H, Fukuda T. In vivo absorption spectroscopy for absolute measurement. Biomed Opt Express 2012;3(10):2587. Available from: https://doi.org/10.1364/BOE.3.002587.

[9] Srinivasan V, Chen Y, Duker J, Fujimoto J. In vivo functional imaging of intrinsic scattering changes in the human retina with high-speed ultrahigh resolution OCT. Opt Express 2009;17 (5):3861. Available from: https://doi.org/10.1364/OE.17.003861.

[10] Hoang K, Kern M. Lighting up the artery: intracoronary imaging with optical coherence tomography | cath lab digest, <https://www.cathlabdigest.com/articles/Lighting-Up-Artery-Intracoronary-Imaging-Optical-Coherence-Tomography>; 2008 [Accessed 13.02.20].

[11] Popescu D, Choo-Smith L, Flueraru C, et al. Optical coherence tomography: fundamental principles, instrumental designs and biomedical applications. Biophys Rev 2011;3(3):155−69. Available from: https://doi.org/10.1007/s12551-011-0054-7.

[12] Webster A. Useful mathematical formulas for transform limited pulses, <http://falsecolour.com/aw/pulses/pulses.pdf>; 2012 [Accessed 01.04.20].

[13] Chen Y, Willett P, Zhu Q. Frequency tracking in optical Doppler tomography using an adaptive notch filter. J Biomed Opt 2007;12(1):014018. Available from: https://doi.org/10.1117/1.2710240.

[14] Vignali L, Solinas E, Emanuele E. Research and clinical applications of optical coherence tomography in invasive cardiology: a review. Curr Cardiol Rev 2014;10(4):369−76. Available from: https://doi.org/10.2174/1573403X10666140604120753.

[15] Given C, Attizzani G, Jones M, et al. Frequency-domain optical coherence tomography assessment of human carotid atherosclerosis using saline flush for blood clearance without balloon occlusion. Am J Neuroradiol 2013;34(7):1414—18. Available from: https://doi.org/10.3174/ajnr.A3411.

[16] De Boer J, Leitgeb R, Wojtkowski M. Twenty-five years of optical coherence tomography: the paradigm shift in sensitivity and speed provided by Fourier domain OCT. Biomed Opt Express 2017;8(7):3248. Available from: https://doi.org/10.1364/boe.8.003248.

[17] Bub G, Tecza M, Helmes M, Lee P, Kohl P. Temporal pixel multiplexing for simultaneous high-speed, high-resolution imaging. Nat Methods 2010;7(3):209—11. Available from: https://doi.org/10.1038/nmeth.1429.

[18] Považay B, Unterhuber A, Hermann B, Sattmann H, Arthaber H, Drexler W. Full-field time-encoded frequency-domain optical coherence tomography. Opt Express 2006;14(17):7661. Available from: https://doi.org/10.1364/oe.14.007661.

[19] Zhou Y, Tang Y, Yang Y, Hu S. Topography measurement of large-range microstructures through advanced Fourier-transform method and phase stitching in scanning broadband light interferometry. Micromachines 2017;8(11):319. Available from: https://doi.org/10.3390/mi8110319.

[20] Dubois A, Levecq O, Azimani H, et al. Line-field confocal time-domain optical coherence tomography with dynamic focusing. Opt Express 2018;26(26):33534. Available from: https://doi.org/10.1364/oe.26.033534.

[21] Leitgeb R. En face optical coherence tomography: a technology review. Biomed Opt Express 2019;10(5):2177. Available from: https://doi.org/10.1364/boe.10.002177.

[22] Roleder T, Jakała J, Kałuza G, et al. The basics of intravascular optical coherence tomography. Postep w Kardiol Interwencyjnej 2015;11(2):74—83. Available from: https://doi.org/10.5114/pwki.2015.52278.

[23] Prati F, Jenkins M, DiGiorgio A, Rollins A. Intracoronary optical coherence tomography, basic theory and image acquisition techniques. Int J Cardiovasc Imaging 2011;27(2):251—8. Available from: https://doi.org/10.1007/s10554-011-9798-1.

[24] Yamaguchi T, Terashima M, Akasaka T, et al. Safety and feasibility of an intravascular optical coherence tomography image wire system in the clinical setting. Am J Cardiol 2008;101(5):562—7. Available from: https://doi.org/10.1016/j.amjcard.2007.09.116.

[25] Katwal A, Lopez J. Technical considerations and practical guidance for intracoronary optical coherence tomography. Interv Cardiol Clin 2015;4(3):239—49. Available from: https://doi.org/10.1016/j.iccl.2015.02.005.

[26] Papafaklis M. Basic interpretation of intracoronary ultrasound and optical coherence tomography images: examples. Contin Cardiol Educ 2016;2(2):115—21. Available from: https://doi.org/10.1002/cce2.26.

[27] Shin E, Ann S, Singh G, Lim K, Yoon H, Hur S, et al. OCT—defined morphological characteristics of coronary artery spasm sites in vasospastic angina. J Am Coll Cardiol Img 2015;8:1059—67. Available from: https://doi.org/10.1016/j.jcmg.2015.03.010.

[28] Adlam D, Joseph S, Robinson C, Rousseau C, Barber J, Biggs M, et al. Coronary optical coherence tomography: minimally invasive virtual histology as part of targeted post-mortem computed tomography angiography. Int J Legal Med 2013;127(5):991—6. Available from: https://doi.org/10.1007/s00414-013-0837-4.

[29] Bouma B, Villiger M, Otsuka K, Oh W. Intravascular optical coherence tomography. Biomed Opt Express 2017;8(5):2660. Available from: https://doi.org/10.1364/boe.8.002660.

[30] Yabushita H, Bouma B, Houser S, et al. Characterization of human atherosclerosis by optical coherence tomography. Circulation 2002;106(13):1640—5. Available from: https://doi.org/10.1161/01.CIR.0000029927.92825.F6.

[31] Su M, Chen C, Yeh H, Wang K. Concise review of optical coherence tomography in clinical practice. Acta Cardiol Sin 2016;32(4):381—6. Available from: https://doi.org/10.6515/acs20151026a.

[32] Kawasaki M, Bouma B, Bressner J, et al. Diagnostic accuracy of optical coherence tomography and integrated backscatter intravascular ultrasound images for tissue characterization of human coronary plaques. J Am Coll Cardiol 2006;48(1):81—8. Available from: https://doi.org/10.1016/j.jacc.2006.02.062.

[33] Liu S. Tissue characterization with depth-resolved attenuation coefficient and backscatter term in intravascular optical coherence tomography images. J Biomed Opt 2017;22(09):1. Available from: https://doi.org/10.1117/1.jbo.22.9.096004.

[34] Toutouzas K, Karanasos A, Tousoulis D. Optical coherence tomography for the detection of the vulnerable plaque. Eur Cardiol Rev 2016;11(2):90−5. Available from: https://doi.org/10.15420/ecr.2016:29:2.

[35] Hasegawa T, Shimada K. Optical coherence tomography for the assessment of coronary plaque vulnerability. In: Coronary artery disease - assessment, surgery, prevention. InTech; 2015. pp. 99−111. Available from: https://doi.org/10.5772/61615.

[36] Ong D, Lee J, Soeda T, Higuma T, Minami Y, Wang Z, et al. Coronary calcification and plaque vulnerability. An optical coherence tomographic study. Circ: Cardiovasc Imaging 2016;9:e003929. Available from: https://doi.org/10.1161/CIRCIMAGING.115.003929.

[37] Stamper D, Weissman N, Brezinski M. Plaque characterization with optical coherence tomography. J Am Coll Cardiol 2006;47(8):C69−79. Available from: https://doi.org/10.1016/j.jacc.2005.10.067.

[38] Uemura S, Soeda T, Sugawara Y, Ueda T, Watanabe M, Saito Y. Assessment of coronary plaque vulnerability with optical coherence tomography. Acta Cardiol Sin 2014;30(1):1−9.

[39] Kume T, Uemura S. Current clinical applications of coronary optical coherence tomography. Cardiovasc Interv Ther 2018;33(1):1−10. Available from: https://doi.org/10.1007/s12928-017-0483-8.

[40] Kume T, Akasaka T, Kawamoto T, et al. Assessment of coronary arterial thrombus by optical coherence tomography. Am J Cardiol 2006;97(12):1713−17. Available from: https://doi.org/10.1016/j.amjcard.2006.01.031.

[41] Gutiérrez J, Alegría E, Teijeiro R, et al. Optical coherence tomography: from research to practice. Eur Heart J Cardiovasc Imaging 2012;13(5):370−84. Available from: https://doi.org/10.1093/ehjci/jes025.

[42] Yoshimura S, Kawasaki M, Yamada K, et al. Visualization of internal carotid artery atherosclerotic plaques in symptomatic and asymptomatic patients: a comparison of optical coherence tomography and intravascular ultrasound. Am J Neuroradiol 2012;33(2):308−13. Available from: https://doi.org/10.3174/ajnr.A2740.

[43] Lee S, Hong M. Stent evaluation with optical coherence tomography. Yonsei Med J 2013;54(5):1075−83. Available from: https://doi.org/10.3349/ymj.2013.54.5.1075.

[44] Tung K, Shi W, De Silva R, Edwards E, Rueckert D. Automatical vessel wall detection in intravascular coronary OCT. In. 2011 IEEE international symposium on biomedical imaging: from nano to macro; 2011.pp. 610−613. Available from: https://doi.org/10.1109/ISBI.2011.5872481.

[45] Wang Z, Chamie D, Bezerra H, et al. Volumetric quantification of fibrous caps using intravascular optical coherence tomography. Biomed Opt Express 2012;3(6):1413. Available from: https://doi.org/10.1364/BOE.3.001413.

[46] Moraes M, Cardenas D, Furuie S. Automatic lumen segmentation in IVOCT images using binary morphological reconstruction. Biomed Eng Online 2013;12(1):78. Available from: https://doi.org/10.1186/1475-925X-12-78.

[47] Kim H, Lee S, Lee C, Ha J, Yoon Y. Automatic lumen contour detection in intravascular OCT images using Otsu binarization and intensity curve. Conf Proc IEEE Eng Med Biol Soc 2014;2014:178−81. Available from: https://doi.org/10.1109/EMBC.2014.6943558.

[48] Cheimariotis G, Chatzizisis Y, Koutkias V, et al. ARC−OCT: automatic detection of lumen border in intravascular OCT images. Comput Methods Programs Biomed 2017;151:21−32. Available from: https://doi.org/10.1016/j.cmpb.2017.08.007.

[49] Cao Y, Cheng K, Qin X, et al. Automatic lumen segmentation in intravascular optical coherence tomography images using level set. Comput Math Methods Med 2017;2017:4710305. Available from: https://doi.org/10.1155/2017/4710305.

[50] Zhao H, He B, Ding Z, et al. Automatic lumen segmentation in intravascular optical coherence tomography using morphological features. IEEE Access 2019;7:88859−69. Available from: https://doi.org/10.1109/ACCESS.2019.2925917.

[51] Nakao F, Ueda T, Nishimura S, et al. Guide wire shadow assessed by shading index is reduced in sparse spring coil wire in optical coherence tomography. Cardiovasc Interv Ther 2013;28(4):362−7. Available from: https://doi.org/10.1007/s12928-013-0186-8.

[52] Danson E, Hansen P, Bhindi R. Wire bias in coronary measurement using optical coherence tomography. Cardiovasc Interv Ther 2018;33(3):217−23. Available from: https://doi.org/10.1007/s12928-017-0468-7.

[53] Niida T, Murai T, Lee T, et al. Guidewire shadow artifacts in optical coherence tomography. Minerva Cardioangiol 2017;65(2):126−33. Available from: https://doi.org/10.23736/S0026-4725.16.04177-3.

[54] Liu Z, Niu D, Guo J. Radial artery spiral dissection confirmed by OCT without guidewire shadow. J Invasive Cardiol 2020;32(4):E102.

[55] Tsantis S, Kagadis G, Katsanos K, Karnabatidis D, Bourantas G, Nikiforidis G. Automatic vessel lumen segmentation and stent strut detection in intravascular optical coherence tomography. Med Phys 2011;39(1):503−13. Available from: https://doi.org/10.1118/1.3673067.

[56] Ha J, Yoo H, Tearney G, Bouma B. Compensation of motion artifacts in intracoronary optical frequency domain imaging and optical coherence tomography. Int J Cardiovasc Imaging 2012;28(6):1299−304. Available from: https://doi.org/10.1007/s10554-011-9953-8.

[57] Van Soest G, Bosch J, Van der Steen A. Azimuthal registration of image sequences affected by nonuniform rotation distortion. IEEE Trans Inf Technol Biomed 2008;12(3):348−55. Available from: https://doi.org/10.1109/TITB.2007.908000.

[58] Wang T, Pfeiffer T, Regar E, et al. Heartbeat OCT: in vivo intravascular megahertz-optical coherence tomography. Biomed Opt Express 2015;6(12):5021. Available from: https://doi.org/10.1364/boe.6.005021.

[59] Griese F, Latus S, Schlüter M, et al. In-vitro MPI-guided IVOCT catheter tracking in real time for motion artifact compensation. PLoS One 2020;15(3):e0230821. Available from: https://doi.org/10.1371/journal.pone.0230821.

[60] Sawada T, Shite J, Negi N, et al. Factors that influence measurements and accurate evaluation of stent apposition by optical coherence tomography. Circ J 2009;73(10):1841−7. Available from: https://doi.org/10.1253/circj.CJ-09-0113.

[61] Mancuso J, Halaney D, Elahi S, et al. Intravascular optical coherence tomography light scattering artifacts: merry-go-rounding, blooming, and ghost struts. J Biomed Opt 2014;19(12):126017. Available from: https://doi.org/10.1117/1.jbo.19.12.126017.

[62] Phipps J, Hoyt T, Halaney D, et al. Intravascular OCT imaging artifacts. In: Cardiovascular OCT Imaging. Springer Nature Switzerland AG; 2020. pp. 53−66. Available from: https://doi.org/10.1007/978-3-030-25711-8_4.

[63] Varga Z, Rajpurohit N, Li S, Stys T, Stys A. Frequency domain-optical coherence tomography of coronary arteries using a diluted iodinated contrast-saline mix with 5-Fr guide catheters. Cureus 2019;11(6):e4892. Available from: https://doi.org/10.7759/cureus.4892.

[64] Bezerra H, Costa M, Guagliumi G, Rollins A, Simon D. Intracoronary optical coherence tomography: a comprehensive review. Clinical and Research Applications. JACC Cardiovasc Interv 2009;2(11):1035−46. Available from: https://doi.org/10.1016/j.jcin.2009.06.019.

[65] Price M. Intravascular imaging: OCT and IVUS. In: Interventional cardiology clinics. Elsevier Health Sciences; 2015. p. 4.

[66] Shirazi A. Analytical and experimental investigations on non-uniform rotational distortion (NURD) correction. < https://escholarship.org/uc/item/9gb4w0fq > . 2017 [Accessed 13.02.20].

[67] Tearney G, Regar E, Akasaka T, et al. Consensus standards for acquisition, measurement, and reporting of intravascular optical coherence tomography studies: a report from the International Working Group for Intravascular Optical Coherence Tomography Standardization and Validation. J Am Coll Cardiol 2012;59(12):1058−72. Available from: https://doi.org/10.1016/j.jacc.2011.09.079.

[68] Van Soest G, Regar E, Goderie T, et al. Pitfalls in plaque characterization by OCT: image artifacts in native coronary arteries. JACC Cardiovasc Imaging 2011;4(7):810−13. Available from: https://doi.org/10.1016/j.jcmg.2011.01.022.

[69] Subban V, Raffel O, Vasu N, Victor S, Sankardas M. Intravascular ultrasound and optical coherence tomography for the assessment of coronary artery disease and percutaneous coronary intervention optimization: specific lesion subsets. Indian Hear J Interv 2018;1(2):95. Available from: https://doi.org/10.4103/IHJI.IHJI_33_18.

[70] Prati F, Regar E, Mintz G, et al. Expert review document on methodology, terminology, and clinical applications of optical coherence tomography: physical principles, methodology of image acquisition, and clinical application for assessment of coronary arteries and atherosclerosis. Eur Heart J 2010;31(4):401−15. Available from: https://doi.org/10.1093/eurheartj/ehp433.

[71] Miyamoto Y, Okura H, Kume T, et al. Plaque characteristics of thin-cap fibroatheroma evaluated by OCT and IVUS. JACC Cardiovasc Imaging 2011;4(6):638−46. Available from: https://doi.org/10.1016/j.jcmg.2011.03.014.

[72] Virmani R. Are our tools for the identification of TCFA ready and do we know them? JACC Cardiovasc Imaging 2011;4(6):656−8. Available from: https://doi.org/10.1016/j.jcmg.2011.01.019.

[73] Bezzera H. Intravascular OCT in PCI. < https://www.acc.org/latest-in-cardiology/articles/2016/06/13/10/01/intravascular-oct-in-pci >. 2016 [Accessed 16.04.20].

[74] Burzotta F, Leone A, De Maria G, et al. Fractional flow reserve or optical coherence tomography guidance to revascularize intermediate coronary stenosis using angioplasty (FORZA) trial: study protocol for a randomized controlled trial. Trials 2014;15(1):140. Available from: https://doi.org/10.1186/1745-6215-15-140.

[75] Pociask E, Malinowski K, Ślęzak M, Jaworek-Korjakowska J, Wojakowski W, Roleder T. Fully automated lumen segmentation method for intracoronary optical coherence tomography. J Healthc Eng 2018;2018(1):1−13. Available from: https://doi.org/10.1155/2018/1414076.

[76] Sinclair H, Bourantas C, Bagnall A, Mintz G, Kunadian V. OCT for the identification of vulnerable plaque in acute coronary syndrome. JACC Cardiovasc Imaging 2015;8(2):198−209. Available from: https://doi.org/10.1016/j.jcmg.2014.12.005.

[77] Alfonso F, Paulo M, Gonzalo N, et al. Diagnosis of spontaneous coronary artery dissection by optical coherence tomography. J Am Coll Cardiol 2012;59(12):1073−9. Available from: https://doi.org/10.1016/j.jacc.2011.08.082.

[78] Alfonso F, Canales E, Aleong G. Spontaneous coronary artery dissection: diagnosis by optical coherence tomography. Eur Heart J 2009;30(3):385. Available from: https://doi.org/10.1093/eurheartj/ehn441.

[79] Akhtar M, Liu W. Use of intravascular ultrasound versus optical coherence tomography for mechanism and patterns of in-stent restenosis among bare metal stents and drug eluting stents. J Thorac Dis 2016;8(1):E104−8. Available from: https://doi.org/10.3978/j.issn.2072-1439.2016.01.48.

[80] Attizzani G, Capodanno D, Ohno Y, Tamburino C. Mechanisms, pathophysiology, and clinical aspects of incomplete stent apposition. J Am Coll Cardiol 2014;63(14):1355−67. Available from: https://doi.org/10.1016/j.jacc.2014.01.019.

[81] Leistner D, Landmesser U, Fröhlich G. FD-OCT and IVUS for detection of incomplete stent apposition in heavily calcified vessels: novel insights. < https://openheart.bmj.com/content/2/1/e000292?cpe-toc = &utm_term = usage-012019&utm_content = consumer&utm_campaign = oh&utm_medium = cpc&utm_source = trendmd >. 2015 [Accessed 15.02.20].

[82] Im E, Kim B, Ko Y, et al. Incidences, predictors, and clinical outcomes of acute and late stent malapposition detected by optical coherence tomography after drug-eluting stent implantation. Circ Cardiovasc Interv 2014;7(1):88−96. Available from: https://doi.org/10.1161/CIRCINTERVENTIONS.113.000797.

[83] Hernández H, Gonzálvez A, Moreno R, Jiménez S. Longitudinal stent deformation: precise diagnosis with optical coherence tomography. J Invasive Cardiol 2019;31(12):E395 PMID:31786534.

[84] Si D, Tong Y, Yu B, He Y, Liu G. In-stent restenosis and longitudinal stent deformation: a case report. BMC Cardiovasc Disorders 2020;20(1):24. Available from: https://doi.org/10.1186/s12872-020-01335-1.

[85] Okamura T, Gonzalo N, Gutierrez J, et al. Does the second generation OCT improve safety and feasibility in clinical practice? a single center experience. J Am Coll Cardiol 2010;55(A202):E1906. Available from: https://doi.org/10.1016/S0735-1097(10)61907-9.

[86] Takarada S, Imanishi T, Liu Y, et al. Advantage of next-generation frequency-domain optical coherence tomography compared with conventional time-domain system in the assessment of coronary lesion. Catheter Cardiovasc Interv 2010;75:202−6. Available from: https://doi.org/10.1002/ccd.22273.

[87] Kato K, Yasutake M, Yonetsu T, et al. Intracoronary imaging modalities for vulnerable plaques. J Nippon Med Sch 2011;78(6):340−51. Available from: https://doi.org/10.1272/jnms.78.340.

[88] Zafar H, Ullah I, Dinneen K, Matiullah S, Hanley A, Leahy M, et al. Evaluation of hemodynamically severe coronary stenosis as determined by fractional flow reserve with frequency domain

optical coherence tomography measured anatomical parameters. J Cardiol 2014;64(1):19—24. Available from: https://doi.org/10.1016/j.jjcc.2013.11.009.

[89]   Next-generation ILUMIEN OPTIS system from St. Jude Medical provides real-time 360° panoramic view of the arteries. CathLab Digest, https://www.cathlabdigest.com/Next-Generation-ILUMIEN-OPTIS-System-St-Jude-Medical-Provides-Real-Time-360%CB%9A-Panoramic-View-Arteries; 2013 [Accessed 05.04.20].

[90]   Fornell D. Advances in intravascular imaging. Diagnostic and Interventional Cardiology. < https://www.dicardiology.com/article/advances-intravascular-imaging-0 >. 2015 [Accessed 05.04.20].

[91]   Hebsgaard L, Nielsen T, Tu S, et al. Co-registration of optical coherence tomography and X-ray angiography in percutaneous coronary intervention. The Does Optical Coherence Tomography Optimize Revascularization (DOCTOR) fusion study. Int J Cardiol 2015;182:272—8. Available from: https://doi.org/10.1016/j.ijcard.2014.12.088.

[92]   Van der Sijde J, Guagliumi G, Sirbu V, Shimamura K, Borghesi M, Karanasos A, et al. The OPTIS integrated system: real-time, co-registration of angiography and optical coherence tomography. Euro Int 2016;12(7):855—60. Available from: https://doi.org/10.4244/EIJV12I7A140.

[93]   St. Jude Medical Launches Optis Mobile System in Europe and Japan. Diagnostic and Interventional Cardiology, https://www.dicardiology.com/product/st-jude-medical-launches-optis-mobile-system-europe-and-japan; 2016 [Accessed 05.04.20].

[94]   Stone G, Witzenbichler B, Weisz G, et al. Platelet reactivity and clinical outcomes after coronary artery implantation of drug-eluting stents (ADAPT-DES): a prospective multicentre registry study. Lancet 2013;382(9892):614—23. Available from: https://doi.org/10.1016/S0140-6736(13)61170-8.

[95]   Maehara A, Ben O, Wijns W, et al. Comparison of Stent expansion guided by optical coherence tomography versus intravascular ultrasound. JACC Cardiovasc Interventions 2015;8(13):1704—14. Available from: https://doi.org/10.1016/j.jcin.2015.07.024.

[96]   Ali Z, Maehara A, Généreux P, et al. Optical coherence tomography compared with intravascular ultrasound and with angiography to guide coronary stent implantation (ILUMIEN III: OPTIMIZE PCI): a randomised controlled trial. Lancet 2016;338(10060):2618—28. Available from: https://doi.org/10.1016/s0140-6736(16)31922-5.

[97]   Stone G, Landmesser U, Ali Z. Optical coherence tomography (OCT) guided coronary stent implantation compared to angiography: a multicenter randomized trial in PCI. https://clinicaltrials.gov/ct2/show/NCT03507777; 2020 [Accessed 05.04.20].

CHAPTER 2

Technique of cardiac magnetic resonance imaging

Ahmed Abdel Khalek Abdel Razek, Dalia Fahmy and Germeen Albair Ashmalla
Department of Diagnostic Radiology, Faculty of Medicine, Mansoura University, Mansoura, Egypt

2.1 Introduction

Cardiac MRI aimed to assess different congenital and acquired heart diseases, for example, myocardial ischemia or infarction, cardiomyopathies, cardiac masses, valvular disease, pericardial lesions, coronary artery disease (CAD), as well as complex congenital anomalies. The good soft-tissue contrast, the feasibility of a large FOV, multiplanar acquisition adeptness in addition to absence of ionizing radiation are advantages of cardiac MRI. On the other hand, the disadvantage of cardiac MRI compared to CT is the inability to assess coronary arteries calcifications. Other limitations of cardiac MRI include: not being suitable for imaging extremely large, claustrophobic or patients with non-MR compatible implants (e.g., old versions of cardiac pacemaker), also Gadolinium-based MR contrast administration is confined to patients with good renal function, lastly, prolonged scan time compared with computed tomography and echocardiography. Till now there are no reports of any possible drawbacks on fetal viability, yet pregnancy is still included in the list of relative contraindications [1—5].

2.2 Physical principles and pulse sequences

2.2.1 Data acquisition

When dealing with cardiac MRI, there are few obstacles to be overcome. To begin with, the rapid and the multiplex mobility of the heart in addition to the pulsating flow of the great vessels, movement during inspiration and expiration, high ventricular blood flow during systole that may be as high as 200 cm/s. However, this problem is solved now by implementing ECG (cardiac) gating; navigator echo respiratory gating; breath-hold techniques; rapid, high-performance gradients; improved field homogeneity; and advanced pulse sequences [1—4]. ECG gating is done in two ways prospective or retrospective. Prospective method means commencing imaging is initiated at same timing as the R wave, so limited images are gathered. In clinical practice, arrhythmias and frequent change in heart rate during examination even in patients with regular rhythm hinder the application of this technique. On the other hand, retrospective gating means that images are acquired along the whole cardiac cycle followed by selection of specific data later on during postprocessing. Retrospective gating is therefore preferable to overcome problems caused by arrhythmias on the behalf of more time consumption to gain data. Navigator echo respiratory gating permits gathering of images without the need for respiratory holding. An excitation pulse is put at the level of the diaphragm or heart to monitor respiratory movement in order to collect image at the end of expiratory phase [1,2].

2.2.2 Morphologic sequences

Morphologic sequences provide the most value when analyzing complex congenital anomalies and measuring the span of cardiac masses. At least one anatomical series will be done in the standard thoracic axial plane; however, additional oblique planes are imaged as well (horizontal and vertical long-axis views, two- and four-chamber views, short-axis view, views of the valves, outflow tracts, and great vessels) [1–3]. Cardiac MR sequences can be categorized into two groups, according to their myocardium-blood pool native contrast—dark (black) blood (Fig. 2.1) and bright (white) blood (Fig. 2.2) sequences. It is often worthwhile to employ both of them for easier comparison.

Figure 2.1 Dark blood sequence: Double inversion recovery (dark-blood MRI imaging sequence) of the short axis of the heart, showing better delineation of the anatomical details of the myocardium with nullifying of signals from blood.

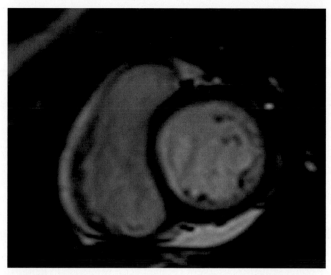

Figure 2.2 Bright blood sequence: SSFP (Bright-blood MRI imaging sequence) of the short axis, showing significant contrast between the myocardial tissue and flowing blood.

2.2.2.1 Dark blood sequences

Dark blood sequence provides a very clear distinction between the vessel wall and blood (Fig. 2.1). They are usually performed at multiple slice locations during diastole to produce a stack of 4—5 mm thick slices. Dark blood images utilize a series of inversion recovery prepulse to cancel unwanted signal—respectively, a double IR prepulse to cancel blood signal or a triple IR prepulse to null blood and fat. Examples of the imaging engines used are TSE, and its faster variant half-Fourier acquired single-shot turbo spin echo. Additionally, the short-tau inversion recovery (STIR) modifier can be of great use for identifying high signal jeopardized myocardium in the setting of acute myocardial infarction. T2-STIR is also used to search for edema associated with acute infarction [1—4].

2.2.2.2 Bright blood sequence with cine functional sequences

Bright blood sequences are built upon the SSFP and EPI gradient engines and are an integral part of CMR examinations. They display a high-intensity signal from fast-flowing blood and are excellent at evaluating cardiac function (Fig. 2.2). These sequences continuously image a single slice across several whole cardiac cycles, creating a short averaged-out movie (cine) of the heart in motion. The cine contains 20—30 frames acquired with 30—50 ms temporal resolution. Classically, a stack of short-axis slices (6—8 mm thick, with 1—2 mm gaps in between) is each turned into individual cine series to achieve adequate coverage [1—4]. Thus, they facilitate accurate estimation of the systolic and diastolic motion of the ventricular walls, both quantitative and

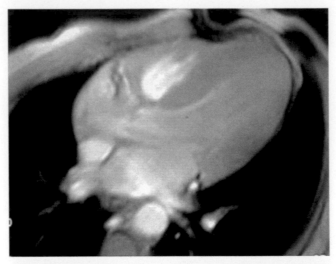

Figure 2.3 Cine functional sequence: Gradient recalled echo sequence in long axis of the heart.

qualitative (Fig. 2.3). Also, measurements can be made of left ventricular end-diastolic and end-systolic volumes, ejection fraction and myocardial mass can be estimated. Additionally, blood velocity and flow direction could be measured using the modifier Phase Contrast (velocity encoded, VENC)—a task impossible for CT, and not easily reproducible with the United States. Phase contrast measures the phase shift from blood protons moving through the magnetic field [without the need for intravenous (IV) contrast material], which is proportional to their speed, allowing for estimation of speed and its direction. A cine series encompassing several phases of the cardiac cycle is created. Velocity is encoded in a way reminiscent of color Doppler in ultrasound. The selected plane is usually at right angle to a vessel, chamber, or valve of interest, with antegrade flow coded in light gray to white and retrograde flow coded in dark gray to black, while stationary tissues appear intermediate gray. Time-velocity and time-flow curves can be generated. VENC is valuable for evaluating shunts and shunt fractions, determining pressure gradients across stenotic valves and determining regurgitated flow (Fig. 2.4) [4,5].

2.2.2.3 T1 and T2 mapping
In the last few years CMR mapping techniques have been introduced, enabling the objective numerical measurement of signal strength in every pixel of either T1-, T2-, or T2*-weighted mapped images (which is impossible to do in images acquired via a different sequence). This technique is mostly used for analyzing diffuse myocardial changes. T1 mapping, for example, is very precise in detecting infiltrative disease—myocarditis, amyloidosis, sarcoidosis, and cardiomyopathies. It is usually performed in two phases

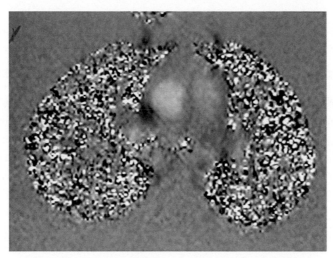

Figure 2.4 Phase-contrast MR sequence: Phase image used for calculation of peak velocity and pressure gradient.

(pre- and postcontrast). T2 mapping is excellent for distinguishing edema, while T2*-mapping is less frequently used, as it demonstrates only myocardial iron overload (e.g., in hemochromatosis).

It is understood that T2 mapping sequences provide quantitative evaluation of myocardial edema (objective T2 relaxation time), not qualitative evaluation (arbitrary signal intensity) unlike the T2-STIR sequences. T1 and T2 mapping play a major role in recognition of minor and subtle myocardial changes not evident in other techniques. Studies are collecting data in order to reach range of T1 and T2 values that are specific to each cardiac disease. This step would be helpful for precise measurement of ECV expansion and assessment of the condition of the myocardium [6−8]. Combined T1 mapping and 4D flow pave the way for a better realization of the consequences of any change in hemodynamics upon the myocardium. The 4D flow technique could enhance the understanding of the pathophysiology of different vascular diseases and the hemodynamic effect of flow abnormalities, in addition to preoperative planning. [9−11].

2.2.2.4 Myocardial perfusion

Perfusion MR imaging can detect perfusion of contrast medium within the tissues that can be used in different regions of the body. CMR perfusion provides a tool of high sensitivity and specificity to assess CAD. Perfusion is done at rest and at (adenosine-induced) stress. Perfusion sequences (balanced SSFP, GRE, or EPI engine) create a short movie of the blood either by using an exogenous IV gadolinium-based tracer or endogenous arterial spins. As the blood washes in and passes through the myocardium, areas with lower signal (hypointense areas) are easily recognized as hypoperfused. It is necessary to get multiple images within a single cardiac cycle so, image quality invariably diminishes, especially in tachycardic patients, where RR intervals are much shorter. Better signal-to-noise ratios for this method can be achieved at 3 Tesla than at 1.5 Tesla [12–20].

Gadolinium-based perfusion is preferred as it allows for strong contrast in T1-weighted images, large coverage of myocardium, and adequate spatial resolution. When doing the stress perfusion examination, adenosine dosed at 140 µg/kg of patient weight per minute is injected over a period of 2–3 minutes. It acts as a vasodilator by influencing the A2A receptors. Its effect is a maximum dilation of the distal arteriolar bed. Coronary flow can be thus increased by about four times in the absence of stenosis. In significantly stenotic arteries, however, there is no change, resulting in a "steal phenomenon" from the stenotic to the normal arteries. The zones supplied by normal arteries demonstrate a multifold flow increase, while the ones corresponding to stenotic arteries show little or no flow increase, appearing hypointense. Usually, the stress test precedes the rest test with roughly 15 minutes in between them, necessary for complete washout of the first Gadolinium bolus. Finally, another 10–15 minutes after the rest test, a late Gd enhancement series can be performed. To clarify further, IV gadolinium is given once during the stress test, and once more during the rest test [20–25].

2.2.2.5 Delayed contrast-enhanced CMR and myocardial viability

Viability studies are mostly performed with late Gd enhancement, using T1-weighted GRE sequences. The images are made with a single IR prepulse, aimed at nulling the signal from normal myocardium, so only the pathologically enhancing structures can be of high signal. Healthy structures are to appear black, while blood within the left ventricle should be of intermediate signal strength—neutral gray. The standard protocol includes precontrast images, first-pass perfusion images with an initial Gd bolus, followed by a second Gd bolus and then, finally, the most important series—delayed imaging at about 10–20 minutes. This is thought to be due to the fact that in acutely infarcted myocytes, the ruptured membranes enable Gd to pass intracellularly via diffusion. Conversely, chronic infarctions consist of scar tissue with greater interstitial space than normal myocardium—therefore, Gd would accumulate within the scar [17–25].

2.2.2.6 CMR angiography

It is usually done through IV injection of gadolinium-based contrast and requires a fast three-dimensional (3D) spoiled GRE sequence. This is a 3D sequence without interslice gaps permitting perfect and smooth multiplanar reformats. This also allows for the building of cast-like volume renderings of the contrast-filled lumen of the vessels as well as cardiac chambers (true 3D models) which are extremely valuable in evaluation of congenital vascular diseases and great vessels of the heart (Fig. 2.5) [26–30].

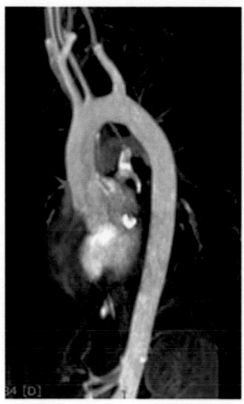

Figure 2.5 Contrast MR angiography: Contrast MRA of the thoracic aorta that can detect thoracic aorta and its main branches.

CAD is considered number one cause of death all over the world. Luminal stenosis occurs due to the buildup of atheromatous plaques over long duration. Early detection of these lesions is necessary to facilitate a proper treatment plan (either percutaneous angioplasty or coronary artery bypass graft surgery) before irreversible damage to myocardial muscle occurs. Coronary arteries could be assessed in bright blood sequences (spoiled gradient echo and SSFP) or after gadolinium injection. One drawback is the incomplete coverage of the whole coronary tree in single breath hold. So, a free-breathing technique and slow infusion (0.3 mL/s) of gadolinium were suggested. This technique facilitates comprehensive imaging of coronary arteries in short duration preserving high sensitivity and specificity compared to conventional cardiac angiography. Coronary artery stiffness could be assessed by measuring degree of dilatation after administration of vasoactive drug or by monitoring change in diameter in systole and diastole. Flow reserve within coronary arteries could be assessed by phase-contrast MR imaging. CMR provides a noninvasive tool to evaluate coronary wall thickness and remodeling. New techniques are developed to overcome motion related to cardiac and respiratory cycles as well as high heart rate and irregular heartbeat (arrhythmia) as these are the main factors hindering the use of CMR in clinical practice [26−35].

2.2.2.7 Arterial spin labeling

Arterial spin labeling is designed for noninvasive quantification of tissue blood flow without the need for contrast media. Radiofrequency pulses (RF) are applied to change the longitudinal magnetization of arterial blood, creating an endogenous label that decays with time constant which has the same duration as the T1 relaxation time. Then a delay time is given to permit passage of labeled blood into tissues, followed by image acquisition. Another group of images is taken without a labeling pulse. The difference between these two image groups represents the amount of labeled blood inflow. It has several applications regarding characterization and evaluation of brain tumors and head and neck cancer. In cardiac imaging, this could be used to replace the first-pass CMR and nuclear medicine [36−42].

2.2.2.8 Magnetic resonance spectroscopy

Magnetic resonance spectroscopy (MRS) is a method designed to evaluate cellular features in vivo by detection of relatively small molecules in intra- and extracellular spaces. MRS proved to be an effective tool in differentiation of various brain and neck tumors. Cardiac MRS applies appropriate RF pulses to the desired tissues with subsequent modification of the magnetic momentum of susceptible nuclei. At the end of the stimulation, a certain amount of energy is released from the excited nuclei and can be collected as a spectrum. In order to avoid signal contamination caused by nearby blood and epicardial fat, the region of interest is placed in the interventricular septum. In vivo, 1H-MRS has been mainly used to assess the cardiac intracellular fat (as TGs and UFAs). Few studies reported that progressive reduction of ventricular function was correlated to increased myocardial TG content, yet available data from different studies are still conflicting. On the other hand, heart failure (HF) showed low Cr that is correlated with LV function. The cardiac PCr/ATP ratio was improved during clinical re-compensation with standard HF treatment and in obese patients losing weight, again correlating with improved LV function [43−47].

2.2.2.9 Cardiac diffusion tensor imaging

Diffusion tensor imaging is commonly used in evaluation of brain tumors and preoperative mapping of gliomas. Diffusion tensor cardiovascular magnetic resonance assumes that the restrained diffusion can be pictorially demonstrated by an ellipsoid shape and mathematically described by a tensor that is measured in at least six different directions. The tensor gives information about how freely water can diffuse in the myocardium via mean diffusivity (MD). The degree of diffusion restriction is expressed by fractional anisotropy (FA) and reflects the underlying organization of the myocardium with grading where 0 represents highly disorganized cells, and 1 represents perfectly linearly organized cells. For example, in myocardial infarction, there was elevated MD and decreased FA in the segment involved in acute infarction compared with the normal segment, attributed to disorganization of ischemic cells [48–57].

2.2.3 Future directions
2.2.3.1 Artificial intelligence
Artificial intelligence recently applied in the cardiac imaging that depends on the automatization tasks, improving diagnostic accuracy, and reducing reading time for image analysis [58,59].

2.2.3.2 Structured reporting
Structured reporting was applied in different regions of the body such as coronary artery, chest, neck, liver, and prostate. Recently structured reporting for cardiovascular magnetic resonance imaging was released that may help to standardized reporting system among radiologists [27,60–69].

References

[1] Jo Y, Kim J, Park CH, et al. Guideline for cardiovascular magnetic resonance imaging from the Korean Society of Cardiovascular Imaging-Part 1: standardized protocol. Korean J Radiol 2019;20:1313–33.

[2] Cui C, Yin G, Lu M, et al. Retrospective electrocardiography-gated real-time cardiac cine MRI at 3T: comparison with conventional segmented cine MRI. Korean J Radiol 2019;20:114–25.

[3] Saeed M, Liu H, Liang CH, et al. Magnetic resonance imaging for characterizing myocardial diseases. Int J Cardiovasc Imaging 2017;33:1395–414.

[4] Situ Y, Birch SCM, Moreyra C, et al. Cardiovascular magnetic resonance imaging for structural heart disease. Cardiovasc Diagn Ther 2020;10:361–75.

[5] Nayak KS, Nielsen JF, Bernstein MA, et al. Cardiovascular magnetic resonance phase contrast imaging. J Cardiovasc Magn Reson 2015;17:71.

[6] Messroghli DR, Moon JC, Ferreira VM, et al. Clinical recommendations for cardiovascular magnetic resonance mapping of T1, T2, T2* and extracellular volume: a consensus statement by the Society for Cardiovascular Magnetic Resonance (SCMR) endorsed by the European Association for Cardiovascular Imaging (EACVI). J Cardiovasc Magn Reson 2017;19:75.

[7] Kim PK, Hong YJ, Im DJ, et al. Myocardial T1 and T2 mapping: techniques and clinical applications. Korean J Radiol 2017;18:113–31.

[8] van den Boomen M, Slart RHJA, Hulleman EV, et al. Native T1 reference values for nonischemic cardiomyopathies and populations with increased cardiovascular risk: a systematic review and meta-analysis. J Magn Reson Imaging 2018;47:891–912.

[9] Kamphuis VP, Westenberg JJM, van der Palen RLF, et al. Unravelling cardiovascular disease using four dimensional flow cardiovascular magnetic resonance. Int J Cardiovasc Imaging 2017;33:1069–81.

[10] Robison S, Hong K, Kim D, et al. Evaluation of modified look-locker inversion recovery and arrhythmia-insensitive rapid cardiac T1 mapping pulse sequences in cardiomyopathy patients. J Comput Assist Tomogr 2018;42:732–8.

[11] Cheung E, Han HC, Hornsey E, et al. Arrhythmia insensitive rapid cardiac T1 mapping: comparison to modified look locker inversion recovery T1 mapping in mitral valve prolapse patients. Int J Cardiovasc Imaging 2020;36:2017−25. Available from: https://doi.org/10.1007/s10554-020-01910-9.

[12] Nordio G, Henningsson M, Chiribiri A, et al. 3D myocardial T1 mapping using saturation recovery. J Magn Reson Imaging 2017;46:218−27.

[13] Seetharam K, Lerakis S. Cardiac magnetic resonance imaging: the future is bright. F1000Res 2019;8 F1000 Faculty Rev-1636.

[14] Dodd JD, Leipsic J. Cardiovascular CT and MRI in 2019: review of key articles. Radiology 2020;297:17−30.

[15] Vieillard-Baron A, Millington SJ, Sanfilippo F, et al. A decade of progress in critical care echocardiography: a narrative review. Intensive Care Med 2019;45:770−88.

[16] Razek AA, Elsorogy LG, Soliman NY, Nada N. Dynamic susceptibility contrast perfusion MR imaging in distinguishing malignant from benign head and neck tumors: a pilot study. Eur J Radiol 2011;77:73−9.

[17] Abdel Razek AA, Gaballa G. Role of perfusion magnetic resonance imaging in cervical lymphadenopathy. J Comput Assist Tomogr 2011;35:21−5.

[18] Abdel Razek AA, Gaballa G, Ashamalla G, et al. Dynamic susceptibility contrast perfusion-weighted magnetic resonance imaging and diffusion-weighted magnetic resonance imaging in differentiating recurrent head and neck cancer from postradiation changes. J Comput Assist Tomogr 2015;39:849−54.

[19] Abdel Razek AA, Samir S, Ashmalla GA. Characterization of parotid tumors with dynamic susceptibility contrast perfusion-weighted magnetic resonance imaging and diffusion-weighted MR imaging. J Comput Assist Tomogr 2017;41:131−6.

[20] François CJ. Current state of the art cardiovascular MR imaging techniques for assessment of ischemic heart disease. Radiol Clin North Am 2015;53:335−44.

[21] Ibanez B, Aletras AH, Arai AE, et al. Cardiac MRI endpoints in myocardial infarction experimental and clinical trials: JACC Scientific Expert Panel. J Am Coll Cardiol 2019;74:238−56.

[22] Fair MJ, Gatehouse PD, DiBella EV, et al. A review of 3D first-pass, whole-heart, myocardial perfusion cardiovascular magnetic resonance. J Cardiovasc Magn Reson 2015;17:68.

[23] Nazir MS, Neji R, Speier P, et al. Simultaneous multi slice (SMS) balanced steady state free precession first-pass myocardial perfusion cardiovascular magnetic resonance with iterative reconstruction at 1.5 T. J Cardiovasc Magn Reson 2018;20:84.

[24] Prosper AE, Colletti PM. Myocardial perfusion SPECT and cardiac MR correlative imaging. Clin Nucl Med 2017;42:941−4.

[25] Benovoy M, Jacobs M, Cheriet F, et al. Robust universal nonrigid motion correction framework for first-pass cardiac MR perfusion imaging. J Magn Reson Imaging 2017;46:1060−72.

[26] Abdel Razek AA, Denewer AT, Hegazy MA, et al. Role of computed tomography angiography in the diagnosis of vascular stenosis in head and neck microvascular free flap reconstruction. Int J Oral Maxillofac Surg 2014;43:811−15.

[27] Abdel Razek AAK, Elrakhawy MM, Yossof MM, et al. Inter-observer agreement of the Coronary Artery Disease Reporting and Data System (CAD-RADS(TM)) in patients with stable chest pain. Pol J Radiol 2018;83:e151−9.

[28] Razek AA, Gaballa G, Megahed AS, et al. Time resolved imaging of contrast kinetics (TRICKS) MR angiography of arteriovenous malformations of head and neck. Eur J Radiol 2013;82:1885−91.

[29] Razek AA, Saad E, Soliman N, et al. Assessment of vascular disorders of the upper extremity with contrast-enhanced magnetic resonance angiography: pictorial review. Jpn J Radiol 2010;28:87−94.

[30] Romeih S, Al-Sheshtawy F, Salama M, et al. Comparison of contrast enhanced magnetic resonance angiography with invasive cardiac catheterization for evaluation of children with pulmonary atresia. Heart Int 2012;7:e9.

[31] Abdel Razek AAK. Imaging findings of Klippel-Trenaunay Syndrome. J Comput Assist Tomogr 2019;43:786−92.

[32] Abdel Razek AA, Al-Marsafawy H, Elmansy M, et al. CT angiography and MR angiography of congenital anomalies of pulmonary veins. J Comput Assist Tomogr 2019;43:399−405.

[33] Abdel Razek AAK, Al-Marsafawy H, Elmansy M. Imaging of pulmonary atresia with ventricular septal defect. J Comput Assist Tomogr 2019;43:906−11.

[34] Ishida M, Sakuma H. Coronary MR angiography revealed: how to optimize image quality. Magn Reson Imaging Clin N Am 2015;23:117−25.

[35] Dweck MR, Puntman V, Vesey AT, et al. MR imaging of coronary arteries and plaques. JACC Cardiovasc Imaging 2016;9:306−16.

[36] Abdel Razek AAK, Talaat M, El-Serougy L, et al. Clinical applications of arterial spin labeling in brain tumors. J Comput Assist Tomogr 2019;43:525−32.

[37] Abdel Razek AAK, Nada N. Arterial spin labeling perfusion-weighted MR imaging: correlation of tumor blood flow with pathological degree of tumor differentiation, clinical stage and nodal metastasis of head and neck squamous cell carcinoma. Eur Arch Otorhinolaryngol 2018;275:1301−7.

[38] Abdel Razek AAK. Arterial spin labelling and diffusion-weighted magnetic resonance imaging in differentiation of recurrent head and neck cancer from post-radiation changes. J Laryngol Otol 2018;132:923−8.

[39] Razek AAKA, El-Serougy L, Abdelsalam M, et al. Differentiation of residual/ recurrent gliomas from postradiation necrosis with arterial spin labeling and diffusion tensor magnetic resonance imaging-derived metrics. Neuroradiology 2018;60:169−77.

[40] Razek AAKA. Multi-parametric MR imaging using pseudo-continuous arterial-spin labeling and diffusion-weighted MR imaging in differentiating subtypes of parotid tumors. Magn Reson Imaging 2019;63:55−9.

[41] Kober F, Jao T, Troalen T, et al. Myocardial arterial spin labeling. J Cardiovasc Magn Reson 2016;18:22.

[42] Jao TR, Nayak KS. Demonstration of velocity selective myocardial arterial spin labeling perfusion imaging in humans. Magn Reson Med 2018;80:272−8.

[43] Abdel Razek AA, Poptani H. MR spectroscopy of head and neck cancer. Eur J Radiol 2013;82:982−9.

[44] Razek AA, Nada N. Correlation of choline/creatine and apparent diffusion coefficient values with the prognostic parameters of head and neck squamous cell carcinoma. NMR Biomed 2016;29:483−9.

[45] El-mewafy Z, Abdel Razek AAAK, El-Eshmawy M, et al. MR spectroscopy of the frontal region in patients with metabolic syndrome: correlation with anthropometric measurement. Polish J Radiol 2018;83:e215−19.

[46] Razek AA, Abdalla A, Ezzat A, et al. Minimal hepatic encephalopathy in children with liver cirrhosis: diffusion-weighted MR imaging and proton MR spectroscopy of the brain. Neuroradiology 2014;56:885−91.

[47] Dellegrottaglie S, Scatteia A, Pascale CE, et al. Evaluation of cardiac metabolism by magnetic resonance spectroscopy in heart failure. Heart Fail Clin 2019;15:421−33.

[48] El-Serougy L, Abdel Razek AA, Ezzat A, et al. Assessment of diffusion tensor imaging metrics in differentiating low-grade from high-grade gliomas. Neuroradiol J 2016;29:400−7.

[49] Razek AA, Fathy A, Gawad TA. Correlation of apparent diffusion coefficient value with prognostic parameters of lung cancer. J Comput Assist Tomogr 2011;35:248−52.

[50] Razek AAKA, Ashmalla GA. Assessment of paraspinal neurogenic tumors with diffusion-weighted MR imaging. Eur Spine J 2018;27:841−6.

[51] Abdel Razek A, Zaki M, Bayoumi D, et al. Diffusion tensor imaging parameters in differentiation recurrent breast cancer from post-operative changes in patients with breast-conserving surgery. Eur J Radiol 2019;111:76−80.

[52] Razek AAKA. Diffusion tensor imaging in differentiation of residual head and neck squamous cell carcinoma from post-radiation changes. Magn Reson Imaging 2018;54:84−9.

[53] Khalek Abdel Razek AA. Characterization of salivary gland tumours with diffusion tensor imaging. Dentomaxillofac Radiol 2018;47:20170343.

[54] Razek AA, Shabana AA, El Saied TO, et al. Diffusion tensor imaging of mild-moderate carpal tunnel syndrome: correlation with nerve conduction study and clinical tests. Clin Rheumatol 2017;36:2319−24.

[55] Razek AAKA, Al-Adlany MAAA, Alhadidy AM, et al. Diffusion tensor imaging of the renal cortex in diabetic patients: correlation with urinary and serum biomarkers. Abdom Radiol 2017;42:1493−500.

[56] Khalique Z, Pennell D. Diffusion tensor cardiovascular magnetic resonance. Postgrad Med J 2019;95:433—8.

[57] MacGowan GA, Parikh JD, Hollingsworth KG. Diffusion tensor magnetic resonance imaging of the heart: looking into the layers of the myocardium. J Am Coll Cardiol 2017;69:677—8.

[58] Razek AAKA. Editorial for "Preoperative MRI-based radiomic machine-learning nomogram may accurately distinguish between benign and malignant soft tissue lesions: a two-center study." J Magn Reson Imaging 2020;52:883—4.

[59] van Assen M, Muscogiuri G, Caruso D, et al. Artificial intelligence in cardiac radiology. Radiol Med 2020;125:1186—99.

[60] Abdel Razek AAK, Abdelaziz TT. Neck imaging reporting and data system: what does radiologist want to know? J Comput Assist Tomogr 2020;44:527—32.

[61] Abdelaziz TT, Abdel Razk AAK, Ashour MMM, et al. Interreader reproducibility of the neck imaging reporting and data system (NI-RADS) lexicon for the detection of residual/recurrent disease in treated head and neck squamous cell carcinoma (HNSCC). Cancer Imaging 2020;20:61.

[62] Abdel Razek AA, Ashmalla GA, Gaballa G, et al. Pilot study of ultrasound parotid imaging reporting and data system (PIRADS): inter-observer agreement. Eur J Radiol 2015;85:2533—8.

[63] Razek AAKA, El Badrawy MK, Alnaghy E. Interstitial lung fibrosis imaging reporting and data system: what radiologist wants to know? J Comput Assist Tomogr 2020;44:656—66.

[64] Abdel Razek AAK, El-Serougy LG, Saleh GA, et al. Liver imaging reporting and data system version 2018: what radiologists need to know. J Comput Assist Tomogr 2020;44:168—77.

[65] Abdel Razek AAK, El-Serougy LG, Saleh GA, et al. Interobserver agreement of magnetic resonance imaging of liver imaging reporting and data system version 2018. J Comput Assist Tomogr 2020;44:118—23.

[66] Abdel Razek AAK, El-Serougy LG, Saleh GA, et al. Reproducibility of LI-RADS treatment response algorithm for hepatocellular carcinoma after locoregional therapy. Diagn Interv Imaging 2020;101:547—53.

[67] Ahmed HN, Ebeed AE, Hamdy A, et al. Inter-observer agreement of prostate imaging—reporting and data system (PI-RADS—V2). Egypt J Radiol Nucl Med 2020;52:5.

[68] Schulz-Menger J, Bluemke DA, Bremerich J, et al. Standardized image interpretation and post-processing in cardiovascular magnetic resonance - 2020 update: Society for Cardiovascular Magnetic Resonance (SCMR): Board of Trustees Task Force on Standardized Post-Processing. J Cardiovasc Magn Reson 2020;22:19.

[69] Huang Y, Zhou H, Feng Y, et al. Structured reporting of cardiovascular magnetic resonance based on expert consensuses and guidelines. Aging Med 2020;3:40—7.

CHAPTER 3

The role of automated 12-lead ECG interpretation in the diagnosis and risk stratification of cardiovascular disease

Salah S. Al-Zaiti[1], Ziad Faramand[2], Khaled Rjoob[3], Dewar Finlay[3] and Raymond Bond[3]

[1]Departments of Acute and Tertiary Care Nursing, Emergency Medicine, and Cardiology, University of Pittsburgh, Pittsburgh, PA, United States
[2]University of Pittsburgh Medical Center (UPMC), Pittsburgh, PA, United States
[3]Faculty of Computing, Engineering and Built Environment, Ulster University, Coleraine, United Kingdom

3.1 Introduction

The surface electrocardiogram (ECG) is a common diagnostic test in clinical settings. It reflects a time-voltage signal of the averaged changes over time in cell membrane polarity of the myocardium (heart tissue), and it constitutes one of the well studied physiological signals of the human body [1–6]. The ECG signal has been widely used for risk stratification in both the general population and in those with cardiovascular disease, with various ECG abnormalities predicting risk of adverse events [7]. Because of this broad applicability, accurate computer-generated diagnostic statements are essential. Basic understanding of both the clinical significance of the ECG waveform and the technological specifications for signal retrieval and processing are needed for designing accurate automated analysis systems of the digital 12-lead ECG.

The association between the ECG and the "digital" computer began over 60 years ago with the early attempts at representing the analog ECG signal as digital samples. As with any time-varying analog quantity, the ECG can be sampled at an appropriate frequency and resolution to allow an accurate representation of the original signal to be stored and processed digitally [8]. Despite the obvious benefits of digital signal processing of the ECG, early investigators were greatly frustrated by limitations in sampling and acquisition hardware which made simultaneous multichannel ECG digitization prohibitive. By the 1970s, however, significant advances in acquisition hardware meant that millions of digital ECGs were being recorded annually [9]. This in turn drew attention to the developments associated with the storage of ECG data. As a result, there are now a plethora of digital file formats for storing the ECG [10]. These file formats can be proprietary or open, and many can be machine readable only, whilst others can be both machine and human readable (e.g., formats based on the eXtensible Markup Language) [11].

Digitizing the ECG enabled computers to process 12-lead ECGs which paved the way for automated interpretation. In the 1960s the first computer algorithm to automatically interpret the 12-lead ECG was developed in the 1960s [12]. Until then, due to the complexity of the signals at hand, interpretation of the ECG was only possible by a skilled human observer [13,14]. Automation of this task had the potential to make the ECG a tool of utility devoid of any clinical expert. In settings where the human observer was accessible, automated interpretation had the potential to assist and augment the human expert. In fact, the automated interpretation of the ECG is a good example of human—computer collaboration in medicine, where the "collaboration" between the human and the computer can improve the accuracy of the final interpretation.

In the USA alone, approximately 100 million ECGs are interpreted by computerized ECG algorithms each year. The automated interpretation of ECGs has become routine in cardiac care. Having an algorithm interpret the ECG has been shown to reduce ECG reading time and more importantly, it has been shown to improve the accuracy of human ECG interpretation, especially for junior interpreters [8]. For instance, the presence of automated ECG interpretation in the emergency department improved physicians' accuracy by 25%, significantly reducing the rate of misdiagnoses [15—17]. Accordingly, current clinical practice guidelines rely on the standard 12-lead ECG in establishing diagnostic criteria of disease abnormalities. The next section will briefly explain how the 12-lead ECG works and will introduce the various diagnostic categories of diseases it can classify.

3.2 Basic knowledge of ECG physiology

In a healthy heart, the ECG signal resembles the normal physiology of the cardiac cycle (Fig. 3.1). When the right and left atria contract, the surface ECG records an electrical signal of a voltage commensurate with the small myocardial tissue in the atria (Fig. 3.1, black arrows #1). When the right and left ventricles contract, the surface ECG records an electrical signal of voltage commensurate with the relatively larger volume of the myocardial tissue of the ventricles (Fig. 3.1, blue arrows #2). As long as this synchrony is maintained, the ECG signal will assume a specific waveform of a morphology (shape of deflections), duration (x-axis), and amplitude (y-axis) dependent on the body surface location of where the ECG electrode is placed. The normal variants of these ECG waveform characteristics have been extensively studied and standardized as normal reference for clinical use [18—20]. Any minor alteration in the function or structure of the myocardium will disrupt the ECG waveform characteristics (i.e., morphology, duration, amplitude), manifesting with varying signatures from one surface electrode to another. Quantifying and phenotyping these deviations from normal limits provide very valuable

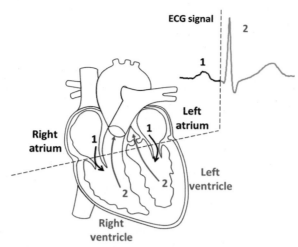

Figure 3.1 The ECG and the cardiac cycle. This figure shows the relationship between the ECG waveform and the mechanical events of the heart. Atria activity (*black* arrows) is denoted by a small ECG deflection while ventricular activity (*blue* arrows) is denoted by larger, more complex deflections on the ECG signal. Arrows indicate the direction of blood flow during the contraction of each chamber. *ECG*, Electrocardiogram.

means for mapping a given distortion in the ECG signal to a specific abnormality or disease pathology.

Given that the heart is a three-dimensional organ, sensing the ECG signal from a single electrode is typically insufficient to detect or map a given waveform distortion to a specific disease pathology. In a similar analogy to why at least three coordinates are needed for optimal location calculations, multiple electrodes are needed for accurate disease detection and classification. The current clinical practice relies on ECG waveform obtained from 12 different leads, hence the term "12-lead ECG." Each of these leads provide unique prognostic information that is independent from, and complements, the other leads.

In a nutshell, depending on where the surface electrode is placed, each ECG lead records waveform deflections in a direction associated with the geometric relationship between that lead location and the specific electrical impulse it senses. This concept is referred to as the cardiac axis and is illustrated in Fig. 3.2. The electrical impulse starts from the right atrium and travels down toward the middle septum of the heart. The impulse distorts the baseline polarity of the cell membrane and is, hence, called depolarization impulse (positively charged). This depolarization impulse generates a small wave on the ECG (Fig. 3.2, black arrows #1), with upward deflection in leads facing the impulse (e.g., lead II), and a downward deflection in leads opposite in direction (e.g., lead aVR). Then, the depolarization impulse propagates in the middle septum (green arrow #2) before it splits into a right bundle branch

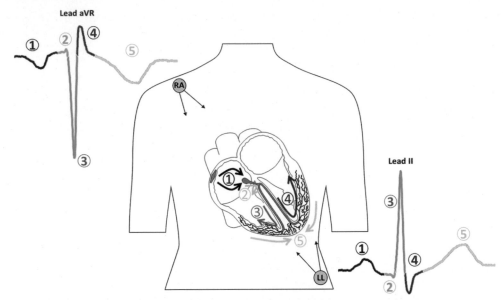

Figure 3.2 The cardiac electrical impulse and the ECG. The electrical impulse travels from the right atrium (pacemaker) to the ventricles in phases: (1) depolarization impulse traveling in the atria (*black* arrows); (2) depolarization impulse traveling through the septum (*green* arrow); (3) depolarization impulse traveling in the right bundle branch (*blue* arrow); (4) depolarization impulse traveling in the left bundle branch (*red* arrow); and (5) repolarization impulse traveling backward through the ventricles (*gold* arrows). The waveform deflections on the ECG depend on the geometric location of the sensing electrode in relation to the direction of each of these five phases. Illustrations are provided for lead II [sensed by left leg (LL) electrode] and lead aVR [sensed by the right arm (RA) electrode] that are approximately opposite in direction. The colors of the ECG waveforms are matched to the color of arrows of the five phases of these electrical impulses. *ECG*, Electrocardiogram.

(blue arrow #3) and a left bundle branch (red arrow #4). This very fast propagation in the myocardium, and given the larger mass of the ventricle, is reflected on the ECG as sharp-peaked deflections, with upward versus downward direction according to the geometric location of the sensing electrode. Since the left bundle branch is more complex, the impulse continues to propagate in this branch a little bit longer to reach the remote portions of the left ventricle. The latter results in a sharp terminal deflection at the end of the ventricular depolarization phase (end of the long red arrow #4).

At the end of ventricular depolarization during which the heart contracts and pumps the blood, the ventricles relax and restore the normal polarity of the cell membrane. This is referred to as repolarization and it generates a negatively charged electrical impulse (Fig. 3.2, gold arrows #5). The repolarization wave moves backward from the remote portions of the ventricles back into the septum. This slow electrical wave generates a dome-shaped wave on the ECG that again depends on the geometric location of the sensing electrode. However, since the repolarization wave is negatively charged, it results in an upward deflection in lead II as it moves away from it, and a downward deflection in lead aVR as it moves toward it.

In electrocardiology, the different electrical phases of the cardiac cycle explained above are labeled as P, Q, R, S, and T (Fig. 3.3). As shown in this figure, atrial depolarization is reflected in the P wave, the ventricular depolarization is reflected in the QRS wave, and the ventricular repolarization is reflected in the T wave. The times the depolarization impulse take to propagate through the atria and through the ventricles correspond to the PR interval and the QRS duration, respectively. The total time of depolarization and repolarization in the ventricles corresponds to the QT interval. In addition to these clinically significant waveforms and intervals, the vulnerable period that corresponds to the overlap between end of ventricular depolarization and beginning of ventricular repolarization is called the ST segment. The latter segment plays a very important role in ECG diagnosis of many cardiac pathologies in the clinical setting.

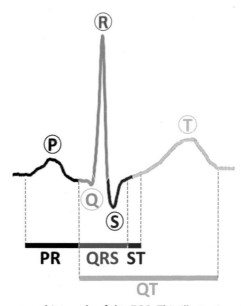

Figure 3.3 Naming the waves and intervals of the ECG. This illustration shows the onset and offset of the P wave, QRS complex, and T wave that correspond to atrial depolarization, ventricular depolarization, and ventricular repolarization, respectively. Other clinically important intervals are also illustrated. *ECG*, Electrocardiogram.

3.3 The 12-lead ECG

As explained before, the heart is a three-dimensional organ and multiple ECG leads are required for optimal detection and phenotyping of cardiac pathologies. The standard 12-lead ECG constitutes the gold standard tool used for disease classification in the clinical setting. Each of these 12 leads look at the heart from a different direction and, hence, has unique waveform characteristics. This waveform morphology is based on the geometric angle between that ECG lead and the instantaneous direction of the cardiac axis at that moment in time. The location of each of these 12 leads on the body surface has been optimized to maximize the spatial coverage in both the frontal plane and the horizontal plane of the heart.

In the frontal plane, three electrodes placed on extremities [right arm (RA), left arm (LA), and left leg (LL)] are needed to construct six bipolar ECG leads (Fig. 3.4). The first three frontal leads (I, II, and III) are each based on two limb electrodes and provide partial coverage of the lateral and inferior walls of the heart (Fig. 3.4, solid

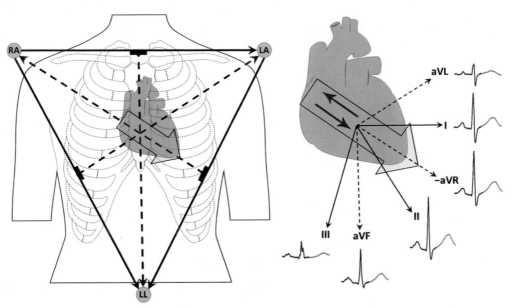

Figure 3.4 The frontal ECG leads. Left panel: using three extremity electrodes, right arm (RA), left arm (LA), and left leg (LL), a total of six dipolar leads can be constructed in the frontal plane. The solid *black* arrows constitute dipolar limb leads (I, II, and III), and the dashed *black* arrows constitute augmented limb leads (aVR, aVL, and aVF). Right panel: the waveform morphology in each frontal lead depends on the geometric angle between each lead and the averaged cardiac axis (large opaque arrow). Note that leads better aligned with the cardiac axis are more likely to have dominant waveform deflections. The color of each ECG waveform morphology is mapped to either a depolarization impulse (*red* arrow) or repolarization impulse (*blue* arrow). *ECG*, Electrocardiogram.

black arrows). To maximize the frontal view, three additional leads (aVR, aVL, and aVF) are computed by augmenting two limb electrodes as one of the bipolar points of the view vector, requiring all three electrodes to compute each augmented lead (Fig. 3.4, dashed black arrows). The new augmented leads maximize the frontal coverage of the heart by providing a true 90 degree inferior viewpoint (lead aVF), a viewpoint of the heart apex that is aligned with the cardiac axis (lead aVR), and a proximal viewpoint of the lateral remote aspects of the left ventricle (lead aVL). The normal cardiac axis in the frontal plane aligns best with lead II and −aVR, both of which have a dominant upward QRS complex and play an important role in disease classification.

In the horizontal plane, six precordial electrodes placed on the chest are used to construct six unipolar ECG leads V1−V6 (Fig. 3.5). The six precordial leads are placed sequentially from the right ventricle to the left ventricle. Given that the impulse propagates in the heart vertically (from atria to ventricles) and laterally (from right to left ventricle), the cardiac axis best aligns with lead V5, which would have the most dominant upward QRS complex and has a unique role in various ECG metric computations.

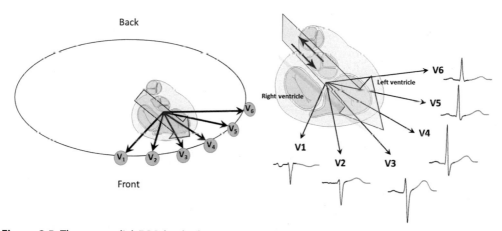

Figure 3.5 The precordial ECG leads (horizontal plane). Left panel: using six precordial electrodes on the chest, a total of six unipolar leads can be constructed in the horizontal plane. The solid *black* arrows constitute unipolar chest leads (V1−V6). Right panel: the waveform morphology in each lead depends on the geometric angle between that lead and the averaged cardiac axis (large opaque arrow). Note that leads better aligned with the cardiac axis are more likely to have dominant waveform deflections. The color of each ECG wave segment is mapped to either a depolarization impulse (*red* arrow) or repolarization impulse (*blue* arrow). Although the illustration implies that the cardiac axis aligns with V3−V4, in a real 3-D model it will align with V5. This is because precordial electrodes are not placed on a parallel line, but rather electrodes V4−V6 are placed 1 in. lower than the other electrodes. *ECG*, Electrocardiogram.

3.4 ECG signal processing

The accurate recording and processing of ECG signal are critical for precise computer-generated diagnostic statements for evidence-based clinical practice. The processing of the ECG signal is governed by methodological standards set forth by ISO/IEC joint working group [21]. Therefore, digital ECG signal processing typically follows a series of steps that are well-outlined in published guidelines [1]: (1) signal acquisition and filtering, (2) beat detection and classification, (3) segmentation of diagnostic waveform, (4) waveform featurization, and (5) diagnostic classification. Technical details and clinical significance of each of these steps are described herein.

The first step in ECG processing is signal acquisition and filtering. The ECG signal is displayed in a temporal resolution of milliseconds and amplitude resolution of microvolts over a 10-second period. Given that sensing electrodes are placed on the body surface, rather than directly on the heart, the ECG signal is significantly attenuated by the varying impedance levels of thoracic tissue. Thus, the ECG signal will first need to be amplified and sampled as well as filtered to ensure noise in the signal is removed. This noise and baseline wander can be caused by movements, and respiration (low-frequency noise); or caused by muscle artifacts, power lines, or radiated electromagnetic interferences (high-frequency noise). The principal frequency of the QRS complex and T wave on the body surface are at approximately 10 and 1–2 Hz, respectively, and most of the diagnostic information in the signal is contained within 0.5–100 Hz in adults. However, using this range for bandwidth filtering has been shown to distort the high- and low-frequency components of the signal, leading to inaccurate detection of R peak and ST segment, respectively. Thus, the current recommendations for routine digital filters require a bandwidth cutoff filter of 0.05–150 Hz. To allow a high-frequency cut-off (low pass filter) of 150 Hz, it has been shown that a minimum sampling rate of 500 samples per second is necessary to limit measurement errors in R peak detection to less than 1% [22]. Additionally, the low-frequency cut-off (high pass filter) of 0.05 Hz has been shown to preserve the fidelity of ST and T wave measurements but would be inadequate for filtering low-frequency noise of respiration that leads to baseline wander. Thus, current electrocardiographs implement additional baseline drift suppression for coherent alignment of sequential P-QRS-T waveform templates (Fig. 3.6). For a more technical and detailed analysis of ECG filtering, readers can refer to the following article [23].

The second step in ECG processing is beat detection and classification. Given that beat-to-beat variations due to noise, respiration, or other intrinsic physiological processes exist, eliminating this unwanted variation within each lead is needed for accurate ECG measurements. This requires forming a "template beat" for each lead to serve as a median representative waveform complex. For this purpose, it is recommended to use the largest-amplitude deflection in each lead as representative of the magnitude for

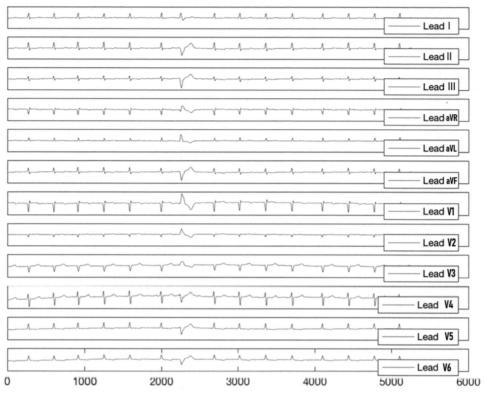

Figure 3.6 ECG acquisition and filtering. The standard 10-s 12-lead ECG is sampled at 500 samples per second and filtered in the bandwidth of 0.05–150 Hz. Baseline drift suppression is needed to ensure the coherent alignment of sequential ECG complexes. ECG, Electrocardiogram.

that measurement. Given that the QRS complex typically contains the largest voltage signal in each lead, most algorithms rely on R peak detection to identify individual ECG beats (Fig. 3.7). However, as seen in this figure, further processing is needed to address two additional challenges before calculating median representative beats that are meaningful. First, accurate alignment of P-QRS-T complexes is needed. Methods for this purpose vary but generally include template matching at R peak and at the fiducial point preceding the Q wave. Second, nondominant waveform templates must be removed from the representative beat calculations (i.e., beat #7 in Fig. 3.7). This is usually achieved using cross-correlation algorithms between individual beats.

Accurate template formation is critical for precise global measurements in subsequent processing steps. Therefore, after creating averaged beats (Fig. 3.7, right), it is recommended to quantify the residual noise in the signal. This is typically computed as the root mean square (RMS) of the aligned templates during representative beat calculations, which provides an estimate of measurement error to be used as a signal

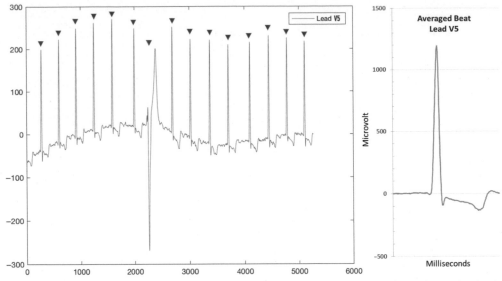

Figure 3.7 Beat detection and classification. This figure focuses on lead V5 from the 12-lead ECG shown in the previous figure. Left panel: Individual beats in a given ECG lead can be detected using R peak detection algorithms (marked as *red* triangles). To remove the evident beat-to-beat variation, further processing involves template alignment to construct a representative median (averaged) beat. In addition, further processing is needed to exclude the nondominant beat templates (beat #7 in this example). Right panel: a representative averaged beat from the same ECG lead following template alignment and removal of nondominant beats. The averaged beat eliminates most of the beat-to-beat variations observed in the raw signal.

quality metric in subsequent steps. Since the representative beat constitutes an arthmic mean of individual templates, the more heartbeats in the 10-second window, the lower the residual error in the signal. It has been shown that an RMS error less than 5 μV is needed to limit estimation error to less than 10% in measuring deflections of 20 μV [22], a clinically significant error in ST segment calculations.

Following the formation of lead-specific averaged beats, the third step in ECG signal processing is the segmentation of the diagnostic waveforms on each of these single-lead representative complexes. As seen in Fig. 3.8 (left panel), various algorithms can be used to detect the onset and offset of each waveform in the P-QRS-T complex. This is usually achieved by using a combination of fiducial points derived from the intercept between signal slope and the signal isoelectric baseline. Next, given that the ECG signal is simultaneously acquired from all 12 leads yielding a time coherent signal, temporal superposition of these 12 representative beats would allow global segmentation of P-QRS-T waveform (Fig. 3.8, middle panel), an approach that has been shown to yield more accurate global measurements. By searching for earliest and latest valid voltage points for P-QRS-T waves on the temporally aligned individual complexes, global onset and offset points can be

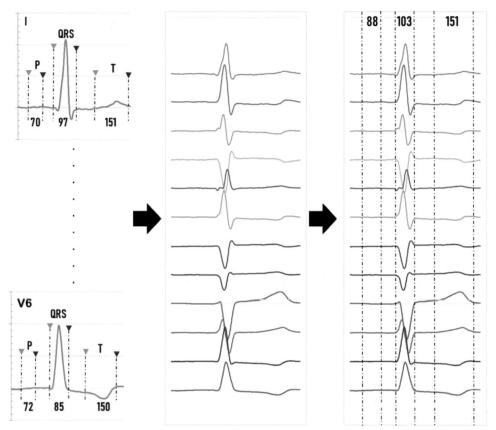

Figure 3.8 ECG waveform segmentation and measurements. Left panel: the onset (*green* triangles) and offset (*red* triangles) of P, QRS, and T waves are initially computed based on lead-specific representative beats. Middle panel: temporal superposition of the simultaneously acquired 12 leads would allow multilead estimation of waveform segments. Right panel: using multilead criteria, electrocardiographs can use the temporally aligned representative beats to search for global onset and offset of waveform segments, which would allow more accurate global interval measurements. *ECG*, Electrocardiogram.

identified (Fig. 3.8, right panel), which would be used for either global interval measures (e.g., QRS duration) or lead-specific measures (ST amplitude).

It is worth noting that the global interval measurements would account for errors in lead-specific measurements. Such errors are attributed to inaccuracies in defining lead-specific onset and offset points due to differences in template formation and alignment. In the example shown in Fig. 3.8, QRS duration measured in lead I and lead V6 was 97 and 85, respectively, likely due to the absent S wave in V6. However, the global QRS duration from all 12 leads was 103, which accounts for the observed lead-to-lead variability in measurements.

The fourth step in ECG signal processing is feature extraction. Initially, beat-to-beat RR interval data are extracted from few leads (e.g., II and V1) for rhythm detection and heart rate computation. Then, from each representative beat in individual leads, the duration and amplitude of the P wave, Q wave, R wave, S wave, ST segment, and T wave are extracted. The presence of secondary P′, R′, S′, and T′ waves (all denoted with prime dash) is extracted for subsequent evaluation of waveform fragmentation, notching, and slurring. Next, using multilead criteria, the electrocardiograph computes the frontal R and T axes and angles in the frontal plane and the horizontal plane of the heart. Finally, using the temporally aligned averaged beats, global measurements of P wave duration, PR interval, QRS duration, and QT duration are extracted. This comprehensive description of global and lead-specific ECG features is needed for accurate and reliable rule-based diagnostic statements as described below.

The fifth and final step in ECG signal processing is making diagnostic classification statements based on the extracted features from the signal. The ECG signal is deterministic in nature, meaning that every waveform characteristic (i.e., morphology, duration, and amplitude) correlates with mechanistic and physiological signatures in the electromechanical function of the heart with a corresponding clinical significance. These waveform characteristics have been extensively studied and standardized for diagnostic statements in established clinical practice guidelines. For example, a global QRS duration greater than 120 ms indicates a defect in the electrical conduction pathway, where an rsR′ morphology in V1 indicating a right bundle branch block (RBBB) and rS morphology indicating a left bundle branch block (LBBB), each with its unique clinical significance (see Section 3.5 below for more details). Thus, the existing commercial interpretation software is primarily considered rule-based or deterministic algorithms and are regulated by the Food and Drug Administration (FDA) for clinical use.

Most commercial interpretation algorithms feed the discrete feature characteristics extracted from the ECG signal into a predetermined algorithm (perhaps akin to a tree of rules) that denote the binary probability of a given diagnostic statement (see Section 3.6 for more details). More recent approaches incorporate data-driven statistical and machine learning (ML) techniques to classify ECGs to account for the probabilistic uncertainty in the decision boundaries. These techniques require large databases of well-documented cases, with adequate distribution of abnormalities and severity, to train, cross-validate, and test reliable and generalizable classifiers (see Section 3.8 for more details).

Finally, it is worth noting that due to the complexity of the serial technical steps needed for ECG processing, it is common to see different diagnostic statements when different algorithms are run on the same ECG signal. The methodological standards summarized in this section can help minimize these variations and promote uniformity of interpretations [1]. Yet, systematic differences in ECG processing and interpretation systems could omit or introduce important diagnostic statements, which translates into current practice standards requiring systematic over-reading of ECGs by experienced clinicians before any therapeutic treatment decision is made [13].

3.5 Cardiovascular diseases diagnosed by the 12-lead ECG

Most functional and structural changes in the heart alter cell membrane voltage duration, velocity, speed, or direction, which manifest as variations in the recorded ECG signal. Accordingly, the ECG provides a valuable bridge between the cellular changes in the myocardium and establishing a specific clinical diagnosis. The ability of the ECG to detect such minimal changes, its noninvasive nature, and its ease of application has made it a robust screening and clinical diagnostic tool. The utility includes both nonemergency situations and urgent life-threatening situations. Nonemergency situations include monitoring patients on heart-altering medications, assessing patients' health before surgeries, and screening for cardiac abnormalities in high-performing athletes (e.g., hypertrophic cardiomyopathy or heart enlargement). More crucially, the ECG is often the first and most important test in cardiovascular emergencies. This includes conditions such as cardiac ischemia and infarction (decreased blood supply to the heart), arrhythmia (an abnormal pattern of heart contraction), and heart blocks (a block in electrical signal conduction across the heart)

Considering the numerous pathologies possible in the heart, corresponding a given ECG finding with a known clinical diagnosis needs a comprehensive evaluation of the patient and the acquired ECG by a trained healthcare provider. When detecting such abnormalities, healthcare providers aim to correspond these changes with the following categories of cardiovascular pathologies, and these subsequent possible clinical diagnoses: rhythm disorders, conduction defects, chamber hypertrophy, or cardiac ischemia or infarction. These cardiac pathologies are briefly explained in the next few sections.

3.5.1 Rhythm disorders

Rhythm disorders, also known as arrhythmia, refer to an abnormal electrical impulse in the heart leading to unusual contraction of the heart muscles. The atria and ventricles are anatomically separate, producing different yet always sequential beats. Since the initial activation of the heart pacemaker occurs in the atria, the sequence of ECG wave deflections is P-QRS-T, corresponding to atrial followed by ventricular contraction. Rhythm disorders occur when this sequence is interrupted due to signals either being produced abnormally from the original heart pacemaker or originating from an abnormal location in the heart.

The causes of arrhythmia are numerous, ranging from benign causes such as anxiety and caffeine intake to life-threatening emergencies such as cardiac ischemia, electrolyte disorders, and drug toxicities. The major concern associated with arrhythmia pertains to

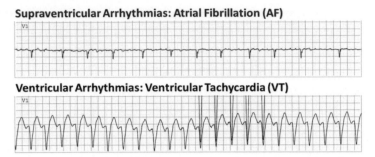

Figure 3.9 Clinically important arrhythmias. This figure shows two examples: atrial fibrillation (AF) (upper strip) and ventricular tachycardia (lower strip). AF is characterized by absent P waves and irregular R-R interval. Ventricular tachycardia is characterized by absent P waves and bizarre-looking QRS complex with discordant T waves (i.e., in opposite direction to the QRS).

the compromised ejection of blood from the heart due to the ineffective abnormal heartbeats. ECG is the mainstay for detecting an arrhythmia, which applies to patients presenting with sudden onset symptoms such as the feeling of rapid heartbeat, and to those continuously being monitored during their in-hospital observation.

Since an arrhythmia is reflected in all axes of the heart, a single lead is often sufficient to discern an ongoing arrhythmia, with that typically being lead II. Identifying the arrhythmia involves assessing for the presence or absence of P waves, the shape and duration of QRS complexes, the relationship between P waves and QRS complex, and whether the heartbeats are produced at regular intervals. Typically, arrhythmias are classified into being supraventricular (above the ventricles) or ventricular arrhythmias, depending on whether the source of the abnormal contractions is the upper portion of the heart or the thicker and stronger ventricles, respectively. Despite the wide range of arrhythmias, the ECG is universally the most vital tool for diagnosis. Fig. 3.9 shows some of the common and most clinically significant arrhythmias, which are explained below as well.

3.5.1.1 Supraventricular arrhythmias

Supraventricular arrhythmia is an abnormal heart rhythm originating from the upper part of the heart. The presentation widely varies and ranges from being detected on a routine ECG screening to a life-threatening drop in blood pressure. Accordingly, the conditions can be managed conservatively with no intervention, to necessitating an urgent treatment. The hallmark of ECG changes in supraventricular arrhythmias revolves around the P waves, including absence of the wave or variations in the shape. Since the QRS reflects changes in the ventricles, the shape of the QRS complex is typically normal. The following are the major types of supraventricular arrhythmias:

1. *Atrial fibrillation:* AF refers to irregular depolarization of the atria, with variable conduction of the signal from the atria to the ventricles. This produces an irregular

beating of the heart, with varying pauses between heartbeats and an irregular ventricular rate. This form of arrhythmia is commonly referred to as an irregularly irregular rhythm. The P waves are absent with a "fibrillatory" isoelectric line due to the ineffective atrial depolarization. AF leads to ineffective ejection of blood from the atria to ventricles and can either present as a chronic and asymptomatic condition or as an acute emergency.

2. *Atrial flutter:* Atrial Flutter is caused by a localized self-perpetuating loop of electrical activity in the atria. This leads to generation of multiple oddly shaped P waves with a single subsequent QRS. The odd-shaped P waves are due to an unusual source of depolarization in the atria, and the shape is often termed "saw tooth" P waves. Similar to AF, the unusual depolarization leads to ineffective ejection of blood from the atria to the ventricles.

3. *Paroxysmal supraventricular tachycardia:* This rhythm is characterized by intermittent episodes of tachycardia with initiation of depolarization occurring in an abnormal focus in the upper part of the heart. Unlike AF and flutter, each atrial contraction is followed by a subsequent ventricular contraction, hence normal QRS complexes. However, the abnormal focus of initial depolarization manifests as abnormally shaped P waves, an abnormal PR interval, or an absent P wave.

3.5.1.2 Ventricular arrhythmias

Ventricular arrhythmias refer to rhythm disorders affecting the contraction of the ventricles. The source of the initial depolarization is from the ventricles, rather than a normally conducted signal through the AV node. Since the ventricles are the main pump in the heart, such arrhythmias often lead to a dysfunctional ejection of blood from the heart to the rest of the body. The potential for pump failure, including cardiac arrest, dictates that all ventricular arrhythmias be treated as an emergency. The hallmark of ventricular arrhythmias is the prolonged and abnormally shaped QRS complexes. This occurs due to the abnormal conduction through the thick ventricular musculature. The following are the two clinically significant ventricular arrhythmias:

1. *Ventricular tachycardia:* This occurs when a focus in the ventricles generates constant electrical impulses leading to ventricular contraction at a rate of more than 100 beats per minute. The QRS complexes are prolonged (>120 ms) and bizarre but with a consistent shape occurring at a regular rate.

2. *Ventricular fibrillation:* Ventricular fibrillation ensues when chaotic depolarizations are generated from the ventricles. The contraction in ventricular fibrillation is erratic and ineffective, leading to failure of the heart pump. This is reflected in the ECG by having prolonged and poorly formed QRS complexes that are inconsistent and shape and occur at an irregular rate. Ventricular fibrillation typically leads to patient collapse and cardiac arrest, and it is considered a life-threatening arrhythmia that needs immediate medical intervention.

3.5.2 Conduction disorders

The electrical conduction system in the heart is finely tuned to facilitate maximum efficiency of contraction. Any alterations in the conduction system would alter the sequence of muscle contraction and potentially affecting its function. The normal signal in the heart travels from the SA node in the right atrium to the AV node followed by the right and left bundle branches, which finally conduct the signal to the ventricular wall. This sequence of conduction enables the atria to contract first, followed by the ventricles. On surface ECG, this translates into every P wave being followed by a QRS complex at a constant time interval. Accordingly, alterations to this synchrony will manifest as an abnormal contraction sequence of the heart, often termed heart blocks. The presentation of blocks can range from being asymptomatic and benign to total loss of heart-pumping ability and death. As shown in Fig. 3.10 and explained below, clinically significant heart blocks are usually a manifestation of delayed conduction either at the AV node or at the subsequent bundle branches in the ventricles:

1. Complete heart block: Complete heart block refers to the state of complete dissociation between atrial and ventricular contractions. This is reflected as a complete lack of synchrony between P waves and QRS complexes on the ECG. The rate of

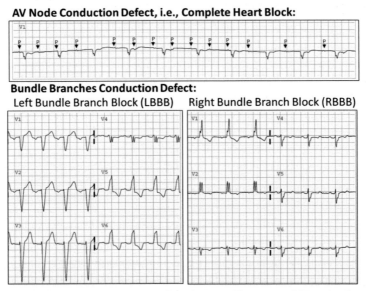

Figure 3.10 Clinically important conduction disturbances. The upper ECG strip shows a complete heart block with complete dyssynchrony between the P waves (*black* arrows) and the QRS complexes. Atrial rate is higher than the ventricular rate. Bottom strips show the precordial leads of two different cases with conduction disturbance due to a block at the right or left bundle branches. P-QRS synchrony is maintained, but QRS duration and morphology are abnormal. *ECG*, Electrocardiogram.

atrial and ventricular contraction will correspondingly differ, with ventricular contraction displaying a slower than usual rate, referred to as bradycardia (heart rate <60 beats/min). Patients with complete heart block are considered high-risk patients requiring urgent evaluation for an intervention.

2. **LBBB:** The left bundle branch conducts the signals from the AV node to the left ventricle. A block in conducting signal in the left bundle branch will lead to delayed activation of the left ventricle. This will disrupt the activation process in the left ventricle, leading to unusually shaped QRS complex with prolonged duration.

3. **RBBB:** Similarly, the right bundle branch conducts the signals from the AV node to the right ventricle. Likewise, disruption in the activation process in the right ventricle leads to unusually shaped QRS complex with prolonged duration.

3.5.3 Chamber enlargement

The size of the atria and the ventricles is determined by the volume of muscle forming these chambers. Analogous to any muscle in the body, the size of the chambers can change due to an increased stress on these muscles. This includes increased resistance in the blood vessels in the form of hypertension, which increases the workload on the left ventricle. Similarly, increased pressure in the lungs can stress the right side of the heart, increasing the size of the right atrium and ventricle. Moreover, dysfunction in the valves of the heart (the leaflets at the exit of each chamber) can influence the size of the involved chambers. An increase in the muscular thickness of one of the chambers affects the ECG since the magnitude of electric signals passing through this chamber is increased. Such chamber size enlargement is often secondary to another ongoing disease, hence, identifying these changes can guide in detecting the primary condition. The most significant of these conditions is left ventricular hypertrophy (LVH), which is often caused by a valvular dysfunction or hypertension. In LVH, the increased magnitude of signals in the left ventricle manifests as higher voltage in the ECG leads mapping this chamber. This is demonstrated by the increased voltage in the R wave in leads V5 and V6. Conversely, the leads opposite to the left side of the heart will have a deeper deflection, hence a deep S wave in V1 and V2 (Fig. 3.11).

3.5.4 Cardiac ischemia or infarction

When blood supply to the heart is not commensurate with its demands, the delivery of oxygen to the cardiac muscle is diminished. This oxygen debt in the heart muscle is known as myocardial ischemia. This usually arises due to a sudden blockage of one of the blood vessels supplying the heart, a condition known as acute coronary syndrome. Often, the vessel blockage is substantial enough to lead to myocardial cell death, known as a myocardial infarction (MI). MI is the most common cause of death in the world, and is a top medical emergency requiring urgent intervention [24].

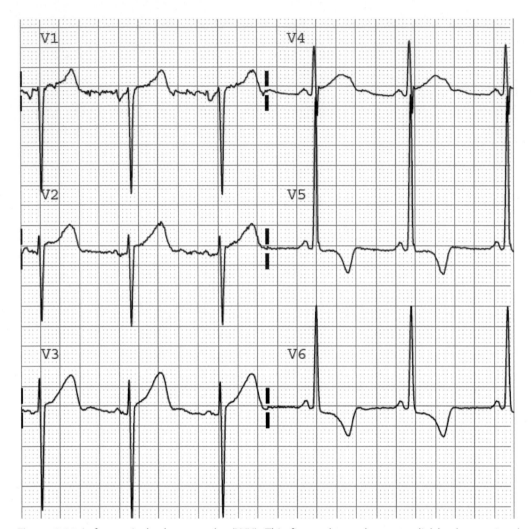

Figure 3.11 Left ventricular hypertrophy (LVH). This figure shows the precordial leads associated with ECG changes of LVH. Note the increased R amplitude in V5 and V6 (facing left ventricle) and the increased S amplitude in V1 and V2 (opposite to left ventricle). Amplitude reflects the voltage in microvolts that is directly related to size of ventricular chamber. *ECG*, Electrocardiogram.

An infarcted area alters the electrical impulse as it travels in this affected tissue. This not only reflects as measurable waveform changes on the ECG but also evolves into localized patterns in specific leads. Characterization and localization of these lead-specific changes can help healthcare providers predict the extent of damage to the myocardium, as well as predict which coronary blood vessel is blocked, leading to the infarction [25].

Indications of the size, site, and severity of ischemia are primarily based on the magnitude and location of ST-segment deviation. Accurate interpretation of these

ECG findings is crucial for clinicians when determining whether to pursue urgent interventions in the operating room in hope of restoring blood flow. Importantly, while the treatment of a myocardial ischemia is individualized, it is important to be aware that the ECG is an indispensable tool to achieve such goal. Angina and MI are the major clinical diagnoses of diminished blood supply that are primarily facilitated by ECG reading, and they are explained below.

3.5.4.1 Stable/unstable angina

Angina is the feeling of chest pain or discomfort that develops due to myocardial ischemia. Various types of angina exist; however, the two primary types of angina are stable and unstable angina. Stable angina occurs due to an unusual state of exertion by the patient, such as when going up the stairs or climbing a steep heel. On the other hand, unstable angina is characterized by the unpredictability of chest pain attacks, with possible attacks occurring even during rest. Such attacks are typically precipitated by an abrupt worsening of a coronary vessel obstruction. Although chest pain occurs during any attack of myocardial ischemia, the diagnosis of an angina is classically used when indicating that no cardiac tissue death has ensued. An ECG would suggest angina when ST–segment depression and T wave inversions are observed (Fig. 3.12).

3.5.4.2 Myocardial infarction

The term MI applies when cardiac muscle death occurs. The death of cardiac tissue leads to leakage of contents from the cardiac cells (Troponin and Creatine Kinase) into the bloodstream, which can be detected by analyzing blood samples in the lab. Such infarctions are termed ST–segment elevation infarctions, demonstrating the remarkably crucial role of an ECG in diagnosing such cases. ST–segment elevations are observed in the leads corresponding to the area of the heart with underlying tissue damage, as demonstrated by the following:

1. *Anterior infarction:* Anterior MIs manifest as ST–segment elevations in precordial leads V1−V4, suggesting an occlusion in the left anterior descending artery.
2. *Lateral infarction:* Lateral MIs manifest as ST–segment elevations in precordial leads V5−V6, and lateral limb leads I and aVL. This occurs due to an occlusion in the circumflex artery.
3. *Inferior infarction:* Inferior MIs manifest as ST–segment elevations in inferior limb leads II, III, and aVF. This occurs due to an occlusion in the right coronary artery.

It is worth noting that these diagnostic categories are not mutually exclusive. A patient might present with an infarction that is due to multivessel occlusion (e.g., anterior and lateral infarction). Moreover, given the vector-based nature of the 12-lead ECG, it is well-documented that ST elevation in one lead might be mirrored as an ST depression in a geometrically opposite lead. These two challenges make ECG diagnosis of ischemia and infarction very challenging clinically.

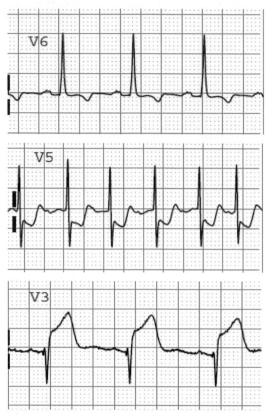

Figure 3.12 ECG patterns associated with cardiac ischemia and infarction. This figure shows three ECG strips from different cases that demonstrate T wave inversion (upper strip), ST depression (middle strip), and ST elevation (bottom strip). T wave inversion and ST depression are commonly associated with ischemia (lack of oxygen supply to the heart), whereas ST elevation is associated with infarction (muscle death). The latter characteristic is used to detect ST-elevation myocardial infarction (STEMI), a clinically significant condition that warrants urgent medical intervention. *ECG*, Electrocardiogram.

3.6 Automated ECG interpretation

By now, the reader should be familiar with the basics of electrophysiology, electrocardiography, ECG signal processing, and cardiovascular disease classifications. In this section we will focus on how ECG interpretation can be automated, including its role in synthesizing diagnostic statements for clinical use.

Computer-aided analysis of the digital 12-lead ECG involves signal processing and diagnostic classification. After signal acquisition, filtering, and preprocessing, the 12-lead ECG visual waveform is displayed on a standard paper in landscape orientation as shown in Fig. 3.13. The ECG leads are presented in 3Ã—4 window

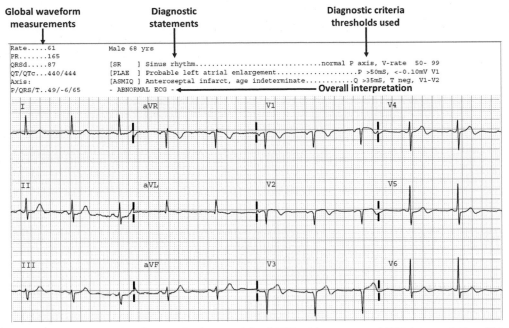

Figure 3.13 An example of a standard 10-s, 12-lead ECG with automated ECG interpretation. This 12-lead ECG was obtained on a 68-year-old male with chest pain in an emergency department. The automated ECG interpretation suggests that this is an "Abnormal ECG," with no rhythm abnormalities but with an old heart attack pattern. An over-reading by a cardiologist confirms these diagnostic statements are accurate but also suggests the abnormal T in precordial leads might be due to an acute process and warrants further evaluation. *ECG*, Electrocardiogram.

preview, with each window measuring 2.5 seconds. All windows on a given row are temporally sequential over 10 seconds, and the windows across columns are temporally aligned over the same 10-second period. The scaling display on the x-axis is 40 ms per small square (1Ã—1 mm in size), and on the y-axis is 100 µV per small square. On the header of the ECG display, global waveform measurements are displayed, including beat-to-beat measures (e.g., heart rate) and the global ECG interval measurements (e.g., QRS duration, QT interval, R axis, etc.). More importantly, standard diagnostic statements are also listed on the header of the ECG display along with the measurement thresholds used in each statement. An overall interpretation statement is also listed on the header. Most of the diagnostic statements listed on the ECG display in commercial interpretation systems are FDA approved for patient safety and are cleared for clinical use.

Although the 12-lead ECG with automated ECG interpretation is widely used in clinical practice, there are no uniform criteria for ECG diagnostic statements. Current clinical practice guidelines suggest 117 primary diagnostic statements in 14 categories and 27 secondary diagnostic statements in two categories [2]. For the sake of

BOX 3.1 Summary of clinically important diagnostic statements

Primary diagnostic category	Clinically important diagnostic statement
1 Overall interpretation	"Normal ECG"; "Abnormal ECG"; "Uninterpretable ECG"
2 Technical conditions	"Misplaced precordial electrodes"; "Artifact"; "Poor quality data"
3 Sinus node rhythms	"Sinus rhythm"; "Sinus bradycardia"; "Sinus arrhythmia"
4 Supraventricular arrhythmia	"Ectopic atrial rhythm"; "Junctional rhythm"
5 Supraventricular tachyarrhythmia	"Atrial fibrillation"; "Atrial flutter"; "Supraventricular tachycardia"
6 Ventricular arrhythmia	"Ventricular premature complex"; "Idioventricular rhythm"
7 Ventricular tachyarrhythmia	"Ventricular tachycardia"; "Ventricular fibrillation"
8 Atrioventricular conduction	"AV block, first degree/second degree/third degree"
9 Intraventricular conduction	"Left bundle-branch block"; "Right bundle-branch block"
10 Axis and voltage	"Right axis deviation"; "Left axis deviation"; "Low voltage"
11 Chamber hypertrophy	"Left ventricular hypertrophy"; "Right ventricular hypertrophy"
12 ST segment and T wave	"T wave abnormality"; "Prolonged QT interval"
13 Myocardial infarction	"Anterior MI"; "Inferior MI"; "Posterior MI"; "Lateral MI"
14 Pacemaker	"Atrial paced rhythm"; "Ventricular pacing"
Secondary diagnostic category	**Clinically important diagnostic statement**
1 Suggests...	"Acute pericarditis"; "Hyperkalemia"
2 Consider...	"Acute ischemia"

simplicity, the most common diagnostic statements with important clinical significance are summarized in Box 3.1. These statements range from benign findings to alert clinicians (e.g., "misplaced leads" → obtain a new ECG) to more serious findings requiring immediate, life-saving medical actions (e.g., "ventricular fibrillation" → evaluate patient and initiate advanced cardiac life support).

The clinically important diagnostic ECG statements summarized in Box 3.1 generally fit into one of four disease pathologies as previously explained: rhythm disorders (diagnostic categories 3–7), conduction defects (diagnostic categories 8–9), chamber hypertrophies (diagnostic categories 10–11), and cardiac ischemia or infarction (diagnostic categories 12–13). For each of these disease categories, automated ECG interpretation algorithms use discrete measurements obtained during signal processing, then map these measurements to rule-based criteria set forth by established clinical practice guidelines. Box 3.2 summarizes few examples of these rule-based ECG criteria associated with selected diagnostic statements of clinical importance.

3.7 "Logic" used in automated ECG interpretation systems

Algorithms that automatically interpret the ECG are typically deterministic or rule-based algorithms [30]. A rule-based algorithm uses a series of "if then else" type logical

BOX 3.2 Rule-based ECG criteria as recommended by clinical guidelines

Disease pathology	Rule-based criteria for selected diagnostic statements	ECG features needed for automated algorithms
Rhythm disorders	"Atrial fibrillation": heart rhythm with no discernible repeating P waves and irregular RR interval [26]	Beat-to-beat RR and PR intervals; global duration of P-QRS-T waves; lead-specific P wave measurements
Conduction defects	"Right bundle branch block": global QRS duration >120 ms; R′ pattern in V1 or V2; S duration >40 ms in V6 [3] "Left bundle branch block": global QRS duration > 120 ms; notched or slurred R in lead I, aVL, V5–V6; ST-T amplitude in opposite direction to QRS amplitude; and abnormal QRS axis [3]	Global QRS duration; lead-specific P-QRS-T measurements; R′ and S′; QRS axis
Chamber hypertrophies	"Left ventricular hypertrophy": there are numerous voltage criteria [5], with the following being the most widely used: $S_{V1} + R_{V5} \geq 35$ mm [27]; or $S_{V3} + R_{aVL} > 28$ mm (men) or >20 mm (women) [28]	Lead-specific R and S amplitude
Cardiac ischemia	"(Anterior/lateral/inferior) infarct": two contiguous leads with (1) ST amplitude $\geq 250\,\mu V$ (men <40 years), $\geq 200\,\mu V$ (men ≥ 40 years), or $\geq 150\,\mu V$ (women) in leads V1 and V2; or $\geq 100\,\mu V$ in other leads; or (2) ST amplitude $\leq 50\,\mu V$ with or without T amplitude $< -100\,\mu V$ [29]	Lead-specific ST and T amplitude; lead-specific Q duration

statements that are used to deduce a computerized diagnosis. The rules are normally knowledge engineered by a computer programmer after considering clinical guidelines and ECG diagnostic criteria. In a way, the rules represent the known ECG knowledge base and diagnostic criteria that physicians use when reading an ECG. However, of course the physician has broader heuristics and knowledge beyond ECG interpretation which is why the physician is ultimately responsible for diagnostics and not the computer. The physician also knows the patient history, context, and other symptoms that the patient exhibits. Hence, the algorithm is an adjunct to the physician, not a replacement.

The question is then what are the rules these computer algorithms reason with? Each individual rule can be considerably basic and binary, for example, a computer program might ask if the heart rate is greater than 120 beats per minute, which is either simply true or false, and depending on whether the rule is true or false, the algorithm will simply fork or move onto the next rule to be processed. However, whilst the rules themselves might be optimized, an algorithm can only reason based on the information that it is given. For example, the rule will not know if the waveform offset was precisely detected and that the ST amplitude was accurately measured. Hence, regardless of how good the rules are, the old adage of "garbage in, garbage out" still applies. Hence, it is clear that the algorithm is not just about the rules, since the preprocessing stage is just as important. This preprocessing stage includes cleaning the ECG signals (removing baseline wander for example) and extracting the information, also known as feature extraction. This includes beat detection, which requires techniques from digital signal processing to detect features such as the R peak, QRS onset, T wave offset, and so on which of course are then used to automatically measure the QRS interval, cardiac axis, ST–amplitude, rhythm, and so on. The veracity of this basic information is critical to the accuracy of the ECG algorithm. Fortunately, ECG printouts typically include the computerized diagnostic statement at the top of the page along with some of the feature measurements, typically including cardiac axis, QRS interval, heart rate, and so on (Fig. 3.13). These measurements could be used by the human reader to validate the computer's "basic information" that is being used to drive the algorithm. Of course, the human has certain perceptual skills that a rule-based algorithm may not have. For example, a human can consider the waveform morphology of the ECG signals and can rely on human level pattern recognition, that is, System 1 thinking [31], whereas the ECG signals are compressed down into "features" for an algorithm to reason with. As an example, the Glasgow ECG program is a well-known ECG algorithm that was developed by Prof. Peter Macfarlane and his team [32].

So, what are the limitations of knowledge-driven, human-curated rule-based logic in automated ECG interpretation systems. Despite the presence of well-established ECG diagnostic guidelines for most cardiovascular disease pathologies (Box 3.2), there remains a wide variation in obtaining similar diagnostic classification statements when the same ECG is interpreted by different computerized analysis systems. Such discrepancy in obtaining similar diagnostic statements can be attributed to few factors [13]. First, ECG signal processing follows multiple stages prior to obtaining automated interval and amplitude measurements of P, QRS, and T waves. Despite the availability of recommendations to standardize ECG processing [1], different manufacturers use different proprietary signal processing approaches leading to statistical differences in the automated measurements of clinically important, and basic, ECG intervals like RR, PR, QRS, and QT [33]. The differences in measurements become even more pronounced when the ECG is abnormal (e.g., nonsinus rhythm), which further limits clinical utility.

A second factor contributing to discrepancy in automated diagnostic statements is the need to account for waveform morphology (e.g., P shape, QRS pattern, and ST-T sloping) and interlead spatial relationships (e.g., contiguous leads) in certain disease pathologies like arrhythmias and MI. These computer-aided statements are usually less reproducible simply because that rule-based systems do not have the visual pattern recognition skills of human readers. It has been shown that, using nine different computer interpretation programs, the overall accuracy of computer-aided ECG diagnosis is $\sim 7\%$ lower than that of cardiologists [34]. Computer-aided diagnostic accuracy was reported to be the lowest in diagnosing arrhythmias and conduction disorders [35], with nearly 15% of rhythm-related diagnostic statements requiring re-evaluation by clinicians [36]. It has been also shown that diagnostic algorithms have wide variability in diagnosing MI, with false positive and false negative prediction rates ranging from 0% to 42% and $22\% - 42\%$, respectively [37,38]. This wide variability has profound implications to clinical management of patients in acute cardiac distress. Consequently, due to the overall suboptimal diagnostic accuracy, the experts' consensus is that all computer-aided ECG interpretations should be systematically over-read by experienced clinicians. Yet, it is worth cautioning that incorrect computer-aided diagnosis would still bias and mislead the clinicians in their ECG interpretation, potentially reducing the accuracy of both specialists and nonspecialists by 43% and 59%, respectively [39].

3.8 Machine learning and automated 12-lead ECG analysis

The previous section described the conventional approach to ECG algorithm development where the algorithm is based on a collection of logical statements that are in the form of rules to infer a diagnosis. As aforementioned, these rules are typically derived from expert knowledge, guidelines, and known diagnostic criteria. Hence, these algorithms can be described as knowledge-driven (deduction) as opposed to being data driven (induction). Whilst knowledge-driven (or knowledge-engineered) algorithms were a popular approach in previous decades (e.g., expert systems), there is a well-known trend towards data-driven algorithms in the form of ML. The phrase "data driven" simply means that the ML algorithm "self-learns" (without much supervision from domain/knowledge experts, i.e., cardiology experts) to infer the diagnosis by deriving its own diagnostic patterns (or even "inducted" rules) after having "seen" a large dataset of "labeled" ECGs. The term "labeled" here means that each ECG that the ML algorithm is exposed to has a reliably "labeled" diagnosis that is either based on a consensus diagnosis from a group of expert cardiologists or that is verified by gold standard tests (e.g., echocardiogram, blood tests, angiograms, etc.).

In a general sense, a data-driven ML algorithm learns the correlates that link the ECG features (e.g., QRS width, ST-amplitude, etc.) to the labeled diagnosis. However, this does run the risk of recognizing confounders and other associations that are unreliable or un-generalizable. Ultimately, an ML algorithm will only be as good as the labeled data; for example, if a single junior clinician labels the ECGs that are used to train an ML algorithm, then the algorithm may make the same diagnostic mistakes as the "labeler." This highlights the importance of using a group of "expert" clinicians and if possible, labels that are verified by other diagnostic tests.

This process of data–driven algorithm development using ML is specifically known as "supervised" ML, since the learning process is driven or "supervised" by existing labels. Learning algorithms such as neural networks update its learning (hyper–parameters or weights) iteratively where the labels are used to supervise and inform the algorithm if its current prediction is correct or incorrect. This could be akin to children learning to recognize cats and dogs where a "learner" initially guesses if the photo includes a cat or a dog, and the parent corrects the learner when they get this wrong, forcing the learner to adjust their understanding. Supervised ML is simply a branch of ML where the algorithm learns using a labeled dataset. Different labels can be used to train ML models. Although most labeling can focus on diagnostic statements, many other ML algorithms have been trained for noise detection [40], lead reversal, and misplacement detection [41,42].

The other two branches of ML include learning using an "unlabeled" dataset and learning using a "semilabeled" dataset (i.e., a mixture of labeled and unlabeled instances), both of which are known as unsupervised ML and semisupervised ML, respectively. While supervised ML is the dominant approach for developing predictive or classification algorithms, unsupervised ML can be useful for discovering patterns or labels in a dataset.

Supervised ML is used to either predict a number (known as a regression problem) or to classify cases into a "class" or "category" (known as a classification problem). Given that ECG interpretation involves categorizing ECG cases into categories (such as Acute MI, Normal ECG, AF, etc.), automated ECG interpretation is known as a classification problem. There are many different supervised ML algorithms for doing classification, including support vector machines (SVMs), artificial neural networks (ANNs), decision trees (DTs), k–nearest neighbor, regularized logistic regression (LR), and Naive Bayes (NB) to name but a few. These supervised ML algorithms are trained using ECG features (e.g., QRS width, P wave, ST amplitude) that characterize each ECG along with its labels (i.e., acute MI, AF, etc.). Data scientists sometimes combine different algorithms, an approach known as ensemble learning, often producing even better results.

Supervised ML algorithms can be trained using 70% of the ECGs in the dataset and tested on the remaining 30%. However, the training and test split is not standardized and can be a ratio of 60:40, 70:30, 80:20, or 90:10. This is typically decided by the data scientist. More importantly, rigorous evaluation techniques such as k–fold cross-validation are typically used on the training set before testing the algorithm on the remaining data. In this case, the typical approach is to use 10-fold cross-validation, meaning the algorithm is trained and validated 10 separate times on the training set, with each iteration having a different subset for validation. The 10-fold cross-validation offers the advantage of attenuating bias, producing results that are more generalizable to the test set.

When the algorithm has finished its "learning" by identifying sets of features that seem to correlate with each of the labels, the algorithm is then tested on a blinded dataset of ECGs to evaluate its performance. After testing, accuracy measures such as sensitivity and specificity can be used to evaluate the performance of the algorithm, however, other metrics such as AUC and F1 scores can also be used. AUC and F1 metrics can be used to benchmark algorithmic performance between different ML algorithms (e.g., SVM, LR, NB, etc.), then choosing the winning algorithm.

This supervised ML technique follows a traditional approach with a standard work-flow pipeline: ECG preprocessing; feature extraction; feature selection; and ECG classification. Such supervised ML techniques are referred to as traditional ML approaches and are usually distinguished from deep learning (DL)-based approaches (to be discussed below). Thus, the feature extraction process in traditional ML can be the same process that is used for rule-based algorithms (except this feature extraction is used for a large number of ECGs to train the algorithm, whereas rule-based algorithms are not trained but use feature extraction to simply get the features from the ECG being interpreted). Data scientists typically use digital signal processing techniques to extract a large set of ECG features for each ECG. Afterward, they use feature selection and/or data reduction (e.g., principal component analysis) techniques to select a set of features (predictors) that seem to have predictive power for classifying the ECGs into the different diseases groups (outcomes). Hence, removing irrelevant features from the dataset. The selected features are then used with a supervised ML algorithm to learn the "labels" [43]. Selecting the features this way is known as "handcrafted" feature selection because the data scientist has assessed the predictive power of each individual feature and made their own case to include them in the model or to exclude them. Unfortunately, handcrafted feature extraction and selection when building ML algorithms can be time consuming, especially in the case where the number of ECG features is large, and there is discrepancy between the feature selection techniques regarding the ranking of feature importance [43]. It is of course important to consult a domain expert (e.g., cardiologist) when selecting features since domain knowledge can also ensure that data science decisions around feature selection are grounded in science and are reasonable and generalizable (ensuring that they are not confounders). And whilst feature selection requires time and effort, this would be minuscule when compared to the labor required to develop knowledge-engineered rule-based algorithms, since they require a programmer to manually codify knowledge into a large set of rules. Automated ECG algorithms based on traditional supervised ML models have been shown to be superior to automated algorithms based on existing rule-based systems [44].

Whilst traditional ML requires a data scientist to do the feature engineering, DL has become a widely used technique that automates the feature engineering process by choosing its own features. DL is a subset of ML and is based on ANNs. DL is bioinspired by the human brain, where activated neurons can connect to other neurons via synapses in a large network. DL can be in the form of different types of networks and structures such as convolutional neural networks, recurrent neural networks, multilayer perceptron, deep belief networks, and long short-term memory. DL has perhaps become more popular given that it automates feature extraction and selection (taking one task away from the data scientist) and is known to outperform traditional supervised ML algorithms.

DL algorithms are also known to improve their accuracy as the training ECG dataset gets larger, whereas the performance of traditional ML techniques may plateau regardless of how large the training dataset gets. Hence, in the era of "big" ECG data, DL is likely to outperform any other approach. However, DL is considered a black box approach as it is difficult to discern the decision-making logic, whereas the decision-making of a rule-based algorithm is clear. Hence, DL algorithms are not as "explainable," "transparent," and "traceable" as other algorithms. The process of feature extraction and feature selection are not transparent to the data scientist, domain expert, or any other end-user. Thus, the gain of accuracy by using DL is usually at the expense of explainability. However, this "black-box" limitation might be solved in the future. Computer scientists have proposed methods to enable DL algorithms to be more explainable and transparent. For example, techniques can be used to generate an "attention map" from the DL algorithm, which is one of the proposed methods that can be used to understand what the DL algorithm "looked" at before making its classification. Another method is to generate a DT that mimics the DL decision-making process since a DT can be interpreted by users.

Although DL has been used for many healthcare applications for decades, ECG interpretation using DL needs to be further explored. DL was used for ECG interpretation in 2009 [45]. Since then, DL has become a popular topic in ECG interpretation according to the accumulative number of published papers in three databases (IEEE, SCOPUS, and PUBMED) as shown in Fig. 3.14. DL showed promising results in ECG interpretation to diagnose different heart abnormalities [46]. In this study, DL was shown to outperform physicians in detecting six abnormalities on the ECG. DL has also outperformed cardiologists to detect 12 different types of cardiac rhythms [47,48]. In addition, DL outperformed 53 physicians who work in cardiology

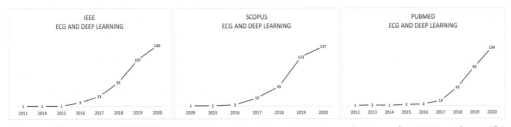

Figure 3.14 Trend in published literature using deep learning techniques for ECG analysis. This figure shows the accumulative number of published articles (*y*-axis) in three main research databases between 2012 and 2020 (*x*-axis). *ECG*, Electrocardiogram.

departments (even for those who have more than 12 years of experience) to detect 21 heart rhythm abnormalities [49].

3.9 Basic principles of risk stratification

By now, the reader should be familiar with the role of ECG in cardiovascular disease classification, as well as the steps involved in automated ECG interpretation, including the different rule-based, ML and DL algorithms. The remaining sections will focus on the role of ECG measurements and diagnostic in risk stratification in the clinical settings. Deep understanding of the role of certain ECG metrics and diagnostic statements in stratifying patients to guide therapeutics is especially important.

Evaluating the risk of a condition poses for a patient is a fundamental task for healthcare providers. This process, known as risk stratification, enables a clinician to classify patients into populations of high risk or low risk for a certain future event. For example, an accurate risk-stratifying strategy enables an emergency physician to classify patients into groups of those needing an immediate intervention in the emergency room, or those requiring further follow-up with their primary care physician, or those who are safe to be immediately sent home. The heart's critical role in the body makes stratifying for potential acute or chronic cardiovascular complications an essential task requiring optimal accuracy.

Accurate selection of outcomes when stratifying risk is integral to the process. Therefore, developing a useful risk stratification tool includes selecting outcomes that are pertinent to the condition at hand and that are easily measurable. Consequently, it is sensible to select outcomes that are true clinical outcomes rather than surrogate outcomes, meaning they are truly related to the disease process and are clinically significant. Moreover, it is practical to select outcomes that are hard outcomes, that is, outcomes that are concrete, clearly definable, and measurable. Therefore, in cardiovascular disease, while the evaluation of a patient ultimately aims to improve a patient's life and avoid morbidity, mortality remains the most important outcome. Mortality as an endpoint offers the advantage of being a hard outcome, is easily measurable without bias, and is obviously clinically significant for both the patient and the clinician. Complying with these characteristics of well-defined endpoints, the following two outcomes are frequently used as the primary mortality outcomes in cardiovascular disease:

1. Cardiovascular death (CV death): Assignment of a cause of death is often scientific and adheres to standardized definitions. CV death aims to capture the primary cause of death, including the disease that initiated the chain of events leading to death [50]. For instance, when a MI leads to heart failure (a weak heart pump) and subsequently death, then the primary cause of death would be the MI. However, the outcome of CV death is often not divided into granular subcategories, such as death resulting from a MI or heart failure, because of the substantial overlap of

such events and the ambiguity of the true trigger of the subsequent death [51]. CV death is then often defined according to (1) certain International Classification of Disease (ICD) codes relevant to the circulatory system (ICD-9 codes 390 to 459 or ICD-10 100 to 199), or (2) as death due to fatal or nonfatal MI.

2. Sudden cardiac death (SCD): SCD is defined as (1) unexpected death within 24 hours of having been observed alive and symptom-free or within 1 hour after the onset of symptoms without any defined cause of death or (2) the presence of resuscitated or nonresuscitated fatal tachyarrhythmia. Compared to the wide cast-net of CV death, SCD alternatively aims to zone in on patients who suffer from a sudden cessation or disruption of normal electrical conduction in the heart. SCD is mostly triggered by the onset of lethal arrhythmia such as ventricular fibrillation.

In addition to these endpoints, many studies use all-cause death for risk stratification. All-cause death is the most unbiased endpoint among mortality endpoints given that it is not subject to observer bias. All-cause death is often defined as a documented death in death certificates, medical records, or national registries, and it is often used as the main mortality endpoint in clinical studies [50]. However, all-cause death is nonspecific and frequently fails in establishing a mechanistic link between a given risk factor and its associated excess risk of mortality. In this chapter, we will primarily focus on CV death and SCD for risk stratification.

3.9.1 The role of ECG in risk stratification

The ECG has proven to be a valuable tool in risk-stratifying patients for mortality outcomes. This is facilitated by the ECG's ability to uncover multiple pathologies that are directly associated with these outcomes. For instance, a variety of arrhythmias are strongly associated with CV death, including AF [52] and other brief spontaneously resolving arrhythmias such as a nonsustained ventricular tachycardia [53]. The ECG is the most important tool in detecting these arrhythmias, particularly during continuous monitoring. Moreover, the ECG is well suited to reflect how frequent and how fast the arrhythmia is occurring, both important elements in stratifying risk of mortality [54]. Similarly, bundle branch blocks are strongly associated with CV death. It is worth noting that, just like many arrhythmias, the ECG is the gold standard method for identifying bundle branch blocks [55]. The characteristics the ECG describes, such as the width of the QRS, provide a vital substrate in risk-stratifying patients with bundle branch blocks for future mortality [56].

Another important role of the ECG in risk stratification centers on coronary artery disease. Coronary disease is the leading cause of mortality worldwide. The ECG plays an integral role in both identifying acute and chronic ischemia and infarction and providing means for predicting future mortality in these patients. This includes the ECG's ability to identify the severity of the ischemia and the location of the obstructed artery, both essential elements in predicting CV death [57]. Crucially, the ECG can be the only prognostic indicator in an otherwise silent acute MI, a significant cause of subsequent mortality [58].

More importantly, coronary artery disease is strongly associated with SCD, which accounts for nearly 80% of all sudden death cases [59]. The ECG is well suited to detect which patients are more likely to develop SCD post a MI, and hence play an essential role in primary prevention of short-term events [60]. In the long term, the interplay between the severity of coronary disease and ejection fraction is an important predictor for which patients are at risk for SCD. The ECG is especially well suited to identify which patients have a compromised ejection fraction, severe coronary disease, and an impaired autonomic nervous system, factors which all interact together, giving rise to SCD.

Identifying patients who are at higher risk of SCD is vital since numerous cases can be prevented by using implantable cardioverter-defibrillator (ICD). ICDs are devices that are implanted into patient's heart and are programmed to generate shocks that halt an ongoing fatal arrhythmia. The role of the ECG in risk-stratifying patients for SCD lies in its distinct ability to detect proarrhythmogenic events and conditions. This includes simple variations captured on resting standard ECG or during continuous monitoring, such as the change in heart rate during exercise or mental stress [61].

Arrhythmic events are central to SCD; therefore, it is natural that arrhythmias detected by an ECG provide value in risk-stratifying patients. This includes events such as transient ventricular tachycardia or as simple as single extra beats originating from the ventricles, known as ventricular ectopy [61]. Moreover, the ECG is the cornerstone in diagnosing inherited arrhythmia syndromes, including Brugada syndrome and Long QT syndrome, conditions that often lead to SCD.

Structural changes that are often diagnosed with routine ECG can lead often to arrhythmia and SCD. This includes conduction defects in the heart such as left bundle branch block and chamber enlargement such as LVH. Both conditions are strongly associated with SCD, and the ability of the ECG to discern the progress of these conditions is vital in risk-stratifying patients.

3.10 ECG-derived markers for risk stratification

The 12-lead ECG constitutes a simple and readily available tool not only to diagnose various cardiovascular pathologies but also to stratify risk of adverse events in the general population and in those with different comorbidities. This ability to stratify patients into categories of risk has important clinical implications. It can help clinicians identify patients who might need more aggressive therapies or closer follow up. As explained in this chapter, the ECG follows a deterministic nature, with each waveform morphology and characteristic resembling a physiological signature in the human body. Distortion in such characteristics does not come in one size fits all, but rather different attributes of this distortion in the signal might suggest different pathological mechanisms involved. For instance, a prolongation in the QTc interval can indicate increased arterial stiffness and systemic vascular resistance [62], not merely longer ventricular activation time, which could explain the repeatedly observed correlation between this marker and CV death. In this section, we will review the ECG-derived risk markers most commonly reported in the literature. These ECG markers can be classified in one of four broad categories: markers associated with conduction disturbances, markers associated with structural changes, markers associated with repolarization abnormalities, and markers associated with distortions in heart rhythm regulation.

3.10.1 ECG risk markers based on conduction disturbances

The most commonly used ECG risk marker associated with conduction disturbances is the QRS duration. A normal QRS duration is ≤ 110 ms in adults older than 16 years of age [3]. A wider QRS duration indicates an abnormal propagation of depolarization impulse originating from the atria and traveling down the ventricles. In adults, an abnormal and prolonged depolarization of QRS ≥ 120 ms usually follows a morphology of either a right or left bundle branch block. The latter is prevalent in nearly half of patients with heart failure and is associated with more advanced myocardial disease, diminished left ventricular function, worse prognosis, and a higher risk of mortality compared with narrow QRS complex [63].

QRS duration has been an important ECG risk marker in evaluating risk and guiding treatment decisions in patients with heart failure, namely, selecting candidates for cardiac resynchronization therapy (CRT). A *meta*-analysis of five randomized clinical trials (pooled sample size = 5813) demonstrated that CRT has been most effective in reducing adverse events in heart failure patients with baseline QRS duration ≥ 150 ms [64]. However, given that QRS narrowing after CRT does not necessarily correlate with hemodynamic improvement [63], as well as the various etiologies involved in altering the ventricular activation cascade, it has been suggested that QRS morphology, not merely QRS widening, is an important predictor in risk stratification [65]. This has been demonstrated in a subsequent study that showed measurable reduction in mortality after CRT in heart failure patients with QRS duration ≥ 150 ms that was specifically observed in those with left bundle branch pattern [66].

Another important ECG risk marker associated with conduction disturbances is the QT interval. The QT interval quantifies the global ventricular depolarization and repolarization time, making it vulnerable to many intrinsic and extrinsic etiologies that can alter the cardiac cycle. A prolonged QT interval on the standard 12-lead ECG has been extensively studied as an established risk factor for SCD, namely, a potentially fatal ventricular tachyarrhythmia called Torsade de Pointes [67]. A prolonged QT interval has not been only shown to predict risk of CV death in clinical populations, like type 2 diabetes [68], but also to predict risk of SCD in the general population. Despite lack of consistency in earlier studies regarding the prognostic value of QT interval in individuals with no preexisting comorbidities [69], a *meta*-analysis that included 16 prospective cohorts and seven case−control studies (pooled sample size >120,000) has shown that a 50 ms increase in QT interval was associated with a relative risk of 1.29 (1.15−1.46) for CV death and 1.24 (0.97−1.60) for SCD [70].

As an established ECG risk marker, perhaps the biggest clinical significance of the QT interval lies in its role in monitoring long QT syndrome that is acquired due to therapeutic drugs [71]. Many drugs interact with cellular ion channels that regulate ventricular action potential, especially the outward potassium channels responsible for late repolarization potentials. The latter constitute a vulnerable proarrhythmic window that can initiate fatal ventricular arrhythmias. In the right context, a drug that alters these channels (referred to as QT prolonging drug) can lead to SCD. Thus, the FDA requires pharmaceutical companies to evaluate drugs under development for any undesirable QT prolongation effects [72].

Despite the seemingly easy computation of the QT interval on the ECG, the high stakes make the ECG processing required for accurate computation a daunting task. The difficulty lies in two challenges. The first challenge is the precise determination of T wave offset, which largely depends on T wave morphology. Given the intra- and inter-individual variabilities, it has been shown that automated QT measurements can be longer or shorter compared to manual measurements by trained human annotators [73], warranting computer assisted validation of QT interval in clinical practice. The second challenge is correcting QT interval for beat-to-beat variability in the heart rate. Although many manufacturers correct the QT interval using the simple Bazett's formula (i.e., QT interval divided by the square root of proceeding RR interval), different correction formulas have been shown to either overcorrect or undercorrect the QT interval at different heart rates, warranting further caution in QT interval interpretation [74].

3.10.2 ECG risk markers based on structural changes

Many of the previously reported pathologies, including chamber hypertrophy and conduction defects, are structural in nature and have been shown to increase risk of CV death, including in healthy individuals independent of traditional risk factors [75]. In terms of ECG risk markers, fragmentation of the QRS complex (Fig. 3.15), a sign of myocardial scarring and remodeling, has been shown as a strong prognostic marker, especially in those with acute MI. In this population, the presence of fragmented QRS on admission ECG was found to be predictive of mortality, adverse events, deterioration of cardiac function, and presence of multivessel disease [76]. Fragmented QRS has been also shown to predict reperfusion failure and in-hospital CV death in ST-elevation MI [77].

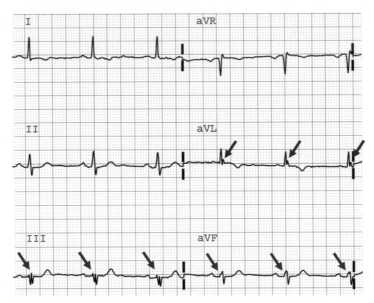

Figure 3.15 QRS fragmentation. This figure shows an evidenced QRS fragmentation in the inferior leads (*red* arrows) of a 48-year-old male evaluated for chest pain.

Another commonly reported ECG marker associated with structural changes is cardiac axis deviation. The mean QRS and T axes project between -30 and $+90$ degrees in the frontal plane [3]. Structural, and repolarization, changes in the ventricles would distort the projection of QRS axis or T axis (or both). Isolated left QRS axis deviation, for example, is associated with altered cardiac function and has been shown to predict CV death, even in healthy asymptomatic individuals [75]. These results have not been consistent in literature though [78]. However, a more interesting concept is the relative relationship between the QRS axis and the T axis, referred to as the QRS-T angle (Fig. 3.16). The QRS-T angle, measured in the frontal or spatial planes, resembles the difference in mean vectors of depolarization and repolarization, and has been consistently described as a strong predictor of both CV death and SCD [79]. A recent *meta*-analysis of 22 studies (pooled sample size 164,171) has shown that a wide QRS-T angle was associated with 71% excess relative risk of mortality in clinical populations as well as in the general population [80]. This marker is explained in further detail under repolarization abnormalities below.

3.10.3 ECG risk markers based on repolarization abnormalities

The repolarization signal on the ECG, or the ST-T waveform, has been extensively studied in the medical literature. It contains a significant amount of prognostic information that play important role in risk stratification [6]. Various pathological processes

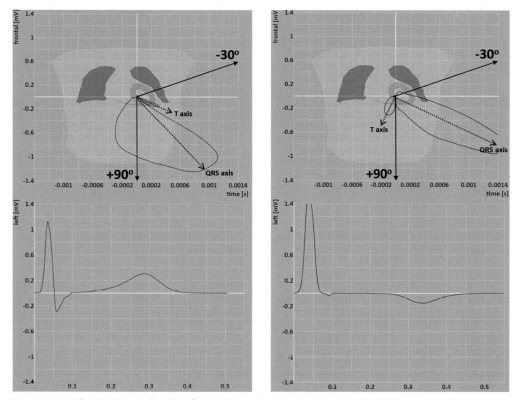

Figure 3.16 The QRS-T angle. This figure shows the angle between the QRS axis and the T axis in the frontal plane. The left panel shows a normal averaged beat with the corresponding projections of the QRS and T axes in the normal range or −30 to +90 degrees, with a frontal QRS-T angle of ∼30 degrees. The right panel shows an abnormal averaged beat with a distorted projection of cardiac axes, resulting in a wider frontal QRS-T angle of ∼90 degrees. *Created using ECGsim v3.0 Â©️ Peacs 2010−2014.*

can alter the repolarization signal, including cardiac ischemia and MI, electrolytes imbalance, chamber hypertrophy and ventricular remodeling, inflammation and oxidative stress, and other systemic and genetic disorders. These varying etiologies make many repolarization abnormalities nonspecific in nature, yet the presence of a repolarization abnormality, even in the absence of an obvious cause, has been linked to increased risk of adverse events.

The role of repolarization characteristics in risk stratification has been demonstrated in a comprehensive *meta*-analysis that included 106 observational studies with a pooled sample size of nearly 350,000 individuals from both the general population and cardiac and noncardiac populations [7]. This *meta*-analysis examined the association between CV death and SCD with repolarization abnormalities clustered in eight categories: T wave duration, T amplitude, isolated T inversion, nonspecific ST-T changes, mean T

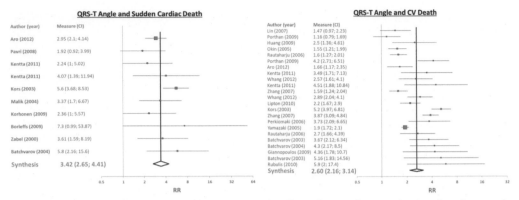

Figure 3.17 Risk stratification using the QRS-T angle. These forest plots synthesize data from published articles that examined the association between widened QRS-T angle and SCD (left panel) and cardiovascular death (right panel). The risk is reported as risk ratio (RR). *Adapted from Al-Zaiti SS. The prognostic value of ventricular repolarization. Ann Arbor, MI, USA: ProQuest LLC; 2013 [81].*

axis, QRS-T angle, T loop morphology, and interlead heterogeneity of T wave. The study showed a consistent increase in risk of SCD (hazard ratio 1.9–4.1) and CV death (hazard ratio 1.6–2.7), with metrics of QRS-T angle showing the strongest and most consistent association with SCD (Fig. 3.17). These findings are intriguing and demonstrate that vector loop criteria (or the equivalent information deduced from simultaneous leads) are sensitive to heterogeneity in repolarization and can be used to assess for arrhythmogenicity in those most vulnerable to sudden death.

An additional ECG risk marker associated with repolarization abnormalities is $T_{peak} - T_{end}$ (i.e., the interval from the peak to the end of the T wave). $T_{peak} - T_{end}$ interval represents a vulnerable window of late repolarization potentials across the myocardium, and $T_{peak} - T_{end}$ prolongation suggests transmural dispersion of ventricular repolarization. This interval has gained tremendous attention in recent years as a useful risk stratification tool for predicting arrhythmic death in various clinical populations. A recent *meta*-analysis of 33 observational studies with pooled sample of more than 150,000 patients showed that a mean $T_{peak} - T_{end}$ interval >100 ms was associated with significant excess odds of ventricular tachyarrhythmia and SCD of 10% and 27%, respectively [82]. This risk was consistent across various disease groups and in the general population. Given that $T_{peak} - T_{end}$ interval would depend on QT interval and its heart rate dependency, some studies examined the arrhythmogenicity of the relative ratio between $T_{peak} - T_{end}$ interval and QT interval. A higher ratio would then, theoretically, represents larger transmural dispersion of ventricular repolarization independent of QTc prolongation. A recent *meta*-analysis demonstrated that a higher $T_{peak} - T_{end}/QT$ ratio is associated with approximately threefold higher risk of SCD after acute MI [83], which has important implications to preventive strategies in clinical practice.

Another ECG risk marker of repolarization abnormalities that gained significant attention in the medical literature is T wave alternans (TWA). TWA reflects excessive beat-to-beat variability and fluctuations in T wave beyond that attributed to noise and artifact in the ECG signal. Excessive fluctuation (or higher TWA) is associated with larger dispersion of ventricular repolarization and, hence, increased risk of arrhythmogenicity and SCD [84]. A *meta*-analysis of 19 studies with pooled sample size of around 2600 patients from a wide range of populations has shown that increased TWA (μV) was associated with more than threefold excess relative risk of SCD [85]. However, this excess risk was not consistent among the different populations studied, with the greatest prognostic value observed in patients with chronic heart failure. A more recent *meta*-analysis demonstrated that the presence of TWA in patients with cardiomyopathy was associated with more than sixfold excess hazard risk of developing subsequent life-threatening ventricular arrhythmias [86]. Finally, it is worth noting that TWA is usually computed on longer ECG recordings (e.g., Holter monitors) to allow higher precision in the statistical estimation of beat-to-beat variability in the T wave. Yet, some recent reports suggest that TWA measured from a standard 10-second 12-lead ECG can still provide important prognostic information in patients with acute MI [87].

3.10.4 ECG risk markers based on distortion in heart rhythm regulation

Although heartbeats are intrinsically initiated in the heart, the oscillations in the intervals between these consecutive heartbeats are regulated by the autonomic nervous system. Through this autonomic control of heart rate regulation, there is now a well-established link between autonomous nervous system and CV death. Resting heart rate on the standard ECG has been specifically shown as a strong prognostic marker. A *meta*-analysis of 45 observational studies demonstrated that an increment of 10 beats/min in resting heart rate is associated with 12% excess relative risk of sudden death in those with preexisting cardiovascular disease [88].

A more intriguing concept to estimate cardiovascular burden is based on the beat-to-beat oscillations of the RR interval (or the consecutive instantaneous heart rates), which is conventionally described as heart rate variability (HRV) [89]. From a mechanistic standpoint, HRV resembles an adaptive change in heart rate by the sympathetic and parasympathetic nervous systems to buffer blood pressure. Hence, a diminished HRV is thought to suggest hemodynamic dysfunction, explaining its long-known association with mortality after MI [90]. A *meta*-analysis of eight observational studies with pooled sample size $>20,000$ patients showed that low HRV is associated with 32%−45% increased risk of CV death. Consistent results were observed in a more recent *meta*-analysis that included 28 cohort studies with pooled sample size of >3000 patients from various clinical populations. In this analysis, reduced HRV was associated with $\sim$45% increased risk of CV death [91]. Both *meta*-analyses evaluated the association between HRV and total CV death, but not specifically against SCD. A recent study in patients with chronic heart failure suggested that, using competing risk analysis, reduced HRV might be preferentially associated with nonsudden CV death rather than sudden arrhythmic death [92].

In terms of SCD prediction, attenuated recovery of beat-to-beat oscillations after a premature ectopic beat, a marker of autonomic dysfunction and remodeling that is usually referred to as heart rate turbulence (HRT), was suggested as a powerful predictor of fatal ventricular tachyarrhythmia in various cardiac populations [93]. In a *meta*-analysis of 45 studies examining the association between SCD and various ECG risk markers described in this section, TWA, but not HRV and HRT, was significantly associated with SCD. However, data on HRT and HRV in this analysis were pooled from only four studies with a pooled sample size <600 patients [94]. In a more recent *meta*-analysis focusing on HRT and pooling data from 15 studies ($n \sim 11,500$), abnormal HRT was a predictive marker for SCD in heart failure and postacute MI patients (relative risk ~ 2.5) [95]. This HRT predictive power of SCD increased significantly when this marker was combined with TWA (relative risk ~ 4.2), making both ECG markers clinically important in stratifying risk postacute MI.

3.11 Challenges and opportunities

The computer might misinterpret the ECG due to different ECG recording problems such as lead misplacement, lead reversals, and noise and artifact in the signal. These "digital" mistakes could mislead the human reader resulting in a misdiagnosis. Automation bias is when the human is biased or anchored to the diagnosis suggested by the computer, even when the computer is incorrect or misleading. Automation bias is a challenge in the application of automated ECG interpretation as the computer diagnoses has an influence on the physician's diagnoses, especially, on less expert interpreters [39]. There is an opportunity to improve and calibrate the trust between the human and the computer. The algorithm needs to be more transparent by providing uncertainty or probability surrounding each prediction [96], or at least its decision logic could be available and metrics could inform the human of how accurate the algorithm is for the respective disease groups.

ML adoption in healthcare is particularly challenging as some ML techniques lack transparency and explainability [97]. Physicians need to understand why and how an ML algorithm made a decision. As aforementioned, data scientists have suggested different methods such as generating attention maps for DL algorithms to show how the final decision was made (or at least what the algorithm "looked at" just before it made a decision). Physicians might also need to understand how ML algorithms generally work. For example, if healthcare systems become more ML reliant, medical schools will have more responsibilities to prepare future physicians for ML-enhanced healthcare systems.

There are also opportunities to improve ECG interpretation as we move towards a paperless healthcare system where ECGs are displayed on digital touchscreens. For example, the ECG can be augmented by complementary visualizations and interactive computing [98]. Interactive ECG interpretation software has been already prototyped as a proof of concept [99]. Such software guides the user through the ECG interpretation process and presents a number of possible diagnoses in a ranked order as part of the final screen. The user can also interrogate the computerized diagnoses by exploring its logic and diagnostic criteria by simply interacting with the user interface.

Finally, whilst standardizing the industry to use a standard algorithm is unlikely, standardizing the outputs of the algorithms should be imperative. A scientific statement list was recommended and approved by the "International Society for Computerized Electrocardiology" that can be used to standardize the outputs of computerized ECG interpretations [2]. As previously mentioned, this statement list consists of diagnostic terms that are used for ECG interpretation. It includes four types of statements: (1) primary statements, (2) secondary statements, (3) modifiers statements, and (4) comparison statements. Standardizing computerized ECG statements is important to ensure that clinicians and machines use consistent nomenclature and diagnostic descriptions when using different ECG machines in different hospitals.

References

[1] Kligfield P, et al. AHA/ACC/HRS scientific statements: recommendations for the standardization and interpretation of the electrocardiogram part I: the electrocardiogram and its technology. A scientific statement from the American Heart Association Electrocardiography and Arrhythmias Committee, Council on Clinical Cardiology; the American College of Cardiology Foundation; and the Heart Rhythm Society Endorsed by the International Society for Computerized Electrocardiology. J Am Coll Cardiol 2007;49(10):1110−29.

[2] Mason J, Hancock E, Gettes L. AHA/ACC Scientific Statements: recommendations for the standardization and interpretation of the electrocardiogram part II: electrocardiography diagnostic statement list a scientific statement from the American Heart Association Electrocardiography and Arrhythmias Committee, Council on Clinical Cardiology; the American College of Cardiology Foundation; and the Heart Rhythm Society Endorsed by the International Society for Computerized Electrocardiology. J Am Coll Cardiol 2007;49(10):1129−37.

[3] Surawicz B, et al. AHA/ACCF/HRS recommendations for the standardization and interpretation of the electrocardiogram: part III: intraventricular conduction disturbances a scientific statement from the American Heart Association Electrocardiography and Arrhythmias Committee, Council on Clinical Cardiology; the American College of Cardiology Foundation; and the Heart Rhythm Society Endorsed by the International Society for Computerized Electrocardiology. J Am Coll Cardiol 2009;53(11):976−81.

[4] Wagner GS, et al. AHA/ACCF/HRS recommendations for the standardization and interpretation of the electrocardiogram: part VI: acute ischemia/infarction a scientific statement from the American Heart Association Electrocardiography and Arrhythmias Committee, Council on Clinical Cardiology; the American College of Cardiology Foundation; and the Heart Rhythm Society Endorsed by the International Society for Computerized Electrocardiology. J Am Coll Cardiol 2009;53(11):1003−11.

[5] Hancock EW, et al. AHA/ACCF/HRS recommendations for the standardization and interpretation of the electrocardiogram: part V: electrocardiogram changes associated with cardiac chamber hypertrophy: a scientific statement from the American Heart Association Electrocardiography and Arrhythmias Committee, Council on Clinical Cardiology; the American College of Cardiology Foundation; and the Heart Rhythm Society: endorsed by the International Society for Computerized Electrocardiology. Circulation 2009;119(10):e251—61.

[6] Rautaharju PM, Surawicz B, Gettes LS. AHA/ACCF/HRS recommendations for the standardization and interpretation of the electrocardiogram: part IV: the ST segment, T and U waves, and the QT interval. J Am Coll Cardiol 2009;53(11):982—91.

[7] Al-Zaiti SS, et al. Electrocardiogram-based predictors of clinical outcomes: a *meta*-analysis of the prognostic value of ventricular repolarization. Heart Lung 2014;43(6):516—26.

[8] Smulyan H. The computerized ECG: friend and foe. Am J Med 2019;132(2):153—60.

[9] Rautaharju PM. Eyewitness to history: landmarks in the development of computerized electrocardiography. J Electrocardiol 2016;49(1):1—6.

[10] Bond RR, et al. A review of ECG storage formats. Int J Med Inform 2011;80(10):681—97.

[11] Conrad E. Chapter 5 — domain 5: security architecture and design. In: Conrad E, editor. Eleventh hour CISSP. Boston: Syngress; 2011. p. 69—87.

[12] Pipberger HV, Arms RJ, Stallmann FW. Automatic screening of normal and abnormal electrocardiograms by means of a digital electronic computer. Proc Soc Exp Biol Med 1961;106(1):130—2.

[13] Schläpfer J, Wellens HJ. Computer-interpreted electrocardiograms: benefits and limitations. J Am Coll Cardiol 2017;70(9):1183—92.

[14] Novotny T, et al. Data analysis of diagnostic accuracies in 12-lead electrocardiogram interpretation by junior medical fellows. J Electrocardiol 2015;48(6):988—94.

[15] Morisbak B, Gjesdal K. Computer-based interpretation of ECG—guiding or misleading? Tidsskr Laegeforen 1999;119(23):3441—4.

[16] Southern WN, Arnsten JH. The effect of erroneous computer interpretation of ECGs on resident decision making. Med Decis Mak 2009;29(3):372—6.

[17] Jakobsson A, Ohlin P, Pahlm O. Does a computer-based ECG-recorder interpret electrocardiograms more efficiently than physicians? Clin Physiol 1985;5(5):417—23.

[18] Willems J, et al. Common standards for quantitative electrocardiography: goals and main results. Methods Inf Med 1990;29(04):263—71.

[19] Mason JW, et al. Electrocardiographic reference ranges derived from 79,743 ambulatory subjects. J Electrocardiol 2007;40(3):228—34 e8.

[20] Rautaharju PM, et al. Normal standards for computer-ECG programs for prognostically and diagnostically important ECG variables derived from a large ethnically diverse female cohort: the Women's Health Initiative (WHI). J Electrocardiol 2013;46(6):707—16.

[21] ISO/IEC, Medical electrical equipmentâ€"Part 2—86: Particular requirements for the basic safety and essential performance of electrocardiographs, including diagnostic equipment, monitoring equipment, ambulatory equipment, electrodes, cables and leadwires, in Respiratory devices and related equipment used for patient care; 2021. Available from: https://www.iso.org/standard/74456.html.

[22] Zywietz C. Sampling rate of ECGs in relation to measurement accuracy. Computerized interpretation of the electrocardiogram. New York, NY: Engineering Foundation; 1986. p. 122—5.

[23] Luo S, Johnston P. A review of electrocardiogram filtering. J Electrocardiol 2010;43(6):486—96.

[24] Virani SS, et al. Heart disease and stroke statistics-2020 update: a report from the American Heart Association. Circulation 2020;141(9):e139—596.

[25] Wellens HJJGA, Doevendans PA, editors. The ECG in acute myocardial infarction and unstable angina: diagnosis and risk stratification. 1st ed Norwell, MA: Kluwer Academic Publishers; 2003.

[26] Hindricks G, et al. 2020 ESC Guidelines for the diagnosis and management of atrial fibrillation developed in collaboration with the European Association of Cardio-Thoracic Surgery (EACTS). Eur Heart J 2020;42(5):373—498. Available from: https://doi.org/10.1093/eurheartj/ehaa612.

[27] Sokolow M, Lyon TP. The ventricular complex in left ventricular hypertrophy as obtained by unipolar precordial and limb leads. Am Heart J 1949;37(2):161—86.

[28] Casale PN, et al. Electrocardiographic detection of left ventricular hypertrophy: development and prospective validation of improved criteria. J Am Coll Cardiol 1985;6(3):572—80.

[29] Thygesen K, et al. Fourth universal definition of myocardial infarction (2018). Eur Heart J 2018;138:e618—51 ehy462-ehy462.

[30] Tison GH, et al. Automated and interpretable patient ECG profiles for disease detection, tracking, and discovery. Circ Cardiovasc Qual Outcomes 2019;12(9):e005289.

[31] Kahneman D. Thinking, fast and slow. Macmillan; 2011.

[32] Macfarlane P, Devine B, Clark E. The University of Glasgow (Uni-G) ECG analysis program. Computers cardiology. IEEE; 2005.

[33] Kligfield P, et al. Comparison of automated measurements of electrocardiographic intervals and durations by computer-based algorithms of digital electrocardiographs. Am Heart J 2014;167 (2):150—9 e1.

[34] Willems JL, et al. The diagnostic performance of computer programs for the interpretation of electrocardiograms. N Engl J Med 1991;325(25):1767—73.

[35] Guglin ME, Thatai D. Common errors in computer electrocardiogram interpretation. Int J Cardiol 2006;106(2):232—7.

[36] Poon K, Okin PM, Kligfield P. Diagnostic performance of a computer-based ECG rhythm algorithm. J Electrocardiol 2005;38(3):235—8.

[37] O'Connor RE, et al. Part 9: acute coronary syndromes. Am Heart Assoc Guidel Update Cardiopulm Resuscitation Emerg Cardiovasc Care Circul 2015;132(18_suppl_2):S483—500.

[38] Garvey JL, et al. Electrocardiographic diagnosis of ST segment elevation myocardial infarction: an evaluation of three automated interpretation algorithms. J Electrocardiol 2016;49(5):728—32.

[39] Bond RR, et al. Automation bias in medicine: the influence of automated diagnoses on interpreter accuracy and uncertainty when reading electrocardiograms. J Electrocardiol 2018;51(6):S6—11.

[40] Abdelazez M, Rajan S, Chan ADC. Detection of noise type in electrocardiogram. In: 2018 IEEE international symposium on medical measurements and applications (MeMeA); 2018.

[41] Rjoob K, et al. Machine learning techniques for detecting electrode misplacement and interchanges when recording ECGs: a systematic review and meta-analysis. J Electrocardiol 2020;62:116—23.

[42] Rjoob K, et al. Data driven feature selection and machine learning to detect misplaced V1 and V2 chest electrodes when recording the 12-lead electrocardiogram. J Electrocardiol 2019;57:39—43.

[43] Bouzid Z, et al. In search of an optimal subset of ECG features to augment the diagnosis of acute coronary syndrome at the Emergency Department. J Am Heart Assoc 2020;e017871.

[44] Al-Zaiti S, et al. Machine learning-based prediction of acute coronary syndrome using only the prehospital 12-lead electrocardiogram. Nat Commun 2020;11(1):1—10.

[45] Jin Z, Sun Y, Cheng AC. Predicting cardiovascular disease from real-time electrocardiographic monitoring: an adaptive machine learning approach on a cell phone. In: 2009 Annual International Conference of the IEEE Engineering in Medicine and Biology Society; 2009.

[46] Ribeiro AH, et al. Automatic diagnosis of the 12-lead ECG using a deep neural network. Nat Commun 2020;11(1):1760.

[47] Minchol Ã© A, Rodriguez B. Artificial intelligence for the electrocardiogram. Nat Med 2019;25 (1):22—3.

[48] Hannun AY, et al. Cardiologist-level arrhythmia detection and classification in ambulatory electrocardiograms using a deep neural network. Nat Med 2019;25(1):65—9.

[49] Zhu H, et al. Automatic multilabel electrocardiogram diagnosis of heart rhythm or conduction abnormalities with deep learning: a cohort study. Lancet Digital Health 2020;2(7):e348—57.

[50] Hicks KA, et al. 2017 cardiovascular and stroke endpoint definitions for clinical trials. J Am Coll Cardiol 2018;71(9):1021—34.

[51] Hicks KA, et al. 2014 ACC/AHA key data elements and definitions for cardiovascular endpoint events in clinical trials: a report of the American College of Cardiology/American Heart Association Task Force on clinical data standards (Writing Committee to Develop Cardiovascular Endpoints Data Standards). Circulation 2015;132(4):302—61.

[52] Singh SM, et al. Population trends in all-cause mortality and cause specific-death with incident atrial fibrillation. J Am Heart Assoc 2020;9(19):e016810.

[53] Lin CY, et al. Long-term outcome of non-sustained ventricular tachycardia in structurally normal hearts. PLoS One 2016;11(8):e0160181.

[54] Rovere MTL, et al. Baroreflex sensitivity and heart rate variability in the identification of patients at risk for life-threatening arrhythmias. Circulation 2001;103(16):2072–7.

[55] Hesse B, et al. Complete bundle branch block as an independent predictor of all-cause mortality: report of 7,073 patients referred for nuclear exercise testing. Am J Med 2001;110(4):253–9.

[56] Zhang Z-m, et al. Different patterns of bundle-branch blocks and the risk of incident heart failure in the Women's Health Initiative (WHI) study. Circ Heart Fail 2013;6(4):655–61.

[57] Hathaway WR, et al. Prognostic significance of the initial electrocardiogram in patients with acute myocardial infarction. GUSTO-I Investigators. Global utilization of streptokinase and t-PA for occluded coronary arteries. JAMA 1998;279(5):387–91.

[58] Yang Y, et al. Prognosis of unrecognised myocardial infarction determined by electrocardiography or cardiac magnetic resonance imaging: systematic review and meta-analysis. BMJ 2020;369:m1184.

[59] Myerburg RJ, Junttila MJ. Sudden cardiac death caused by coronary heart disease. Circulation 2012;125(8):1043–52.

[60] Zaman S, Kovoor P. Sudden cardiac death early after myocardial infarction: pathogenesis, risk stratification, and primary prevention. Circulation 2014;129(23):2426–35.

[61] Wellens HJ, et al. Risk stratification for sudden cardiac death: current status and challenges for the future. Eur Heart J 2014;35(25):1642–51.

[62] Al-Zaiti S, et al. Arterial stiffness is associated with QTc interval prolongation in patients with heart failure. Biol Res Nurs 2017;20(3):255–63.

[63] Kashani A, Barold SS. Significance of QRS complex duration in patients with heart failure. J Am Coll Cardiol 2005;46(12):2183–92.

[64] Sipahi I, et al. Impact of QRS duration on clinical event reduction with cardiac resynchronization therapy: meta-analysis of randomized controlled trials. Arch Intern Med 2011;171(16):1454–62.

[65] Poole JE, Singh JP, Birgersdotter-Green U. QRS duration or QRS morphology: what really matters in cardiac resynchronization therapy? J Am Coll Cardiol 2016;67(9):1104–17.

[66] Peterson PN, et al. QRS duration, bundle-branch block morphology, and outcomes among older patients with heart failure receiving cardiac resynchronization therapy. JAMA 2013;310(6):617–26.

[67] Algra A, et al. QTc prolongation measured by standard 12-lead electrocardiography is an independent risk factor for sudden death due to cardiac arrest. Circulation 1991;83(6):1888–94.

[68] Cox AJ, et al. Heart rate–corrected QT interval is an independent predictor of all-cause and cardiovascular mortality in individuals with type 2 diabetes: the Diabetes Heart Study. Diabetes Care 2014;37(5):1454–61.

[69] Montanez A, et al. Prolonged QTc interval and risks of total and cardiovascular mortality and sudden death in the general population: a review and qualitative overview of the prospective cohort studies. Arch Intern Med 2004;164(9):943–8.

[70] Zhang Y, et al. Electrocardiographic QT interval and mortality: a meta-analysis. Epidemiol (Cambridge, Mass) 2011;22(5):660.

[71] Shah RR. The significance of QT interval in drug development. Br J Clin Pharmacol 2002;54 (2):188.

[72] Stockbridge N, et al. Practice and challenges of thorough QT studies. J Electrocardiol 2012;45 (6):582–7.

[73] Darpo B, et al. Man versus machine: is there an optimal method for QT measurements in thorough QT studies? J Clin Pharmacol 2006;46(6):598–612.

[74] Luo S, et al. A comparison of commonly used QT correction formulae: the effect of heart rate on the QTc of normal ECGs. J Electrocardiol 2004;37:81–90.

[75] Sawano M, et al. Independent prognostic value of single and multiple non-specific 12-lead electrocardiographic findings for long-term cardiovascular outcomes: a Prospective Cohort Study. PLoS One 2016;11(6):e0157563.

[76] Güngör B, et al. Prognostic value of QRS fragmentation in patients with acute myocardial infarction: a meta-analysis. Ann Noninvasive Electrocardiol 2016;21(6):604–12.

[77] Kewcharoen J, et al. Fragmented QRS predicts reperfusion failure and in-hospital mortality in ST-Elevation myocardial infarction: a systematic review and *meta*-analysis. Acta Cardiol 2019;1—14.

[78] Ostrander L. Left axis deviation: prevalence, associated conditions, and prognosis. Ann Intern Med 1971;75(1):23—8.

[79] Oehler A, et al. QRS-T angle: a review. Ann Noninvasive Electrocardiol 2014;19(6):534—42.

[80] Zhang X, et al. Spatial/frontal QRS-T angle predicts all-cause mortality and cardiac mortality: a *meta*-analysis. PLoS One 2015;10(8):e0136174.

[81] Al-Zaiti SS. The prognostic value of ventricular repolarization. Ann Arbor, MI: ProQuest LLC; 2013.

[82] Tse G, et al. The Tpeak — Tend interval as an electrocardiographic risk marker of arrhythmic and mortality outcomes: a systematic review and *meta*-analysis. Heart Rhythm 2017;14(8):1131—7.

[83] Tse G, et al. *Meta*-analysis of T-wave indices for risk stratification in myocardial infarction. J Geriatric Cardiol 2017;14(12):776—9.

[84] Narayan SM. T-wave alternans and the susceptibility to ventricular arrhythmias. J Am Coll Cardiol 2006;47(2):269—81.

[85] Gehi AK, et al. Microvolt T-wave alternans for the risk stratification of ventricular tachyarrhythmic events: a *meta*-analysis. J Am Coll Cardiol 2005;46(1):75—82.

[86] Sammani A, et al. Predicting arrhythmic risk in dilated cardiomyopathy: a systematic review & *meta*-analysis of clinical parameters. Eur Heart J 2019;40(Suppl_1).

[87] Al-Zaiti S, et al. Evaluation of beat-to-beat ventricular repolarization lability from standard 12-lead ECG during acute myocardial ischemia. J Electrocardiol 2017;50(6):717—24.

[88] Zhang D, Wang W, Li F. Association between resting heart rate and coronary artery disease, stroke, sudden death and noncardiovascular diseases: a *meta*-analysis. CMAJ 2016;188(15):E384—92.

[89] Malik M, et al. Heart rate variability standards of measurement, physiological interpretation, and clinical use. Eur Heart J 1996;17(3):354—81.

[90] La Rovere MT, et al. Baroreflex sensitivity and heart-rate variability in prediction of total cardiac mortality after myocardial infarction. Lancet 1998;351(9101):478—84.

[91] Fang S-C, Wu Y-L, Tsai P-S. Heart rate variability and risk of all-cause death and cardiovascular events in patients with cardiovascular disease: a *meta*-analysis of cohort studies. Biol Res Nurs 2020;22(1):45—56.

[92] Al-Zaiti SS, et al. The role of heart rate variability, heart rate turbulence, and deceleration capacity in predicting cause-specific mortality in chronic heart failure. J Electrocardiol 2019;52:70—4.

[93] Huikuri HV, et al. Attenuated recovery of heart rate turbulence early after myocardial infarction identifies patients at high risk for fatal or near-fatal arrhythmic events. Heart Rhythm 2010;7(2):229—35.

[94] Goldberger JJ, et al. Sudden cardiac death risk stratification in patients with nonischemic dilated cardiomyopathy. J Am Coll Cardiol 2014;63(18):1879—89.

[95] Disertori M, et al. Heart rate turbulence is a powerful predictor of cardiac death and ventricular arrhythmias in postmyocardial infarction and heart failure patients: a systematic review and *meta*-analysis. Circ Arrhythmia Electrophysiol 2016;9(12):e004610.

[96] Knoery CR, et al. SPICED-ACS: study of the potential impact of a computer-generated ECG diagnostic algorithmic certainty index in STEMI diagnosis: towards transparent AI. J Electrocardiol 2019;57:S86—91.

[97] Singh RP, et al. Current challenges and barriers to real-world artificial intelligence adoption for the healthcare system, provider, and the patient. Transl Vis Sci Technol 2020;9(2):45.

[98] Bond RR, et al. Methods for presenting and visualising electrocardiographic data: from temporal signals to spatial imaging. J Electrocardiol 2013;46(3):182—96.

[99] Cairns AW, et al. A decision support system and rule-based algorithm to augment the human interpretation of the 12-lead electrocardiogram. J Electrocardiol 2017;50(6):781—6.

CHAPTER 4

Extracting heterogeneous vessels in X-ray coronary angiography via machine learning

Binjie Qin[1], Mingxin Jin[1] and Song Ding[2]
[1]Biomedical Engineering School, Shanghai Jiao Tong University, Shanghai, China
[2]Department of Cardiology, Ren Ji Hospital, School of Medicine, Shanghai Jiao Tong University, Shanghai, China

4.1 Introduction

Cardiovascular disease remains the leading cause of death in the world. Percutaneous coronary intervention with the guidance of X-ray coronary angiography (XCA) has been routinely applied into the clinic since XCA is an imaging modality capable of observing internal structures and functions with superior spatiotemporal resolution. Apart from interventional guidance, XCA is assumed to be an important reference for better detection and treatment of impaired myocardial perfusion. Current XCA-guided coronary artery revascularization via stent implantation solely reconstructs the perfusion of main epicardial arteries. However, whether this artery revascularization could improve the distal microcirculation and accordingly lead to desired therapeutic effect on the acute myocardial ischemic heart diseases is not easily evaluated in preoperative and postoperative assessment. This is because the distal microcirculation on the most important parts of the coronary tree is poorly assessed by traditional XCA analysis. To solve this challenging problem, this chapter introduces machine-learning-based XCA analysis methods to extract and visualize the heterogeneous XCA vessels at pixel-level resolution.

Although XCA images are widely used in the clinic, the visibility of vessels (especially distal vessels) in XCA images is very poor due to complex spatiotemporal patterns of disturbances with the following reasons. XCA represents complex 2D/3D (2D + time) low-contrast structures of contrast-filled vessels by 2D projection of low dose X-ray imaging, which is badly overlapped by various background structures (e.g., catheters, bones, diaphragms, and lungs) and be simultaneously degraded by tissue-dependent noises and different motion patterns (i.e., respiratory and cardiac motions, as well as other tissue deformations during intervention). Furthermore, due to the bad effect of fastly evanesced contrast agents that are rapidly diffused inside the vessel networks, XCA vessels have fast change of inhomogeneous intensities that are disturbed with different vessel-like noisy structures and motion patterns.

Recently, extracting contrast-filled vessels from XCA data has gradually attracted attention and achieved some developments along with some advancements in medical imaging and machine learning [1]. Specifically, robust subspace learning [2] via decomposition into low-rank plus sparse matrices [3] has proven to effectively separate moving objects from the background. Based on the fact that XCA sequence can be modeled as a sum of low-rank background structures and sparsely distributed foreground contrast-filled vessels, robust principal component analysis (RPCA) [4—8] is effectively exploited to extract the moving contrast agents of vessel networks from the noisy complex backgrounds. However, various RPCA-based methods [5—11] still cannot perfectly extract the contrast-filled vessels from the dynamic and complex backgrounds that have nonlocally coupled properties of low rankness, motion patterns, and vessel-like noisy artifacts.

With the popularity of data-driven deep learning in medical imaging including cardiac image segmentation [12], recent patch-based [13,14] or image-based [15,16] deep learning works have designed convolutional neural networks (CNN) [13,17] and encoder-decoder architectures [14—16,18] to segment entire vessel networks from the XCA sequences. By exploring various prior knowledges with image enhancement [13,16], attention mechanism [15], and transfer learning strategy [16,17], these deep learning-based methods have indeed improved the vessel segmentation performances. But there are still challenges or limitations in the noisy annotated datasets [19,20] and class imbalance problems [15].

By embracing the challenge in highlighting the minority class of foreground vessels from the majority class of complex backgrounds in XCA, we were inspired to enjoy the advantage of having taken the opposite tack by masking the initially segmented vessels as missing entries of backgrounds, such that our recently published work [21] completed the whole backgrounds of XCA via tensor completion of background layer and then subtracted the completed background layer from whole XCA sequence to well recover the heterogeneous vessels' shape and intensity. This chapter provides an overview of these related works in Section 4.2, and introduces our recent machine learning-based works on the RPCA-based vessel extraction in Section 4.3, encoder—decoder-based deep vessel segmentation networks with XCA-dedicated architecture design in Section 4.4, and heterogeneous vessel recovery with tensor completion of background layer in Section 4.5. The final discussion and conclusion are given in Section 4.6.

4.2 Related works

Most blood vessel extraction or vessel segmentation methodologies were reviewed in the papers [22,23] and recently updated in the works [24—27]. These review papers have mostly focused on various medical imaging modalities such as magnetic resonance angiography, computed-tomography angiography but rarely on XCA. Currently, there are few works dealing with vessel extraction for XCA, except for the review [28] on reconstruction of high-contrast coronary arteries from X-ray angiography by focusing on the theoretical features in model-based tomographic reconstruction of coronary arteries. Generally, XCA vessel extraction works can be classified as three types of methodologies. First, earlier works extract blood vessels via digital subtraction angiography (DSA) that subtracts a precontrast mask image from later contrast images to clearly visualize the contrast-enhanced blood vessels and remove the interfering backgrounds. However, this simple technique has difficulty in handling vessels with a lot of motion artifacts since the vessels' surrounding backgrounds always have local tissue motions, noisy intensity variations, and interventional changes during DSA imaging. To reduce the motion artifact, image registration method is required to match the locally deformed mask images to the live images for minimizing their dissimilarity. Coupling with RPCA-based vessel enhancement method, the authors in the work [29] have generated a vascular roadmap that enables visualization of an entire blood vessel by combining multiple enhanced images with image registration. However, the registration-based vessel extraction methods have an unsolved challenging problem of nonrigid image registration with local large deformations and noncorresponding outlier features [30,31], therefore they cannot ensure the efficiency in reducing the sensitivity to the outlier features and motion artifacts of XCA imaging with the locally deformed backgrounds.

Second, most XCA vessel extraction methods generally belong to the machine learning-based algorithms by combining various model-based methods with various vessel filtering techniques including nonlinear and nonlocal filtering methods [24–27,32,33]. These integrated vessel extraction approaches usually involve two steps: a filtering step for enhancing and extracting vessel-like features and a mode-based classification step for highlighting the featured vessel pixels from the backgrounds. After the XCA images were denoised and enhanced, the model-based methods usually have highlighted the target vessels for further vessel refinements by formulating it as an energy optimization problem [1], which have included motion layer separation such as low-rank plus sparse decomposition modeling [4] (see Section 4.3), deformable models such as active contour [34], graph-based modeling [35], minimal path optimization [36–38], and tube-like or tree-like structure tracking model [39]. Among these model-based methods, the active contour models with level set evolution are developed and classified into region-based and edge-based models with various improvements for image segmentation. It has recently been proven that the hybrid variants combining both region and edge information [34] can improve the vessel segmentation performance. But these methods are usually sensitive to model initialization and have limited performances in extracting the real vessels with intensity inhomogeneity as well as varied vessel shapes and topologies from many vessel-like blurry edges in complex backgrounds. Furthermore, the tube-like structure tracking models [36–38] have attracted some research attentions recently. However, due to the low-contrast intensity inhomogeneities, complex noise distributions, background overlaps, pathology and surgical changes, vessel tracking methods always result in early termination of vessel evolution when the matching between the vessel model itself and the image data in the current model neighborhood is not easily computed by both the deterministic and statistical tracking approaches.

For the filtering methods, more advanced vessel filtering methods are proposed to lift original low-dimensional image data to a high-dimensional space exploring the lifted data's multidimensional and multiscale information about the local and nonlocal curvilinear features such as orientations, phases, intensity profiles, and high-level topological and geometric features [28,33]. The nonlocal similarity-based filtering [40,41] has proven to perform well in aggregating similar patches for X-ray image denoising. In addition, new nonlocal computation schemes including the multiscale superpixels handling different vessel scales [42], nonlocal weighted fuzzy energy term in active contour models [43], and the fractional calculus [44,45] enabling long-range interaction have proven to well enhance the edge- and ridge-like features from the noisy backgrounds in medical imaging. Furthermore, inspired by the phase congruency model [46] having robustness to noise and being invariant to changes in contrast, some image enhancement methods have exploited the phase congruency based feature indicator called phase symmetry and phase asymmetry [44,47,48] to detect edge- and ridge-like features such as 2D/3D vessels. The high-level vessel feature representations have benefited subsequent classification of enhanced vessel features from complex and dynamic backgrounds. However, this vessel-feature enhancement filtering simultaneously enhances the background structures with similar vessel-like features to introduce more difficulty in subsequent vessel classification or vessel tracking. The vessel feature representations are also very important in the model-based vessel tracking methods after model initialization, where the current model's neighboring topological and geometric features are exploited to steer the evolution of model-based vessel tracking.

Third, as medical imaging data and computer power become increasingly available in our life, various data-driven deep learning network architectures have learned the end-to-end mapping between training images and their corresponding manually annotated binary ground truth maps for medical image segmentation [49,50]. By assigning a vessel or nonvessel label to each pixel, typical supervised vessel segmentation generally consists of training and testing. In the training stage, the method simultaneously learns the features and classification parameters for classifying the pixels from known labels (ground truth). After that, in test stage, the trained classifier is examined on previously unseen pixels. Generally, most current deep learning-based vessel segmentation methods are built from the encoder—decoder architectures including fully convolutional networks and U-Net [15,16,18], which learn to map input data of arbitrary sizes into a high-level feature representation with contextual information by an encoding function and then predict the output with the same size from the feature representation and recover the pixel-wise spatial detail back to the original domain. On the one hand, fusing prior knowledge about target vessels into neural network architecture such as channel attention and loss function [15], as well as preprocessing and postprocessing modules (such as conditional random field module) will certainly improve the vessel segmentation performance. On the other hand, incorporating graphical models [14] and classical model-based machine learning such as active contour models [50] into multiscale data-driven deep neural networks will enable a full exploration of contextual information about geometrical and topological features to effectively refine the vessel segmentation. Unfortunately, most existing vessel segmentation methods are solely developed for the purpose of vessel shape recovery. To the best of our knowledge, automated vessel extraction with inhomogeneous intensity recovery from XCA images is currently an unexplored task. This chapter therefore for the first time presents the complete procedures for heterogeneous vessel extraction with intensity recovery. Fig. 4.1 displays the whole procedure of this chapter: we first present motion coherency regularized RPCA called MCR-RPCA (https://github.com/Binjie-Qin/ MCR-RPCA) [5] for extracting foreground vessels from the noisy backgrounds in Section 4.3. Our sequential vessel segmentation network called SVS-net [15] is presented in Section 4.4 to demonstrate its segmentation of entire XCA vessel networks. In Section 4.5, we introduce the work of vessel region background completion with t-TNN tensor completion (VRBC-t-TNN) for accurately recovering the heterogeneous vessel network's shapes and intensities. This heterogeneous-vessel extraction is ready for further microcirculation analysis in the clinic.

4.3 MCR-RPCA: motion coherency regularized RPCA for vessel extraction

4.3.1 Motivation and problems

We viewed the XCA images as high dimensional video frames that have moving contrast agents continuously flowing inside vascular networks, which are distributed and overlapped within the complex backgrounds and artifacts, resulting in a big challenge for XCA analysis [5]. Fortunately, we have observed that XCA data have two specific structural characteristics, for example, the sparsity of moving contrast agent, and the similarity of background tissue structures. Then we naturally asked ourselves the question: How to simultaneously leverage the sparsity of foreground contrast agents and the similarity of the sequential backgrounds? Low-rank plus sparse modeling [2] is an effective tool to detect sparse outliers from the observed background images that are approximated with low rankness. Specifically, RPCA has been proposed in the classic work of Candès et al. [3] by decomposing the whole video data into low-rank plus sparse matrices with a convex optimization problem. Thereafter various RPCA models are exploited to outperform the state-of-the-art algorithms in many applications [4].

To directly extract the contrast-filled blood flow in vessel trajectories, the spatio-temporal sparseness and consistency of vessel trajectories within RPCA framework have been exploited in our work MCR-RPCA [5]. Specifically, based on the sparse

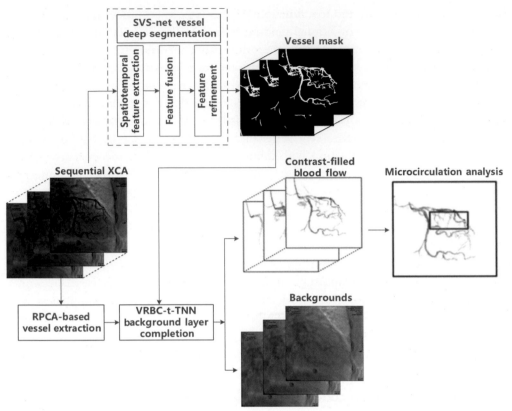

Figure 4.1 The whole procedure of extracting heterogeneous vessels in XCA for microcirculation analysis. (1) The MCR-RPCA directly separated the heterogeneous foreground vessels from the backgrounds. (2) The deep network SVS-net segmented the vessel masks from the sequential XCA images. (3) The VRBC-t-TNN method was used to complete the background regions of vessel masks for subsequently subtracting the completed background layers from the overall XCA data to recover the heterogeneous vessel network's shapes and intensities. *XCA*, X-ray coronary angiography; *MCR-RPCA*, motion coherency regularized RPCA.

and low-rank modeling of foreground/background in XCA imaging, MCR–RPCA used a statistically structured RPCA first to identify all candidate foreground vessels. Then, we imposed total variation minimization on the foreground vessel trajectories in modeling the spatiotemporal contiguity and smoothness within RPCA modeling to eliminate the backgrounds remained in the candidates.

4.3.2 Candidate contrast-filled vessel detection via statistically structured MoG-RPCA

Observing that the candidate foreground vessel regions are sparsely clustered and correlated within curvilinear structures, we introduced structured sparsity constraint in RPCA for extracting all candidate contrast-filled vessels. However, the real structural pattern in foreground regions is full of the overlapping structures of vessels and other tissues via 2D X-ray projection. To sparsely regularized the complex contrast-filled vessels in the sparse matrix $\mathbf{S}$, we associated the matrix $\mathbf{S}$ with noisy disturbances to model the moving contrast agents as a mixture of statistical structures and complex noise. Specifically, we applied mixture of Gaussian (MoG) model to statistically construct MoG-based RPCA [51] for separating the candidate contrast-filled vessels from the complex backgrounds. In fact, this MoG-RPCA has proven to achieve high detection rate of foreground moving object in some rigorous experimental evaluations using both synthetic and real videos [52].

Assuming $\mathbf{D} = \mathbf{L} + \mathbf{S}$ where $\mathbf{D}, \mathbf{L}, \mathbf{S} \in \mathbb{R}^{m \times n}$ are the original XCA sequence, low-rank backgrounds, and sparsely distributed vessels, respectively, we set each s_{ij} in sparse matrix $\mathbf{S}$ with the following MoG distribution:

$$p\left(s_{ij} \middle| \mu, \tau, \mathbf{z}_{ij}\right) = \prod_{k=1}^{K} \mathcal{N}\left(s_{ij} \middle| \mu_k, \tau_k^{-1}\right)^{z_{ijk}} p\left(\mathbf{z}_{ij} \middle| \pi\right) = \prod_{k=1}^{K} \pi_k^{z_{ijk}} \tag{4.1}$$

where $\mathbf{z}_{ij}$ is associated with s_{ij} to have a 1-of-K indicator vector $z_{ijk} \in \{0, 1\}, \sum_{k=1}^{K} z_{ijk} = 1$. $\pi = (\pi_1, \ldots \pi_K)$ is a mixing coefficient vector with $\pi_k \in \{0, 1\}$ representing the existence probability of the kth Gaussian component having $\sum_{k=1}^{K} \pi_k = 1$. $\mu = (\mu_1, \ldots, \mu_K)$ and $\tau = (\tau_1, \ldots, \tau_K)$ with μ_k and τ_k being the mean and precision (inverse variances) of the k-th Gaussian component, respectively. Here $\mathbf{Z}$ is an $m \times n \times K$ array with the (i, j, k)th element denoted by z_{ijk} to facilitate the following description.

The Gaussian-Gamma distribution was used to model the parameters μ_k and τ_k with the Dirichlet distribution modeling the mixing coefficient π

$$p(\mu_k, \tau_k) = \mathcal{N}\left(\mu_k \middle| \mu_{0k}, \beta_0^{-1} \tau_k^{-1}\right) \cdot \mathrm{Gam}\left(\tau_k \middle| \alpha_0, \chi_0\right) \quad p(\pi) = \mathrm{Dir}\left(\pi \middle| \eta_0\right) \tag{4.2}$$

where μ_{0k} is the mean of the $k$thGaussian component, $\mathrm{Gam}(\cdot)$ is the Gamma distribution with hyperparameters α_0, β_0, and χ_0 being set to be small deterministic value (e.g., 10^{-5}) to obtain broad hyperpriors. $\mathrm{Dir}\left(\pi \middle| \eta_0\right)$ denotes the Dirichlet distribution parameterized by $\eta_0 = (\eta_{01}, \ldots, \eta_{0K})$.

For low-rank background modeling in MoG-RPCA, the $\mathbf{L} \in \mathbb{R}^{m \times n}$ with rank $l \leq \min(m, n)$ was set to be the product of $\mathbf{U} \in \mathbb{R}^{m \times R}$ and $\mathbf{V} \in \mathbb{R}^{n \times R}$ with $R > l$:

$$\mathbf{L} = \mathbf{U}\mathbf{V}^T = \sum_{r=1}^{R} \mathbf{u}_{\cdot r} \mathbf{v}_{\cdot r}^T \tag{4.3}$$

where $\mathbf{u}_{\cdot r}(\mathbf{v}_{\cdot r})$ is the rth column of $\mathbf{U}(\mathbf{V})$. The low-rank nature of $\mathbf{L}$ is to achieve column sparsity in $\mathbf{U}$ and $\mathbf{V}$ by setting the following priors on $\mathbf{U}$ and $\mathbf{V}$:

$$p(\mathbf{u}_{\cdot r}) = \mathcal{N}\left(\mathbf{u}_{\cdot r} \middle| \mathbf{0}, \gamma_r^{-1} \mathbf{I}_m\right), p(\mathbf{v}_{\cdot r}) = \mathcal{N}\left(\mathbf{v}_{\cdot r} \middle| \mathbf{0}, \gamma_r^{-1} \mathbf{I}_n\right) \tag{4.4}$$

where $\mathbf{I}$ denotes identity matrix. The conjugate prior on each precision variable is

$$p(\gamma_r) = \mathrm{Gam}\big(\gamma_r | a_0, b_0\big) \propto \gamma_r{}^{a_0 - 1} \exp\big(-b_0 \gamma_r\big) \tag{4.5}$$

where a_0 and b_0 are treated as small deterministic parameters to obtain broad hyperpriors. The common precision variable γ_r leading to large precision values of some γ_rs can result in a good low-rank estimate of $\mathbf{L}$ [53]. After the above-mentioned combination of equations, we modeled the MoG-RPCA to achieve the candidate contrast-filled vessel detection, which turned to infer the posterior $p(\mathbf{U}, \mathbf{V}, \mathbf{Z}, \mu, \tau, \pi, \gamma | \mathbf{D})$ of all involved variables, where $\mathbf{Z} = \{\mathbf{z}_{ij}\}, \mu = (\mu_1, \ldots, \mu_K), \tau = (\tau_1, \ldots, \tau_K)$, and $\gamma = (\gamma_1, \ldots, \gamma_R)$.

To get variational inference of the posterior of MoG-RPCA, we computed the true posterior $p(\mathbf{x} | \mathcal{D})$ with an approximation distribution $q(\mathbf{x})$ by minimizing the Kullback–Leibler (KL) divergence between $p(\mathbf{x} | \mathcal{D})$ and $q(\mathbf{x})$, that is, $\min_{q \in \mathcal{C}} \mathrm{KL}(q \| p) = -\int q(\mathbf{x}) \ln \{p(x | D) / q(\mathbf{x})\}\, d\mathbf{x}$, where $\mathcal{C}$ denotes the set of probability densities with certain constraints to make the minimization tractable. If we partition the elements of $\mathbf{x}$ into disjoint groups $\{\mathbf{x}_i\}$, $q(\mathbf{x})$ is then generally assumed to be factorized as $q(\mathbf{x}) = \prod_i q_i(\mathbf{x}_i)$. The solution for each group $\{\mathbf{x}_j\}$, with the others fixed, can then be obtained by

$$q_j^*(\mathbf{x}_j) = \frac{\exp\big(\mathbb{E}_{i \neq j}\big[\ln p(\mathbf{x}, \mathcal{D})\big]\big)}{\int \exp\big(\mathbb{E}_{i \neq j}\big[\ln p(\mathbf{x}, \mathcal{D})\big]\big) d\mathbf{x}_j} \tag{4.6}$$

where $p(\mathbf{x}, \mathcal{D})$ is the joint distribution of parameter $\mathbf{x}$ and observations $\mathcal{D}$, and $\mathbb{E}_{i \neq j}[\cdot]$ denotes the expectation with respect to $\mathbf{x}_i$s except $\mathbf{x}_j$. The solution for each group $\{\mathbf{x}_j\}$ can then be approached by alternatively optimizing each $q_j(\mathbf{x}_j)$ by Eq. (4.6). The posterior distribution of MoG-RPCA is factorized as the following form:

$$q(\mathbf{U}, \mathbf{V}, \mathbf{Z}, \mu, \tau, \pi, \gamma) = \prod_i q(\mathbf{u}_{i\cdot}) \prod_j q(\mathbf{v}_{j\cdot}) \prod_{ij} q(\mathbf{z}_{ij}) \prod_k q(\mu_k, \tau_k) q(\pi) \prod_r q(\gamma_r) \tag{4.7}$$

where $\mathbf{u}_{i\cdot} (\mathbf{v}_{j\cdot})$ is the ith (jth) row of $\mathbf{U}(\mathbf{V})$. The estimation of candidate foreground and low-rank background components via MoG-RPCA can then be derived by estimating all the factorized distributions involved in the above equation as follows.

4.3.2.1 Estimation of candidate foreground component

To estimate the parameters $\mu, \tau, \mathbf{Z}$ and π involved in the foreground vessel detection, we got the following update equation for each parameter using the prior imposed in Eq. (4.2) and its conjugate property:

$$q(\mu_k, \tau_k) = \mathcal{N}\big(\mu_k | m_k, (\beta_k \tau_k)^{-1}\big) \cdot \mathrm{Gam}\big(\tau_k | \alpha_k, \chi_k\big) \tag{4.8}$$

where

$$\beta_k = \beta_0 + \sum_{ij} \mathbb{E}[z_{ijk}],$$

$$m_k = \frac{1}{\beta_k}\left(\beta_0 \mu_{0k} + \sum_{ij} \mathbb{E}[z_{ijk}]\left(d_{ij} - \mathbb{E}[\mathbf{u}_{i\cdot}]\mathbb{E}[\mathbf{v}_{j\cdot}]^T\right)\right), \alpha_k = \alpha_0 + \frac{1}{2}\sum_{ij}\mathbb{E}[z_{ijk}]$$

$$\chi_k = \chi_0 + \frac{1}{2}\left\{\sum_{ij}\mathbb{E}[z_{ijk}]\mathbb{E}\left[\left(d_{ij} - \mathbf{u}_{i\cdot}\mathbf{v}_{j\cdot}^T\right)^2\right] + \beta_0\mu_{0k}^2\right.$$

$$\left. - \frac{1}{\beta_k}\left(\sum_{ij}\mathbb{E}[z_{ijk}]\left(d_{ij} - \mathbb{E}[\mathbf{u}_{i\cdot}]\mathbb{E}[\mathbf{v}_{j\cdot}]^T\right) + \beta_0\mu_0\right)^2\right\}$$

The posterior mixing coefficients π is similarly updated using the equation $q(\pi) = \mathrm{Dir}(\pi|\eta)$, where $\boldsymbol{\eta} = (\eta_1, \ldots, \eta_K)$, $\eta_k = \eta_{0k} + \sum_{ij}\mathbb{E}[z_{ijk}]$. The variational posterior for the indicators $\mathbf{Z}$ is computed by $q(\mathbf{z}_{ij}) = \prod_k r_{ijk}^{z_{ijk}}$, where $r_{ijk} = \delta_{ijk}/\sum_k \delta_{ijk}$,

$$\delta_{ijk} = 0.5\mathbb{E}[\ln\tau_k] - 0.5\ln 2\pi - 0.5\mathbb{E}[\tau_k]\mathbb{E}\left[\left(d_{ij} - \mathbf{u}_{i\cdot}\mathbf{v}_{j\cdot}^T - \mu_k\right)^2\right] + \mathbb{E}[\ln\pi_k] \qquad (4.9)$$

4.3.2.2 Estimation of low-rank background component

The posterior distribution for each row $\mathbf{u}_{i\cdot}$ of $\mathbf{U}$ (and $\mathbf{v}_{j\cdot}$ of $\mathbf{V}$) involved in low-rank background component can be approximated by

$$q(\mathbf{u}_{i\cdot}) = \mathcal{N}\left(\mathbf{u}_{i\cdot}\middle|\boldsymbol{\mu}_{\mathbf{u}_{i\cdot}}, \sum_{\mathbf{u}_{i\cdot}}\right), q(\mathbf{v}_{j\cdot}) = \mathcal{N}\left(\mathbf{v}_{j\cdot}\middle|\boldsymbol{\mu}_{\mathbf{v}_{j\cdot}}, \sum_{\mathbf{v}_{j\cdot}}\right) \qquad (4.10)$$

where

$$\boldsymbol{\mu}_{\mathbf{u}_{i\cdot}}^T = \sum_{\mathbf{u}_{i\cdot}}\left\{\sum_k \mathbb{E}[\tau_k]\sum_j \mathbb{E}[z_{ijk}]\left(d_{ij} - \mathbb{E}[\mu_k]\right)\mathbb{E}[\mathbf{v}_{j\cdot}]\right\}^T$$

$$\sum_{\mathbf{u}_{i\cdot}} = \left\{\sum_k \mathbb{E}[\tau_k]\sum_j \mathbb{E}[z_{ijk}]\mathbb{E}\left[\mathbf{v}_{j\cdot}^T\mathbf{v}_{j\cdot}\right] + \Gamma\right\}^{-1}$$

$$\boldsymbol{\mu}_{\mathbf{v}_{j\cdot}}^T = \sum_{\mathbf{v}_{j\cdot}}\left\{\sum_k \mathbb{E}[\tau_k]\sum_i \mathbb{E}[z_{ijk}]\left(d_{ij} - \mathbb{E}[\mu_k]\right)\mathbb{E}[\mathbf{v}_{j\cdot}]\right\}^T$$

$$\sum_{\mathbf{v}_{j\cdot}} = \left\{\sum_k \mathbb{E}[\tau_k]\sum_i \mathbb{E}[z_{ijk}]\mathbb{E}\left[\mathbf{u}_{i\cdot}^T\mathbf{u}_{i\cdot}\right] + \Gamma\right\}^{-1}, \quad \Gamma = \mathrm{diag}(\mathbb{E}[\gamma])$$

We displayed the experimental results for the candidate vessel extraction (see the middle column of Fig. 4.2), which leave some noisy artifacts in the vessel layers for the subsequent vessel refinement via trajectory decomposition in MCR–RPCA.

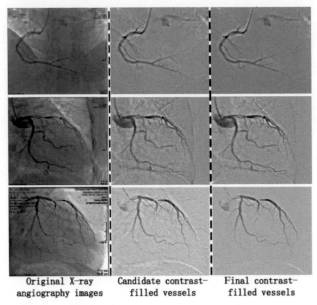

Original X-ray   Candidate contrast-   Final contrast-
angiography images   filled vessels   filled vessels

Figure 4.2 Vessel extraction examples via MCR-RPCA [5]. From left to right: the original images, the candidate foreground vessels via the statistically structured MoG-RPCA, the final vessels via the motion coherency regularized RPCA.

4.3.3 Motion coherency regularized RPCA for trajectory decomposition

Since the statistically structured RPCA is unable to encode the long-term temporal coherency of XCA sequence, there still have some parts of noisy backgrounds in the extracted candidate foregrounds. Inspired by the trajectory decomposition works [54] that have preserved temporal consistency by assigning similar lables to the pixels belonging to the same trajectories, we exploited the trajectory properties of blood vessels by directly representing the motion coherency as spatiotemporal contiguity and smoothness of the image pixels to refine the vessel extraction in the subsequent trajectory decomposition.

The sparsely distributed sinuous courses of blood flow in vessels make the foreground trajectories occupy a set of contiguous regions throughout image sequences. Therefore, being different from the traditional $L_{2,1}$ norm-based group sparsity constraint $\|\mathbf{S}\|_{2,1}$ [2] that treats each column of matrix as a whole, the L_1-norm-based pixel-wise sparsity constraint is more appropriate for the foreground trajectory extraction task. Then, the total variation minimization is further exploited as a motion coherency constraint for the contrast-filled vessel extraction. Based on a difference operator, the weighted TV regularization of matrix $\mathbf{S}$ can be defined as $\|\mathbf{S}\|_{\text{TV}} = w_x \|\nabla_x \mathbf{S}\|_1 + w_y \|\nabla_y \mathbf{S}\|_1 + w_z \|\nabla_z \mathbf{S}\|_1$ with default setting $w_x = w_y = w_z = 1$, where ∇_x, ∇_y, and ∇_z correspond to difference operations performed along x (or row), y (or column), and z (or frame) directions, respectively. The combination of TV and L_1-norm of matrix **S** will encourage the proximate trajectories with similar appearances to be grouped into the same foreground vessels. The motion coherency regularized RPCA model is carried out as follows:

$$\min\nolimits_{\mathbf{L},\mathbf{S}} \left\|\mathbf{L}\right\|_* + \lambda_1 \left\|\mathbf{S}\right\|_1 + \lambda_2 \left\|\mathbf{S}\right\|_{\mathrm{TV}} \quad \text{s.t. } \mathbf{D} = \mathbf{L} + \mathbf{S} \tag{4.11}$$

where **D** represents the candidate foreground matrix, **L** and **S** represent new low-rank background and sparse foreground trajectories, respectively. The λ_1 and λ_2 are regularizing parameters. We used alternating direction method (ADM) to solve the minimization problem in Eq. (4.11) with the solver Inexact Augmented Lagrangian Multiplier Method (IALM) [53] by rewriting the Eq. (4.11) into another form:

$$\min\nolimits_{\mathbf{L},\mathbf{S},\mathbf{T}} \left\|\mathbf{L}\right\|_* + \lambda_1 \left\|\mathbf{S}\right\|_1 + \lambda_2 \left\|\mathbf{T}\right\|_{\mathrm{TV}}, \quad \text{s.t. } \mathbf{D} = \mathbf{L} + \mathbf{S} \quad \mathbf{T} = \mathbf{S} \tag{4.12}$$

The augmented Lagrangian function of Eq. (4.12) is given by

$$
\begin{aligned}
\mathcal{L}(\mathbf{L},\mathbf{S},\mathbf{T},\mathbf{X},\mathbf{Y};\mu) = \quad & \left\|\mathbf{L}\right\|_* + \lambda_1 \left\|\mathbf{S}\right\|_1 + \lambda_2 \left\|\mathbf{T}\right\|_{\mathrm{TV}} + \frac{\mu}{2}\left\|\mathbf{D}-\mathbf{L}-\mathbf{S}\right\|_F^2 \\
& + \langle \mathbf{X},\mathbf{D}-\mathbf{L}-\mathbf{S}\rangle + \frac{\mu}{2}\left\|\mathbf{T}-\mathbf{S}\right\|_F^2 + \langle \mathbf{Y},\mathbf{T}-\mathbf{S}\rangle
\end{aligned}
\tag{4.13}
$$

where **X** and **Y** are the Lagrangian multipliers, and μ is a positive penalty scalar. We summarized the solutions of the subproblems based on the ADM strategy in Algorithm 1.

Algorithm 1 ADM for motion coherency regularized RPCA

Input: Matrix $\mathbf{D} \in \mathbb{R}^{m \times n}$, $\lambda_1 > 0$, $\lambda_2 > 0$
1: Initializing: $\mathbf{L}$, $\mathbf{S}$ and $\mathbf{X}$, $\mathbf{Y}$
2: **while** not converged **do**
3:     **L sub-problem:**

$$\mathbf{L}_{k+1} = \arg\min_{\mathbf{L}} \mathcal{L}(\mathbf{L}, \mathbf{S}_k, \mathbf{T}_k, \mathbf{X}_k, \mathbf{Y}_k, \mu)$$
$$= \arg\min_{\mathbf{L}} \|\mathbf{L}\|_* + \frac{\mu}{2}\|(\mathbf{D} - \mathbf{S}_k + \mu^{-1}\mathbf{X}_k) - \mathbf{L}\|_F^2$$

solved by:

$$(\mathbf{U}, \mathbf{\Sigma}, \mathbf{V}) = \mathrm{svd}(\mathbf{D} - \mathbf{S}_k + \mu^{-1}\mathbf{X}_k)$$
$$\mathbf{L}_{k+1} = \mathbf{U}\mathcal{S}_{\mu^{-1}}(\mathbf{\Sigma})\mathbf{V}^T$$

4:     **S sub-problem:**

$$\mathbf{S}_{k+1} = \arg\min_{\mathbf{S}} \mathcal{L}(\mathbf{L}_{k+1}, \mathbf{S}, \mathbf{T}_k, \mathbf{X}_k, \mathbf{Y}_k, \mu)$$

solved by the soft shrinkage operator.
5:     **T sub-problem:**

$$\mathbf{T}_{k+1} = \arg\min_{\mathbf{T}} \mathcal{L}(\mathbf{L}_{k+1}, \mathbf{S}_{k+1}, \mathbf{T}, \mathbf{X}_k, \mathbf{Y}_k, \mu)$$
$$= \arg\min_{\mathbf{T}} \lambda_2\|\mathbf{T}\|_{TV} + \frac{\mu}{2}\|\mathbf{T} - \mathbf{S}_{k+1}\| + \langle \mathbf{Y}_k, \mathbf{T} - \mathbf{S}_{k+1}\rangle$$
$$= \arg\min_{\mathbf{T}} \lambda_2\|\mathbf{T}\|_{TV} + \frac{\mu}{2}\|\mathbf{T} - \mathbf{S}_{k+1} + \mu^{-1}\mathbf{Y}_k\|_F^2$$

solved by split Bregman method.
6:     Update Lagrange multiplier $\mathbf{X}$ and $\mathbf{Y}$:

$$\mathbf{X}_{k+1} = \mathbf{X}_k + \mu(\mathbf{D} - \mathbf{L}_{k+1} - \mathbf{S}_{k+1})$$
$$\mathbf{Y}_{k+1} = \mathbf{Y}_k + \mu(\mathbf{T}_{k+1} - \mathbf{S}_{k+1})$$

7: **end while**
Output: $(\mathbf{L}_k, \mathbf{S}_k)$

Using the ADM algorithm, we alternately optimized one variable ($\mathbf{L}$, or $\mathbf{S}$, or $\mathbf{T}$) with the other two variables fixed: for $\mathbf{L}$ subproblem optimization, it has closed-form solution by a soft shrinkage operator $\mathcal{S}_{\mu^{-1}}(\gamma) = \mathrm{sgn}(\gamma)\max(|\gamma| - \mu^{-1}, 0)$ with a threshold μ^{-1} for a scalar γ, which operator is extended entry-wisely to vectors and matrices; $\mathbf{S}$ subproblem is solved by a shrinkage operator with the implementation detail at the following section; the split Bregman method [55] is adopted to solve $\mathbf{T}$ subproblem optimization. In Algorithm 1, $\lambda_1 = 0.5/\sqrt{\max(m, n)}$ and $\lambda_2 = 0.2/\sqrt{\max(m, n)}$, which can perform well on most experimental data.

For the $\mathbf{S}$ subproblem optimization in Algorithm 1, the objective function is

$$\mathbf{S}_{k+1} = \arg\min_{\mathbf{S}} \mathcal{L}(\mathbf{L}_{k+1}, \mathbf{S}, \mathbf{T}_k, \mathbf{X}_k, \mathbf{Y}_k, \mu)$$

$$= \arg\min_{\mathbf{S}} \lambda_1 \|\mathbf{S}\|_1 + \frac{\mu}{2} \|\mathbf{D} - \mathbf{L}_{k+1} - \mathbf{S}\|_F^2 + \langle \mathbf{X}_k, \mathbf{D} - \mathbf{L}_{k+1} - \mathbf{S} \rangle$$

$$+ \frac{\mu}{2} \|\mathbf{T}_k - \mathbf{S}\|_F^2 + \langle \mathbf{Y}_k, \mathbf{T}_k - \mathbf{S} \rangle$$

$$= \arg\min_{\mathbf{S}} \lambda_1 \|\mathbf{S}\|_1 + \mu \|\mathbf{Q} - \mathbf{S}\|_F^2 \tag{4.14}$$

where we denote $\mathbf{Q} = \frac{\mathbf{D} - \mathbf{L}_{k+1} + \mathbf{T}_k + \mu^{-1}(\mathbf{X}_k + \mathbf{Y}_k)}{2}$. The objective function can be further expressed as

$$\mathbf{S}_{k+1} = \arg\min_{\mathbf{S} \in \mathbb{R}^{m \times n}} \sum_{i=1}^{m} \sum_{j=1}^{n} (\lambda_1 |\mathbf{S}_{i,j}| + \mu |\mathbf{Q}_{i,j} - \mathbf{S}_{i,j}|^2) \tag{4.15}$$

Eq. (4.15) can be minimized for each $\mathbf{S}_{i,j}$ separately. The solution $\mathbf{S}_{k+1}$ for $\mathbf{S}$ subproblem is obtained by the soft shrinkage operator $\mathbf{S}_{k+1} = \mathcal{S}_{\lambda_1(2\mu)^{-1}}(\mathbf{Q})$, where the operator $\mathcal{S}$ is performed element-wisely.

As for the $\mathbf{T}$ subproblem optimization in Algorithm 1, the objective function is as follows:

$$\mathbf{T}_{k+1} = \arg\min_{\mathbf{T}} \mathcal{L}(\mathbf{L}_{k+1}, \mathbf{S}_{k+1}, \mathbf{T}, \mathbf{X}_k, \mathbf{Y}_k, \mu)$$

$$= \arg\min_{\mathbf{T}} \lambda_2 \|\mathbf{T}\|_{TV} + \frac{\mu}{2} \|\mathbf{T} - \mathbf{S}_{k+1}\| + \langle \mathbf{Y}_k, \mathbf{T} - \mathbf{S}_{k+1} \rangle$$

$$= \arg\min_{\mathbf{T}} \lambda_2 \|\mathbf{T}\|_{TV} + \frac{\mu}{2} \|\mathbf{T} - (\mathbf{S}_{k+1} - \mu^{-1}\mathbf{Y}_k)\|_F^2$$

$$= \arg\min_{\mathbf{T}} \lambda_2 (\|\nabla_x \mathbf{T}\|_1 + \|\nabla_y \mathbf{T}\|_1 + \|\nabla_z \mathbf{T}\|_1 + \frac{\mu}{2} \|\mathbf{T} - (\mathbf{S}_{k+1} - \mu^{-1}\mathbf{Y}_k)\|_F^2 \tag{4.16}$$

To apply Bregman splitting method, we first replaced $\nabla_x \mathbf{T}$ by d_x, $\nabla_y \mathbf{T}$ by d_y, and $\nabla_z \mathbf{T}$ by d_z to yield the following constrained problem:

$$\mathbf{T}_{k+1} = \arg\min_{\mathbf{T}} \lambda_2 \left(\|d_x\|_1 + \|d_y\|_1 + \|d_z\|_1 \right) + \frac{\mu}{2} \|\mathbf{T} - \mathbf{K}\|_F^2 \quad \text{s.t.} d_x = \nabla_x \mathbf{T}, d_y$$

$$= \nabla_y \mathbf{T}, d_z = \nabla_z \mathbf{T} \tag{4.17}$$

where $\mathbf{K} = \mathbf{S}_{k+1} - \mu^{-1}\mathbf{Y}_k$. To weakly enforce the constraints in this formulation, we added penalty function terms to obtain the following objective function:

$$\mathbf{T}_{k+1} = \arg \min_{d_x, d_y, d_z, \mathbf{T}} \lambda_2(||d_x||_1 + ||d_y||_1 + ||d_z||_1) + \frac{\mu}{2}||\mathbf{T} - \mathbf{K}||_F^2$$

$$+ \frac{\lambda_t}{2}||d_x - \nabla_x \mathbf{T}||_F^2 + \frac{\lambda_t}{2}||d_y - \nabla_y \mathbf{T}||_F^2 + \frac{\lambda_t}{2}||d_z - \nabla_z \mathbf{T}||_F^2 \quad (4.18)$$

where λ_t represents the weight of penalty function. Finally, we strictly enforced the constraints by applying the Bregman iteration [55] to get

$$\mathbf{T}_{k+1} = \arg \min_{d_x, d_y, d_z, \mathbf{T}} \lambda_2(||d_x||_1 + ||d_y||_1 + ||d_z||_1) + \frac{\mu}{2}||\mathbf{T} - \mathbf{K}||_F^2 + \frac{\lambda_t}{2}$$

$$||d_x - \nabla_x \mathbf{T} - b_x^k||_F^2 + \frac{\lambda_t}{2}||d_y - \nabla_y \mathbf{T} - b_y^k||_F^2 + \frac{\lambda_t}{2}||d_z - \nabla_z \mathbf{T} - b_z^k||_F^2 \quad (4.19)$$

where the proper values of b_x^k, b_y^k, and b_z^k are chosen through Bregman iteration. We can efficiently solve the minimization problem in Eq. (4.19) by iteratively minimizing it with respect to d and $\mathbf{T}$ separately. For the solution of $\mathbf{T}$, we have the following subproblem:

$$\mathbf{T}_{k+1} = \arg \min_{\mathbf{T}} \frac{\mu}{2}||\mathbf{T} - \mathbf{K}||_F^2 + \frac{\lambda_t}{2}||d_x^k - \nabla_x \mathbf{T} - b_x^k||_F^2 + \frac{\lambda_t}{2}||d_y^k - \nabla_y \mathbf{T} - b_y^k||_F^2$$

$$+ \frac{\lambda_t}{2}||d_z^k - \nabla_z \mathbf{T} - b_z^k||_F^2 \quad (4.20)$$

with an optimality condition

$$(\mu \mathbf{I} - \lambda_t \Delta)\mathbf{T}_{k+1} = \mu \mathbf{K} + \lambda_t \nabla_x \mathbf{T}(d_x^k - b_x^k) + \lambda_t \nabla_y \mathbf{T}(d_y^k - b_y^k) + \lambda_t \nabla_z \mathbf{T}(d_z^k - b_z^k). \quad (4.21)$$

In order to achieve optimal efficiency, we used a fast iterative algorithm to get an approximate solution to the problem in Eq. (4.20). Due to the problem being strictly diagonally dominant, a natural component-wise solution of Gauss–Seidel method for this problem should be represented as $\mathbf{T}_{i,j}^{k+1} = \mathbf{G}_{i,j}^k$

$$\mathbf{G}_{i,j}^k = \frac{\lambda_t}{\mu + 6\lambda_t}(\mathbf{T}_{i+1,j,l}^k + \mathbf{T}_{i-1,j,l}^k + \mathbf{T}_{i,j+1,l}^k + \mathbf{T}_{i,j-1,l}^k + \mathbf{T}_{i,j,l+1}^k + \mathbf{T}_{i,j,l-1}^k$$

$$+ d_{x,i-1,j,l}^k - d_{x,i,j,l}^k + d_{y,i,j-1,l}^k - d_{y,i,j,l}^k + d_{z,i,j,l-1}^k - d_{z,i,j,l}^k \quad (4.22)$$

$$- b_{x,i-1,j,l}^k + b_{x,i,j,l}^k - b_{y,i,j-1,l}^k + b_{y,i,j,l}^k - b_{z,i,j,l-1}^k + b_{z,i,j,l}^k) + \frac{\mu}{\mu + 6\lambda_t}\mathbf{K}_{i,j,l}$$

where $\mathbf{T}^{k+1}$ has the same meaning as $\mathbf{T}_{k+1}$ in Eqs. (4.17) and (4.21), here is for the sake of convenience.

Table 4.1 demonstrates the performance comparison of vessel extraction via our MCR-RPCA and other classical RPCA-based methods. The performance is evaluated in terms of detection rate, precision, F-measure, and contrast-to-noise ratio (CNR) that measure the contrast between the foreground and background pixel intensities in relation to the standard deviation of the background pixel intensities. A larger CNR value implies a better contrast and thus a better performance of foreground/background separation. We used two different versions of CRN by defining two different background masks in XCA images. We refer the interested readers to Ref. [5] and the references therein.

4.4 SVS-net: sequential vessel segmentation via channel attention network

Recently, deep learning has become the most widely used approach for cardiac image segmentation [12] which covers common imaging modalities including MRI, CT, and ultrasound. However, due to the overlapping structures, low contrast, and the presence of complex and dynamic background artifacts in XCA images, accurately segmenting contrast-filled vessels from the XCA image sequence is particularly challenging for both classical modal-driven and modern data-driven deep learning methods. Being different from current several works that solely focused on segmenting main vessel from XCA [63−65], we have developed a novel encoder−decoder deep sequential vessel segmentation network (SVS-net, https://github.com/Binjie-Qin/SVS-net) [15] for entire XCA vessel network segmentation, which exploits several contextual frames of 2D + t sequential

Table 4.1 Performance comparison of eight RPCA methods on the X-ray coronary angiography sequences.

Method	Detection rate	Precision	F-measure	CNR1	CNR2	Time
MCR-PCA[1]	0.71258	0.83955	0.76976	2.88208	3.27754	919.34 s
Block-RPCA [56][2]	0.70313	0.83132	0.7591	2.57224	2.93497	4 h
DECOLOR [57][3]	0.68435	0.84038	0.75024	2.62923	2.69954	148.5 s
IALM-BLWS [58][4]	0.68957	0.84053	0.75618	2.58344	2.95259	74.84 s
FPCP [59][5]	0.67088	0.76977	0.71303	2.39507	2.22859	0.98 s
GoDec [60][6]	0.656308	0.77700	0.70826	2.34807	2.12574	1.41 s
TFOCS-EC [61][7]	0.63397	0.79817	0.70273	2.34603	2.11375	304.37 s
PRMF [62][8]	0.68573	077546	0.72556	2.56356	2.45889	42.06 s

[1]https://github.com/Binjie-Qin/MCR-RPCA.
[2]https://www.ece.nus.edu.sg/stfpage/eleclf/.
[3]http://bioinformatics.ust.hk/decolor/decolor.html.
[4]https://www.ccc.nus.edu.sg/stfpage/eleclf/.
[5]https://sites.google.com/a/istec.net/prodrig/Home/en/pubs.
[6]https://github.com/andrewssobral/godec/.
[7]https://github.com/cvxr/TFOCS.
[8]http://winsty.net/prmf.html.

images in a sliding window centered at current frame to continuously segment 2D vessel masks from the current frame in the XCA sequence.

4.4.1 Architecture of sequential vessel segmentation-network

Being modified from classical U–net architecture [66,67], the SVS–net architecture has three main modules that are equipped with spatiotemporal (2D + t) feature extraction in encoder module, 3D feature fusion operation (FFO) in skip connections, and channel attention block (CAB) in decoder module (See Fig. 4.3). Specifically, (1) A sequence of 3D convolutional layers hierarchically extracted spatiotemporal 3D

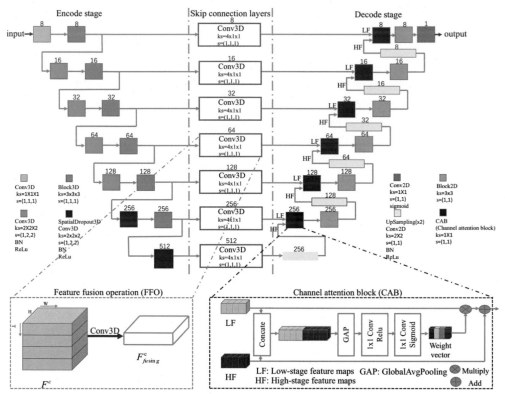

Figure 4.3 The proposed sequential vessel segmentation-network architecture, which is based on U-Net with the encoder network extracting 3D feature from the input sequence and the decoder network learning the salient feature via upsampling and operation of CAB, between the encoder and decoder network is the skip connection layer with FFO. The numbers 8, 16, 32,... above each block denote the number of output channels for that block. Each block has different convolutional kernel sizes and strides (s: strides). In the FFO and CAB in the bottom, the $F \in \mathbb{R}^{C \times T \times H \times W}$ denotes the temporal-spatial feature maps, C denotes channel axis, T denotes temporal axis, H denotes height axis, W denotes width axis, $F^c \in \mathbb{R}^{C \times H \times W}$: the cth channel of temporal-spatial feature maps. $F^c_{fusing} \in \mathbb{R}^{H \times W}$ denotes the cth channel of fused temporal-spatial feature map through Conv3D with kernel size $4 \times 1 \times 1$ and strides (1,1,1) [15].

features in the encoder module. We introduced 3D residual blocks to extract multi-scale spatiotemporal features while easing network optimization in the encoder module; (2) Skip connections that connect the encoder and decoder subsequently fused the spatiotemporal feature maps along temporal axis and delivered the fused 2D spatial feature maps to the corresponding decoder stages. Through the 3D feature fusion in the left bottom of Fig. 4.3, the feature maps' dimension mismatch problems between the 3D encoder stage and the 2D decoder stage was solved with computation cost being simultaneously reduced; (3) The decoder module utilized CAB to refine the intermediate feature maps from skip connections by learning discriminative feature representation and suppressing the complex and noisy artifacts in the XCA images; (4) Dice loss function was further implemented to train the SVS-net in order to solve the class imbalance problem in the XCA data causing by the imbalanced ratio between backgrounds and foreground vessels.

4.4.1.1 Modification of U-net

The U-Net was chosen as a fundamental architecture for SVS-net due to its being a classical and powerful segmentation network architecture widely used for biomedical imaging, which can improve the spatial accuracy of a deep neural network for final high-resolution segmentation results by effectively exploring underlying both high-resolution and low-resolution information in biomedical images and transmitting multiscale information from encoder network to decoder network via skip connections. Specifically, to accurately segment vessels from XCA with low contrast and fuzzy boundary, the skip connection mechanism in U-Net allowed high-resolution information delivery to the decoder network for detail recovery. Furthermore, the low-resolution semantic information about the internal tissues and their topologies in XCA images can be simply provided by multiple downsampling operations in U-Net's encoder network for the target vessel recognition.

To achieve accurate XCA vessel segmentation, we have designed a U-Net-based deep learning architecture with several notable features: (1) The encoder network was modified to extract 3D spatiotemporal contexts through 3D convolutions followed by 3D residual convolutional blocks except the last convolutional operation. There were totally seven stages of 3D convolutions with the first six convolutional stages followed by 3D residual convolutional block, which were utilized to extract rich spatiotemporal feature contexts for subsequent vessel mask extraction in the decoder network. The output of each 3D residual convolutional block was linked to the next 3D convolutional stage and skip connection layer, respectively. The spatial dropout (0.5) at the last two 3D convolutional stages was employed before executing convolution to avoid overfitting. The encoder network was capable of effectively extracting 3D spatiotemporal features from the context of sequential XCA images which contain long-range vessel details of different scales and different vessel types that may not appear in a single image.

(2) In the skip connection layer, the spatiotemporal feature representations were fused by mapping from 3D space to 2D space via $4 \times 1 \times 1$ convolutional kernels in FFO block, where the first dimension of convolutional kernel indicates four channels (frames) in the temporal axis. The temporal domain features from these four frames were then fused together by temporal axis convolution. The computation of FFO can be formulated as follows:

$$X_{F_l} = \text{Squeeze}(X_F \otimes W) \qquad (4.23)$$

where $X_F \in \mathbb{R}^{C \times T \times H \times W}$ is the spatiotemporal feature map outputted from each 3D convolutional stage in the encoder network with the C, T, H, W being features' channel dimension, temporal dimension, height, and width, respectively. $X_{F_L} \in \mathbb{R}^{C \times H \times W}$ fuses the spatiotemporal feature map. W is a $4 \times 1 \times 1$ convolutional kernel with $\otimes$ representing convolution operation. Squeeze denotes dimension compress.

(3) In the decoder network, the parameter-free bilinear upsampling strategy rather than transposed convolutional operations was adopted to gradually recover the feature maps' spatial resolution, which can reduce the number of trainable parameters without degrading the segmentation performance. A sequence of CAB modules that follow upsampling layer was designed to gradually fuse low-stage and high-stage XCA feature maps, whose output was further linked to 2D residual convolutional blocks (Block2D, see Fig. 4.3). The two outputs of low-stage feature maps from the skip connection layer and the high-stage feature maps from the upsampling layer were feed simultaneously in CAB (as illustrated in the right bottom of Fig. 4.3) to learn the most discriminative features from noisy and complex background artifacts (see details in Section 4.4.1.4). After the last 2D residual convolutional block in the end of sequential decoder networks, we employed 1×1 convolution followed by sigmoid activation function to yield final high-resolution vessel mask.

4.4.1.2 3D spatiotemporal feature encoder

For a set of frames $(F_1, F_2, \ldots F_n)$ in the XCA image sequence, the contextual information such as the low contrast intensity distribution and the similar appearances embedded in the successive frames are helpful to infer whether one pixel of each frame belongs to either the foreground or background. Specifically, in these successive frames, blood flow in the contrast-filled vessel regions moves fast and consistently through the contiguous frames and the noisy backgrounds fluctuate synchronously along with human breathing and heart beating. Therefore these consistent contexts can provide spatiotemporal information to accurately identify vessels from backgrounds. The SVS-net accepts inputs from the successive four frames (i.e., $F_{i-2}, F_{i-1}, F_i, F_{i+1}$) to predict a binary probability map (i.e., P_i) where the foreground vessel pixel values equal 1 while other background pixel values equal 0.

To verify the choice of four frames as an appropriate input configuration, we chose different frames, that is, 2, 3, 4, 5 frames, as the input of network to investigate the network's different convergence performances. We observed some subtle differences of convergence results on Dice loss function in our experiment results [15]. When inputs from four frames were fed in the network, the loss function converged at about -0.86, which is the smallest compared with those of other input strategies. The choice of four frames is thus appropriate to be served as the input configuration for accurate vessel segmentation.

4.4.1.3 2D and 3D residual convolutional blocks

Increasing the depth of a neural network can improve network generalization capacity, but it introduces the difficulty in promoting gradient backpropagation for the training of deep neural network. To ease the training of deep neural network, He et al. [68] developed deep residual network to facilitate gradient backpropagation by explicitly reformulating the network layers as learning residual functions with reference to the layer inputs instead of learning unreferenced functions. As demonstrated in the work of wide residual networks [69], two stacked convolutional layers in single residual block are optimal architecture compared with other settings. Inspired by these works, we employed 3D residual blocks and 2D residual blocks in encoder and decoder networks respectively. Between the encoder and decoder networks, the skip connection layer with FIFO was added to increase the depth and improve the accuracy of deep CNNs.

4.4.1.4 Channel attention mechanism

Aiming to highlight the most dominant target regions in an image, visual attention mechanism has been widely developed from traditional model-driven image computation to modern data-driven deep learning for visual saliency detection in both cognitive and computational sciences. The visual saliency computations for single image, image pair, and video sequence have been widely exploited in numerous applications to improve their performance for object detection [70], image retrieval [71], image registration [72–74], image cosegmentation [75,76], and video analysis [77]. Attention mechanism in deep learning can be viewed as a generalization of estimating weights for a weighted average in a regression model, where weights encode the relevance of the training instance to the query. Visual attention has become popular in many deep learning-based computer vision tasks to focus on relevant regions within the image and capture structural long-range dependencies between the images of video sequences. Furthermore, attention modeling is particularly important for the interpretability of deep learning architectures since the magnitude of attention is assumed to be a particular weight that correlates with how relevant a specific region of input is for the prediction of output at each position in a spatiotemporal sequence.

To represent rich multiscale features for extracting target vessels from complex and dynamic backgrounds, the SVS-net first exploits encoder network to extract multiple types of features from the whole XCA images by multiple convolutional kernels in every convolutional stage of the encoder module (see Fig. 4.3). Through the attention mechanism of CAB assigning different weights to the extracted features, the SVS-net can adaptively highlight some channel information meanwhile suppress the trivial channel information containing noisy background disturbances. Hence, the predicted probability map is gradually improved. Specifically, the feature maps of the low-stage output from the skip connection layer are weighted in CAB and then combined with the corresponding high-stage feature maps output from the upsampling layer. Since high-stage output feature maps provide more advanced global semantic information while low-stage feature maps contain more detailed yet noisy information, the high-stage features can then be used as guide clues to filter useful information from low-stage feature maps and achieve more pure feature representation for target vessel. The core modules of CAB is presented as follows (see the CAB in the bottom right of Fig. 4.3):

Global average pooling (GAP) can be considered as a simplest version of channel-wise attention, which computes the channel-wise statistic $G \in \mathbb{R}^{C \times 1 \times 1}$ of the given input feature maps by averaging across each $H \times W$ spatial dimension. The cth channel statistic s_c of s is computed as follows:

$$G_c(X) = \frac{1}{H \times W} \sum_{h=1}^{H} \sum_{w=1}^{W} X_c(h, w) \tag{4.24}$$

where $X_c \in \mathbb{R}^{H \times W}$, $\forall c \in \{1, \ldots, C\}$ refers to the cth feature of the input feature map. In our work, the low-stage feature maps $X_{F_l} \in \mathbb{R}^{C \times H \times W}$ and the corresponding high-stage feature maps $X_{F_h} \in \mathbb{R}^{C \times H \times W}$ are concatenated together to make feature maps $X_F \in \mathbb{R}^{2C \times H \times W}$. Then a GAP is performed on the concatenated feature maps to generate a weighted vector $W^{X_F} \in \mathbb{R}^{2C \times 1 \times 1}$. Two 1×1 convolutional operations, which are followed by the rectified linear unit function and sigmoid function, respectively, are performed on $W_{X_F} \in \mathbb{R}^{2C \times 1 \times 1}$ to learn interchannel relationship and the final channel attention weight vector $W_{X_F} \in \mathbb{R}^{C \times 1 \times 1}$ is achieved. The obtained attention vector multiplies low-stage feature maps in channel-wise manner, then the weighted feature maps from low stage are added with the corresponding high-stage feature maps to be subsequently passed to the next layer. The whole process of generating attention weights can be expressed as:

$$W_{X_F} = \phi(\varphi(G(X_F))) \tag{4.25}$$

where G means the operation of GAP, φ denotes 1×1 convolution followed by rectified linear unit and ϕ indicates 1×1 convolution followed by sigmoid activation. An intuitive display of CAB is shown in the left bottom of Fig. 4.4. Under the guidance of high-stage features, the attention weights are learned and used to obtain discriminative

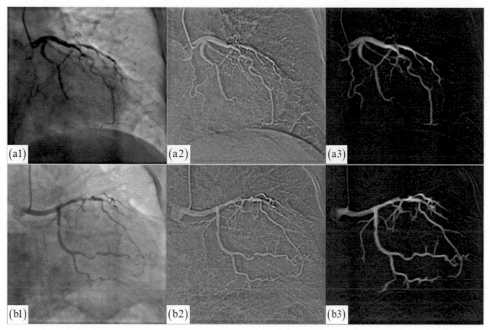

Figure 4.4 Illustrating the CAB's effects on suppressing the noises in the background areas while highlighting the foreground vessel feature. From left to right, each row displays the original XCA image; the second channel of fused spatial feature maps in the output of the second skip connection layer (Fig. 4.3) before inputting to the CAB, which contains noise pollution from the background areas; the second channel of refined feature maps from the output of CAB in the decoder stage (Fig. 4.3).

salient features for target vessels. As displayed in Fig. 4.4(a3)(b3), CAB has successfully refined the low stage feature map from the output of skip connection. The background disturbances in Fig. 4.4(a2)(b2) are greatly suppressed while the foreground vessel features are highlighted.

4.4.1.5 Data augmentation

Since there are several limitations in annotated data for supervised segmentation deep network, including scarce annotations where only limited labeled data are available for training, as well as weak and noisy annotations where the training data have sparse and erroneous annotations. Especially, for vessel annotation in XCA images, the contrast-filled vessel networks are distributed and overlapped in the complex noisy backgrounds with similar appearances to the foreground vessels, which make it very difficult and time-consuming for manually labeling vessel networks (especially with distal vessels) from backgrounds. To improve the network's generalization and accuracy based on small labeled datasets, data augmentation techniques increasing both the size and diversity of labeled training datasets are required to generate new labeled data points for training via transformations of existing image.

SVS–net used various sample transformations to augment data from existing data, which include rotations by the angles ranging in $[-10°, 10°]$, flipping both horizontally and vertically, scaling by a factor of 0.2 random crop, and affine transformations. For the images in our dataset, there is a 50% probability to perform each of the above transformations to generate new samples in real-time during the training process.

4.4.1.6 Loss function for class imbalance problem

Class imbalance is a common problem in which a dataset consists of examples primarily from one specific class. This could manifest itself in XCA vessel segmentation problems such that there is a clear majority—minority class distinction between the backgrounds and foreground vessels due to the contrast-filled vessels being sparsely visualized in the spatio-temporal sequence. Specifically, the class imbalance problem is typically represented as two aspects in XCA vessel segmentation: first, the number of negative pixels (being 0 for background) is much greater than the number of positive pixels (being 1 for the vessel pixels); second, the ratio between the two classes varies a lot in terms of both interframe differences in the same XCA sequence and intersequence differences in the different XCA sequences.

In supervised deep learning, imbalanced datasets are harmful because they bias deep learning models toward majority class predictions and render accuracy as a deceitful performance metric. Many data-level and algorithm-level solutions [78] are proposed to deal with class imbalance in big data in deep learning. The above-mentioned data augmentation falls under a data-level solution to class imbalance.

Among the algorithm-level solutions, the design of loss function [79] is very important in the deep learning to evaluate how well the predicted segmentation matches the ground truth. Currently, there is no widely accepted common view about the best loss function for image segmentation. However, there are some insights from existing literature. For example, the Dice loss or generalized Dice loss has proven to perform well for the mildly imbalanced problems [79]. Being different from the cross entropy highlighting each pixel equally to the CE loss, the Dice loss function measures the overlap ratio between ground truth mask and the predicted vessel mask such that it is appropriate to be adopted in SVS-net to guide parameters learning. Dice loss is defined as follows:

$$L_{\text{DiceCoef}} = -\frac{2\sum_{1}^{N} p_i y_i + \epsilon}{\sum_{1}^{N} p_i + \sum_{1}^{N} y_i + \epsilon} \tag{4.26}$$

where $y_i \in \{0, 1\}$ is the ground truth label and $p_i \in [0, 1]$ is a predicted value for location i. N is the total number of pixels, ϵ is a very small constant used to keep value stable.

From Eq. (4.26) we can find that the Dice loss is applied to the whole mask and it measures the overall loss for that mask rather than the average loss across all the pixels.

Recently, Kervadec et al. [80] have demonstrated that combining boundary loss with generalized Dice loss can address highly imbalanced segmentation tasks, we assume that not only using compound loss functions but also highlighting the boundary information with the overlap ratio between ground truth mask and the predicted vessel mask may be a more better choice for segmenting the dynamically and sparsely distributed vessel networks from the complex background.

4.4.2 Segmentation experimental results

4.4.2.1 Materials

All the experiments performed in this work were approved by our institutional review board. Our experiments were implemented on GPU (i.e., NVIDIA 1080 Ti, 11GB) and acquired 120 sequences of real clinical X-ray coronary angiography images from Ren Ji Hospital of Shanghai Jiao Tong University. Each sequence has a length of 30–140 frames. Three experts manually labeled the images from 120 sequences to constitute the ground truth. To eliminate the differences in the resolution, the noise distribution, and the pixels' intensity range of different frames in these XCA sequences that are acquired from different machines (i.e., 800 mAh digital silhouette angiography X-ray machine from Siemens, medical angiography X-ray system from Philips), we resized the images from the XCA sequence into 512×512 resolution with 8 bits per pixel, and employed Poisson denoising methods to smooth the noise and normalize the pixels' intensity range into 0–1. The dataset is stored in mat array format according to the corresponding filenames and will be available on the website https://github.com/Binjie-Qin/SVS-net.

Due to the varieties of XCA images with different directions and angles of X-ray penetration as well as different patient sources with different dosages of contrast agents, the visibility of different vessel sequences in the clinic is quite changeable such that designing a robust vessel segmentation algorithm is necessary for the XCA data with this poor visual quality. In addition, proper selection of frames from each sequence for experiment is crucial especially when both the background and foreground are dynamic and contain many artifacts. From the 120 annotated sequences, we selected the XCA images that contain most vessel structures with good visual quality as a total of 332 experiment samples. The dataset is randomly divided into training dataset, validation dataset, and test data at approximately 0.5, 0.25, and 0.25 ratios, respectively.

We validated the SVS-net's performance on the above-mentioned dataset by plotting the loss curves for both the training and validation set in the training process [15]. For both the training and validation set, the loss reduced quickly at the beginning stage of training process and gradually converged, indicating the SVS-Net having no problem of over-fitting or under-fitting state. Meanwhile, the size of our dataset was assumed to be properly matched into the size of our model.

4.4.2.2 Performance comparison

We compared SVS-net with three traditional vessel segmentation algorithms, that is, Coye's method [81], Jin's spatially adaptively filtering method (Jin's) [11], Kerkeni's multiscale region growing method (Kerkeni's) [82], and four deep learning-based methods that include Retinal-net [67,83], bridge-style U-Net with salient mechanism (S–UNet) [84], X-ray net [85], and short connected deep supervised net (BTS-DSN) [86].

In Fig. 4.5, the deep learning methods surpassed traditional methods with higher performances in terms of some metrics [15]. The patch-based Retinal-net method introduced more background residuals since it lacked more global contextual information to guide the segmentation. X-ray net simply accepted the current frame image with its first three frames as the inputs to the network and cannot effectively extract the temporally consistent information. Therefore it not only increased temporal information but also introduced disturbances at the same time. BTS-DSN adopted deeply supervised strategy to achieve relative higher metrics with some false positives in the vessel regions. Being different from the above deep network methods, SVS-net not only robustly detected the vessels with entire structures and continuous branches but also effectively removed the noisy backgrounds. The continuity and integrity of the segmented vessel branches were due to the contextual information inferred in the spatiotemporal features extracted by the encoder network and feature fusion in the skip connections. The noise suppression in the segmented vessel regions was mostly derived from the

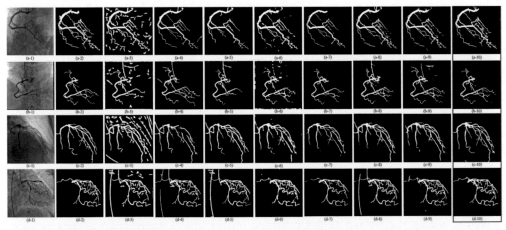

Figure 4.5 Vessel segmentation examples for real XCA image sequence by different vessel segmentation methods [15]. From left to right, each row displays the original XCA image, the ground truth vessel segmentation, the vessel images segmented by Coye's, [71] Jin's, [11] Kerkeni's, [72] Retinal-net, [73] SU-Net, [74] X-ray net, [75] BTS-DSN, [76] and SVS-net, [15] respectively.

discriminative feature selection implemented by the channel attention mechanism. Therefore the spatiotemporal feature extraction, feature fusion, and the discriminative feature learning adopted in SVS-net were helpful to improve the segmentation performances.

However, there is a small number of thin-vessel branches unrecognized by SVS-net. A new design of a hybrid loss function combined with network architectures is desirable to efficiently differentiate the thick and thin vessels with their different weights. That is, the deep gives more weight to these thin vessels via topology-preserving loss function [87] and pays more attention to these thin vessels. Topology-preserving vessel segmentation is definitely a very promising direction for improving the clinical value of XCA images.

4.5 VRBC-t-TNN: accurate heterogeneous vessel extraction via tensor completion of X-ray coronary angiography backgrounds

By modeling XCA sequence with low-rank plus sparse decomposition, motion coherency regularized RPCA [5] has been successfully exploited to recover the sparsely distributed contrast agent in the vessel networks from the low-rank subspace of backgrounds [21]. However, current RPCA-based methods have the following limitations: (1) Some parts of XCA vessel have low rank properties due to the underlying pattern of periodic heartbeat and the contrast agent's adhesion along the vessel wall, current RPCA methods therefore always have vessel residue as part of the low-rank backgrounds such that the extracted vessels suffer from severe distortion or loss of vessel intensity. This intensity loss results in an incomplete vessel recovery and makes it impossible for accurately analyzing the contrast agent concentration and the corresponding blood flow perfusion. (2) Vectorizing the XCA sequence into a matrix in RPCA ignores the 3D spatiotemporal information between the consecutive frames of the XCA sequence. For example, X-ray imaging produces a lot of dense noisy artifacts, whose positions change in gradually moving patterns in the XCA frames. The RPCA methods often mistakenly recognize these moving artifacts as foreground objects. (3) XCA sequence has serious signal-dependent noises that locally affect every entry of the data matrix and result in unsatisfying foreground vessels that are contaminated with residual artifacts. Though MCR-RPCA takes advantage of Bayesian RPCA that models data noise as MoGs, current RPCA-based methods cannot tackle the challenging problem of spatially varying noise in low-rank plus sparse decomposition.

To extract the foreground vessels that are overlapped with backgrounds, we assume that the overlap between foreground vessels and the backgrounds is present in the vessel regions. Once contrast-filled vessel regions are masked by the SVS-net vessel segmentation with high detection rates, all the other pixels in the remaining regions can be regarded as sequential background layers. Furthermore, based on the spatiotemporal consistency and low-rankness of the sequential background layers, the missing parts of the background layers masked with the foreground vessels can be fully completed using the state–of–the–art tensor completion method. Then, the challenging problem of foreground vessel extraction can be tackled by subtracting the completed background layers from the overall XCA data (see Fig. 4.6). Therefore we exploited the low-rank tensor completion [88] to recover a low-rank tensor from noisy partial observations of its entries. Tensors [89,90] refer to multidimensional arrays, which can naturally reserve more spatiotemporal information than do the matrices. Different from RPCA using matrix representation for XCA sequence, the tensor-based completion methods infer the unknown missing pixels from the known pixels in the spatiotemporal contexts of XCA sequence. Mathematically, the low-rank tensor completion problem can be written as

$$\min_{\mathcal{X}} \mathrm{rank}(\mathcal{X}), \quad \text{s.t. } P_{\Omega}(\mathcal{X}) = P_{\Omega}(\mathcal{M}) \tag{4.27}$$

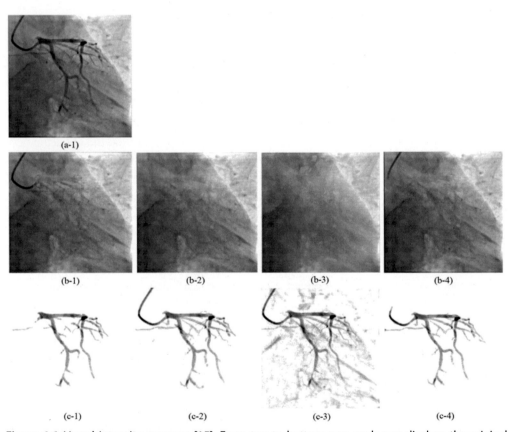

Figure 4.6 Vessel intensity recovery [15]. From top to bottom row, each row displays the original XCA image, the background and foreground vessel images recovered from SU-Net [74], X-ray net [75], BTS-DSN [76] and SVS-net [15], respectively.

where $\mathcal{M}$ is the corrupted tensor, $\mathcal{X}$ is the underlying tensor, and $\mathcal{P}_\Omega(\mathcal{X})$ refers to the projection of $\mathcal{X}$ on the observed entries Ω.

Based on different definitions of tensor ranks, many tensor completion models have been proposed. Typically, tensor nuclear norm (TNN) [91] that is designed for 3D tensors based on tensor singular value decomposition (t-SVD) [92] has proven effective at 3D tensor completion [88]. Hu et al. have further optimized the TNN model for the video completion task by integrating a twist operation [93].

According to Beer–Lambert Law, a given X-ray image is assumed to reflect the X-ray exponential attenuation composition (or sum) of material linear attenuation coefficients for the foreground contrast-filled vessels and background layers along the X-ray projection paths. The additive property of X-ray exponential attenuation composition along the vessel and background layers in XCA can be directly exploited to exactly decompose the whole XCA image into the vessel and background layers. Therefore this X-ray attenuation sum model justifies the above-mentioned foreground vessel extraction strategy via completion and subtraction of the background layers from the whole XCA images. Specifically, we proposed an accurate heterogeneous vessel extraction framework in a logarithmic domain, into which the raw XCA image is first mapped. We extracted the vessel mask regions via SVS-net and subsequently recovered vessel intensities in these regions by a tensor completion method called t-TNN (twist tensor nuclear norm) [93]. By focusing on the vessel intensity recovery problem only in the small parts of vessel regions, the proposed vessel recovery method called VRBC-t-TNN can extract vessel layers with accurate recovery of vessel structures and intensities.

4.5.1 Global intensity mapping

A global logarithm mapping was carried out on the whole XCA image data to perfectly fit the X-ray attenuation sum model of angiograms. In X-ray imaging, photons coming through human body are attenuated by contrast agents and various human tissues. The intensity of rays is reduced exponentially by the sum of attenuation coefficients, as the following equation:

$$X_{\text{out}} = X_{\text{in}} e^{-\int_d \mu \mathrm{d}x} \tag{4.28}$$

where X_{in} and X_{out} represent the intensities of X-rays that come into and out of human body, respectively, μ denotes the attenuation coefficient, and d denotes the path of rays.

By applying the log operator on both sides, we got

$$-\ln(X_{\text{out}}/X_{\text{in}}) = \int_d \mu \mathrm{d}x. \tag{4.29}$$

The XCA image intensity normalized to the range [0,1] can be regarded as the normalization of its intensity, that is, the ratio of X_{out} to X_{in}. Then we got the following equation:

$$-\ln(I_{\text{XCA}}) = -\ln(X_{\text{out}}/X_{\text{in}}) = \int_{d_1} \mu dx + \int_{d_2} \mu dx = A_F + A_B, \qquad (4.30)$$

where A_F and A_B represent the attenuation sums caused by foreground vessels and complex backgrounds, respectively. This equation demonstrates that the XCA image is a sum of vessel/background layers in the logarithm domain, accordingly the multiplication of the two layers in the original image domain.

After this logarithm mapping, the linear sum model was ready for vessel/background separation via low-rank plus sparse matrix decomposition in RPCA (Illustrated in Section 4.3), as well as low-rank background plus foreground vessel extraction in tensor completion (Illustrated in Section 4.6). Therefore we used the logarithm operation as a preprocessing of image data and performed exponentiation operation afterward for the whole experiments in this work.

4.5.2 Background completion using t-TNN

Considering the vessel mask regions as missing entries of the background layer, we recovered the intensities of these entries for the construction of background layers by adopting the t-TNN tensor completion algorithm [93], which can effectively exploit the temporal redundancy and low-rank prior between the neighboring frames more efficiently. Specifically, the original XCA sequence was represented as a tensor $\mathcal{D}$ with each slice being a matrix representation of each frame. All areas except the vessel mask regions, denoted as Ω, were presumed to be the known background layer pixels. Each vessel mask region was first morphologically dilated by a 5×5 mask to ensure that Ω does not contain edge pixels of the vessels. Therefore the background regions of all the frames constituted Ω for the subsequent t-TNN-based tensor completion.

The t-TNN model is based upon a tensor decomposition scheme called t-SVD [92,94]. Having a similar structure to the matrix SVD, t-SVD models a tensor in the matrix space through a defined t-product operation [92]. For a 3-way tensor $\mathcal{X} \in \mathbb{R}^{n_1 \times n_2 \times n_3}$, the notation $\mathcal{X}(k,:,:)$, $\mathcal{X}(:,k,:)$, and $\mathcal{X}(:,:,k)$ denote the k-th horizontal, lateral, and frontal slices, respectively. Particularly, $\mathcal{X}^{(k)}$ denotes $\mathcal{X}(:,:,k)$. For $\mathcal{X} \in \mathbb{R}^{n_1 \times n_2 \times n_3}$, the $\mathcal{X}^{(k)}$ values can be used to form the block circulant matrix

$$\mathbf{bcirc}(\mathcal{X}) = \begin{bmatrix} \mathcal{X}^{(1)} & \mathcal{X}^{(n_3)} & \cdots & \mathcal{X}^{(2)} \\ \mathcal{X}^{(2)} & \mathcal{X}^{(1)} & \cdots & \mathcal{X}^{(3)} \\ \vdots & \vdots & \ddots & \vdots \\ \mathcal{X}^{(n_3)} & \mathcal{X}^{(n_3-1)} & \cdots & \mathcal{X}^{(1)} \end{bmatrix}, \qquad (4.31)$$

The block vectorizing and its opposite operation are defined as

$$\mathbf{bvec}(\mathcal{X}) = \begin{bmatrix} \mathcal{X}^{(1)} \\ \mathcal{X}^{(2)} \\ \vdots \\ \mathcal{X}^{(n_3)} \end{bmatrix}, \mathbf{bvfold}(\mathbf{bvec}(\mathcal{X})) = \mathcal{X} \tag{4.32}$$

The **bdiag** operator which maps the tensor to the block diagonal matrix and its opposite operation **bdfold** are defined as

$$\mathbf{bdiag}(\mathcal{X}) = \begin{bmatrix} \mathcal{X}^{(1)} & & \\ & \ddots & \\ & & \mathcal{X}^{(n_3)} \end{bmatrix}, \mathbf{bdfold}(\mathbf{bdiag}(\mathcal{X})) = \mathcal{X}. \tag{4.33}$$

Based on these notations, the t-product is defined as follows [92]:

$$\mathcal{M} = \mathcal{A} * \mathcal{B} = \mathbf{bvfold}(\mathbf{bcirc}(\mathcal{A})\mathbf{bvec}(\mathcal{B})).$$

The t product is analogous to the matrix product except that the circular convolution replaces the product operation between the elements. The following equation shows that original t-product corresponds to the matrix multiplication of the frontal slices in the Fourier domain:

$$\mathcal{M}_f^{(k)} = \mathcal{A}_f^{(k)} * \mathcal{B}_f^{(k)}, \quad k = 1, \cdots, n_3. \tag{4.34}$$

where $\mathcal{X}_f = \mathbf{fft}(\mathcal{X}, [\ ], 3)$ denotes the Fourier transform of $\mathcal{X}$ along the third dimension. Accordingly, $\mathcal{X} = \mathbf{ifft}(\mathcal{X}_f, [], 3)$. Based on the definition of t-product, the tensor–SVD (t-SVD) [94] of $\mathcal{X} \in \mathbb{R}^{n_1 \times n_2 \times n_3}$ is given by

$$\mathcal{X} = \mathcal{U} * \mathcal{S} * \mathcal{V}^T, \tag{4.35}$$

where $\mathcal{U} \in \mathbb{R}^{n_1 \times n_1 \times n_3}$ and $\mathcal{V} \in \mathbb{R}^{n_2 \times n_2 \times n_3}$ are orthogonal tensors, respectively. $\mathcal{S} \in \mathbb{R}^{n_1 \times n_2 \times n_3}$ is a rectangular f-diagonal tensor in which all of its frontal slices are diagonal matrices, and the entries in $\mathcal{S}$ are called the singular values of $\mathcal{X}$.

Based on the Fourier domain property of t-product as Eq. (4.34), t-SVD can be efficiently computed in the Fourier domain [92,94]. Each frontal slice of $\mathcal{U}_f$, $\mathcal{S}_f$, and $\mathcal{V}_f$ can be obtained via the matrix SVD, that is, $[\mathcal{U}_f^{(k)}, \mathcal{S}_f^{(k)}, \mathcal{V}_f^{(k)}] = \mathbf{SVD}(\mathcal{X}_f^{(k)})$. Then the t-SVD of $\mathcal{X}$ can be obtained by $\mathcal{U} = \mathbf{ifft}(\mathcal{U}_f, [], 3), \mathcal{S} = \mathbf{ifft}(\mathcal{S}_f, [], 3), \mathcal{V} = \mathbf{ifft}(\mathcal{V}_f, [], 3)$. The TNN of $\mathcal{X} \in \mathbb{R}^{n_1 \times n_2 \times n_3}$ is defined as the average of the nuclear norms of all the frontal slices of $\mathcal{X}_f$ [94], that is,

$$||\mathcal{X}||_\circledast = \frac{1}{n_3} \sum_{i=1}^{n_3} ||\mathcal{X}_f^{(i)}||_* = \frac{1}{n_3} ||\mathbf{bcirc}(\mathcal{X})||_* \tag{4.36}$$

Using the definition of TNN, the TNN-based tensor completion [93] can be represented by

$$\min_{\mathcal{X}} ||\mathcal{X}||_{\circledast}, \quad \text{s.t. } \mathcal{P}_{\Omega}(\mathcal{X}) = \mathcal{P}_{\Omega}(\mathcal{M}), \tag{4.37}$$

where $\mathcal{M}$ is the corrupted tensor, $\mathcal{P}_{\Omega}(\mathcal{X})$ refers to the projection of $\mathcal{X}$ on the observed entries Ω. Accordingly, $\mathcal{P}_{\Omega^{\perp}}(\mathcal{X})$ is the complementary projection, that is, $\mathcal{P}_{\Omega}(\mathcal{X}) + \mathcal{P}_{\Omega^{\perp}}(\mathcal{X}) = \mathcal{X}$. The tensor completion problem can be solved using the t-SVD mentioned above.

TNN can simultaneously characterize the low-rankness of a tensor along various modes and therefore is a general model for 3D data completion problems. Based on the TNN, Hu et al. [93] proposed twist TNN (called t-TNN) via twist operator on the tensor. That is, for $\mathcal{X} \in \mathbb{R}^{n_1 \times n_2 \times n_3}$, the twist tensor $\vec{\mathcal{X}}$ is an $n_1 \times n_2 \times n_3$ tensor whose lateral slice $\vec{\mathcal{X}}(:, k, :) = \mathcal{X}(:, :, k)$. Though this twist operation is simply a dimension shift of tensors, it emphasizes the temporal connections between frames. The t-TNN norm $\left\| \mathcal{X} \right\|_{\vec{\circledast}}$ of tensor $\mathcal{X}$ is then defined as follows:

$$\left\| \mathcal{X} \right\|_{\vec{\circledast}} = \frac{1}{n_3} \left\| \mathbf{bcirc}(\vec{\mathcal{X}}) \right\|_{*}, \tag{4.38}$$

where the twist operation $\vec{\mathcal{X}}$ is a dimension shift of $\mathcal{X}$, and $\overleftarrow{\mathcal{Y}}$ shifts it back. By equalizing the nuclear norm of the block circulant matriculation of the twist tensor, t-TNN can not only exploit the correlations between all the modes simultaneously but also take advantage of the low-rank prior along a certain mode, for example, X-ray image sequence over the time dimension. Specifically, by exploiting the low-rank prior along the horizontal translation relationship between frames in XCA image sequences due to patient's breath and movement, we have found that the t-TNN model is more suitable than TNN for our XCA background completion work. Therefore by minimizing the t-TNN norm-based rank of the input tensor subject to certain constraints, the tensor completion work for XCA background recovery can be addressed by solving the following convex model [93]:

$$\min_{\mathcal{X}} \left\| \mathcal{X} \right\|_{\vec{\circledast}}, \quad \text{s.t. } \mathcal{P}_{\Omega}(\mathcal{X}) = \mathcal{P}_{\Omega}(\mathcal{D}) \tag{4.39}$$

where $\mathcal{D}$ and $\mathcal{X}$ refer to the original corrupted data tensor (original XCA sequence) and the reconstructed tensor (background layer), respectively.

The alternating direction method of multipliers algorithm [95] can be used to solve the Eq. (4.39) by the following minimization model [93]:

$$\operatorname{argmin}_{\mathcal{X}, \mathcal{Y}, \mathcal{W}} \left\| \mathcal{Y} \right\|_{\vec{\circledast}} + \mathbf{1}_{\mathcal{X}_{\Omega} = \mathcal{D}_{\Omega}} + \langle \mathcal{W}, \mathcal{X} - \mathcal{Y} \rangle + \frac{\rho}{2} \left\| \mathcal{X} - \mathcal{Y} \right\|_F^2, \tag{4.40}$$

where a new variable $\mathcal{Y} = \mathcal{X}$ is introduced, $\mathbf{1}_{\mathcal{X}_{\Omega} = \mathcal{D}_{\Omega}}$ is an indicator function that indicates whether the elements of $\mathcal{X}$ and $\mathcal{D}$ on the support of Ω are equal, $\mathcal{W}$ is the Lagrangian multiplier, and μ is a positive penalty scalar. Variables $\mathcal{X}$, $\mathcal{Y}$, and $\mathcal{W}$ can be optimized alternately with the other variable fixed. The detailed deduction of this algorithm is too long and out of the scope of this chapter. We refer the interested reader to the work in Ref. [93].

After the construction of background layer $\mathcal{X}$ by t-TNN, the final vessel layer can be obtained by subtracting $\mathcal{X}$ from the original data $\mathcal{D}$. This subtraction was done in the logarithm domain such that the corresponding operation for original image data would be division. The whole procedure of the t-TNN background completion step is shown in Algorithm 2.

Algorithm 2 t-TNN based background completion

Input: Original XCA data $\mathcal{D} \in \mathbb{R}^{n_1 \times n_2 \times n_3}$, non-vessel mask region Ω.

1: **Initialize:** $\rho^0 > 0, \eta > 1, k = 0, \mathcal{X} = \mathcal{P}_\Omega(\mathcal{D}), \mathcal{Y} = \mathcal{W} = 0$.

2: **while** $\|\mathcal{X} - \mathcal{Y}\|_F / \|\mathcal{X}\|_F > tol$ **and** $k < K$ **do**

3:     $\mathcal{X}$ **sub-problem:**

$$\mathcal{X}^{k+1} = \arg\min_{\mathcal{X}:\mathcal{X}_\Omega = \mathcal{D}_\Omega^k} \left\| \mathcal{X} - \mathcal{Y}^k + \frac{1}{\rho^k}\mathcal{W}^k \right\|_F^2$$

solved by:

$$\mathcal{X}^{k+1} = \mathcal{P}_\Omega(\mathcal{D}^k) + \mathcal{P}_{\Omega^\perp}(\mathcal{Y}^k - \frac{1}{\rho^k}\mathcal{W}^k);$$

4:     $\mathcal{Y}$ **sub-problem:**

$$\mathcal{Y}^{k+1} = \arg\min_{\mathcal{Y}} \|\mathcal{Y}\|_\circledast + \frac{\rho^k}{2}\left\| \mathcal{X}^{k+1} - \mathcal{Y} + \frac{1}{\rho^k}\mathcal{W}^k \right\|_F^2$$

solved by:

$\tau = \frac{1}{\rho^k}, \tau' = \tau \lceil \frac{n_2+1}{2} \rceil, \mathcal{Z} - \mathcal{X}^{k+1} + \tau\mathcal{W}^k;$

$\vec{\mathcal{Z}}_f = \mathbf{fft}(\vec{\mathcal{Z}}, [], 3);$

for $j = 1, \cdots, \lceil \frac{n_2+1}{2} \rceil$ **do**

$[\mathcal{U}_f^{(j)}, \mathcal{S}_f^{(j)}, \mathcal{V}_f^{(j)}] = \mathbf{SVD}(\vec{\mathcal{Z}}_f^{(j)});$

$\mathcal{J}_f^{(j)} = \mathbf{diag}\{(1 - \frac{\tau'}{\mathcal{S}_f^{(j)}(i,i)})_+\};$

$\mathcal{S}_{f,\tau'}^{(j)} = \mathcal{S}_f^{(j)} \mathcal{J}_f^{(j)};$

$\mathcal{H}_f^{(j)} = \mathcal{U}_f^{(j)} \mathcal{S}_{f,\tau'}^{(j)} \mathcal{V}_f^{(j)T}$

end for

for $j = \lceil \frac{n_2+1}{2} \rceil + 1, \cdots, n_2$ **do**

$\mathcal{H}_f^{(j)} = \mathrm{conj}\left(\mathcal{H}_f^{(n_2-j+2)}\right);$

end for

$\mathcal{H} = \mathbf{ifft}(\mathcal{H}_f, [], 3), \mathcal{Y}^{k+1} = \overleftarrow{\mathcal{H}};$

5:     $\mathcal{W}^{k+1} = \mathcal{W}^k + \rho^k(\mathcal{X}^{k+1} - \mathcal{Y}^{k+1});$

6:     $\rho^{k+1} = \eta\rho^k, k = k+1$

7: **end while**

8: Vessel layer $\mathcal{V} = \mathcal{D} - \mathcal{X};$

Output: Background layer tensor $\mathcal{X}$, vessel layer tensor $\mathcal{V}$.

4.5.3 Experimental results

4.5.3.1 Synthetic X-ray coronary angiography data

To accurately evaluate the performance of vessel intensity recovery, we constructed 10 synthetic XCA images which include ground truth background images (GTBL) and foreground vessel layer images (GTVL). All the original 12 XCA sequences were obtained from Ren Ji Hospital of Shanghai Jiao Tong University. Each sequence has 80 frames whose image resolution is 512×512 pixels with 8 bits per pixel. All the experiments were approved by our institutional review board.

To get GTVLs, we performed a vessel extraction algorithm similar to Section 4.2 on the real XCA data. Then some artifacts were manually removed from the extracted rough vessel images to obtain the GTVLs. The GTBLs were the consecutive frames selected from the real XCA data. Because an XCA image is the product of the vessel layer and the background layer according to the X-ray imaging mechanism (see Section 4.5.1), we multiplied a sequence of GTVLs to the clean regions of GTBLs from a different sequence to obtain the synthetic XCA data. An example synthetic image with GTBL and GTVL is shown in Fig. 4.7A.

4.5.3.2 Experiment demonstration

We performed experiments similar to the algorithm shown in Fig. 4.1 to illustrate the effect of tensor completion on vessel intensity recovery. The real vessel segmentation algorithm (see details in Ref. [11]) is different from that of Section 4.4 in Fig. 4.1, it makes little influence on vessel intensity performances. We validated the performances from the VRBC-t-TNN and other layer separation methods for comparison purpose. The median subtraction method (MedSubtract) used by Baka et al. constructs a static background layer image as the median of the first 10 frames of a sequence and subtract it from all the frames [96]. Several open-source RPCA algorithms, including PRMF [97], MoG-RPCA [51], IALM-RPCA, [5], and MCR–RPCA in Section 4.3 [5] were tested. The proposed framework VRBC can use other matrix completion and tensor completion methods to replace t-TNN. We tested some open source data completion methods including PG-RMC [98], MC-NMF [99], ScGrassMC [100], LRTC [101], and tSVD [102] as comparison, whose codes were obtained from Sobral's library lrslibrary [103] and mctc4bmi [104].

4.5.3.3 Performance comparison

The layer separation results of the synthetic data are shown in Fig. 4.7. As can be seen, all these layer separation methods can remove noises and increase the vessel visibility to some extent. Among these algorithms, because MedSubtracted constructs a static background layer image that does not change over time, the extracted vessel layer image with lots of remaining noise was the worst among these extracted results. The four RPCA-based methods achieved much better vessel extraction results with more

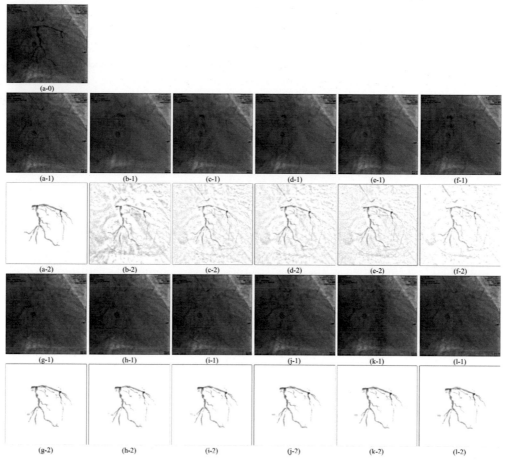

Figure 4.7 Examples of vessel layer extraction results from synthetic data [21]. Each group of results contains a background layer image labeled 1 and a vessel layer image labeled 2. (a-0) Synthetic XCA image. (a-1,2) Ground truth background layer and vessel layer image. (b)–(l) Layer separation results: (b) Med Subtract [83]. (c) PRMF [84]. (d) MoG-RPCA [49]. (e) IALM-RPCA [51]. (f) MCR-RPCA [5]. (g) VRBC-PG-RMC. (h) VRBC-MC-NMF. (i) VRBC-ScGrassMC. (j) VRBC-LRTC [21]. (k) VRBC-tSVD. (l) VRBC-t-TNN [21].

noises being removed. Among these four RPCA-based methods, MCR-RPCA [5] achieved the best vessel extraction results with the least residual artifacts. However, though RPCA-based methods can nicely capture the vessel structures in the vessel layer images, the vessel intensities were not fully extracted since obvious vessel residuals can be observed in their resulting background layer images. This observation is consistent with the fact that some contrast agents being pushed against the vessel wall have reduced their flow rate and behaved low-rankness property, such that these contrast agents remained in the backgrounds after RPCA-based decomposition.

In contrast, the VRBC framework embedded within all the tensor–completion methods greatly improved the performances of vessel extraction and intensity recovery. The recovered vessel intensities were further compared to those from RPCA algorithms. Among all these algorithms, the result images of VRBC-t-TNN achieved the best visual performances. Both the background layer images and the vessel layer images were visually appealing and seemed to be well recovered in terms of structure and intensity recovery. To quantitatively measure the accuracy of vessel intensity recovery, we directly calculated the differences between the extracted vessel layers and the ground truths. The reconstruction error of vessels is defined as follow:

$$E_{recon} = \frac{\sum_{(x,y) \in V} |I_{result}(x, y) - I_{groundtruth}(x, y)|}{\sum_{(x,y) \in V} I_{groundtruth}(x, y)} \tag{4.41}$$

where V denotes the vessel regions, I_{result} and $I_{groundtruth}$ denote the intensities of the resulting vessel layer images and the ground truth vessel layer images, respectively. For each synthetic XCA sequence, the E_{recon} of the whole sequence is calculated. Fig. 4.8 shows the general performances of different algorithms on the 10 synthetic sequences.

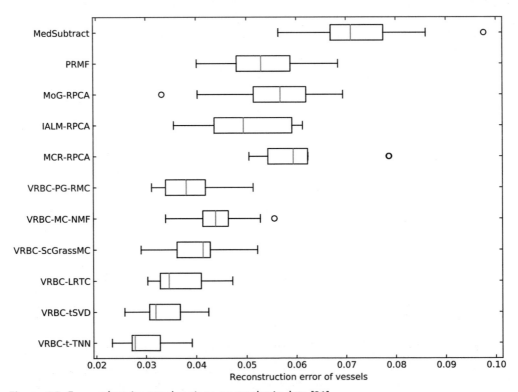

Figure 4.8 E_{recon} values in vessel regions on synthetic data [21].

E_{recon} measured the vessel intensity difference between the separation result and the ground truth. A small E_{recon} indicated an accurate vessel layer extraction. We can see that VRBC framework achieved smaller E_{recon} values than other existing methods. Among them, VRBC-t-TNN achieved the best performance. This E_{recon} evaluation indicated that VRBC-t-TNN can accurately recover the intensities of contrast-filled vessels from XCA images.

4.6 Conclusion

In this chapter, we demonstrated the entire framework to effectively extract the contrast-filled vessels and their intensities from the complex and noisy backgrounds in XCA sequences. To the best of our knowledge, this is the first work to perform such complete work for the benefit of microcirculation analysis in minimally invasive vascular interventions. Current XCA-guided coronary artery revascularization via stent implantation solely performs epicardial artery-based revascularization. However, whether this artery revascularization could improve the distal microcirculation and accordingly lead to a desired therapeutic effect on the acute myocardial ischemic heart diseases is not easily evaluated in preoperative and postoperative assessment in current vascular interventions. We hope our work could be helpful to appropriately assess the microcirculation and other cardiovascular diseases by extracting and analyzing the heterogeneous XCA vessels.

Acknowledgments

This work was supported in parts by the Science and Technology Commission of Shanghai Municipality under Grant 19dz1200500 and Grant 19411951507, the National Natural Science Foundation of China under Grant 61271320 and 82070477, Shanghai ShenKang Hospital Development Center (SHDC12019X12), and the Shanghai Jiao Tong University Cross Research Fund for Translational Medicine under Grant ZH2018ZDA19, YG2021QN122 and YG2021QN99.

References

[1] Theodoridis S. Machine learning: a Bayesian and optimization perspective. 2nd ed. Elsevier; 2020.
[2] Lin Z, Zhang H. Low-rank models in visual analysis: theories, algorithms, and applications. Academic Press; 2017.
[3] Candès EJ, Li X, Ma Y, Wright J. Robust principal component analysis? J ACM 2011;58(3):1–37.
[4] Bouwmans T, Javed S, Zhang H, Lin Z, Otazo R. On the applications of robust PCA in image and video processing. Proc IEEE 2018;106(8):1427–57.
[5] Jin M, Li R, Jiang J, Qin B. Extracting contrast-filled vessels in X-ray angiography by graduated RPCA with motion coherency constraint. Pattern Recognit 2017;63:653–66.
[6] Ma H, Hoogendoorn A, Regar E, Niessen WJ, van Walsum T. Automatic online layer separation for vessel enhancement in X-ray angiograms for percutaneous coronary interventions. Med Image Anal 2017;39:145–61.

[7]   Song S, Du C, Ai D, Huang Y, Song H, Wang Y, et al. Spatio-temporal constrained online layer separation for vascular enhancement in X-ray angiographic image sequence. IEEE Trans Circuits Syst Video Technol 2020;30(10):3558−70.

[8]   Xia S, Zhu H, Liu X, Gong M, Huang X, Xu L, et al. Vessel segmentation of X-ray coronary angiographic image sequence. IEEE Trans Biomed Eng 2020;67(5):1338−48.

[9]   Zhu L, Jiang X, Li J, Hao Y, Tian Y. Motion-aware structured matrix factorization for foreground detection in complex scenes. ACM Trans Multimedia Comput Commun Appl (TOMM) 2020;16(4):1−23.

[10] Hu Z, Nie F, Wang R, Li X. Low rank regularization: a review. Neural Netw 2021;136:218−32.

[11] Jin M, Hao D, Ding S, Qin B. Low-rank and sparse decomposition with spatially adaptive filtering for sequential segmentation of 2D + t vessels. Phys Med Biol 2018;63(17):17LT01.

[12] Chen C, Qin C, Qiu H, Tarroni G, Duan J, Bai W, et al. Deep learning for cardiac image segmentation: a review. Front Cardiovasc Med 2020;7:25.

[13] Nasr-Esfahani E, Karimi N, Jafari MH, Soroushmehr SMR, Samavi S, Nallamothu BK, et al. Segmentation of vessels in angiograms using convolutional neural networks. Biomed Signal Process Control 2018;40:240−51.

[14] Shin SY, Lee S, Yun ID, Lee KM. Deep vessel segmentation by learning graphical connectivity. Med Image Anal 2019;58:101556.

[15] Hao D, Ding S, Qiu L, Lv Y, Fei B, Zhu Y, et al. Sequential vessel segmentation via deep channel attention network. Neural Netw 2020;128:172−87.

[16] Samuel PM, Veeramalai T. VSSC Net: vessel specific skip chain convolutional network for blood vessel segmentation. Comput Methods Prog Biomed 2021;198:105769.

[17] Zhu X, Cheng Z, Wang S, Chen X, Lu G. Coronary angiography image segmentation based on PSPNet. Comput Methods Prog Biomed 2021;200:105897.

[18] Fan J, Yang J, Wang Y, Yang S, Ai D, Huang Y, et al. Multichannel fully convolutional network for coronary artery segmentation in X-ray angiograms. IEEE Access 2018;6:44635−43.

[19] Wang L, Liang D, Yin X, Qiu J, Yang Z, Xing J, et al. Coronary artery segmentation in angiographic videos utilizing spatial-temporal information. BMC Med Imaging 2020;20(1):1−10.

[20] Zhang J, Wang G, Xie H, Zhang S, Huang N, Zhang S, et al. Weakly supervised vessel segmentation in X-ray angiograms by self-paced learning from noisy labels with suggestive annotation. Neurocomputing 2020;417:114−27.

[21] Qin B, Jin M, Hao D, Lv Y, Liu Q, Zhu Y, et al. Accurate vessel extraction via tensor completion of background layer in X-ray coronary angiograms. Pattern Recognit 2019;87:38−54.

[22] Kirbas C, Quek F. A review of vessel extraction techniques and algorithms. ACM Comput Surv (CSUR) 2004;36(2):81−121.

[23] Lesage D, Angelini ED, Bloch I, Funka-Lea G. A review of 3D vessel lumen segmentation techniques: models, features and extraction schemes. Med Image Anal 2009;13(6):819−45.

[24] Moccia S, De Momi E, El Hadji S, Mattos LS. Blood vessel segmentation algorithms-review of methods, datasets and evaluation metrics. Comput Methods Prog Biomed 2018;158:71−91.

[25] Zhao F, Chen Y, Hou Y, He X. Segmentation of blood vessels using rule-based and machine-learning-based methods: a review. Multimed Syst 2019;25(2):109−18.

[26] Mookiah MRK, Hogg S, MacGillivray TJ, Prathiba V, Pradeepa R, Mohan V, et al. A Review of machine learning methods for retinal blood vessel segmentation and artery/vein classification. Med Image Anal 2020;68:101905.

[27] Jia D, Zhuang X. Learning-based algorithms for vessel tracking: a review. Computerized Med Imaging Graph 2021;89:101840.

[28] Çimen S, Gooya A, Grass M, Frangi AF. Reconstruction of coronary arteries from X-ray angiography: a review. Med Image Anal 2016;32:46−68.

[29] Kawabe M, Ohnishi T, Nakano K, Kato H, Ooka Y, Haneishi H. Vascular roadmap generation by registration and blending of multiple enhanced X-ray angiograms. IEEE Access 2021;9:36356−67.

[30] Qin B, Shen Z, Zhou Z, Zhou J, Lv Y. Structure matching driven by joint-saliency-structure adaptive kernel regression. Appl Soft Comput 2016;46:851−67.

[31] Qin B, Shen Z, Fu Z, Zhou Z, Lv Y, Bao J. Joint-saliency structure adaptive kernel regression with adaptive-scale kernels for deformable registration of challenging images. IEEE Access 2017;6:330−43.

[32] Smets BMN, Portegies J, St-Onge E, Duits R. Total variation and mean curvature PDEs on the homogeneous space of positions and orientations. J Math Imaging Vis 2021;63:237−62.

[33] Wang C, Oda M, Hayashi Y, Yoshino Y, Yamamoto T, Frangi AF, et al. Tensor-cut: a tensor-based graph-cut blood vessel segmentation method and its application to renal artery segmentation. Med Image Anal 2020;60:101623.

[34] Zhang W, Wang X, Chen J, You W. A new hybrid level set approach. IEEE Trans Image Process 2020;29:7032−44.

[35] Liu X, Hou F, Qin H, Hao A. Robust optimization-based coronary artery labeling from X-ray angiograms. IEEE J Biomed Health Inform 2016;20(6):1608−20.

[36] Chen D, Zhang J, Cohen LD. Minimal paths for tubular structure segmentation with coherence penalty and adaptive anisotropy. IEEE Trans Image Process 2019;28(3):1271−84.

[37] Fang H, Ai D, Cong W, Yang S, Zhu J, Huang Y, et al. Topology optimization using multiple-possibility fusion for vasculature extraction. IEEE Trans Circuits Syst Video Technol 2020; 30(2):442−56.

[38] Yang G, Lv T, Shen Y, Li S, Yang J, Chen Y, et al. Vessel structure extraction using constrained minimal path propagation. Artif Intell Med 2020;105:101846.

[39] Liu M, Chen W, Wang C, Peng H. A multiscale ray-shooting model for termination detection of tree-like structures in biomedical images. IEEE Trans Med Imaging 2020;38(8):1923−34.

[40] Huang Z, Zhang Y, Li Q, Zhang T, Sang N. Spatially adaptive denoising for X-ray cardiovascular angiogram images. Biomed Signal Process Control 2018;40:131−9.

[41] Hariharan SG, Strobel N, Kaethner C, et al. Data-driven estimation of noise variance stabilization parameters for low-dose x-ray images. Phys Med Biol 2020;65(22):225027.

[42] Fazlali HR, Karimi N, Soroushmehr SMR, Shirani S, Nallamothu BK, Ward KR, et al. Vessel segmentation and catheter detection in X-ray angiograms using superpixels. Med Biol Eng Comput 2018;56(9):1515−30.

[43] Lv H, Fu S, Zhang C, Liu X. Non-local weighted fuzzy energy-based active contour model with level set evolution starting with a constant function. IET Image Process 2019;13(7):1115−23.

[44] Mei K, Hu B, Fei B, Qin B. Phase asymmetry ultrasound despeckling with fractional anisotropic diffusion and total variation. IEEE Trans Image Process 2020,29.2845−59.

[45] Shukla AK, Pandey RK, Pachori RB. A fractional filter based efficient algorithm for retinal blood vessel segmentation. Biomed Signal Process Control 2020;59:101883.

[46] Kovesi P. Image features from phase congruency. Videre: J Comput Vis Research 1999;1(3):1−26.

[47] Zhao Y, Zheng Y, Liu Y, Zhao Y, Luo L, Yang S, et al. Automatic 2-D/3-D vessel enhancement in multiple modality images using a weighted symmetry filter. IEEE Trans Med Imaging 2018; 37(2).438−50.

[48] Reisenhofer R, King EJ. Edge, ridge, and blob detection with symmetric molecules. SIAM J Imaging Sci 2019;12(4):1585−626.

[49] Tajbakhsh N, Jeyaseelan L, Li Q, Chiang JN, Wu Z, Ding X. Embracing imperfect datasets: a review of deep learning solutions for medical image segmentation. Med Image Anal 2020;63:101693.

[50] Minaee S, Boykov YY, Porikli F, Plaza AJ, Kehtarnavaz N, Terzopoulos D. Image segmentation using deep learning: a survey. IEEE Trans Pattern Anal Mach Intell 2021.

[51] Zhao Q, Meng D, Xu Z, Zuo W, Zhang L. Robust principal component analysis with complex noise[C]//International conference on machine learning. PMLR 2014;55−63.

[52] Bouwmans T, Sobral A, Javed S, Jung SK, Zahzah EH. Decomposition into low-rank plus additive matrices for background/foreground separation: a review for a comparative evaluation with a large-scale dataset. Comput Sci Rev 2017;23:1−71.

[53] Lin Z, Chen M, Ma Y The augmented lagrange multiplier method for exact recovery of corrupted low-rank matrices. *arXiv:1009.5055*; 2010.

[54] Ren Z, Chia LT, Rajan D, Gao S Background subtraction via coherent trajectory decomposition. In: Proceedings of the twenty-first ACM international conference on multimedia; 2013, pp. 545−548.

[55] Goldstein T, Osher S. The split Bregman method for L1-regularized problems. SIAM J Imaging Sci 2009;2(2):323−43.

[56] Gao Z, Cheong LF, Wang YX. Block-sparse RPCA for salient motion detection. IEEE Trans Pattern Anal Mach Intel 2014;36(10):1975−87.

[57] Zhou X, Yang C, Yu W. Moving object detection by detecting contiguous outliers in the low-rank representation. IEEE Trans Pattern Anal Mach Intel 2012;35(3):597−610.

[58] Lin Z., Wei S. A block Lanczos with warm start technique for accelerating nuclear norm minimization algorithms. arXiv preprint arXiv:1012.0365, 2010.

[59] Rodriguez P., Wohlberg B. Fast principal component pursuit via alternating minimization. 2013 IEEE International Conference on Image Processing. IEEE, 2013;69-73.

[60] Zhou T., Tao D. Godec: Randomized low-rank & sparse matrix decomposition in noisy case. Proceedings of the 28th International Conference on Machine Learning, ICML 2011.

[61] Becker SR, Candès EJ, Grant MC. Templates for convex cone problems with applications to sparse signal recovery. Math Program Comput 2011;3(3):165.

[62] Wang N., Yao T., Wang J., et al. A probabilistic approach to robust matrix factorization. European Conference on Computer Vision. Springer, Berlin, Heidelberg, 2012:126-139.

[63] Xian Z, Wang X, Yan S, Yang D, Chen J, Peng C. Main coronary vessel segmentation using deep learning in smart medical. Math Probl Eng 2020;2020:8858344.

[64] Yang S, Kweon J, Roh JH, Lee JH, Kang H, Park LJ, et al. Deep learning segmentation of major vessels in X-ray coronary angiography. Sci Rep 2019;9(1):1−11.

[65] Jun TJ, Kweon J, Kim YH, Kim D. T-net: nested encoder−decoder architecture for the main vessel segmentation in coronary angiography. Neural Netw 2020;128:216−33.

[66] Liu L, Cheng J, Quan Q, Wu FX, Wang YP, Wang J. A survey on U-shaped networks in medical image segmentations. Neurocomputing 2020;409:244−58.

[67] Ronneberger O, Fischer P, Brox T U-net: convolutional networks for biomedical image segmentation. In: Proceedings of the international conference on medical image computing and computer-assisted intervention. Cham: Springer; 2015, pp. 234−241.

[68] He K, Zhang X, Ren S, Sun J. Deep residual learning for image recognition. In: Proceedings of the IEEE conference on computer vision and pattern recognition; 2016, pp. 770−778.

[69] Zagoruyko S, Komodakis N Wide residual networks. *arXiv:1605.07146*; 2016.

[70] Wang W, Lai Q, Fu H, et al. Salient object detection in the deep learning era: an in-depth survey. IEEE Trans Pattern Anal Mach Intell 2021. Available from: https://doi.org/10.1109/TPAMI.2021.3051099.

[71] Liu GH, Yang JY, Li ZY. Content-based image retrieval using computational visual attention model. Pattern Recognit 2015;48(8):2554−66.

[72] Qin B, Gu Z, Sun X, Lv Y. Registration of images with outliers using joint saliency map. IEEE Signal Process Lett 2010;17(1):91−4.

[73] Gu Z, Qin B. Nonrigid registration of brain tumor resection MR images based on joint saliency map and keypoint clustering. Sensors 2009;9(12):10270−90.

[74] Ou Y, Sotiras A, Paragios N, Davatzikos C. DRAMMS: deformable registration via attribute matching and mutual-saliency weighting. Med Image Anal 2011;15(4):622−39.

[75] Li H, Ngan KN. A co-saliency model of image pairs. IEEE Trans Image Process 2011; 20(12):3365−75.

[76] Gong X, Liu X, Li Y, Li H. A novel co-attention computation block for deep learning based image co-segmentation. Image Vis Comput 2020;101:103973.

[77] Wang W, Shen J, Yang R, Porikli F. Saliency-aware video object segmentation. IEEE Trans Pattern Anal Mach Intell 2018;40(1):20−33.

[78] Johnson JM, Khoshgoftaar TM. Survey on deep learning with class imbalance. J Big Data 2019;6 (1):1−54.

[79] Ma J, Chen J, Ng M, Huang R, Li Y, Li C, et al. Loss Odyssey in medical image segmentation. Med Image Anal 2021;71:102035.

[80] Kervadec H, Bouchtiba J, Desrosiers C, et al. Boundary loss for highly unbalanced segmentation. Med Image Anal 2021;67:101851.

[81] Coye T A novel retinal blood vessel segmentation algorithm for fundus images. MATLAB Cent File Exch (Jan 2017); 2017.

[82] Kerkeni A, Benabdallah A, Manzanera A, Bedoui MH. A coronary artery segmentation method based on multiscale analysis and region growing. Computerized Med Imaging Graph 2016;48:49—61.

[83] Liskowski P, Krawiec K. Segmenting retinal blood vessels with deep neural networks. IEEE Trans Med Imaging 2016;35(11):2369—80.

[84] Hu J, Wang H, Gao S, Bao M, Liu T, Wang Y, et al. S-unet: a bridge-style u-net framework with a saliency mechanism for retinal vessel segmentation. IEEE Access 2019;7:174167—77.

[85] Ambrosini P, Ruijters D, Niessen WJ, Moelker A, van Walsum T Fully automatic and real-time catheter segmentation in X-ray fluoroscopy. In: Proceedings of the international conference on medical image computing and computer-assisted intervention. Cham: Springer; 2017, pp. 577—585.

[86] Guo S, Wang K, Kang H, Zhang Y, Gao Y, Li T. BTS-DSN: deeply supervised neural network with short connections for retinal vessel segmentation. Int J Med Inform 2019;126:105—13.

[87] Clough J.R., Byrne N., Oksuz I., et al. A topological loss function for deep-learning based image segmentation using persistent homology. IEEE Trans Pattern Anal Mach Intel 2021. Preprint.

[88] Song Q, Ge H, Caverlee J, Hu X. Tensor completion algorithms in big data analytics. ACM Trans Knowl Discovery Data (TKDD) 2019;13(1):1—48.

[89] Kolda TG, Bader BW. Tensor decompositions and applications. SIAM review 2009;51 (3):455—500.

[90] Panagakis Y, Kossaifi J, Chrysos GG, et al. Tensor Methods in Computer Vision and Deep Learning. Proc IEEE 2021;109(5):863—90.

[91] Ely G, Aeron S, Hao N, Kilmer ME. 5D and 4D pre-stack seismic data completion using tensor nuclear norm (TNN). In: SEG technical program expanded abstracts 2013. Society of Exploration Geophysicists; 2013, pp. 3639—3644.

[92] Kilmer ME, Braman K, Hao N, Hoover RC. Third-order tensors as operators on matrices: A theoretical and computational framework with applications in imaging. SIAM J Matrix Anal Appl 2013,34(1).148—72.

[93] Hu W, Tao D, Zhang W, Xie Y, Yang Y. The twist tensor nuclear norm for video completion. IEEE Trans Neural Netw Learn Syst 2017;28(12):2961—73.

[94] Lu C, Feng J, Chen Y, Liu W, Lin Z, Yan S. Tensor robust principal component analysis with a new tensor nuclear norm. IEEE Trans Pattern Anal Mach Intell 2020;42(4):925—38.

[95] Boyd S, Parikh N, Chu E. Distributed optimization and statistical learning via the alternating direction method of multipliers. Now Publishers Inc.; 2011.

[96] Baka N, Metz CT, Schultz CJ, van Geuns RJ, Niessen WJ, van Walsum T. Oriented Gaussian mixture models for nonrigid 2D/3D coronary artery registration. IEEE Trans Med imaging 2014, 33(5):1023—34.

[97] Wang N, Yao T, Wang J, Yeung DY A probabilistic approach to robust matrix factorization. In: European conference on computer vision. Berlin, Heidelberg: Springer; 2012, pp. 126—139.

[98] Cherapanamjeri Y., Gupta K., Jain P. Nearly optimal robust matrix completion. In: International conference on machine learning. PMLR; 2017, pp. 797—805.

[99] Xu Y, Yin W, Wen Z, Zhang Y. An alternating direction algorithm for matrix completion with nonnegative factors. Front Math China 2012;7(2):365—84.

[100] Ngo TT, Saad Y Scaled gradients on grassmann manifolds for matrix completion. In: NIPS 2012; 2012, pp. 1412—1420.

[101] Liu J, Musialski P, Wonka P, Ye J. Tensor completion for estimating missing values in visual data. IEEE Trans Pattern Anal Mach Intell 2013;35(1):208—20.

[102] Zhang Z, Ely G, Aeron S, Hao N, Kilmer M Novel methods for multilinear data completion and de-noising based on tensor-SVD. In: Proceedings of the IEEE conference on computer vision and pattern recognition; 2014, pp. 3842—3849.

[103] Sobral A, Bouwmans T, Zahzah E. Lrslibrary: low-rank and sparse tools for background modeling and subtraction in videos. Robust low-rank and sparse matrix decomposition: applications in image and video processing. CRC Press, Taylor and Francis Group; 2016.

[104] Sobral A, hadi Zahzah E. Matrix and tensor completion algorithms for background model initialization: a comparative evaluation. Pattern Recognit Lett 2017;96:22—33.

CHAPTER 5

Assessing coronary artery disease using coronary computed tomography angiography

Mina M. Benjamin, Marco Shaker and Mark G. Rabbat
Department of Cardiology, Loyola University Medical Center, Maywood, IL, United States

5.1 Introduction

Coronary artery disease (CAD) accounts for approximately one-third to one-half of the total cases of cardiovascular disease, with ischemic heart disease as the number one cause of death in adults from both low- and high-income countries [1,2]. Coronary computed tomography angiography (CCTA) has been increasingly used as an imaging modality for diagnosing CAD and as a first-line test in many scenarios. Technological advances in CCTA acquisition and processing have allowed coronary artery assessment at a low dose of radiation and high accuracy. CCTA also has prognostic implications for patient management. CCTA stands out among other diagnostic modalities with an excellent negative predictive value and an ability to image various stages of atherosclerosis.

5.1.1 The utility of CCTA in Coronary artery disease diagnosis and prognostication

CCTA represents a widely available and well tolerated examination that visualizes the presence and extent of CAD noninvasively both in the acute and nonacute settings. CCTA has the highest diagnostic accuracy for the detection of obstructive CAD in major epicardial vessels as detected by invasive coronary angiography because of its high sensitivity and phenomenally low rate of false negatives. CCTA accuracy has markedly increased over time. Earlier studies showed high sensitivity (86%−100%) and negative predictive value (93%−100%) for detection of significant stenosis compared to invasive coronary angiography, with lower specificity and positive predictive values (50%−90%) [3]. A pooled study of different reports showed sensitivity, specificity, negative predictive value, and positive predictive value of 96%, 91%, 96%, and 91%, respectively, for the 64 slice scanner [4]. Another *meta*-analysis reported a mean sensitivity of 93% and specificity of 96% for stenosis detection by 64-slice CT on a per-segment basis. On a per-patient basis, sensitivity was as high as 99% [5]. CCTA has

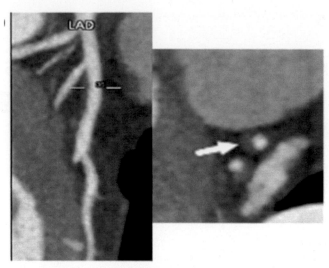

Figure 5.1 Noncalcified plaque and positive remodeling of the midleft anterior descending artery (arrow).

shown an excellent correlation with coronary intravascular ultrasound (IVUS) in several studies comparing the two modalities measurements of minimal lumen area and plaque volume, in addition to identifying adverse plaque characteristics such as positive remodeling, spotty calcifications, and low attenuation [6,7] (Fig. 5.1). In a *meta*-analysis including 946 patients, CCTA had an excellent predictive value when compared to IVUS, with a sensitivity of 90% and specificity of 92%. Plaque area and volume were the same between IVUS and CCTA. CCTA overestimated the lumen area by $0.46\,\mathrm{mm}^2$, likely due to partial volume effects [8]. Another *meta*-analysis included 1360 patients from 42 studies that found no significant differences between CCTA and IVUS measurements of the vessel lumen cross-sectional area, plaque area and volume, or percentage of area stenosis. The sensitivity and specificity of CCTA compared to IVUS were 93% and 92%, respectively [9]. The emerging role of CCTA has been acknowledged by the 2019 Guidelines of the European Society of Cardiology recommending the use of CT as a first-line tool for the evaluation of patients with stable chest pain with a class I, level of evidence B recommendation.

CCTA can also be of utility following invasive coronary angiography to differentiate between true right coronary artery or left main artery lesions versus spasms during catheterization. CCTA can also be used for defining bypass grafts not identified during the invasive coronary angiogram [10].

CCTA also has an important prognostication value for identifying patients at low risk for future major adverse cardiovascular events [11–14]. The CONFIRM (Coronary CT Angiography Evaluation For Clinical Outcomes: an International

Multicenter Registry) registry was a large international multicenter study, which included 14,064 patients at 12 centers and showed that CCTA predicts all-cause mortality. The absence of CAD by CCTA was associated with a low rate of incident death (annualized death rate: 0.28%) [15].

Another utility of the noncontrast portion of a CCTA is the ability to calculate a coronary artery calcium (CAC) score. Also known as an Agatston score, a CAC score can be used to risk-stratify patients for future development of cardiac events. CAC scores are useful in identifying asymptomatic patients where more intensive preventative treatment regimens would be appropriate. The Multimodality Appropriate Use Criteria for the Detection of Stable Ischemic Heart Disease guidelines from the American College of Cardiology and American Heart Association (ACC/AHA) suggested that CAC scoring may be appropriate in select patients who are asymptomatic but at intermediate risk for CAD. CAC scoring alone is rarely appropriate in symptomatic patients [16].

5.2 Patient selection

The ideal patient for CCTA would have an intermediate pretest probability (10%—90%) for significant CAD (as defined by the Diamond–Forrester score) without established CAD or in those with equivocal or nondiagnostic functional test results [17,18]. CCTA is also appropriate as the initial test in patients without known CAD who present with chest pain or possible acute coronary syndrome when highly sensitive troponin assay testing and the clinical evaluation cannot confidently exclude acute coronary syndrome [18]. CCTA should not be performed in patients who are unstable with ongoing chest pain who have acute coronary syndrome since transporting them is unsafe and CT suites are generally not equipped to deal with these patients [19,20]. CCTA can also be appropriate as an alternative to stress testing or invasive coronary angiography in selected patients without previously known CAD who are diagnosed with non-ST-elevation acute coronary syndrome with clinically low-risk presentation (e.g., absence of heart failure, hemodynamic or electrical instability, or refractory ischemic symptoms), and in whom there is a clinician or patient desire to avoid invasive coronary angiography [21,22].

CCTA is generally not recommended in asymptomatic patients. CCTA is also not typically recommended as a first-line test in patients with prior coronary artery revascularization. For patients with prior percutaneous coronary intervention, stent material often results in "blooming" on CCTA images, a phenomenon that can obscure a portion of the coronary lumen within the stent and limit diagnostic accuracy. Patients with stents also often have extensive coronary calcification that can negatively impact diagnostic accuracy [23]. However, there may be clinical scenarios where it is useful to guide patient management. CCTA is highly accurate for the evaluation of bypass graft patency and is considered an appropriate study when the patency of bypass graft conduits is the primary clinical question [24].

5.2.1 Other utilities of computed tomography angiography, that is, other than in coronary artery disease

As mentioned earlier, CCTA protocols typically involve an initial noncontrast, low-radiation dose phase. This noncontrast portion of the study can yield high-quality data about cardiac anatomical structures that may not be as adequately visualized with other noninvasive imaging modalities, for example, trans-thoracic echocardiography or cardiac magnetic resonance imaging, including valvular abnormalities [25–27]. Functional assessment is also feasible with every retrospectively acquired ECG-gated CCTA. Dedicated postprocessing tools are needed for image analysis. Despite the inferior temporal resolution of CCT, previous studies have shown a close correlation between end-diastolic, end-systolic LV volume, ejection fraction, and regional wall motion abnormalities obtained by multislice CCT compared to two-dimensional echocardiography [28].

CCT can identify intracavitary thrombi. In clinical practice, transesophageal echocardiography is recommended for this purpose, but it is an invasive procedure with a risk of bleeding and esophageal perforation [29]. Recent meta-analyses have shown a high sensitivity of CCTA in detecting thrombi in the left ventricle [30], and in the left atrial appendage [31] even in the presence of a left atrial appendage occluder device [32].

CCTA can also be applied toward the diagnosis of coronary anomalies. Professional guidelines from the ACC/AHA released in 2018 listed CCTA as a class I indication for initial screening of adult patients with suspected congenital anomalous coronary arteries of ectopic origin [33]. CCTA is also of utility in patients with congenital cardiac anomalies and is a class I indication study in patients with several congenital anomalies including suspected Williams syndrome, significant coarctation of the aorta, supravalvular aortic stenosis, and anomalous pulmonary venous return [33].

5.2.2 CCTA technique and quality factors

CCTA technique has developed significantly over the last 20 years. As mentioned above, CCTA protocols typically involve an initial noncontrast, low-radiation dose phase for the delineation of cardiac structures and calculation of the CAC. A bolus dose of iodinated contrast (typically 50–120 mL) is administered intravenously. Nitroglycerin, typically sublingual tablet or spray is given approximately 5 minutes prior to the examination to dilate the coronary arteries and facilitate assessment of luminal narrowing. Patients should be screened for compliance to breath-hold and heart rate stability. Depending on the temporal resolution of the scanner, patients with irregular heart rate or a rate above a certain limit (typically 65 beats/min) are premedicated with beta-blockers both to improve image quality and to reduce radiation exposure. Calcium channel blockers can also be used. Ivabradine, a selective and specific inhibitor of the I_f current, which is one of the most important ionic currents for regulating pacemaker activity in the sinoatrial node, is an alternative drug that has been validated as an alternative to beta-blockers for reducing the heart rate prior to CCTA. It can be used in conjunction with beta-blockers or exclusively in patients with baseline systolic blood pressure < 100−110 mmHg, severe left ventricular dysfunction, peripheral vascular disease, or severe obstructive airway disease [34−38].

The acquisition of a CCTA is performed using ECG-gating either in a retrospective or prospective way [39]. The retrospectively ECG-gated approach captures the heart throughout the whole cardiac cycle, acquiring images at multiple cardiac phases and, thus delivering high-quality images even at high heart rates, yet at increased radiation exposure compared to prospective modes. For prospectively acquired ECG-gated scans, sequential and high-pitch helical techniques are available, which are chosen depending on heart rate and rhythm, as well as patient habitus. The sequential mode acquires images of different anatomic regions during preselected cardiac phases, the so-called "step-and-shoot" method; whereas high-pitch helical scans cover the entire heart with a single gantry rotation, so that the image is obtained in a single cardiac cycle. The latter is associated with a drastic dose reduction to an average effective dose of 2.2 milliSievert (mSv) [40,41]; scans with a dose less than 1 mSv have also been shown to be feasible [42,43].

5.3 Spatial resolution

Spatial resolution is defined as the ability to distinguish two neighboring structures as separated. Spatial frequency with the unit of "line pairs per centimeter" is used for object dimension measurement. Spatial resolution improved from 0.5 with a 64-slice CT to 0.4 mm with a 128-slice scanner, until 0.35 mm in a 320-slice CT scanner and 0.17 mm in 640-slice CT [44]. A basic requirement for adequate multiplanar reconstruction is that the resolution is isotropic meaning that the resolution is equal in all directions. Increasing the number of detector rows allows for covering the whole heart in a single heart beat without moving the CT table; however, progressive deformation of the reconstructed object is an issue in the peripheral regions of the field of view. Correction algorithms have been developed to mitigate this issue through the years [44].

Detectors must have several features to deliver good diagnostic image quality: accuracy, dynamic range, stability, uniformity, speed of response, resolution, geometric efficiency, detector quantum efficiency, and cross-talk. Filtering kernels can affect spatial resolution. Convolution filters are applied to reduce the blurring that occurs with back projection alone. Each convolution kernel uses the value of nearby pixels to create a filtered profile. There are different types of kernel filters that can be roughly classified as standard, smooth, and sharp. The type of filter determines spatial resolution and noise [45]. Iterative reconstruction starts from the images obtained from the filtered back projection, generates new projection data that are compared to the original ones, then noise corrections are made. This process is repeated (i.e., iterated) several times. Iterative reconstruction has been shown to have a great utility in reducing radiation dose while preserving good image quality [46,47].

5.4 Temporal resolution

Temporal resolution is the time needed to acquire the data to generate an image. High temporal resolution is needed for CCTA scans to reduce respiratory motion artifacts and to overcome cardiac motion artifacts. Temporal resolution is affected by the gantry rotation speed, image reconstruction (i.e., prospective vs retrospective triggering), pitch and postprocessing algorithm. Multisegment reconstruction techniques have been introduced where some portions of projections from different heartbeats are used; these data are then collected to compose a full reconstruction, reaching a higher temporal resolution [44]. Another advancement came with the introduction of Dual Source CT which allowed an instant doubling of temporal resolution. Newer generations of the Dual Source CT have allowed a high-pitch single-heartbeat acquisition with the scan of the whole heart volume in a single cardiac cycle [47].

The pitch is another element to be considered; it corresponds to the speed of motion of the CT table per rotation of the gantry, divided by the amplitude of the detectors. A typical CCT pitch is between 0.2 and 0.4 depending on the heart rate of the patient during the scan. Cardiac imaging in spiral mode requires low pitch because high-quality 3D images with minimal artifacts require data overlap [48]. A high pitch is not possible when using dual-source CT techniques, which are defined as acquisitions of two separate datasets utilizing two different X-ray spectra energies [e.g., low and high kilovoltage peak (kVp) spectra]. It has been shown to enhance diagnostic accuracy, provide added value for more comprehensive diagnosis, improve image quality, and/or reduce both radiation and contrast media requirements [47].

5.5 Technical issues in specific patient subgroups

As mentioned above, the amount of radiation needed has decreased significantly with technical advances but may remain an issue in individuals with a higher body mass index (BMI). Patients with a high BMI or with fat predominance in the upper portion of the body may require higher values of kV and mA to obtain diagnostic images. While there is a linear relationship between the dose delivered to the patient and the tube current (mA), tube voltage (kVp) has an exponential relationship to the radiation exposure [49]. Automatic exposure control is a technology that adapts the mA automatically according to the patient's size, allowing up to a third in radiation dose reduction. Another method for dose reduction in CCT is to decrease the tube voltage (kVp). The main disadvantage of kV reduction is the potential reduction of diagnostic accuracy and noise increase. This effect can be mitigated by an increased mA delivery which increases tube power to an adequate level with a significant reduction of radiation dose [50].

Coronary calcification is a major factor that influences the rate of evaluable arteries by CCTA and its diagnostic accuracy resulting in a considerable rate of false-positive studies [51]. CORE-64 study involved 371 patients who underwent CCTA and cardiac angiography for detection of obstructive CAD. The diagnostic accuracy of CCTA was reduced in patients with calcium scores of >600 versus those with scores <600 Agatston units [3]. Although calcification clearly makes coronary evaluation more difficult, even pronounced calcifications often do not hinder the evaluation of a coronary segment if no motion artifacts are present. However, the presence of motion artifacts makes calcified segments challenging to evaluate with confidence [52].

Another issue is in patients with irregular rhythms, most commonly atrial fibrillation. Only a few studies have investigated the diagnostic accuracy of CCTA in these patient subgroups. The diagnostic accuracy of CCTA has been typically suboptimal, particularly when high heart rate coexists with high variability [53,54]. However, with the recent advances in CCTA hardware and software, sensitivity and specificity for detection of CAD have been reported similar to in patients with no arrhythmias [55,56].

5.5.1 The future of CCTA

The primary focus of recent advances has been the addition of a physiologic assessment either by CT myocardial perfusion imaging (CTP) or by measuring the degree of flow limitation, that is, CT-derived fractional flow reserve (FFR$_{CT}$).

5.5.1.1 Computed tomography perfusion imaging

A perfusion study can be done using vasodilation-inducing drugs as adenosine, dipyridamole, or regadenoson. The premise of a vasodilator study is creating preferential vasodilation by increasing myocardial blood flow during stress three to five times that of resting myocardial blood flow and in case of coronary stenosis, the blood will preferentially supply the normal vessel over the stenosed vessels [57]. CT Perfusion (CTP) was first used to detect perfusion defects during rest but has evolved to detect perfusion during stress with the recent advances in technology including the use of multidetectors with high temporal resolution, and less motion artifact [58–63]. Alternative protocols include either rest followed by stress perfusion or stress perfusion first followed by rest. It could be dynamic or static perfusion. The static depends on obtaining data from the left ventricle at the peak myocardial enhancement at the first arterial pass. The images obtained during rest can be used to assess the coronaries. Images depend on the comparison between the hypodense and normal myocardium. The limitation of this technique is it can miss the perfusion defects if the ischemia is balanced among the three vessels [64]. Dynamic perfusion depends on imaging of the left ventricular myocardium overtime after the contrast bolus injection to create myocardial time attenuation curves. It can be done with the table in the stationary position with a wide detector CT scanner (i.e., 320 slice CT) or axial shuttle mode with dual-source CT scanners [65]. Quantitative software for myocardial perfusion has been developed as well [63]. In a substudy of the CORE320 (Coronary Artery Evaluation Using 320-row Multidetector Computed Tomography Angiography and Myocardial Perfusion) trial which included 381 patients who underwent both CTA-CTP and SPECT myocardial perfusion imaging preceding invasive coronary angiography, the prevalence of flow-limiting CAD defined by invasive coronary angiography with an associated SPECT defect was only 45% and 23% in males and females, respectively. Patient-based diagnostic accuracy defined by the area under the receiver operating curve for detecting flow-limiting CAD was improved by CTA-CTP versus CTA alone from 0.83 to 0.92 in females and from 0.82 to 0.84 in males [66].

The main limitations of dynamic CTP include heterogeneity of normal perfusion values, underestimation of perfusion value compared to PET and CMR in addition to significantly higher radiation doses needed. Dynamic and static radiation doses are 5—15 and 2—9 mSv, respectively [67—71].

5.5.1.2 Viability and fibrosis

Delayed enhancement imaging (performed 5—10 minutes after contrast injection) with CCT is possible. The aim of this technique is viability assessment (i.e., the detection of necrosis, fibrosis, and microvascular obstruction). An infarcted territory can be characterized based on hyper- and hypoenhancement on delayed enhancement images signaling an infarcted territory or microvascular obstruction. In the case of hyperenhancement in acute infarction, membrane dysfunction lets iodine molecules pass into the intracellular space where contrast accumulates. Hyperenhancement in scar tissue, however, is believed to be caused by an increase of the intercellular space due to cell necrosis. Microvascular obstruction, on the other hand, appears as hypoattenuation due to blockage of capillaries caused by cell debris despite restored flow [72].

While focal myocardial scar tissue can be reliably detected on CT images, diffuse myocardial fibrosis has mainly been quantified using MRI [73]. The idea behind both techniques is the calculation of the extracellular volume fraction of the myocardium, which is increased in myocardial fibrosis and associated with various cardiomyopathies and heart failure [74]. For the calculation of ECV, HU attenuation values in the myocardium and blood pool were measured in pre- and postcontrast images, and the ratio of these changes (change in myocardial attenuation/change in blood pool attenuation) was set in relation with the patient's hematocrit level. CT-obtained extracellular volume values demonstrated a good correlation with MRI measures ($r = 0.82$) and were elevated in patients with heart failure [74]. Contrast-enhanced dual-energy CT is also being evaluated for the quantification of myocardial fibrosis by measuring overlay attenuation values of the myocardium and blood pool on iodine attenuation maps. Again, the results were comparable with MRI as the reference standard [75].

5.5.1.3 CCTA-derived FFR (FFR$_{CT}$)

The Achilles heel of CCTA alone is not being able to define the hemodynamic significance of coronary lesions [76]. Invasive fractional flow reserve (FFR) measures the pressures proximal to (aortic pressure) and distal to (guidewire pressure) stenotic lesions at maximal flow and creates a pressure ratio, representing the proportion of flow across that stenosis. Identifying patients with both anatomically and functionally significant CAD before catheterization using noninvasive testing could dramatically reduce the need for unnecessary invasive and downstream testing. FFR$_{CT}$ (HeartFlow, Redwood City, CA) is a technology whereby machine learning has been utilized to construct patient-specific models of blood flow from CCTA images allowing for a noninvasively derived FFR (Fig. 5.2) [77,78]. The technology uses deep learning algorithms to extract lumen boundaries from CCTA using an approach validated against OCT, and it creates a patient specific physiologic model based on form function principles and computational fluid dynamic analysis to compute the blood flow solution [79,80].

Several recent reports have examined the relationship between various CCTA-derived plaque characteristics and the ability to predict ischemia, as measured by various techniques including myocardial perfusion and FFR [81−83]. The NXT (Analysis of Coronary Blood Flow Using CT Angiography: Next Steps) trial demonstrated that the diagnostic accuracy of FFR$_{CT}$ [AUC: 0.90; 95% confidence interval (CI), 0.87−0.94] was significantly greater than that of CCTA alone (0.81; 95% CI, 0.76−0.87).[84] The PACIFIC (Prospective Comparison of Cardiac PET/CT, SPECT/CT Perfusion Imaging and CCTA With Invasive Coronary Angiography) study compared the diagnostic accuracy of various modalities using invasive 3-vessel FFR as the gold standard and found that the AUC on a per-vessel basis was significantly greater for FFR$_{CT}$ (0.94) compared to CCTA (0.83), SPECT (0.70), and PET (0.87) ($P < .001$ for all) [85]. FFR$_{CT}$ is being investigated as a tool in clinical decision-making. Rabbat et al. reported the safe deferral of invasive coronary angiography in patients with stable CAD using a diagnostic strategy of FFR$_{CT}$ [86]. Ongoing prospective, pragmatic, randomized clinical trials such as PRECISE (Prospective Randomized Trial of the Optimal Evaluation of Cardiac Symptoms and Revascularization) will shed light on the role of using FFR$_{CT}$ as a diagnostic strategy for patients with suspected CAD. FFR$_{CT}$ can also be used for virtual planning of percutaneous coronary interventions. HeartFlow Planner has been approved by the Food and Drug

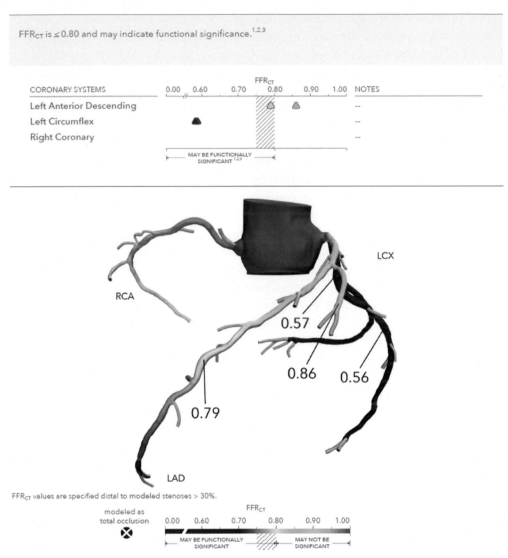

Figure 5.2 Example of FFR$_{CT}$ report showing no flow-limiting disease in the right coronary, border-line flow-limiting disease in the left anterior descending (FFR$_{CT}$ = 0.79), and flow-limiting disease in the circumflex (FFR$_{CT}$ = 0.56) coronary arteries. There is a lesion in the first diagonal artery that is not flow-limiting (FFR$_{CT}$ = 0.86). The cutoff for normal FFR$_{CT}$ is 0.8 with borderline or grey zone values between 0.75 and 0.8.

Administration as a real–time virtual modeling tool for CAD intervention. HeartFlow Planner provides luminal remodeling using computer software enabling recalculation of the FFR after virtual removal of coronary artery stenoses and prediction of post-PCI FFR$_{CT}$ [87,88].

5.6 Clinical trials comparing CCTA to other modalities

Landmark trials, including the Prospective Multicenter Imaging Study for Evaluation of chest pain (PROMISE) and Scottish Computed Tomography of the Heart (SCOT-HEART), have contributed to a better understanding of how CCTA may play a role in more efficient management and improved health outcomes in patients with suspected CAD.

The PROMISE trial recruited 10,003 symptomatic stable outpatients who were due to undergo noninvasive investigation for suspected CAD. Participants were randomized to undergo either anatomical assessment with CCTA or functional testing with exercise electrocardiography, stress echocardiography, or radionucleotide perfusion imaging. The primary outcome of the PROMISE study was a composite of all-cause mortality, myocardial infarction, hospitalization for unstable angina, and major complications of cardiovascular procedures or diagnostic testing. At 12 months of follow-up, the risk of death or nonfatal myocardial infarction was lower in the CCTA group than in the functional imaging group [hazard ratio (HR), 0.66, 95% CI, 0.44−1.00, $P = .049$). However, at 25 months of follow-up, there was no difference in the primary outcome between the two groups (events 3.3 vs 3.0%, HR, 1.04, 95% CI, 0.83−1.29, $P = .75$). PROMISE showed that CCTA is a safe alternative to functional testing in a low-risk population with similar outcomes in both groups after 2 years of follow-up [89].

The SCOT-HEART trial randomized 4146 outpatients with suspected angina due to CAD to standard care or standard care plus CCTA. Participants were recruited from cardiology outpatient clinics. The primary endpoint of the SCOT-HEART trial was the certainty of diagnosis of angina pectoris secondary to significant CAD at 6 weeks. At 6 weeks, the diagnosis was changed in 23% of patients undergoing CCTA compared to 1% in the standard care group. CCTA improved the certainty of the diagnosis for both the presence of CAD and the diagnosis of angina due to CAD (RR 2.56 and 1.79, respectively). CCTA increased the frequency of the diagnosis of CAD (RR 1.09). At 1.7 years of follow-up, the CCTA group had a 38% lower rate of fatal and nonfatal myocardial infarction compared to the control group, but this difference did not quite reach statistical significance (HR, 0.62, $P = .0527$) [90] The overall event rate was low, similar to the PROMISE study, occurring in just 2% of participants. However, in a post hoc landmark analysis censored to the median time of treatment alteration (50 days), there was a 50% reduction in fatal and nonfatal myocardial infarction in the CCTA group (HR, 0.50, $P = 0.020$) [91]. At 5 years follow-up, the rate of the primary endpoint was lower in the CTA group than in the standard care group (2.3% vs 3.9%). Although the rates of invasive coronary angiography and coronary revascularization were higher in the CCTA group than in the standard care group in the first few months of follow-up, overall rates were similar at 5 years. More preventive therapies were initiated in patients in the CCTA group (OR 1.40), as were more anti-anginal therapies (OR 1.27). There were no significant between-group differences in the rates of cardiovascular or noncardiovascular deaths or deaths from any cause [92].

Another study assessed 3306 patients undergoing CCTA versus 2752 who underwent routine care. The incidence of acute coronary syndrome and repeated ER visits decreased significantly in CCTA arm (RR 0.26 and 0.58, respectively) compared to regular care [93]. A similar study by Foy et al. of 20,092 patients concluded that CCTA showed reduced MI but higher coronary revascularization, with no statistically significant difference for death or cardiac hospitalization [94]. CTA was also superior to functional testing as a first-line strategy in symptomatic patients with diabetes in the PROMISE trial [95].

A *meta*-analysis of four randomized controlled trials including 2567 patients presenting to the emergency department with chest pain concluded that patients with CCTA were more likely to undergo revascularization, with an OR of 1.88 with a reduced time to diagnosis by 7.28 hour and reduction of ED cost by $680 [96]. Another *meta*-analysis by Hulten et al. included 3266 patients in the ED found that CCTA had similar mortality, incidence of MI, or rehospitalization compared to usual care. The length of stay and the cost of care were decreased with CCTA [20].

5.7 Conclusion

As detailed above, with the technical advances in CCTA, it is now possible to obtain an accurate anatomic assessment of the coronary arteries with an excellent negative predictive value and prognostic information. CCTA also offers valuable information about different cardiac structures and major vessels. Patient selection and adequate preparation are key to obtaining interpretable studies. The newer technologies specifically FFR$_{CT}$ and CTP are promising of providing functional information pertaining to the degree of myocardial ischemia and the flow-limiting nature of atherosclerotic lesions, but more validation studies and some technical advances are needed before these technologies are ready for prime time.

References

[1] Benjamin EJ, et al. Heart disease and stroke statistics-2019 update: a report from the American Heart Association. Circulation 2019;139(10):e56—e528.
[2] Dai H, et al. Global, regional, and national burden of ischemic heart disease and its attributable risk factors, 1990—2017: results from the global Burden of Disease Study 2017. Eur Heart J Qual Care Clin Outcomes 2020;.
[3] Arbab-Zadeh A, et al. Diagnostic accuracy of computed tomography coronary angiography according to pre-test probability of coronary artery disease and severity of coronary arterial calcification. The

CORE-64 (Coronary Artery Evaluation Using 64-Row Multidetector Computed Tomography Angiography) International Multicenter Study. J Am Coll Cardiol 2012;59(4):379−87.

[4] Gopalakrishnan P, Wilson GT, Tak T. Accuracy of multislice computed tomography coronary angiography: a pooled estimate. Cardiol Rev 2008;16(4):189−96.

[5] Vanhoenacker PK, et al. Diagnostic performance of multidetector CT angiography for assessment of coronary artery disease: *meta*-analysis. Radiology 2007;244(2):419−28.

[6] Boogers MJ, et al. Automated quantification of coronary plaque with computed tomography: comparison with intravascular ultrasound using a dedicated registration algorithm for fusion-based quantification. Eur Heart J 2012;33(8):1007−16.

[7] Nakazato R, et al. Quantification and characterisation of coronary artery plaque volume and adverse plaque features by coronary computed tomographic angiography: a direct comparison to intravascular ultrasound. Eur Radiol 2013;23(8):2109−17.

[8] Voros S, et al. Coronary atherosclerosis imaging by coronary CT angiography: current status, correlation with intravascular interrogation and *meta*-analysis. JACC Cardiovasc Imaging 2011;4 (5):537−48.

[9] Fischer C, Hulten E, Belur P, Smith R, Voros S, Villines TC. Coronary CT angiography versus intravascular ultrasound for estimation of coronary stenosis and atherosclerotic plaque burden: a *meta*-analysis. J Cardiovasc Comput Tomogr 2013;7(4):256−66.

[10] Ilia R, Shimony A, Shalev A, Cafri C, Weinstein JM. The incremental value of coronary computerized tomography angiography following invasive coronary angiography with an emphasis on equivocal left main stenosis. Int J Cardiol 2015;201:119−20.

[11] Andreini D, et al. A long term prognostic value of coronary CT angiography in suspected coronary artery disease. JACC Cardiovasc Imaging 2012;5(7):690−701.

[12] Pundziute G, et al. Prognostic value of multislice computed tomography coronary angiography in patients with known or suspected coronary artery disease. J Am Coll Cardiol 2007;49(1):62−70.

[13] Schlett CL, et al. Prognostic value of CT angiography for major adverse cardiac events in patients with acute chest pain from the emergency department: 2-year outcomes of the ROMICAT trial. JACC Cardiovasc Imaging 2011;4(5):481−91.

[14] Chow BJ, et al. Prognostic value of 64-slice cardiac computed tomography severity of coronary artery disease, coronary atherosclerosis, and left ventricular ejection fraction. J Am Coll Cardiol 2010;55(10):1017−28.

[15] Min JK, et al. Age- and sex-related differences in all-cause mortality risk based on coronary computed tomography angiography findings results from the International Multicenter CONFIRM (Coronary CT Angiography Evaluation for Clinical Outcomes: an international multicenter registry) of 23,854 patients without known coronary artery disease. J Am Coll Cardiol 2011;58(8):849−60.

[16] Fihn SD, et al. 2014 ACC/AHA/AATS/PCNA/SCAI/STS focused update of the guideline for the diagnosis and management of patients with stable ischemic heart disease: a report of the American College of Cardiology/American Heart Association Task Force on Practice Guidelines, and the American Association for Thoracic Surgery, Preventive Cardiovascular Nurses Association, Society for Cardiovascular Angiography and Interventions, and Society of Thoracic Surgeons. J Am Coll Cardiol 2014;64(18):1929−49.

[17] Knuuti J, et al. 2019 ESC guidelines for the diagnosis and management of chronic coronary syndromes. Eur Heart J 2020;41(3):407−77.

[18] Rybicki FJ, et al. 2015 ACR/ACC/AHA/AATS/ACEP/ASNC/NASCI/SAEM/SCCT/SCMR/ SCPC/SNMMI/STR/STS appropriate utilization of cardiovascular imaging in emergency department patients with chest pain: a joint document of the American College of Radiology Appropriateness Criteria Committee and the American College of Cardiology Appropriate Use Criteria Task Force. J Am Coll Cardiol 2016;67(7):853−79.

[19] Collet JP, et al. 2020 ESC guidelines for the management of acute coronary syndromes in patients presenting without persistent ST-segment elevation. Eur Heart J 2020;42(14):1289−367.

[20] Hulten E, et al. Outcomes after coronary computed tomography angiography in the emergency department: a systematic review and *meta*-analysis of randomized, controlled trials. J Am Coll Cardiol 2013;61(8):880−92.

[21] Smulders MW, et al. Initial imaging-guided strategy versus routine care in patients with non-ST-segment elevation myocardial infarction. J Am Coll Cardiol 2019;74(20):2466—77.

[22] Linde JJ, et al. Coronary CT angiography in patients with non-ST-segment elevation acute coronary syndrome. J Am Coll Cardiol 2020;75(5):453—63.

[23] Dai T, Wang JR, Hu PF. Diagnostic performance of computed tomography angiography in the detection of coronary artery in-stent restenosis: evidence from an updated *meta*-analysis. Eur Radiol 2018;28(4):1373—82.

[24] Barbero U, et al. 64 slice-coronary computed tomography sensitivity and specificity in the evaluation of coronary artery bypass graft stenosis: a *meta*-analysis. Int J Cardiol 2016;216:52—7.

[25] Jongbloed MR, et al. Noninvasive visualization of the cardiac venous system using multislice computed tomography. J Am Coll Cardiol 2005;45(5):749—53.

[26] Klass O, et al. Quantification of aortic valve area at 256-slice computed tomography: comparison with transesophageal echocardiography and cardiac catheterization in subjects with high-grade aortic valve stenosis prior to percutaneous valve replacement. Eur J Radiol 2011;80(1):151—7.

[27] Koo HJ, et al. Cardiac computed tomography for the localization of mitral valve prolapse: scallop-by-scallop comparisons with echocardiography and intraoperative findings. Eur Heart J Cardiovasc Imaging 2019;20(5):550—7.

[28] Palazzuoli A, et al. Left ventricular remodelling and systolic function measurement with 64 multi-slice computed tomography versus second harmonic echocardiography in patients with coronary artery disease: a double blind study. Eur J Radiol 2010;73(1):82—8.

[29] January CT, et al. 2014 AHA/ACC/HRS guideline for the management of patients with atrial fibrillation: a report of the American College of Cardiology/American Heart Association Task Force on Practice Guidelines and the Heart Rhythm Society. J Am Coll Cardiol 2014;64(21):e1—e76.

[30] Singh M, Aldiwani H, Abidov A. Utilization of coronary computed tomography angiogram in evaluation of left ventricular thrombus. J Cardiovasc Comput Tomogr 2020;14(5):e82—4.

[31] Romero J, Husain SA, Kelesidis I, Sanz J, Medina HM, Garcia MJ. Detection of left atrial appendage thrombus by cardiac computed tomography in patients with atrial fibrillation: a *meta*-analysis. Circ Cardiovasc Imaging 2013;6(2):185—94.

[32] Banga S, et al. CT assessment of the left atrial appendage post-transcatheter occlusion - a systematic review and meta analysis. J Cardiovasc Comput Tomogr 2020;15(4):348—55.

[33] Stout KK, et al. 2018 AHA/ACC guideline for the management of adults with congenital heart disease: a report of the American College of Cardiology/American Heart Association Task Force on clinical practice guidelines. J Am Coll Cardiol 2019;73(12):e81—e192.

[34] Bayraktutan U, et al. Efficacy of ivabradin to reduce heart rate prior to coronary CT angiography: comparison with beta-blocker. Diagn Interv Radiol 2012;18(6):537—41.

[35] Guaricci AI, et al. Heart rate control with oral ivabradine in computed tomography coronary angiography: a randomized comparison of 7.5 mg versus 5 mg regimen. Int J Cardiol 2013;168(1) 362—8.

[36] Guaricci AI, et al. Incremental value and safety of oral ivabradine for heart rate reduction in computed tomography coronary angiography. Int J Cardiol 2012;156(1):28—33.

[37] Adile KK, et al. Safety and efficacy of oral ivabradine as a heart rate-reducing agent in patients undergoing CT coronary angiography. Br J Radiol 2012;85(1016):e424—8.

[38] Lambrechtsen J, Egstrup K. Pre-treatment with a sinus node blockade, ivabradine, before coronary CT angiography: a retrospective audit. Clin Radiol 2013;68(10):1054—8.

[39] Abbara S, et al. SCCT guidelines for the performance and acquisition of coronary computed tomographic angiography: a report of the society of Cardiovascular Computed Tomography Guidelines Committee: endorsed by the North American Society for Cardiovascular Imaging (NASCI). J Cardiovasc Comput Tomogr 2016;10(6):435—49.

[40] Halliburton SS, et al. SCCT guidelines on radiation dose and dose-optimization strategies in cardiovascular CT. J Cardiovasc Comput Tomogr 2011;5(4):198—224.

[41] Taron J, Foldyna B, Eslami P, Hoffmann U, Nikolaou K, Bamberg F. Cardiac computed tomography - more than coronary arteries? a clinical update. Rofo 2019;191(9):817—26 Kardinale CT: Mehr als nur Koronarien? Ein Abgleich mit dem Alltag.

[42] Park CH, Lee J, Oh C, Han KH, Kim TH. The feasibility of sub-millisievert coronary CT angiography with low tube voltage, prospective ECG gating, and a knowledge-based iterative model reconstruction algorithm. Int J Cardiovasc Imaging 2015;31(2):197—203.

[43] Kawaguchi Y, et al. Submillisievert imaging protocol using full reconstruction and advanced patient motion correction in 320-row area detector coronary CT angiography. Int J Cardiovasc Imaging 2018;34(3):465—74.

[44] Flohr TG, Raupach R, Bruder H. Cardiac CT: how much can temporal resolution, spatial resolution, and volume coverage be improved? J Cardiovasc Comput Tomogr 2009;3(3):143—52.

[45] Kumamaru KK, Hoppel BE, Mather RT, Rybicki FJ. CT angiography: current technology and clinical use. Radiol Clin North Am 2010;48(2):213—35.

[46] Chen MY, et al. Simulated 50% radiation dose reduction in coronary CT angiography using adaptive iterative dose reduction in three-dimensions (AIDR3D). Int J Cardiovasc Imaging 2013;29(5):1167—75.

[47] Albrecht MH, et al. Dual-energy CT of the heart current and future status. Eur J Radiol 2018;105:110—18.

[48] Mahesh M, Cody DD. Physics of cardiac imaging with multiple-row detector CT. Radiographics 2007;27(5):1495—509.

[49] Gerber TC, Kantor B, McCollough CH. Radiation dose and safety in cardiac computed tomography. Cardiol Clin 2009;27(4):665—77.

[50] Maffei E, et al. Low dose CT of the heart: a quantum leap into a new era of cardiovascular imaging. Radiol Med 2010;115(8):1179—207.

[51] Leschka S, et al. Accuracy of MSCT coronary angiography with 64-slice technology: first experience. Eur Heart J 2005;26(15):1482—7.

[52] Burgstahler C, et al. Cardiac dual-source computed tomography in patients with severe coronary calcifications and a high prevalence of coronary artery disease. J Cardiovasc Comput Tomogr 2007;1(3):143—51.

[53] Xu L, Yang L, Fan Z, Yu W, Lv B, Zhang Z. Diagnostic performance of 320 detector CT coronary angiography in patients with atrial fibrillation: preliminary results. Eur Radiol 2011;21(5):936—43.

[54] Zhang JJ, Liu T, Feng Y, Wu WF, Mou CY, Zhai LH. Diagnostic value of 64-slice dual-source CT coronary angiography in patients with atrial fibrillation: comparison with invasive coronary angiography. Korean J Radiol 2011;12(4):416—23.

[55] Matveeva A, et al. Coronary CT angiography in patients with atrial fibrillation: standard-dose and low-dose imaging with a high-resolution whole-heart CT scanner. Eur Radiol 2018;28(8):3432—40.

[56] Andreini D, et al. Atrial fibrillation: diagnostic accuracy of coronary CT angiography performed with a whole-heart 230-microm spatial resolution CT scanner. Radiology 2017;284(3):676—84.

[57] Wilson RF, Wyche K, Christensen BV, Zimmer S, Laxson DD. Effects of adenosine on human coronary arterial circulation. Circulation 1990;82(5):1595—606.

[58] Vavere AL, et al. Diagnostic performance of combined noninvasive coronary angiography and myocardial perfusion imaging using 320 row detector computed tomography: design and implementation of the CORE320 multicenter, multinational diagnostic study. J Cardiovasc Comput Tomogr 2011;5(6):370—81.

[59] Treibel TA, Rossi A, Pugliese F, Davies LC. Functional assessment of coronary artery disease by cardiac computed tomography. Expert Rev Cardiovasc Ther 2017;15(9):657—65.

[60] Pontone G, et al. Incremental diagnostic value of stress computed tomography myocardial perfusion with whole-heart coverage CT scanner in intermediate- to high-risk symptomatic patients suspected of coronary artery disease. JACC Cardiovasc Imaging 2019;12(2):338—49.

[61] Pontone G, et al. Dynamic stress computed tomography perfusion with a whole-heart coverage scanner in addition to coronary computed tomography angiography and fractional flow reserve computed tomography derived. JACC Cardiovasc Imaging 2019;12(12):2460—71.

[62] Pontone G, et al. Stress computed tomography perfusion versus fractional flow reserve CT derived in suspected coronary artery disease: the perfection study. JACC Cardiovasc Imaging 2019;12(8):1487—97 Pt 1.

[63] Pontone G, et al. Quantitative versus qualitative evaluation of static stress computed tomography perfusion to detect haemodynamically significant coronary artery disease. Eur Heart J Cardiovasc Imaging 2018;19(11):1244—52.

[64] Pelgrim GJ, et al. Optimal timing of image acquisition for arterial first pass CT myocardial perfusion imaging. Eur J Radiol 2017;86:227—33.

[65] Kikuchi Y, et al. Quantification of myocardial blood flow using dynamic 320-row multi-detector CT as compared with (1)(5)O-H(2)O PET. Eur Radiol 2014;24(7):1547—56.

[66] Penagaluri A, et al. Computed tomographic perfusion improves diagnostic power of coronary computed tomographic angiography in women: analysis of the CORE320 trial (Coronary Artery Evaluation Using 320-Row Multidetector Computed Tomography Angiography and Myocardial Perfusion) according to gender. Circ Cardiovasc Imaging 2016;9:11.

[67] Bamberg F, et al. Accuracy of dynamic computed tomography adenosine stress myocardial perfusion imaging in estimating myocardial blood flow at various degrees of coronary artery stenosis using a porcine animal model. Invest Radiol 2012;47(1):71—7.

[68] Ho KT, Ong HY, Tan G, Yong QW. Dynamic CT myocardial perfusion measurements of resting and hyperaemic blood flow in low-risk subjects with 128-slice dual-source CT. Eur Heart J Cardiovasc Imaging 2015;16(3):300—6.

[69] George RT, et al. Quantification of myocardial perfusion using dynamic 64-detector computed tomography. Invest Radiol 2007;42(12):815—22.

[70] Morton G, et al. Quantification of absolute myocardial perfusion in patients with coronary artery disease: comparison between cardiovascular magnetic resonance and positron emission tomography. J Am Coll Cardiol 2012;60(16):1546—55.

[71] Motwani M, Kidambi A, Uddin A, Sourbron S, Greenwood JP, Plein S. Quantification of myocardial blood flow with cardiovascular magnetic resonance throughout the cardiac cycle. J Cardiovasc Magn Reson 2015;17(1):4.

[72] Lardo AC, et al. Contrast-enhanced multidetector computed tomography viability imaging after myocardial infarction: characterization of myocyte death, microvascular obstruction, and chronic scar. Circulation 2006;113(3):394—404.

[73] Schelbert EB, et al. Late gadolinium-enhancement cardiac magnetic resonance identifies postinfarction myocardial fibrosis and the border zone at the near cellular level in ex vivo rat heart. Circ Cardiovasc Imaging 2010;3(6):743—52.

[74] Nacif MS, et al. Interstitial myocardial fibrosis assessed as extracellular volume fraction with low-radiation-dose cardiac CT. Radiology 2012;264(3):876—83.

[75] Lee HJ, et al. Myocardial extracellular volume fraction with dual-energy equilibrium contrast-enhanced cardiac CT in nonischemic cardiomyopathy: a prospective comparison with cardiac MR imaging. Radiology 2016;280(1):49—57.

[76] Patel MR, et al. Low diagnostic yield of elective coronary angiography. N Engl J Med 2010;362 (10):886—95.

[77] Meijboom WB, et al. Comprehensive assessment of coronary artery stenoses: computed tomography coronary angiography versus conventional coronary angiography and correlation with fractional flow reserve in patients with stable angina. J Am Coll Cardiol 2008;52(8):636—43.

[78] Rabbat MG, et al. Interpreting results of coronary computed tomography angiography-derived fractional flow reserve in clinical practice. J Cardiovasc Comput Tomogr 2017;11(5):383—8.

[79] Taylor CA, Fonte TA, Min JK. Computational fluid dynamics applied to cardiac computed tomography for noninvasive quantification of fractional flow reserve: scientific basis. J Am Coll Cardiol 2013;61(22):2233—41.

[80] Uzu K, et al. Lumen boundaries extracted from coronary computed tomography angiography on computed fractional flow reserve (FFRCT): validation with optical coherence tomography. EuroIntervention 2019;14(15):e1609—18.

[81] Bakhshi H, et al. Comparative effectiveness of CT-derived atherosclerotic plaque metrics for predicting myocardial ischemia. JACC Cardiovasc Imaging 2019;12(7):1367—76 Pt 2.

[82] Gaur S, et al. Coronary plaque quantification and fractional flow reserve by coronary computed tomography angiography identify ischaemia-causing lesions. Eur Heart J 2016;37(15):1220—7.

[83] Driessen RS, et al. Effect of plaque burden and morphology on myocardial blood flow and fractional flow reserve. J Am Coll Cardiol 2018;71(5):499—509.

[84] Norgaard BL, et al. Diagnostic performance of noninvasive fractional flow reserve derived from coronary computed tomography angiography in suspected coronary artery disease: the NXT trial (Analysis of coronary blood flow using CT angiography: next steps). J Am Coll Cardiol 2014;63 (12):1145—55.

[85] Driessen RS, et al. Comparison of coronary computed tomography angiography, fractional flow reserve, and perfusion imaging for ischemia diagnosis. J Am Coll Cardiol 2019;73(2):161—73.

[86] Rabbat M, et al. Fractional flow reserve derived from coronary computed tomography angiography safely defers invasive coronary angiography in patients with stable coronary artery disease. J Clin Med 2020;9:2.

[87] Modi BN, et al. Predicting the physiological effect of revascularization in serially diseased coronary arteries. Circ Cardiovasc Interv 2019;12(2):e007577.

[88] Conte E, et al. FFRCT and CT perfusion: a review on the evaluation of functional impact of coronary artery stenosis by cardiac CT. Int J Cardiol 2020;300:289—96.

[89] Douglas PS, et al. Outcomes of anatomical versus functional testing for coronary artery disease. N Engl J Med 2015;372(14):1291—300.

[90] investigators S-H. CT coronary angiography in patients with suspected angina due to coronary heart disease (SCOT-HEART): an open-label, parallel-group, multicentre trial. Lancet 2015;385(9985): 2383—91.

[91] Williams MC, et al. Use of coronary computed tomographic angiography to guide management of patients with coronary disease. J Am Coll Cardiol 2016;67(15):1759—68.

[92] Investigators S-H, et al. Coronary CT angiography and 5-year risk of myocardial infarction. N Engl J Med 2018;379(10):924—33.

[93] Bittencourt MS, et al. Clinical outcomes after evaluation of stable chest pain by coronary computed tomographic angiography versus usual care: a meta-analysis. Circ Cardiovasc Imaging 2016;9(4): e004419.

[94] Foy AJ, Dhruva SS, Peterson B, Mandrola JM, Morgan DJ, Redberg RF. Coronary computed tomography angiography versus functional stress testing for patients with suspected coronary artery disease: a systematic review and meta-analysis. JAMA Intern Med 2017;177(11):1623—31.

[95] Sharma A, et al. Stress testing versus CT angiography in patients with diabetes and suspected coronary artery disease. J Am Coll Cardiol 2019;73(8):893—902.

[96] D'Ascenzo F, et al. Coronary computed tomographic angiography for detection of coronary artery disease in patients presenting to the emergency department with chest pain: a meta-analysis of randomized clinical trials. Eur Heart J Cardiovasc Imaging 2013;14(8):782—9.

CHAPTER 6

Multimodality noninvasive cardiovascular imaging for the evaluation of coronary artery disease

Chris Anthony, Reza Reyaldeen and Bo Xu
Section of Cardiovascular Imaging, Robert and Suzanne Tomsich Department of Cardiovascular Medicine, Sydell and Arnold Miller Family Heart, Vascular and Thoracic Institute, Cleveland Clinic, Cleveland, OH, Unites States

6.1 Introduction

Coronary artery disease (CAD) is highly prevalent and is associated with significant morbidity and mortality [1]. Due to its prevalence and the adverse impact on the well-being and health resources of the community at large, accurate and expedient diagnosis of flow-limiting CAD is of paramount importance [1]. In addition to coronary artery anatomy and morphology, functional evaluation of the adequacy of myocardial perfusion and myocyte metabolism are of paramount importance, as patients with both anatomically and functionally significant stenoses have been demonstrated to benefit from revascularization [2]. In a study of 541 patients, who were referred for cardiac evaluation and underwent both coronary cardiac CT (CCT) and myocardial perfusion imaging (MPI) [2], CCT emerged as an independent predictor of events with an incremental prognostic value to MPI with an annualized hard event rate (all-cause mortality and nonfatal infarction) in patients with none or mild CAD (CCT <50% stenosis) of 1.8% versus 4.8% in patients with significant CAD (CCT ≥50% stenosis). Patients who had either an abnormal or normal MPI result were three times as likely to suffer from an adverse event [2]. MPI and CCT were synergistic, as the authors demonstrated that combined use resulted in significantly improved prediction of adverse outcomes with a P-value of <.005 [2].

While the severity of ischemia is often related to the degree of flow-limiting stenosis, this correlation is not always linear [3]. The presence of collateral circulation distal to the site of flow-limiting coronary artery stenosis may result in false-negative testing despite the presence of downstream ischemia, distal to the site of stenosis. The phenomenon of collateralization further highlights the importance of functional assessment of CAD to better guide treatment decisions made by treating clinicians to endure optimal benefit from revascularization, be that percutaneous or surgical [4]. The ultimate goal of a multimodality imaging approach to the assessment of CAD is to clearly outline flow-limiting

147

CAD and its physiologic flow dynamic related implications, as opposed to purely anatomic information which is often the case when only one modality is used. A combined multimodality approach enables patients with actual flow-limiting CAD to be better stratified with a more personalized evidence-based approach to optimal risk factor modification therapy and ultimately revascularization strategy.

A diverse range of multimodality cardiovascular imaging techniques are available for the evaluation of CAD, including stress echocardiogram (TTE), cardiac computed tomography (CCT), stress cardiac magnetic resonance imaging (CMR), single-photon emission computed tomography (SPECT), or a combination of positron emission tomography (PET) and CT or PET with magnetic resonance imaging (MRI). MPI is a representation of the regional myocardial blood flow and the metabolic activity of myocytes as a functional marker of adequate perfusion.

The goal of this chapter is to clearly outline the different noninvasive imaging modalities that include stress TTE, CCT, stress CMR, SPECT, PET, and fusion imaging for the evaluation of CAD.

6.2 Ischemic cascade

Myocardial ischemia occurs in a sequence of pathophysiologic events, in which various markers of myocyte dysfunction can be observed in a well-defined time sequence [5]. The cascade of events are characterized by reduced left ventricular (LV) compliance or diastolic dysfunction, a reduction in myocardial contractile function, increased end-diastolic pressure, electrocardiogram signals of myocardial ischemia specifically ST-segment changes, and lastly clinical symptoms such as angina or shortness of breath on exertion (Fig. 6.1). Myocardial ischemia is caused by insufficient blood flow between

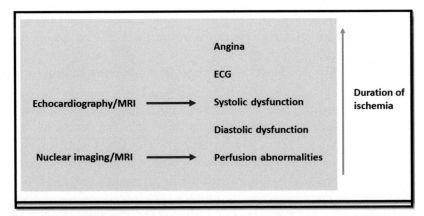

Figure 6.1 The ischemic cascade demonstrating the sequence of pathophysiologic events as detected by various imaging modalities.

the subendocardial and subepicardial layers, which results in myocyte dysfunction and consequent mechanical and contractile dysfunction [5].

The concept of the ischemic cascade is a key concept in allowing clinicians to better appreciate the different role various imaging and stress techniques play in making the diagnosis of flow-limiting CAD and consequent myocardial ischemia. There are strengths and weaknesses to the various modalities, which highlight the importance of answering a specific clinical question, as evidenced by the fact that subtle changes in myocardial function form the basis of various new physiologic markers for the detection of ischemia, namely, the demonstration of a reduction in coronary flow reserve (CFR) irrespective of the imaging modality used [6].

Myocardial ischemia as described within the ischemic cascade often manifests as inducible regional or global myocardial dysfunction, depicted by abnormal ventricular cavity size and thickening of the myocardium at peak stress [6,7]. In the absence of CAD, CFR can be reduced due to microvascular disease or insufficient blood flow at the level of the microcapillary beds, uncontrolled hypertension which can result in reduced myocyte perfusion or LV hypertrophy which can once again impact the microcirculation within the myocardium [8–10]. These common clinical entities are important confounders in all diagnostic tests for the detection of myocardial ischemia and must form part of the differential diagnosis in all positive imaging tests.

6.3 Exercise stress echocardiography

The exercise stress echocardiogram is a combination of cardiac ultrasound-based tomographic imaging exercise induced "stress" as per the various stress protocols that have been standardized and widely incorporated into global practice such as the Bruce protocol or the modified Bruce protocol (Fig. 6.2; Table 6.1) [11]. During stress echocardiography clinicians utilize qualitative visual assessment for wall-motion abnormality and concurrent reduction in LV chamber size during peak exercise for the detection and exclusion of flow-limiting CAD-induced myocardial ischemia [11,12]. This qualitative approach is made more reproducible by the assignment of various descriptions of wall motion abnormality at peak exercise, with terms such as hypokinesis, akinesis, or dyskinesis often used as nomenclature to describe areas of dysfunction within the myocardium.

The American Society of Echocardiography advocated for a more quantitative and reproducible approach to the grading of wall motion abnormality during stress echocardiogram, with the introduction of a 17 segments model [11]. The ASE advocates that each segment in this 17 segment model be assigned a regional wall motion score from 1 to 4, with 1 being normal, 2 being hypokinetic, 3 being akinetic, and 4 being dyskinetic [11]. This score can then be tabulated as an index [12]. More advanced quantitative methods include determination of LV volumes in diastole and systole

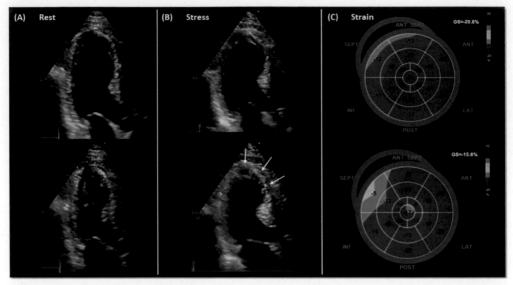

Figure 6.2 (A) Resting echocardiography three-chamber view shows normal wall thickening in systole (bottom panel). (B) Following stress, there is hypokinesis of the mid anteroseptum and apical segments (*white arrows* bottom panel). Note also the lack of relative reduction in overall left ventricular end-systolic cavity size, consistent with LAD territory ischemia (C) This panel demonstrates the corresponding global longitudinal strain plots at rest (top panel) and stress (bottom panel), highlighting a reduction in peak global longitudinal strain following stress.

from which stroke volume and ejection fraction can be calculated, evaluation of diastolic dysfunction at peak exercise and strain which will be described further in this chapter [13].

Stress echocardiography has formed the backbone for functional ischemic testing due to its high sensitivity and specificity, as evidence by a pooled analysis of studies of 1849 patients by Schuijf et al. [14], who demonstrated a sensitivity and specificity of 84% and 82%, respectively, for the detection of flow-limiting CAD [14]. There have been several studies that have reported a higher sensitivity for detecting patients with multivessel CAD as opposed to a single vessel disease [15]. The literature has defined 70% stenosis as clinically significant and flow-limiting, resulting in improved sensitivity but lower specificity for the detection of flow-limiting CAD [16].

Exercise stress echocardiography is preferred for patients who are physically capable of achieving an adequate level of exercise for the accurate evaluation of flow-limiting CAD [11].

6.4 Pharmacologic stress echocardiography

Pharmacologic stress testing with either dobutamine or vasodilator can also be utilized for the detection of myocardial ischemia when a patient is incapable of exercising

Table 6.1 Various approaches of stress echocardiography in coronary artery disease.

	Exercise stress echocardiogram	Dobutamine stress echocardiogram	Myocardial perfusion stress echocardiogram
Suitability	Patients who are capable of attaining adequate level of exercise for exclusion of CAD	Patients who are unable to exercisePatients who require myocardial viability assessment	Patients who have poor endocardial definition
Contraindications	• Unstable angina • Hypertensive urgency • Serious cardiac dysrhythmia • Severe aortic stenosis	• Significant LVOT obstruction • Unstable angina • Serious cardiac dysrhythmia • Hypertensive urgency	• Unstable angina • Serious cardiac dysrhythmia • Hypertensive urgency
Limitations	• Left bundle branch block • Cardiac pacing • Poor acoustic imaging windows	• Left bundle branch block • Cardiac pacing • Poor acoustic imaging windows	• Left bundle branch block • Cardiac pacing • Poor acoustic imaging windows

Note: CAD, Coronary artery disease.

capacity due to physical or physiologic limitations [11]. Dobutamine stress echocardiography (DSE) is the most commonly used method for the assessment of myocardial viability in the setting of determining if revascularization will indeed salvage or improve myocardial function in a hibernating myocardium [11]. Dobutamine is usually delivered in graded doses starting at 5 μg/kg per minute and is increased at 3 minute intervals if tolerated by the patient or in the absence of dobutamine-induced hypertension or dysrhythmia [11]. When target heart rate cannot be achieved with dobutamine alone, atropine can be added to increase the sensitivity of DSE, particularly in patients taking beta-blockers and in those with single-vessel disease [11].

The diagnostic accuracy of DSE was evaluated in 141 patients who underwent coronary arteriography within 2 weeks of DSE [17]. All patients were being evaluated for known or suspected CAD. Marcovitz and Armstrong [17] demonstrated that DSE had a sensitivity of 96% and a specificity of 66% for the detection of flow-limiting CAD. DSE had a sensitivity of 87% and specificity of 91% for the exclusion of flow-limiting CAD if there was normal resting wall motion, which was the case in 53 patients in the study cohort [17].

Eleven studies (749 participants) met the inclusion criteria. The sensitivity of DSE varied from 1.7% to 93.8%, and specificity, from 54.8% to 98.8%. Pooled sensitivity was 60.2% (95% confidence interval (CI), 33.0%−82.3%) and specificity 85.7% (95% CI, 73.8%−92.7%). DSE had an overall diagnostic odds ratio (OR) of 9.1 (95% CI, 4.6−17.8), positive likelihood ratio of 4.1 (95% CI, 2.8−6.1), negative likelihood ratio of 0.47 (95% CI: 0.23−0.73), and area under curve of 0.73 [18].

6.5 Myocardial perfusion stress echocardiography

Myocardial perfusion stress echocardiography (MPSE), which utilizes ultrasound enhancing agents (UEA) during exercise stress echocardiography, improves the detection of ischemia, as perfusion abnormalities often occur before regional dysfunction within the myocardium, once again as depicted in the ischemic cascade [19]. In addition, the use of UEA during stress echocardiography improves the sensitivity for detection of ischemia and improves prediction of risk, as it aids the visual appreciation of focal and often subtle areas of regional dysfunction within the myocardium at peak exercise [19]. MPSE with UEA can be used in both exercise and DSE [20]. MPSE may also have particular advantages in improving sensitivity in the context of resting wall motion abnormalities and confounders that make interpretation of regional wall motion abnormalities even more challenging such as conduction delays or dyssynchrony due to left bundle branch block (LBBB) [21]. In addition, the use of UEA and perfusion enables a more parametric evaluation of myocardial perfusion and can also be used to appreciate areas of microvascular obstruction and/or early ischemic dysfunction [22].

In a study by Porter et al. [23] of 100 patients who were referred for invasive coronary angiography (ICA) and had myocardial contrast echocardiography, the sensitivity and specificity for the detection of a concurrent region of impaired myocardial perfusion that corresponded to an anatomic >50% diameter stenosis was 80% and 74%, respectively [23]. This is a useful supplementary technique, however, due to the time requirement, it is not often performed.

6.6 Left ventricular strain in exercise stress echocardiography

Combining stress echocardiography with strain analysis is a novel and promising technique for the detection of subclinical cardiac dysfunction due to myocardial ischemia that is not apparent on visual assessment of myocardial recruitment at peak exercise [24,25]. In a study of 50 healthy adolescents and young adults, von Scheidt et al. [25] demonstrated that strain and strain rate (SR) increased during progressive exercise stress [25]. The authors reported that the mean longitudinal strain was −20.4% ± 1.3%, SR −1.1 ± 0.15/s at rest, where the mean heart rate was 79.4 ± 12.0 beats/min, increasing to −22.6% ± 1.6% and −1.5 ± 0.16/s at low stress level at a heart rate of 117.1 ± 8.7 beats/min and −23.7% ± 1.1% and −1.9 ± 0.29/s at submaximal stress level at a heart rate of 154.2 ± 7.0 beats/min, respectively, returning to $-20.6\% \pm 1.4\%$ and -1.2 ± 0.16/s postexercise at a heart rate of 90.1 ± 9.4 beats/min [25]. The authors also noted that interobserver variability for strain was acceptable even during submaximal stress [25]. Further studies on the comprehensive assessment of segmental ventricular strain at rest and during a standardized exercise are necessary for the creation of accepted and validated normal and abnormal thresholds, however, represent a promising additional tool in the evaluation of flow-limiting CAD.

6.7 Limitations of stress echocardiography

The pitfalls with stress echocardiography include suboptimal imaging windows resulting in poor endocardial definition of dropout of wall segments [12]. This limitation can be aided with the utility of UEA for the improvement of endocardial border definition [12].

The development of global ventricular dysfunction should increase the interpreter's suspicion of multivessel disease. The detection of single-vessel stenosis is also challenging, as the ischemic region will need to incorporate a substantial portion of the myocardium to enable detection of a regional abnormality, which may be underappreciated with distal disease or collateral supply to an occluded arterial bed. The identification of ischemia within preexisting or baseline areas of resting wall motion abnormalities is challenging and may require the administration of pharmacological agents to demonstrate a biphasic response for the confirmation of inducible ischemia within an infarct zone.

Baseline electrical conduction abnormality such as LBBB or significant intra- or interventricular conduction delay resulting in mechanical dyssynchrony may result in added difficulty in accurately assessing myocardial recruitment at peak exercise. Xu et al. have proposed an additional algorithm that incorporates various multimodality imaging techniques to aid clinicians with navigating this difficult clinical conundrum [26]. This impact of LBBB on the diagnostic accuracy of exercise stress echocardiography is further highlighted in a study of 191 consecutive patients with LBBB undergoing exercise stress echocardiography [27]. Of 62 patients who had demonstrated abnormal LV contractile response to exercise and subsequently underwent confirmatory anatomic imaging of the coronary arteries, only 29 had significant flow-limiting CAD, conferring an overall suboptimal specificity for the detection of significant CAD in the setting of LBBB of 21% and accuracy of 52% [27].

6.8 Computed tomography coronary calcium score

CT coronary artery calcium scores (CAC) is a quantitative imaging technique that is used for the screening of risk for adverse cardiac events in asymptomatic individuals (Fig. 6.3) [28,29,30]. CAC or the Agatston method is defined as highly attenuated lesions above a threshold of 130 Hounsfield units with an area of ≥ 3 pixels on noncontrast-enhanced

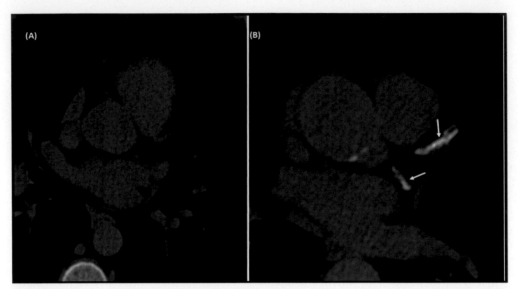

Figure 6.3 (A) Example of a patient with a calcium score of zero. (B) In comparison, this patient has calcification in the left anterior descending artery (*white arrow*) and left circumflex artery (*yellow arrow*), with a total calcium score of 1008, placing the patient at the 90th percentile for age and gender.

CCT [31]. The CAC cut-points that are often used for the purpose of stratification in categorizing the risk of CAD: 0 (very low), 1—99 (mild), 100—400 (moderate), >400 (severe) based on large prospective observational studies [29,30].

CAC is highly predictive of future risk of adverse cardiac events [29,30]. Nasir et al. [30] demonstrated that in a study population of 4758 participants, patients who had a CAC score of 0 was associated with an extremely low adverse cardiac event rate of 1.5 per 1000 person years [30]. Sarwar et al. [32] conducted a *meta*-analysis of 49 studies totaling 90,000 patients over a period of 18 years, to evaluate the diagnostic and prognostic performance of a zero CAC score in asymptomatic and symptomatic individuals. In their analysis, only 146 of 25,903 patients without CAC experienced a cardiovascular event, providing evidence that a zero CAC score is associated with a very low risk of future cardiovascular events [32].

This has been incorporated into the American College of Cardiology (ACC) guidelines document for the management of blood cholesterol, where if the coronary calcium score is zero, it is reasonable to withhold statin therapy and reassess in 5—10 years in the absence of higher-risk conditions, such as diabetes mellitus, family history of premature cardiac events, or cigarette smoking. In addition, if the CAC score is 1—99, as per the guidelines statement, it is reasonable to initiate statin therapy for patients who are ≥ 55 years of age and lastly, if the CAC score is 100 or higher or in the 75th percentile or higher, it is reasonable to initiate statin therapy [33].

In addition, Miedema et al. [34] and Ajufo et al. [35] demonstrated that CAC score can be used for guiding the prescription of aspirin for primary prevention of adverse cardiac events. Participants with CAC score ≥ 100 had a benefit from aspirin use, while individuals with a zero CAC score would likely experience more harm than benefit [34,35]. In 4229 participants from the Multi-Ethnic Study of Atherosclerosis who were not on aspirin at baseline and were free of diabetes mellitus, individuals with CAC ≥ 100 had an estimated net benefit with aspirin regardless of their traditional risk status (estimated 5-year number needed to treat 173 for individuals $<10\%$ FRS and 92 for individuals $\geq 10\%$ FRS, estimated 5-year number needed to harm of 442 for a major bleed) [34]. Conversely, individuals with zero CAC had unfavorable estimations (estimated 5-year number needed to treat of 2036 for individuals $<10\%$ FRS and 808 for individuals $\geq 10\%$ FRS, estimated 5-year number needed to harm of 442 for a major bleed) [34].

In 2191 participants from the Dallas Heart Study cohort who were free from atherosclerotic cardiovascular disease and not taking aspirin at baseline, higher CAC categories (CAC $1-99$ and ≥ 100 vs CAC 0) were associated with both ASCVD and bleeding events [hazard ratio (HR), 1.6; 95% CI, 1.1–2.4; HR, 2.6; 95% CI, 1.5–4.3; HR, 4.8; 95% CI, 2.8–8.2; $P < .001$; HR, 5.3; 95% CI, 3.6–7.9; $P < .001$], but aspirin use was estimated to result in net harm in individuals at low ($<5\%$) and intermediate (5%–20%) 10-year ASCVD risk and net benefit in those at high ($\geq 20\%$) ASCVD risk [35].

Apart from its proven predictive role, CAC scoring is easily performed, noninvasive, has very low radiation, is highly reproducible, and provides a quantitative assessment based on the absolute score and risk percentiles.

6.9 Limitations of coronary artery calcium

The severity of calcium deposition in a particular vessel is not considered in risk prediction, as the overall degree of CAC is predictive of the risk of adverse events [36].

Regional distribution of CAC can be very heterogeneous from the total CAC score [36].

CAC may result in unnecessary referral for invasive correlation due to the inability to detect flow-limiting disease, as it is a measure of extraluminal calcification and not specifically intraluminal obstruction. CAC can also miss significant noncalcified, cholesterol-based CAD, which can potentially be flow-limiting [36].

6.10 Computed tomography coronary angiogram

Cardiac CT angiogram (CCTA) in addition to the calculation of a CAC enables direct anatomic visualization of CAD in coronary arteries, with low radiation exposure

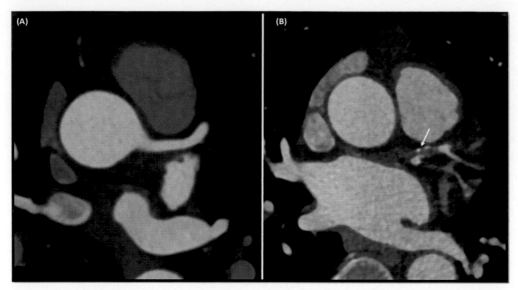

Figure 6.4 (A) Computed tomography coronary angiogram demonstrating no atherosclerotic disease (this image shows a patient left main and proximal LAD). (B) This patient has evidence of mixed plaque and spotty calcification (*white arrow*) in the proximal LAD causing high-grade stenosis (>70%) extending into the distal left main. *LAD*, Left anterior descending artery.

(Fig. 6.4) [37]. Improvement in CCTA scanner technology has improved the speed and diagnostic accuracy, enabling the acquisition of large data sets within seconds and with excellent spatial resolution [38]. CCTA also enables the assessment of atherosclerotic plaque burden and plaque characteristics noninvasively and has been reported to be comparable to the invasive intravascular ultrasound that is performed during invasive coronary angiogram [39].

The ACCURACY or Assessment by Coronary Computed Tomographic Angiography of Individuals Undergoing ICA trial by Budoff et al. [40] was the first prospective multicenter trial to evaluate the diagnostic accuracy of CCTA in symptomatic patients without known CAD [40]. In the 230 patients that were studied and had both CCTA and ICA, CCTA demonstrated high accuracy for the detection of CAD with greater than 70% luminal stenosis with a high negative predictive value (NPV) of 99% [40].

A prospective study of 360 symptomatic patients with acute and stable angina by Meijboom et al. [41] reported a sensitivity, specificity, and both positive predictive value (PPV) and NPV for the detection of CAD which the authors defined as greater than 50% of the luminal diameter of 99%, 64%, 86%, and 97%, respectively. Both studies highlight the high sensitivity and NPV of CCTA in the evaluation of CAD confirming the safety of a CCTA-based screening strategy for the evaluation for CAD [42].

The SCOT—HEART study, a multicenter prospective open-label randomized study of 4146 patients with stable angina, demonstrated that CCTA in addition to standard care, with subsequent changes in management, resulted in a statistically significant reduction in death from CAD or nonfatal myocardial infarction, driven by non-fatal myocardial infarction events, than standard care alone at 5 years of follow up [43]. They did not find that CCTA increased the use of angiography or coronary revascularization [43]. The findings also raise the possibility that CCTA detects patients with nonobstructive lesions to target with preventative therapy that would be otherwise missed by standard evaluations, which may mitigate downstream cardiac events due to earlier detection and optimal risk reduction.

The Prospective Multi-Centre Imaging Study for Evaluation of Chest Pain (PROMISE) trial, a parallel randomized study of 10,003 patients, compared clinical outcomes in symptomatic patients evaluated using CCTA or functional testing with either exercise electrocardiography, nuclear stress testing, or stress echocardiography [44]. The adjusted HR for a CCTA strategy, compared to a composite of all the aforementioned functional testing modalities was 1.04 (95% CI, 0.83—1.29), with adjustment for age, sex, and cardiovascular risk factors [44]. Douglas et al. also demonstrated a trend toward reduced rates of adverse clinical events at 12 months for individuals undergoing CCTA. The data from the PROMISE trial demonstrate that an initial strategy of CCTA as an index investigation is comparable to outcomes obtained with an initial strategy of functional testing [44].

The prognostic value of CCTA for predicting adverse cardiac outcomes was demonstrated by utilizing data from the Coronary CT Angiography Evaluation for Clinical Outcomes:

International Multicenter (CONFIRM) registry study, where Min et al. [45] examined the all-cause mortality in relation to CAD severity in 24,775 patients undergoing ≥ 64-detector row CCTA without known CAD using the CONFIRM registry [20]. In risk adjusted analysis, both per patient obstructive ($> 50\%$ stenosis) (HR, 2.60; 95% CI, 1.94—3.49; $P < .0001$) and nonobstructive (HR, 1.60; 95% CI, 1.18—2.16; $P = .002$) CAD conferred increased risk of mortality compared with patients without evidence of CAD [45]. These data bring to light the importance of nonobstructive CAD and its strong relationship with adverse cardiac outcomes.

The ACC recommended the use of functional testing for patients who are able to exercise, while CCTA can be considered for patients who are able to exercise but have an uninterpretable electrocardiogram [46]. The British National Institute for Health and Care Excellence guidelines have updated recommendations to state that the majority of patients with stable angina should be investigated with an anatomical imaging test, namely, CCTA [47]. Functional tests, such as stress echocardiography, have been downgraded as second-line investigations in patients who cannot have a CCTA or when CCTA is inconclusive [47].

The European Society of Cardiology (ESC) recommends the use of functional tests or CCTA as the first-line investigations in symptomatic patients when obstructive CAD cannot be excluded by clinical assessment [48]. The ESC Task Force comment that CCTA is preferable in patients with a lower range of clinical likelihood of CAD and characteristics associated with good image quality. The stance for the use of functional testing is further outlined in their guideline document by citing the better specificity of functional testing in the evaluation for flow-limiting CAD [48].

6.11 Limitations of computed tomography coronary angiogram

One of the main limitations of CCTA is the distinction of flow-limiting disease in patients who have densely calcified plaque. A high degree of extra-luminal calcification can lead to "blooming artifact" which often results in the segment of coronary artery being deemed noninterpretable [49]. This reduces the overall sensitivity of CCTA for the detection of CAD [49].

CCTA imaging often requires heart rates within a narrow range and the absence of dysrhythmia for optimal image quality [49]. Retrospective imaging acquisition can be used in these patients; however, this comes at the cost of increased radiation dose and exposure [49]. In addition, CCTA requires the use of exogenous contrast agents, which may be a contraindication or exclusionary criteria for patients with renal impairment or contrast-related hypersensitivity reactions.

6.12 Computed tomography in combination with single-photon emission tomography

SPECT imaging studies provide added diagnostic accuracy for detecting significant CAD compared to CCTA alone, by the addition of a functional element to the evaluation of stenosis (Table 6.2) [50]. In addition, SPECT imaging provides three-dimensional evaluation of the heart and coronary vessels, which is then fused with CT images resulting in increased specificity for the detection of flow-limiting CAD in comparison to CT alone [51]. In the United States, MPI is the most commonly used imaging modality, with an estimated 9 million stress perfusion studies performed annually [52]. This has been reviewed recently in detail by Chetrit et al. [53].

A study by Sato et al. [54] demonstrated that coronary artery segments that were uninterpretable due to severe calcification, motion artifacts, and/or poor opacification on CT when combined with SPECT improved specificity and the PPV for the detection of flow-limiting CAD. SPECT/CT imaging may also provide better sensitivity than SPECT alone as demonstrated by side-by-side analysis of SPECT and coronary CT images in patients with multivessel disease [55].

Table 6.2 Comparison between positron emission tomography and SPECT in coronary artery disease.

Modality	PET	SPECT
Sensitivity	87%	57%
Specificity	84%	94%

Additional functional information	LV ejection fraction
	  Viability
		LV ejection fraction
		  Viability

Limitations	Cost
	  Reduced specificity
	  Less impacted by left bundle branch block
	  Less susceptible to artifact
		Higher radiation
		  Miss balanced ischemia
		  Reduced sensitivity
		  Reduced cost
		  Impacted by left bundle branch block
		  More susceptible to artifact

Radiation dose	2−3 mSV	6−11 mSV (Technetium) 41 mSV (Thallium)

Note: CAD, coronary artery disease; PET, Positron emission tomography; SPECT, single-photon emission computed tomography.

In addition, CT/SPECT imaging helps reduce unnecessary downstream ICA and improves the sensitivity of SPECT alone [55]. In keeping with this, guidelines advocate for the addition of a functional test in patients who have an undefined degree of stenosis on CCTA before referral for invasive anatomical evaluation of CAD [56].

The combination of CT and SPECT has additional prognostic value, as demonstrated by a study by van Werkhoven et al. [2], where 517 (96%) patients with an interpretable MSCT, significant CAD (MSCT ≥50% stenosis) was detected in 158 (31%) patients, and abnormal perfusion summed stress score (SSS): ≥4 was observed in 168 (33%) patients. During follow-up (median 672 days; 25th, 75th percentile: 420, 896), an event occurred in 23 (5.2%) patients [2]. A normal MPI defined by the authors as a SSS <4 and an abnormal MPI defined by the authors as a SSS ≥4 were associated with an annualized hard event rate of 1.1% and 3.8%, respectively [2]. Both MSCT and MPI were synergistic, and combined use resulted in significantly improved prediction (log-rank test P-value <.005). Another study by Pazenkhottil et al. [57] further demonstrated the prognostic capacity of a combined CT and SPECT imaging approach, with higher death rates demonstrate for patients with abnormal findings on both modalities, in comparison to mismatched or normal findings.

A *meta*-analysis by Danad et al. [58] reviewing 23 studies with a total of 3788 patients and 5323 vessels comparing SPECT to invasively measured fraction flow reserve gave an overall sensitivity of 70% (95% CIs, 59%−80%) and a specificity of 78% (95% CIs, 68%−87%) for the diagnosis of CAD. Of note, based on the per-vessel analysis, SPECT had a 57% sensitivity and 75% specificity, largely owing to the lack of anatomical data.

6.13 Computed tomography in combination with positron emitting tomography

PET is a nuclear medicine modality that utilizes signals emitted from positron-emitting radionuclides that are the target of certain regions of interest such as myocardium in order to generate images [59]. PET imaging has the advantage of both improved spatial resolution and tissue contrast in comparison to SPECT imaging (Fig. 6.5) [60]. Multiple studies have demonstrated high sensitivity and specificity PET for detection of significant CAD, with high NPV [61,62].

An additional advantage of a combined CT and PET imaging approach is the ability to evaluate for microvascular disease [62]. PET adenosine stress testing allows for better evaluation of triple vessel disease, as it offers the added advantage of anatomic correlation as the interpreter can evaluate the degree of luminal stenosis directly on CT. Conversely, PET can confirm or refute the presence of flow-limiting CAD on CT by demonstrating the presence or absence of concomitant perfusion defects [62]. PET and CCTA hybrid imaging can also be used to help clinicians better select the right patients for ICA. In a study by Kajander et al. [62], of 375 patients with suspected CAD [62]. PET and CCTA and SPECT and CCTA are good options for clinicians to better select patients who might benefit from ICA and subsequent revascularization as opposed to optimal medical therapy [63].

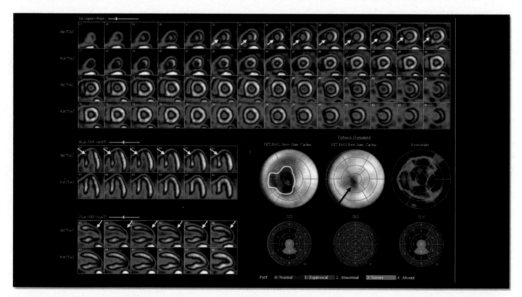

Figure 6.5 Gated Rb-82 Regadenoson stress PET study with evidence of stress perfusion defects in the apex, mid inferoseptal/anteroseptal, and mid anterior segments (*white arrows*—top rows are stress perfusion images and bottom are rest, best appreciated on the perfusion polar map—*white trace*) consistent with moderate (10%—20%) ischemia in the LAD territory. There was also evidence of a small area of scar (*black arrow* rest perfusion polar map) in the LAD territory (<10%). *PET*, Positron emission tomography; *LAD*, left anterior descending artery.

Hybrid imaging by PET and CT has great utility in the area of chronic total occlusion, where the decision for revascularization can be challenging [64,65].

6.14 Limitations and strengths of positron emission tomography and SPECT imaging

In addition to the exposure to radiation (Table 6.1) [66], balanced ischemia is a potential significant confounder in SPECT imaging [20,67]. This occurs in SPECT imaging when there is equivalent "balanced" flow limitation of all three coronary vessels, resulting in a false-positive result.

SPECT and PET imaging are generally widely available and interestingly demonstrated a cost—benefit in comparison to CCTA as evidenced by Shaw et al. in a study of 11,372 patients [68]. An average excess cost ranging from $500 to $1500 without a major difference in rates of death or MI at 3-year follow-up when favoring an initial anatomical approach over a functional approach namely, PET or SPECT ($P>.20$) [68].

In the PROMISE trial there was an average cost at 90 days ranging between $946 and $1132 for a nuclear imaging strategy and an average cost between $2200 and $2400 for a CCTA or invasive testing. Interestingly, early CCTA testing costs were on average $332 lower than functional testing costs; however, downstream testing was $600 higher [69].

Overall, the mean cost difference between the groups remained small after 3 years. PET is on average more costly than SPECT imaging, and even more so, with the addition of any hybrid technique [69].

6.15 CTCA and fractional flow reserve

An additional novel functional parameter to the evaluation of flow-limiting CAD with CTCA imaging is the utility of fluid dynamic-based technology, referred to as fractional flow reserve CTCA (FFR-CCTA). The feasibility of FFR-CCTA has been demonstrated in several studies with excellent sensitivity, specificity, and NPV [70]. The NXT trial by Nørgaard et al. was a prospective multicenter trial of 254 patients scheduled to undergo clinically indicated ICA for suspected CAD [70]. The authors demonstrated that when FFR-CCTA was compared to invasively measured FFR, the area under the receiver-operating characteristic curve for FFR (CCTA) was 0.90 (95% CI, 0.87—0.94) versus 0.81 (95% CI, 0.76—0.87), $P = .0008$ [70]. The sensitivity and specificity for the detection of ischemia for each individual patient were 86% and 79% for FFR(CCTA) compared to 94% and 34% for coronary CTA, compared to 64% and 83% for invasive angiogram, respectively [70]. A study by Koo et al. evaluating the computation of FFR from CCTA data was performed on 159 vessels in 103 patients undergoing CCTA, ICA, and FFR [71]. They demonstrated that the sensitivity, specificity, PPV, and NPV were 87.9%, 82.2%, 73.9%, 92.2% for FFR(CCTA) and 91.4%, 39.6%, 46.5%, 88.9% for CCTA detection of stenosis, respectively [71]. The area under the receiver—operator characteristics curve was 0.90 for FFR (CTCA) and 0.75 for CCTA ($P = .001$) [71]. The FFR(CTCA) and FFR demonstrated a good correlation for the detection of CAD ($r = 0.717$, $P < .001$). Min et al. [72] conducted a multicenter diagnostic performance study involving 252 stable patients with suspected or known CAD from 17 centers in five countries who underwent CT, ICA, FFR, and FFR(CCTA) [72]. They demonstrated that the respective sensitivity, specificity, PPV, and NPV for FFR(CT) plus CT were 90%, 54%, 67%, and 84%, respectively [72].

An exciting application of FFR-CCTA is its use to perform virtual stenting by computational modeling of coronary flow after CT-guided reconstruction [73]. Kim et al. prospectively enrolled 44 patients from three different centers (48 lesions) who had coronary CT angiography before angiography and stenting, and invasively measured FFR before and after stenting. FFR-CCTA was computed in a blinded fashion using coronary CT angiography and computational fluid dynamics before and after virtual coronary stenting [73]. They demonstrated an excellent correlation between FFR-CCTA and invasive FFR pre- and postpercutaneous coronary revascularization as evidenced by a measured invasive FFR prior to intervention was 0.70 ± 0.14 and increased to 0.90 ± 0.05 after stenting [73]. FFR-CCTA prior to intervention was 0.70 ± 0.15 and increased to 0.88 ± 0.05 after virtual coronary stenting. There was modest correlation between invasive FFR and FFR-CCTA before ($R = 0.60$, $P < .001$) and after intervention ($R = 0.55$, $P < .001$) [73]. The mean difference between FFR-CCTA and FFR was 0.006 for preintervention (95% limit of agreement: -0.27 to 0.28) and 0.024 for postintervention (95% limit of agreement: -0.08 to 0.13) [73]. Intraclass correlation coefficient was 0.71 ($P < .001$) [73]. The diagnostic accuracy of FFR-CCTA to predict ischemia (FFR ≤ 0.8) prior to stenting of 77% (sensitivity: 85.3%, specificity: 57.1%, PPV: 83%, and NPV: 62%) and after stenting of 96% (sensitivity: 100%, specificity: 96% positive predictive value: 50%, and NPV: 100%) [73].

This is an exciting development in the CT imaging and will enable functional assessment of coronary lesions in a single study without the addition of additional contrast agents or radiation.

6.16 Limitations of FFR CCTA

Although a highly promising technique, FFR-CCTA is not widely available and is not commonly used at the Cleveland Clinic. With regard to cost, Hiatky et al. demonstrated in 96 patients from the Diagnosis of Ischemia-Causing Stenoses Obtained Via Noninvasive Fractional Flow Reserve study that initial management costs were highest for the ICA/visual strategy ($10,702), and lowest for the CTA/FFR-CCTA/ICA strategy ($7674). The use of FFR–CCTA to select patients for ICA and PCI would result in 30% lower costs and 12% fewer events at 1 year compared with the most commonly used ICA/visual strategy [74]. Despite this overall saving, this technique is still limited due to the aforementioned lack of widespread availability.

6.16.1 Cardiac magnetic resonance imaging in coronary artery disease

CMR has an excellent spatial and temporal resolution in addition to its major advantage over other imaging modalities, which is the delineation of soft-tissue contrast [75]. These characteristics enable the comprehensive evaluation of cardiac morphology, function, regional wall motion abnormality, and early pathologic changes within myocardial tissue including edema or scar formation. The superior spatial resolution afforded by CMR enables the delineation between subendocardial and transmural perfusion defects, which is an added advantage in comparison to CT and SPECT imaging, as subendocardial perfusion defects are often difficult to visualize on other imaging modalities [75].

6.16.2 Cardiac magnetic resonance perfusion imaging

Regional myocardial perfusion can be assessed by first-pass techniques using ultrafast T1-weighted sequences [76]. MR coronary angiography has become feasible in recent years, and high-resolution imaging with or without contrast enhancement may allow for characterization of atherosclerotic plaque.

CMR MPI is a technique that utilized contrast administration, namely, a gadolinium-based contrast agent at rest and during the administration of a pharmacological agent to vasodilate the coronary arteries (Fig. 6.6) [76]. The administration of contrast agents shortens the T1 relaxation time of the myocardium, resulting in an increase in the signal intensity of the areas of myocardium that is being perfused [76]. Regions that are ischemic regions are then clearly identified due to the significantly reduced signal intensity in the corresponding region [76]. Several studies have demonstrated sensitivities and specificities of 84% and 85% for CMR perfusion techniques in the diagnosis of myocardial ischemia [76–78].

The vastly improved spatial resolution afforded by CMR enables the delineation between subendocardial and transmural perfusion defects, which is an added advantage in comparison to CT and SPECT imaging, where subendocardial perfusion defects are often difficult to objectively appreciate [76].

6.17 Cardiac magnetic resonance angiography

CMR enables the direct visualization of coronary arteries with or without gadolinium [79]. CMRA also enables the simultaneous visualization of the coronary veins, which is exceedingly useful for preprocedural planning of pacemaker lead implantation for cardiac resynchronization therapy [80].

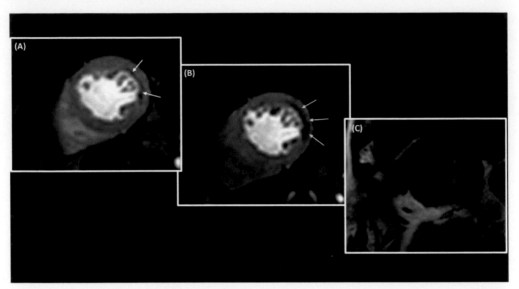

Figure 6.6 (A) This CMR image shows a short-axis stack at the mid-left ventricle level with rest perfusion revealing evidence of mild—moderate ischemia in the basal-mid anterolateral segments (*white arrows*). (B) After vasodilator stress (0.4 mg Regadenoson over 4 min), there is worsening ischemia in this territory as demonstrated by a more prominent hypointense rim in the subendocardium (*yellow arrows*). (C) Delayed gadolinium-enhancement analysis reveals no evidence of prior ischemic damage/scar in the corresponding ischemic segments. *CMR*, cardiac magnetic resonance imaging.

Balanced steady-state free precession sequences with the addition of parallel imaging techniques using multichannel surface coils, in addition to improved respiratory gating with navigator echo software have resulted in vastly improved temporal resolution [81]. Pooled data, a total of 51 studies comparing CCTA and CMRA for the detection of flow-limiting CAD, demonstrated that the sensitivities and specificities were higher for CCTA 85% and 95% compared with CMRA 72% and 87%, respectively [82]. The OR for the presence of flow-limiting CAD was higher in CCTA in comparison to CMRA (16.9 compared to 6.4, $P < .0001$).

The CMR sequences that were utilized in this studies, however, were subject to suboptimal gating techniques and were also impacted by a reduced signal-to-noise ratio. These findings highlight the promise of CMRA, however, necessitate further development in CMR image acquisition and optimization techniques.

Future developments in the area of CMRA, including higher field strengths and improved contrast techniques, such as the development of blood pool contrast agents, will likely improve diagnostic accuracy. Importantly, CMRA-based evaluation of plaque morphology and composition in addition to accurate evaluation of coronary flow may better demonstrate the presence, severity, composition, and the degree of flow limitation of CAD [83].

6.17.1 Limitations of cardiac magnetic resonance

While MRI provides excellent spatial resolution, it is time-consuming and more expensive than the other diagnostic tests [84].

Very obese patients may not be able to fit comfortably within the MRI machine, and patients with severe heart failure may struggle to lie flat for the duration of the test. Some patients will suffer from claustrophobia to a degree that will not allow them to tolerate an MRI scan. In patients with very fast heart rates, or frequent irregular beats, ECG gating may prove unreliable [84].

In addition, patients who have implanted medical devices such as certain types of pacemakers or defibrillators, or who may have retained pacemaker device leads, orthopedic screws or implants, or metal fragments in their eyes, are not suitable for MRI investigation [84].

6.18 Conclusion

A multimodality noninvasive cardiovascular imaging approach to the detection and evaluation of CAD enables the anatomical and functional evaluation of atherosclerotic plaque, by providing objective data on the degree of stenosis, and impact on downstream flow. Combining both anatomic and functional information is key for guiding patient management, as there is an often variable relationship between the anatomic degree of a stenotic lesion and the severity of myocardial ischemia. The additional information with a hybrid combined multimodality imaging approach does result in increased radiation exposure and higher costs; however, the synergistic approach may be justified if there is a clear benefit from the information obtained which will optimize downstream patient-specific management.

References

[1] Virani SS, Alonso A, Benjamin EJ, et al. Heart disease and stroke statistics-2020 update: a report from the American Heart Association. Circulation 2020;141:e139—596.
[2] van Werkhoven JM, Schuijf JD, Gaemperli O, et al. Prognostic value of multislice computed tomography and gated single-photon emission computed tomography in patients with suspected coronary artery disease. J Am Coll Cardiol 2009;53:623—32.
[3] Meinel FG, Schoepf UJ, Townsend JC, et al. Diagnostic yield and accuracy of coronary CT angiography after abnormal nuclear myocardial perfusion imaging. Sci Rep 2018;8:9228.
[4] De Bruyne B, Pijls NH, Kalesan B, et al. Fractional flow reserve-guided PCI vs medical therapy in stable coronary disease. N Engl J Med 2012;367:991—1001.
[5] Nesto RW, Kowalchuk GJ. The ischemic cascade: temporal sequence of hemodynamic, electrocardiographic and symptomatic expressions of ischemia. Am J Cardiol 1987;59:23c—30c.
[6] Cerqueira MD, Weissman NJ, Dilsizian V, et al. Standardized myocardial segmentation and nomenclature for tomographic imaging of the heart. A statement for healthcare professionals from the Cardiac Imaging Committee of the Council on Clinical Cardiology of the American Heart Association. Circulation 2002;105:539—42.

[7]   Ross Jr. J. Mechanisms of regional ischemia and antianginal drug action during exercise. Prog Cardiovasc Dis 1989;31:455−66.

[8]   Camici PG, Gistri R, Lorenzoni R, et al. Coronary reserve and exercise ECG in patients with chest pain and normal coronary angiograms. Circulation 1992;86:179−86.

[9]   Kaski JC, Rosano GM, Collins P, Nihoyannopoulos P, Maseri A, Poole-Wilson PA. Cardiac syndrome X: clinical characteristics and left ventricular function. Long-term follow-up study. J Am Coll Cardiol 1995;25:807−14.

[10] Picano E, Pálinkás A, Amyot R. Diagnosis of myocardial ischemia in hypertensive patients. J Hypertens 2001;19:1177−83.

[11] Pellikka PA, Arruda-Olson A, Chaudhry FA, et al. Guidelines for performance, interpretation, and application of stress echocardiography in ischemic heart disease: from the American Society of Echocardiography. J Am Soc Echocardiography 2020;33(1−41):e8.

[12] Pellikka PA, Nagueh SF, Elhendy AA, Kuehl CA, Sawada SG. American Society of Echocardiography recommendations for performance, interpretation, and application of stress echocardiography. J Am Soc Echocardiogr 2007;20:1021−41.

[13] Ejlersen JA, Poulsen SH, Mortensen J, May O. A comparison of the diagnostic value of 2D strain stress echocardiography, myocardial perfusion scintigraphy, and Duke treadmill score in patients suspected of coronary artery disease. Echocardiography 2016;33:1523−31.

[14] Schuijf JD, Shaw LJ, Wijns W, et al. Cardiac imaging in coronary artery disease: differing modalities. Heart 2005;91:1110−17.

[15] Heijenbrok-Kal MH, Fleischmann KE, Hunink MG. Stress echocardiography, stress single-photon-emission computed tomography and electron beam computed tomography for the assessment of coronary artery disease: a meta-analysis of diagnostic performance. Am Heart J 2007;154:415−23.

[16] Yao S-S, Wever-Pinzon O, Zhang X, Bangalore S, Chaudhry FA. Prognostic value of stress echocardiogram in patients with angiographically significant coronary artery disease. Am J Cardiol 2012;109:153−8.

[17] Marcovitz PA, Armstrong WF. Accuracy of dobutamine stress echocardiography in detecting coronary artery disease. Am J Cardiol 1992;69:1269−73.

[18] Elkaryoni A, Abu-Sheasha G, Altibi AM, Hassan A, Ellakany K, Nanda NC. Diagnostic accuracy of dobutamine stress echocardiography in the detection of cardiac allograft vasculopathy in heart transplant recipients: a systematic review and meta-analysis study. Echocardiography 2019;36:528−36.

[19] Leong-Poi H, Rim SJ, Le DE, Fisher NG, Wei K, Kaul S. Perfusion vs function: the ischemic cascade in demand ischemia: implications of single-vessel vs multivessel stenosis. Circulation 2002;105:987−92.

[20] Abdelmoneim SS, Mulvagh SL, Xie F, et al. Regadenoson stress real-time myocardial perfusion echocardiography for detection of coronary artery disease: feasibility and accuracy of two different ultrasound contrast agents. J Am Soc Echocardiogr 2015;28:1393−400.

[21] Hayat SA, Dwivedi G, Jacobsen A, Lim TK, Kinsey C, Senior R. Effects of left bundle-branch block on cardiac structure, function, perfusion, and perfusion reserve: implications for myocardial contrast echocardiography vs radionuclide perfusion imaging for the detection of coronary artery disease. Circulation 2008;117:1832−41.

[22] Mattoso AA, Kowatsch I, Tsutsui JM, et al. Prognostic value of qualitative and quantitative vasodilator stress myocardial perfusion echocardiography in patients with known or suspected coronary artery disease. J Am Soc Echocardiogr 2013;26:539−47.

[23] Porter TR, Adolphson M, High RR, et al. Rapid detection of coronary artery stenoses with real-time perfusion echocardiography during regadenoson stress. Circ Cardiovasc Imaging 2011;4:628−35.

[24] Stewart GM, Chan J, Yamada A, et al. Impact of high-intensity endurance exercise on regional left and right ventricular myocardial mechanics. Eur Heart J Cardiovasc Imaging 2016;18:688−96.

[25] von Scheidt F, Kiesler V, Kaestner M, Bride P, Krämer J, Apitz C. Left ventricular strain and strain rate during submaximal semisupine bicycle exercise stress echocardiography in healthy adolescents and young adults: systematic protocol and reference values. J Am Soc Echocardiogr 2020;33:848−57 e1.

[26] Xu B, Cremer P, Jaber W, Moir S, Harb SC, Rodriguez LL. Which test for CAD should be used in patients with left bundle branch block? Clevel Clin J Med 2018;85:224−30.

[27] Xu B, Dobson L, Mottram PM, Nasis A, Cameron J, Moir S. Is exercise stress echocardiography useful in patients with suspected obstructive coronary artery disease who have resting left bundle branch block? Clin Cardiol 2018;41:360−5.

[28] Kocyigit D, Scanameo A, Xu B. Multimodality imaging for the prevention of cardiovascular events: Coronary artery calcium and beyond. Cardiovasc Diagn Ther 2020;11(3):840−58.

[29] Yeboah J, McClelland RL, Polonsky TS, et al. Comparison of novel risk markers for improvement in cardiovascular risk assessment in intermediate-risk individuals. JAMA 2012;308:788−95.

[30] Nasir K, Bittencourt MS, Blaha MJ, et al. Implications of coronary artery calcium testing among statin candidates according to American College of Cardiology/American Heart Association Cholesterol Management Guidelines: MESA (Multi-Ethnic Study of Atherosclerosis). J Am Coll Cardiol 2015;66:1657−68.

[31] Agatston AS, Janowitz WR, Hildner FJ, Zusmer NR, Viamonte Jr. M, Detrano R. Quantification of coronary artery calcium using ultrafast computed tomography. J Am Coll Cardiol 1990;15:827−32.

[32] Sarwar A, Shaw LJ, Shapiro MD, et al. Diagnostic and prognostic value of absence of coronary artery calcification. JACC Cardiovasc Imaging 2009;2:675−88.

[33] Grundy SM, Stone NJ, Bailey AL, et al. AHA/ACC/AACVPR/AAPA/ABC/ACPM/ADA/AGS/APhA/ASPC/NLA/PCNA guideline on the management of blood cholesterol: a report of the American College of Cardiology/American Heart Association Task Force on Clinical Practice Guidelines. J Am Coll Cardiol 2019;73:e285−350.

[34] Miedema MD, Duprez DA, Misialek JR, et al. Use of coronary artery calcium testing to guide aspirin utilization for primary prevention: estimates from the multi-ethnic study of atherosclerosis. Circ Cardiovasc Qual Outcomes 2014;7:453−60.

[35] Ajufo E, Ayers CR, Vigen R, et al. Value of coronary artery calcium scanning in association with the net benefit of aspirin in primary prevention of atherosclerotic cardiovascular disease. JAMA Cardiol 2021;6:179−87.

[36] Ramanathan S. Coronary artery calcium data and reporting system: strengths and limitations. World J Radiol 2019;11:126−33.

[37] Pontone G, Bertella E, Mushtaq S, et al. Coronary artery disease: diagnostic accuracy of CT coronary angiography—a comparison of high and standard spatial resolution scanning. Radiology 2014;271:688−94.

[38] Abdulla J, Abildstrom SZ, Gotzsche O, Christensen E, Kober L, Torp-Pedersen C. 64-multislice detector computed tomography coronary angiography as potential alternative to conventional coronary angiography: a systematic review and meta-analysis. Eur Heart J 2007;28:3042−50.

[39] Fischer C, Hulten E, Belur P, Smith R, Voros S, Villines TC. Coronary CT angiography versus intravascular ultrasound for estimation of coronary stenosis and atherosclerotic plaque burden: a meta-analysis. J Cardiovasc Comput Tomogr 2013;7:256−66.

[40] Budoff MJ, Dowe D, Jollis JG, et al. Diagnostic performance of 64-multidetector row coronary computed tomographic angiography for evaluation of coronary artery stenosis in individuals without known coronary artery disease: results from the prospective multicenter ACCURACY (Assessment by Coronary Computed Tomographic Angiography of Individuals Undergoing Invasive Coronary Angiography) trial. J Am Coll Cardiol 2008;52:1724−32.

[41] Meijboom WB, Meijs MF, Schuijf JD, et al. Diagnostic accuracy of 64-slice computed tomography coronary angiography: a prospective, multicenter, multivendor study. J Am Coll Cardiol 2008;52:2135−44.

[42] Taylor AJ, Cerqueira M, Hodgson JM, et al. ACCF/SCCT/ACR/AHA/ASE/ASNC/NASCI/SCAI/SCMR 2010 appropriate use criteria for cardiac computed tomography. A report of the American College of Cardiology Foundation Appropriate Use Criteria Task Force, the Society of Cardiovascular Computed Tomography, the American College of Radiology, the American Heart Association, the American Society of Echocardiography, the American Society of Nuclear Cardiology, the North American Society for Cardiovascular Imaging, the Society for Cardiovascular

Angiography and Interventions, and the Society for Cardiovascular Magnetic Resonance. J Am Coll Cardiol 2010;56:1864—94.

[43] Newby DE, Adamson PD, Berry C, et al. Coronary CT angiography and 5-year risk of myocardial infarction. N Engl J Med 2018;379:924—33.

[44] Douglas PS, Hoffmann U, Patel MR, et al. Outcomes of anatomical versus functional testing for coronary artery disease. N Engl J Med 2015;372:1291—300.

[45] Min JK, Dunning A, Lin FY, et al. Age- and sex-related differences in all-cause mortality risk based on coronary computed tomography angiography findings results from the International Multicenter CONFIRM (Coronary CT Angiography Evaluation for Clinical Outcomes: An International Multicenter Registry) of 23,854 patients without known coronary artery disease. J Am Coll Cardiol 2011;58:849—60.

[46] Fihn S, Gardin JM, Abrams J, et al. ACCF/AHA/ACP/AATS/PCNA/SCAI/STS guideline for the diagnosis and management of patients with stable ischemic heart disease: a report of the American College of Cardiology Foundation/American Heart Association task force on practice guidelines, and the American College of Physicians, American Association for Thoracic Surgery, Preventive Cardiovascular Nurses Association, Society for Cardiovascular Angiography and Interventions, and Society of Thoracic Surgeons. Circulation 2012;126(25):e354—471.

[47] Kelion AD, Nicol ED. The rationale for the primacy of coronary CT angiography in the National Institute for Health and Care Excellence (NICE) guideline (CG95) for the investigation of chest pain of recent onset. J Cardiovasc Comput Tomogr 2018;12:516—22.

[48] Knuuti J, Wijns W, Saraste A, et al. ESC Guidelines for the diagnosis and management of chronic coronary syndromes: the task force for the diagnosis and management of chronic coronary syndromes of the European Society of Cardiology (ESC). Eur Heart J 2019;41:407—77.

[49] Narula J, Chandrashekhar Y, Ahmadi A, et al. SCCT 2021 expert consensus document on coronary computed tomographic angiography: a report of the society of cardiovascular computed tomography. J Cardiovasc Comput Tomogr 2020;15(3):192—217.

[50] Greulich S, Sechtem U. Multimodality imaging in coronary artery disease — "the more the better?". Cor et Vasa 2015;57:e462—9.

[51] Rispler S, Keidar Z, Ghersin E, et al. Integrated single-photon emission computed tomography and computed tomography coronary angiography for the assessment of hemodynamically significant coronary artery lesions. J Am Coll Cardiol 2007;49:1059—67.

[52] Strauss HW. Stress myocardial perfusion imaging - the beginning. JACC Cardiovasc Imaging 2008;1:238—40.

[53] Chetrit M, Verma BR, Xu B. Choosing the appropriate stress test for myocardial perfusion imaging. Curr Cardiovasc Imaging Rep 2019;12:12.

[54] Sato A, Nozato T, Hikita H, et al. Incremental value of combining 64-slice computed tomography angiography with stress nuclear myocardial perfusion imaging to improve noninvasive detection of coronary artery disease. J Nucl Cardiol 2010;17:19—26.

[55] Santana CA, Garcia EV, Faber TL, et al. Diagnostic performance of fusion of myocardial perfusion imaging (MPI) and computed tomography coronary angiography. J Nucl Cardiol 2009;16:201—11.

[56] Klocke FJ, Baird MG, Lorell BH, et al. ACC/AHA/ASNC guidelines for the clinical use of cardiac radionuclide imaging—executive summary. Circulation 2003;108:1404—18.

[57] Pazhenkottil AP, Nkoulou RN, Ghadri J-R, et al. Prognostic value of cardiac hybrid imaging integrating single-photon emission computed tomography with coronary computed tomography angiography. Eur Heart J 2011;32:1465—71.

[58] Danad I, Szymonifka J, Twisk JWR, et al. Diagnostic performance of cardiac imaging methods to diagnose ischaemia-causing coronary artery disease when directly compared with fractional flow reserve as a reference standard: a meta-analysis. Eur Heart J 2017;38:991—8.

[59] Camici PG. Positron emission tomography and myocardial imaging. Heart 2000;83:475—80.

[60] Schindler TH, Schelbert HR, Quercioli A, Dilsizian V. Cardiac PET imaging for the detection and monitoring of coronary artery disease and microvascular health. JACC: Cardiovasc Imaging 2010;3:623—40.

[61] Nandalur KR, Dwamena BA, Choudhri AF, Nandalur SR, Reddy P, Carlos RC. Diagnostic performance of positron emission tomography in the detection of coronary artery disease: a *meta*-analysis. Acad Radiol 2008;15:444–51.

[62] Kajander S, Joutsiniemi E, Saraste M, et al. Cardiac positron emission tomography/computed tomography imaging accurately detects anatomically and functionally significant coronary artery disease. Circulation 2010;122:603–13.

[63] Thomassen A, Petersen H, Diederichsen ACP, et al. Hybrid CT angiography and quantitative 15O-water PET for assessment of coronary artery disease: comparison with quantitative coronary angiography. Eur J Nucl Med Mol Imaging 2013;40:1894–904.

[64] Opolski MP, Achenbach S, Schuhbäck A, et al. Coronary computed tomographic prediction rule for time-efficient guidewire crossing through chronic total occlusion. JACC: Cardiovasc Interventions 2015;8:257–67.

[65] Luo C, Huang M, Li J, et al. Predictors of interventional success of antegrade PCI for CTO. JACC: Cardiovasc Imaging 2015;8:804–13.

[66] Shi L, Dorbala S, Paez D, et al. Gender differences in radiation dose from nuclear cardiology studies across the world: findings from the INCAPS registry. JACC Cardiovasc Imaging 2016;9:376–84.

[67] Proctor P, Al Solaiman F, Hage FG. Myocardial perfusion imaging prior to coronary revascularization: from risk stratification to procedure guidance. J Nucl Cardiol 2019;26:954–7.

[68] Shaw LJ, Hachamovitch R, Berman DS, et al. The economic consequences of available diagnostic and prognostic strategies for the evaluation of stable angina patients: an observational assessment of the value of precatheterization ischemia. Economics of Noninvasive Diagnosis (END) Multicenter Study Group. J Am Coll Cardiol 1999;33:661–9.

[69] Mark DB, Federspiel JJ, Cowper PA, et al. Economic outcomes with anatomical versus functional diagnostic testing for coronary artery disease. Ann Intern Med 2016;165:94–102.

[70] Nørgaard BL, Leipsic J, Gaur S, et al. Diagnostic performance of noninvasive fractional flow reserve derived from coronary computed tomography angiography in suspected coronary artery disease: the NXT trial (Analysis of Coronary Blood Flow Using CT Angiography: Next Steps). J Am Coll Cardiol 2014;63:1145–55.

[71] Koo BK, Erglis A, Doh JH, et al. Diagnosis of ischemia-causing coronary stenoses by noninvasive fractional flow reserve computed from coronary computed tomographic angiograms. Results from the prospective multicenter DISCOVER-FLOW (Diagnosis of Ischemia-Causing Stenoses Obtained Via Noninvasive Fractional Flow Reserve) study. J Am Coll Cardiol 2011;58:1989–97.

[72] Min JK, Leipsic J, Pencina MJ, et al. Diagnostic accuracy of fractional flow reserve from anatomic CT angiography. JAMA 2012;308:1237–45.

[73] Kim KH, Doh JH, Koo BK, et al. A novel noninvasive technology for treatment planning using virtual coronary stenting and computed tomography-derived computed fractional flow reserve. JACC Cardiovasc Interv 2014;7:72–8.

[74] Hlatky MA, Saxena A, Koo BK, Erglis A, Zarins CK, Min JK. Projected costs and consequences of computed tomography-determined fractional flow reserve. Clin Cardiol 2013;36:743–8.

[75] Kramer CM, Barkhausen J, Flamm SD, et al. Standardized cardiovascular magnetic resonance (CMR) protocols 2013 update. J Cardiovasc Magn Reson 2013;15:91.

[76] Paetsch I, Jahnke C, Wahl A, et al. Comparison of dobutamine stress magnetic resonance, adenosine stress magnetic resonance, and adenosine stress magnetic resonance perfusion. Circulation 2004;110:835–42.

[77] Wolff SD, Schwitter J, Coulden R, et al. Myocardial first-pass perfusion magnetic resonance imaging: a multicenter dose-ranging study. Circulation 2004;110:732–7.

[78] Al-Saadi N, Nagel E, Gross M, et al. Noninvasive detection of myocardial ischemia from perfusion reserve based on cardiovascular magnetic resonance. Circulation 2000;101:1379–83.

[79] Weber OM, Martin AJ, Higgins CB. Whole-heart steady-state free precession coronary artery magnetic resonance angiography. Magn Reson Med 2003;50:1223–8.

[80] Chiribiri A, Kelle S, Götze S, et al. Visualization of the cardiac venous system using cardiac magnetic resonance. Am J Cardiol 2008;101:407–12.

[81] McCarthy RM, Shea SM, Deshpande VS, et al. Coronary MR angiography: true FISP imaging improved by prolonging breath holds with preoxygenation in healthy volunteers. Radiology 2003;227:283–8.

[82] Schuijf JD, Bax JJ, Shaw LJ, et al. *Meta*-analysis of comparative diagnostic performance of magnetic resonance imaging and multislice computed tomography for noninvasive coronary angiography. Am Heart J 2006;151:404–11.

[83] Dirksen MS, Lamb HJ, van der Geest R, de Roos A. Toward comparability of coronary magnetic resonance angiography: proposal for a standardized quantitative assessment. Eur Radiol 2003;13:2353–7.

[84] Ripley DP, Musa TA, Dobson LE, Plein S, Greenwood JP. Cardiovascular magnetic resonance imaging: what the general cardiologist should know. Heart 2016;102:1589–603.

CHAPTER 7

Magnetic resonance imaging of ischemic heart disease

Ahmed Abdel Khalek Abdel Razek, Dalia Fahmy and Germeen Albair Ashmalla
Department of Diagnostic Radiology, Faculty of Medicine, Mansoura University, Mansoura, Egypt

7.1 Introduction

Detection of nonviable myocardium in early contrast–enhanced (ECE) images, whether associated or not with enhanced scar in the delay postcontrast images is crucial in the diagnosis of ischemic cardiomyopathy. Treatment plan is influenced by the ratio of viable to nonviable myocardium, in addition to the presence of any indicators determining severe myocardial ischemia such as size and extent of infarct, microvascular obstruction, heterogeneity of infarct, myocardial hemorrhage, and multiple silent or right ventricular (RV) infarcts. All these issues will be discussed in this chapter.

7.2 Cardiac MR imaging of myocardial infarction

7.2.1 CMR of acute infarction

CMR is usually done in the first 2−5 days following acute MI. Imaging in this situation is mainly directed to assess the cardiac structure and function. Cardiac function is evaluated through dedicated visualization of cardiac wall mobility, valve leaflet mobility and there is associated regurgitation or stenosis in SSFP cine imaging along various cardiac axes [1−4]. Myocardial perfusion patterns are recognized by watching the early images taken after IV injection of gadolinium derivatives. Microvascular obstruction (MVO) manifests as areas of incomplete myocardial reperfusion that appears of low SI and nonenhancing in the ECE images. On the other hand, myocardial infarct manifests by subendocardial enhancement in late contrast–enhanced (LCE) images obtained 10−15 after contrast injection. The addition of cine imaging provides a combined viability-functional imaging [3,4]. In case of co-excitant valve disease, phase-contrast or velocity-encoded cine techniques are used for quantitative assessment of regurgitant flow volumes and/or measure peak velocities/transvalvular gradients [1−5].

Cardiovascular and Coronary Artery Imaging
DOI: https://doi.org/10.1016/B978-0-12-822706-0.00003-2
171

7.2.2 CMR with clinical suspicion of acute coronary syndrome

Patients who suffer from symptoms suggesting acute coronary syndrome but routine imaging and lab tests show no clear evidence of ischemia require a specific CMR protocol designed to look for signs of coronary artery stenosis or alternatively other underlying diseases that present with acute severe specifically; acute dissection of the ascending aorta and acute pulmonary artery embolism. Imaging protocol includes stress perfusion alone as a single test or with rest perfusion. Injection of vasodilator (e.g., adenosine, dipyridamole) directs more blood flow to the normally perfused myocardium with less blood flow to areas supplied by stenotic artery. As mentioned earlier, hypo-perfused myocardium shows no enhancement in ECE images. The addition of rest-stress perfusion allows measurement of myocardial perfusion reserve. Bright blood (SSFP) imaging and contrast-enhanced 3D mono-phasic or time-resolved CMR angiography are applied to exclude the presence of acute dissection of the ascending aorta or filling defects (emboli) at the pulmonary artery [6–14].

7.2.3 Visualization and characterization of jeopardized myocardium

Jeopardized myocardium is a term used to describe the myocardium devoid of blood supply distal to coronary artery occlusion. It is important to be reperfused properly before turning necrotic. Presence of myocardial edema is a clue of the infarct-related artery, while its absence excludes acute ischemia. Alternatively, myocardial edema is present in other "acute" cardiac pathologies like myocarditis and stress cardiomyopathy, thus correlation with findings gained from LCE and cine imaging is mandatory. Myocardial edema is routinely depicted in T2 WI, yet other sequences namely, pre-contrast T1 mapping and T2 mapping are promising in this issue [15,16]. On the other hand, myocardial infarct is detected in contrast-enhanced images. The application of an inversion-recovery pre-pulse improves infarct visualization as it nullifies signal of normal myocardium which enable accurate delineation of infarcted myocardium (infarct volumes as small as or even less than 1 g). Infarct images are acquired in LCE (Fig. 7.1). Using multislice 2D or 3D sequences covering the ventricles, the presence and exact size of infarcted myocardium can be visualized and quantified either as a volume or as a percentage of LV mass. Classic myocardial infarct is located at coronary perfusion territory and shows subendocardial enhancement with variable transmural extent [9–14,17–24].

A myocardial salvage ratio is defined as the relation between infarct size measured in LCE imaging to an area at risk measured in T2 WI. This ratio reflects the extent of irreversibly damaged myocardium. The presence of myocardial edema in T2 WI that lacks enhancement in LCE equals aborted MI, while the presence of enhanced myocardium in LCE that matches the same size of myocardial edema represents a ratio of 0. This ratio is directly related to post-reperfusion ST-segment resolution, and inversely to adverse LV remodeling and is considered an independent prognostic value [17–20].

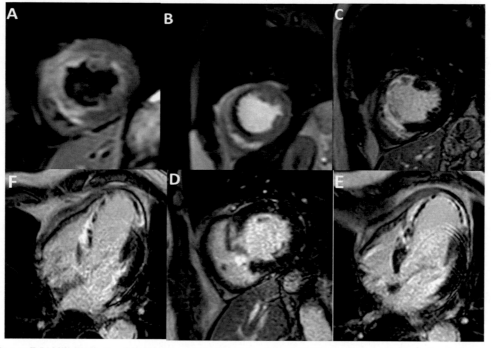

Figure 7.1 MRI findings of ischemic scar in 64 years old male: Inversion recovery short-axis images before (A) and after (B) arrival of gadolinium chelate in the left ventricle show perfusion defect in the anteroseptal wall, multilevel short axis (C, D) and long axis delayed gadolinium enhancement (E, F) show anteroseptal and apical subendocardial and transmural enhancement denoting ischemic scar involving more than 50% of the thickness of the myocardium. *MRI*, Magnetic resonance imaging.

7.3 MR indicators of myocardial infraction severity

7.3.1 Infarct size and extent of transmural involvement

Myocardial tissue is characterized by low regenerative capacity with replacement of irreversibly damaged myocardium by nonfunctional fibrotic scar. Thus the amount of lost contractile tissue is strongly correlated with worse LV remodeling and patient outcome. LCE imaging proved to be a well-validated, accurate, and reproducible way to correctly measure the size of myocardial infarct no matter the age of infarct. It can detect small-sized infarcts that are not detected by ECG or other imaging modalities such as SPECT. Moreover, assessment of infarct transmurality is the second clue of infarct severity. Several studies stated that the more mural thickness involved by infarct the less inotropic reserve, less functional recovery of contractility, more severe residual adverse effects; severe post-infarct thinning of myocardial wall, ventricular wall aneurysm, and ventricular wall remodeling [18–22].

Early measurement of the infarct size is usually overestimated as it will be affected by the presence of edema and other cellular elements [21]. Progressive decrease of the infarct size occurs due to improvement of tissue edema and gradual shrinkage of scar tissue (by as much as 25% over a period of 4—8 weeks). Another factor is the increase in the remaining myocardial mass attributed to compensatory hypertrophy. So, the scar to normal myocardium ratio appears to become smaller by time. These changes are not well represented in calculations of LV total volume and mass [22].

7.3.2 Microvascular obstruction

Although endothelial cells can withstand prolonged ischemia better than myocytes, yet "no-reflow" or "MVO" could still occur following successful coronary arterial reperfusion. It is believed that other factors including reperfusion injury, distal embolization, and individual susceptibility contribute to the development of MVO. Presence and extent of MVO are directly related to the actual duration of ischemic event, development of collaterals, and how effective it could substitute major vessel occlusion. It is independently linked to no functional recovery, adverse remodeling, and far worse patient outcomes. In the case of MVO, the involved segment myocardium shows no enhancement in the ECE phase, which requires a long inversion time to depict MVO. On the other hand, several studies reported that persistent MVO at LCE is more valuable ECE and is stronger indicator of adverse clinical events [25,26].

7.3.3 Intramyocardial hemorrhage

When an irreversibly damaged myocardium is reperfused, intramyocardial hemorrhage (IMH) with excess extracellular blood extravasation occurs. It is seen after both pharmacological and mechanical reperfusion. Considering the presence of hemoglobin breakdown product deoxyhemoglobin that displays low SI in T2 and T2*WI, so hemorrhagic infarct appears in T2 WI as segment of high SI with dark center, while nonhemorrhagic infarcts display homogenous high SI. IMH is linked to more infarcts that have greater transmural extension and lower baseline ejection fraction. IMH is independently related to adverse regional and global LV remodeling, no functional recovery, late arrhythmia, and worse patient outcomes [21—27].

7.3.4 Myocardial infarct heterogeneity

Patients with a recent history of MI are at high risk for arrhythmias. The center of the necrotic tissue contains mainly dense fibrotic scar that does not depolarize, but the infarct margin contains a mixture of nonviable and viable cells that act as an arrhythmogenic focus initiating ventricular arrhythmias that may end with sudden cardiac death. Dense fibrotic myocardium displays high SI in LCE defined as 5SD above the SI of normal myocardium. Lower SI—that is between 2SD and 5SD—the so-called "gray" myocardium representing areas with variable ratio of fibrosis/myocytes. The gray myocardium is not limited to the infarct margin, it could be seen also in central segments, in addition to papillary muscles [21–28].

7.3.5 Right ventricular infarction

Isolated RV infarction is a rare event, that is why RV infarction is dealt with as a biventricular MI. There is a wide variety in infract extent along the anterior or inferior RV wall resulting in RV dysfunction. No functional recovery is linked with high death rate. RV wall is trabeculated and relatively thin, which does not make detection of ischemic changes easy, even with recent techniques. Nevertheless, CMR is extremely valuable in assessment of reversible and irreversible RV damage using a dedicated protocol composed of T2 WI, LCE, and cine sequences [21].

7.3.6 Missed infarcts

Unfortunately, about 40%–60% of MIs are silent [29,30]. Unfortunately, any scar in a person who did not suffer from chest pain is linked to high risk of adverse events. Delayed-enhancement MR imaging allowed the discovery of silent MI 76%–390% more frequently than ECG [23].

7.3.7 Chronic myocardial infarction

In chronic MI, cine images depict thinned wall with abnormal mobility (hypo, dys, or akinetic). Edema is not detected on T2 WI. LCE reveals wall thinning and subendo-cardial/transmural late enhancement in typical vascular distribution [23].

7.4 Myocardial infarction complications

7.4.1 Thrombus

Left ventricular thrombus is a common adverse effect following myocardial infarction. It may be associated with formation of arterial emboli causing stroke, mostly seen in large anterior wall MIs with anteroapical aneurysm. On cine imaging, a thrombus is shown as an intracavitary mass adherent to an akinetic LV apex (Fig. 7.2).

Long inversion times (TI-value >422 ms), sequences immediately after the injection of gadolinium and following a 15-minute delay time can discriminate an intracavitary thrombus from cardiac tumors accurately. A thrombus consistently demonstrates a characteristic pattern of hypo-intensity within the core lesion at early and delayed scans while the core lesion of hyper- and hypovascularized tumors appears hyperintense in delayed scan [21,22].

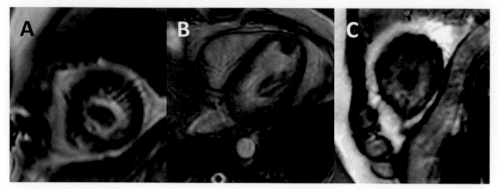

Figure 7.2 Left ventricular thrombus: Short axis cine (A) and four chamber view cine (B) show hypointense thrombus within the lumen of the left ventricle near the apex. Delayed postcontrast short-axis view (C) shows no enhancement.

7.4.2 LV aneurysm

LV aneurysm is one of the rare complications of myocardial infarction; yet, it is associated with high morbidity and mortality. A true LV aneurysm appears as a dyskinetic thin well—demarcated myocardial wall bulge that apparently lacks muscle fibers on cine images. As a result of disorganized weak myocardial muscle contraction, there will be significant deterioration of LV function. On delayed enhancement inversion recovery imaging, the wall of the aneurysm shows transmural LGE owing to scarred fibrotic wall [23,31].

7.5 Future directions

Application of advanced MR sequences including MR spectroscopy that gives information about metabolic changes within the infarction part of the myocardium [32—35], diffusion tensor imaging that gives date about cellularity and chronicity of myocardial infarction [36—42], perfusion with contrast MR imaging for characterization of myocardial lesions [1—4], arterial spin labeling that gives information about vascularity of the lesions [43—46], and contrast MR angiography for evaluation of the coronary artery is still limited. It may also be used in the preparative assessment of aorta and pulmonary artery for any associated or incidental findings [47—50]. Also the use of structured reporting as for CT of coronary artery disease [51—57] and artificial inelegance [58,59] in the future will increase the clinical validity. And it may also be used for MR imaging in the evaluation of patients with ischemic heart disease.

References

[1] Jo Y, Kim J, Park CH, et al. Guideline for cardiovascular magnetic resonance imaging from the Korean Society of cardiovascular imaging-part 1: standardized protocol. Korean J Radiol 2019;20:1313–33.

[2] Cui C, Yin G, Lu M, et al. Retrospective electrocardiography-gated real-time cardiac cine MRI at 3T: comparison with conventional segmented cine MRI. Korean J Radiol 2019;20:114–25.

[3] Saeed M, Liu H, Liang CH, et al. Magnetic resonance imaging for characterizing myocardial diseases. Int J Cardiovasc Imaging 2017;33:1395–414.

[4] Situ Y, Birch SCM, Moreyra C, et al. Cardiovascular magnetic resonance imaging for structural heart disease. Cardiovasc Diagn Ther 2020;10:361–75.

[5] Nayak KS, Nielsen JF, Bernstein MA, et al. Cardiovascular magnetic resonance phase contrast imaging. J Cardiovasc Magn Reson 2015;17:71.

[6] Seetharam K, Lerakis S. Cardiac magnetic resonance imaging: the future is bright. F1000Res 2019;8 F1000 Faculty Rev-1636.

[7] 14Dodd JD, Leipsic J. Cardiovascular CT and MRI in 2019: review of key articles. Radiology 2020;297:17–30. Available from: https://doi.org/10.1148/radiol.2020200605.

[8] Vieillard-Baron A, Millington SJ, Sanfilippo F, et al. A decade of progress in critical care echocardiography: a narrative review. Intensive Care Med 2019;45:770–88.

[9] François CJ. Current state of the art cardiovascular MR imaging techniques for assessment of ischemic heart disease. Radiol Clin North Am 2015;53:335–44.

[10] Ibanez B, Aletras AH, Arai AE, et al. Cardiac MRI endpoints in myocardial infarction experimental and clinical trials: JACC Scientific Expert Panel. J Am Coll Cardiol 2019;74:238–56.

[11] Fair MJ, Gatehouse PD, DiBella EV, et al. A review of 3D first-pass, whole-heart, myocardial perfusion cardiovascular magnetic resonance. J Cardiovasc Magn Reson 2015;17:68.

[12] Nazir MS, Neji R, Speier P, et al. Simultaneous multi slice (SMS) balanced steady state free precession first-pass myocardial perfusion cardiovascular magnetic resonance with iterative reconstruction at 1.5 T. J Cardiovasc Magn Reson 2018;20:84.

[13] Prosper AE, Colletti PM. Myocardial perfusion SPECT and cardiac MR correlative imaging. Clin Nucl Med 2017;42:941–4.

[14] Benovoy M, Jacobs M, Cheriet F, et al. Robust universal nonrigid motion correction framework for first-pass cardiac MR perfusion imaging. J Magn Reson Imaging 2017;46:1060–72.

[15] Messroghli DR, Moon JC, Ferreira VM, et al. Clinical recommendations for cardiovascular magnetic resonance mapping of T1, T2, T2* and extracellular volume: A consensus statement by the Society for Cardiovascular Magnetic Resonance (SCMR) endorsed by the European Association for Cardiovascular Imaging (EACVI). J Cardiovasc Magn Reson 2017;19:75.

[16] Kim PK, Hong YJ, Im DJ, et al. Myocardial T1 and T2 mapping: techniques and clinical applications. Korean J Radiol 2017;18:113–31.

[17] Kendziora B, Dewey M. Prognostic value of the myocardial salvage index measured by T2-weighted and T1-weighted late gadolinium enhancement magnetic resonance imaging after ST-segment elevation myocardial infarction: a systematic review and meta-regression analysis. PLoS One 2020;15:e0228736.

[18] Bulluck H, Dharmakumar R, Arai AE, et al. Cardiovascular magnetic resonance in acute ST-segment-elevation myocardial infarction: recent advances, controversies, and future directions. Circulation 2018;137:1949–64.

[19] Bulluck H, Hammond-Haley M, Weinmann S, et al. Myocardial infarct size by CMR in clinical cardioprotection studies: insights from randomized controlled trials. JACC Cardiovasc Imaging 2017;10:230–40.

[20] Garg P, Broadbent DA, Swoboda PP, et al. Acute infarct extracellular volume mapping to quantify myocardial area at risk and chronic infarct size on cardiovascular magnetic resonance imaging. Circ Cardiovasc Imaging 2017;10:e006182.

[21] Reindl M, Eitel I, Reinstadler SJ. Role of cardiac magnetic resonance to improve risk prediction following acute ST-elevation myocardial infarction. J Clin Med 2020;9:1041.

[22] Pontone G, Carità P, Rabbat MG, et al. Role of cardiac magnetic resonance imaging in myocardial infarction. Curr Cardiol Rep 2017;19:101.

[23] Rajiah P, Desai MY, Kwon D, et al. MR imaging of myocardial infarction. RadioGraphics 2013;33:1383—412.

[24] Gräni C, Eichhorn C, Bière L, et al. Comparison of myocardial fibrosis quantification methods by cardiovascular magnetic resonance imaging for risk stratification of patients with suspected myocarditis. J Cardiovasc Magn Reson 2019;21:14.

[25] van Kranenburg M, Magro M, Thiele H, et al. Prognostic value of microvascular obstruction and infarct size, as measured by CMR in STEMI patients. JACC Cardiovasc Imaging 2014;7:930—9.

[26] Galea N, Dacquino GM, Ammendola RM, et al. Microvascular obstruction extent predicts major adverse cardiovascular events in patients with acute myocardial infarction and preserved ejection fraction. Eur Radiol 2019;29:2369—77.

[27] Carrick D, Haig C, Ahmed N, et al. Myocardial hemorrhage after acute reperfused ST-segment-elevation myocardial infarction: relation to microvascular obstruction and prognostic significance. Circ Cardiovasc Imaging 2016;9:e004148.

[28] Bogaert J, Eitel I. Role of cardiovascular magnetic resonance in acute coronary syndrome. Glob Cardiol Sci Pract 2015;2015:24.

[29] Ahmed AH, Shankar K, Eftekhari H, et al. Silent myocardial ischemia: current perspectives and future directions. Exp Clin Cardiol 2007;12:189—96.

[30] Prasad DS, Kabir Z, Revathi Devi K, et al. Prevalence and RIsk factors for Silent Myocardial ischemia (PRISM): a clinico observational study in patients of type 2 diabetes. Indian Heart J 2019;71:400—5.

[31] Olivas-Chacon CI, Mullins C, Solberg A, et al. Assessment of ischemic cardiomyopathy using cardiovascular magnetic resonance imaging: a pictorial review. J Clin Imaging Sci 2015;5:28.

[32] Razek AA, Nada N. Correlation of choline/creatine and apparent diffusion coefficient values with the prognostic parameters of head and neck squamous cell carcinoma. NMR Biomed 2016;29:483—9.

[33] El-mewafy Z, Abdel Razek AAAK, El-Eshmawy M, et al. MR spectroscopy of the frontal region in patients with metabolic syndrome: correlation with anthropometric measurement. Pol J Radiol 2018;83:e215—19.

[34] Razek AA, Abdalla A, Ezzat A, et al. Minimal hepatic encephalopathy in children with liver cirrhosis: diffusion-weighted MR imaging and proton MR spectroscopy of the brain. Neuroradiology 2014;56:885—91.

[35] Dellegrottaglie S, Scatteia A, Pascale CE, et al. Evaluation of cardiac metabolism by magnetic resonance spectroscopy in heart failure. Heart Fail Clin 2019;15:421—33.

[36] Razek A.A.A. Ashmalla G. Assessment of paraspinal neurogenic tumors with diffusion-weighted MR imaging. Eur Spine J 2018;27:841-846.

[37] Abdel Razek AA, Elkhamary S, Al-Mesfer S, Alkatan HM. Correlation of apparent diffusion coefficient at 3T with prognostic parameters of retinoblastoma. Am J Neuroradiol 2012;33:944—8.

[38] El-Serougy L, Abdel Razek AA, Ezzat A, et al. Assessment of diffusion tensor imaging metrics in differentiating low-grade from high-grade gliomas. Neuroradiol J 2016;29:400—7.

[39] Razek AAKA. Diffusion tensor imaging in differentiation of residual head and neck squamous cell carcinoma from post-radiation changes. Magn Reson Imaging 2018;54:84—9.

[40] Razek AA, Fathy A, Gawad TA. Correlation of apparent diffusion coefficient value with prognostic parameters of lung cancer. J Comput Assist Tomogr 2011;35:248—52.

[41] Khalek Abdel Razek AA. Characterization of salivary gland tumours with diffusion tensor imaging. Dentomaxillofac Radiol 2018;47:20170343.

[42] Khalique Z, Pennell D. Diffusion tensor cardiovascular magnetic resonance. Postgrad Med J 2019;95:433—8.

[43] Abdel Razek AAK, Talaat M, El-Serougy L, et al. Clinical applications of arterial spin labeling in brain tumors. J Comput Assist Tomogr 2019;43:525—32.

[44] Abdel Razek AAK. Arterial spin labelling and diffusion-weighted magnetic resonance imaging in differentiation of recurrent head and neck cancer from post-radiation changes. J Laryngol Otol 2018;132:923—8.

[45] Razek AAKA. Multi-parametric MR imaging using pseudo-continuous arterial-spin labeling and diffusion-weighted MR imaging in differentiating subtypes of parotid tumors. Magn Reson Imaging 2019;63:55—9.

[46] Kober F, Jao T, Troalen T, et al. Myocardial arterial spin labeling. J Cardiovasc Magn Reson 2016;18:22.

[47] Abdel Razek AA, Al-Marsafawy H, Elmansy M, et al. CT angiography and MR angiography of congenital anomalies of pulmonary veins. J Comput Assist Tomogr 2019;43:399—405.

[48] Abdel Razek AAK, Al-Marsafawy H, Elmansy M. Imaging of pulmonary atresia with ventricular septal defect. J Comput Assist Tomogr 2019;43:906—11.

[49] Abdel Razek AAK, Elrakhawy MM, Yossof MM, et al. Inter-observer agreement of the coronary artery disease reporting and data system (CAD-RADS(TM)) in patients with stable chest pain. Pol J Radiol 2018;83:e151—9.

[50] Ishida M, Sakuma H. Coronary MR angiography revealed: how to optimize image quality. Magn Reson Imaging Clin N Am 2015;23:117—25.

[51] Abdel Razek AAK, El-Serougy LG, Saleh GA, et al. Liver imaging reporting and data system version 2018: what radiologists need to know. J Comput Assist Tomogr 2020;44:168—77.

[52] Abdel Razek AAK, El-Serougy LG, Saleh GA, et al. Reproducibility of LI-RADS treatment response algorithm for hepatocellular carcinoma after locoregional therapy. Diagn Interv Imaging 2020;101:547—53.

[53] Razek AAKA, El Badrawy MK, Alnaghy E. Interstitial lung fibrosis imaging reporting and data system: what radiologist wants to know? J Comput Assist Tomogr 2020;44:656—66.

[54] Abdel Razek AA, Ashmalla GA, Gaballa G, et al. Pilot study of ultrasound parotid imaging reporting and data system (PIRADS): inter-observer agreement. Eur J Radiol 2015;85:2533—8.

[55] Abdel Razek AAK, Abdelaziz TT. Neck imaging reporting and data system: what does radiologist want to know? J Comput Assist Tomogr 2020;44:527—32.

[56] Abdelaziz TT, Abdel Razk AAK, Ashour MMM, et al. Interreader reproducibility of the Neck Imaging Reporting and Data system (NI-RADS) lexicon for the detection of residual/recurrent disease in treated head and neck squamous cell carcinoma (HNSCC). Cancer Imaging 2020;20:61.

[57] Huang Y, Zhou H, Feng Y, Zhou M, Tang H, Zhou G, et al. Structured reporting of cardiovascular magnetic resonance based on expert consensuses and guidelines. Aging Med 2020;3:40—7.

[58] Razek AAKA. Editorial for "Preoperative MRI-based radiomic machine-learning nomogram may accurately distinguish between benign and malignant soft tissue lesions: a two-center study". J Magn Reson Imaging 2020;52:883—4.

[59] Jiang B, Guo N, Ge Y, Zhang L, Oudkerk M, Xie X. Development and application of artificial intelligence in cardiac imaging. Br J Radiol 2020;93:20190812.

CHAPTER 8

CT angiography of anomalous pulmonary veins

Ahmed Abdel Khalek Abdel Razek[1], Maha Elmansy[1], Mahmoud Abd El-Latif[2] and Hala Al-Marsafawy[3]

[1]Department of Diagnostic Radiology, Faculty of Medicine, Mansoura University, Mansoura, Egypt
[2]Mansoura University Hospital, Mansoura, Egypt
[3]Pediatric Cardiology Unit, Pediatrics Department, Faculty of Medicine, Mansoura University, Mansoura, Egypt

8.1 Introduction

There is a wide spectrum of congenital anomalies affecting pulmonary veins and appears in pediatric patients due to abnormal embryonic vascular development. Those anomalies vary from small isolated lesions to large complex anomalies with multiple associated abnormalities. Accurate assessment of pulmonary vascular anomalies is very important in the treatment plans of those patients [1—6]. Pulmonary veins are four vascular structures carrying oxygenated blood from the right and left lungs and drain it to the left atrium as following: (1) *Right superior pulmonary vein:* carries blood from upper and middle right lung lobes, (2) *Right inferior pulmonary vein:* carries blood from the lower lobe of the right lung, (3) *Left superior pulmonary vein:* carries blood from the upper lobe of the left lung and the lingual, and (4) *Left inferior pulmonary vein:* carries blood from the left lower lung lobe. The normal venous drainage of the lungs is considerably variable among the population [2—5].

Different imaging modalities such as MR angiography, ultrasound, and CT angiography (CTA) are used for emulation of pulmonary veins [7—11]. Echocardiography is an initial imaging modality but it is operator-dependent and cannot delineate the course of extracardiac vascular structures [12—14] and MR angiography is used but it takes long time for data acquisition and postprocessing time [1—18]. CTA is used for diagnosis of congenital pulmonary veins in children, detection of associated cardiac or extracardiac congenital anomalies, and used for postsurgical follow-up of these cases [19,20]. Dual energy CT (DECT) may be used to decrease the time of examination and improve the image quality [21,22] and CT perfusion may give an idea about perfusion and of the lung [22,23].

The purpose of this chapter is to review the role of CTA in pulmonary venous anomalies in cases with congenital heart diseases.

Cardiovascular and Coronary Artery Imaging
DOI: https://doi.org/10.1016/B978-0-12-822706-0.00004-4

Table 8.1 Classification of anomalous pulmonary veins.

Pulmonary veins

Caliber anomalies
- Stenosis
- Hypoplasia
- Atresia
- Varix

Total anomalous pulmonary venous return
- Supracardiac
- Cardiac
- Infracardiac
- Mixed

Partial anomalous pulmonary venous return
- Ass sinus venosus defect
- Veno-venous bridge
- Scimitar syndrome
- Pseudo-scimitar
- Cortriatriatum
- Levoatriocardial vein

8.2 Classification

The Classification of anomalous pulmonary veins has been represented in Table 8.1. It is divided into two main sections: total and partial. See Table 8.1.

8.3 Anomalous in caliber of pulmonary veins

8.3.1 Stenosis of pulmonary vein

It is a very rare entity and accounts approximately for 0.4% of congenital cardiac diseases. Single or more than one vein may be involved. As regard histology; this lesion is characterized mostly by thickening of the fibrous intima and to less extent by hypertrophy of the media. It may lead to death even in unilateral cases (Fig. 8.1) [24,25].

8.3.2 Atresia of pulmonary vein

It means that there is no communication of the pulmonary vein with the left atrium but it differs from the total anomalous pulmonary venous return (TAPVR) that in this case, pulmonary veins do not have drainage to the systemic vein or the right atrium. Decompression of pulmonary venous obstruction is done in small amounts by small venous collaterals. The patient presented in the neonatal period with severe cyanosis. It may occur in any of the two lungs, with an equal incidence of both right and left side affection [26,27].

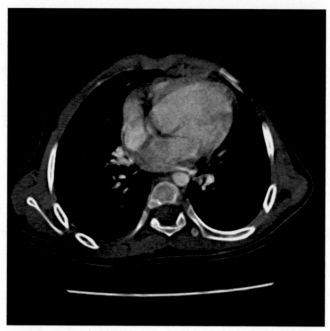

Figure 8.1 Stenosis of pulmonary vein.

8.3.3 Pulmonary venous varix

It is a congenital abnormal dilatation of the pulmonary vein at the site of its connection with the left atrium. Radiologically it is characterized by a mass with a lobulated outline seen posterior to the cardiac shadow. The most common veins involved are the right lower and the left upper pulmonary veins [28,29].

8.4 Total anomalous pulmonary venous return

TAPVR is a rare anomaly with its incidence of about 1%−2% of congenital cardiac anomalies. It consists of abnormal drainage of the pulmonary venous blood that drains into returns to the systemic venous circulation instead of normal left atrial drainage. This results in pulmonary vascular congestion that causes pulmonary hypertension crisis in those cases. Associated obstruction of the pulmonary veins should be reported as it decreases the cardiac output significantly. Regarding the level of pulmonary venous drainage, TAPVR is classified into four types: supracardiac, cardiac, infracardiac, and mixed types [30−35].

8.4.1 Supracardiac type

The commonest type accounting for 45% of TAPVR. In this type, all the four pulmonary veins are draining into an anomalous vertical vein that originates from a venous confluence located posteriorly to the left atrium and anteriorly to the left main pulmonary artery. It may also be seen passing behind the dilated pulmonary artery and so become entrapped between it and the left main bronchus causing subsequent compression and obstruction of pulmonary venous blood flow. The vertical vein has an ascending course that ends in the dilated brachiocephalic vein and then to the superior vena cava (SVC). The right cardiac chambers are usually dilated due to the volume overload. There is always an ASD or patent foramen ovale, which is the only source of flow to the left heart (Fig. 8.2) [32].

8.4.2 Cardiac type

It comes after the supracardiac type as the second most common type accounting for about 15%—30% of TAPVD. It means that the four pulmonary veins are seen draining into an anomalous vertical vein that drains to the heart at the level of the coronary sinus (which is markedly enlarged) or in the right atrium near the interatrial septum at its posterior wall through a short channel or multiple openings [33].

8.4.3 Infracardiac type

This accounts for about 26% of TAPVR. It is characterized by abnormal drainage of the four pulmonary veins in a site below the level of the diaphragm. The site of anomalous drainage in this type includes inferior vena cava, azygos vein, the portal vein, or one of the hepatic veins. The external compression of the diaphragm on the anomalous vein commonly causes an obstruction that result in pulmonary edema in the neonatal period. Infracardiac TAPVR is the commonest type of TAPVR that is associated with pulmonary venous obstruction accounting for up to 78% of cases (Fig. 8.3) [34].

8.4.4 Mixed type

The least common type accounting for 2%—10% of TAPVD. This type is characterized by abnormal pulmonary venous drainage in two or more different sites whether supracardiac (as innominate vein or SVC), cardiac (as coronary sinus or right atrium), or infracardiac (as IVC or portal vein). The most common form of mixed TAPVR is drainage of the left side to the left brachiocephalic vein and drainage of the right side to the coronary sinus or the right atrium. A mixed type of TAPVR is usually accompanied by other congenital cardiac anomalies [35].

Previously, the only way for good visualization of the pulmonary venous drainage anomalies was the conventional angiography, but with rapid advances in sectional imaging CTA as well as MR angiography now allows the excellent depiction of the pulmonary veins with superadded benefits of extracardiac structures visualization. CTA not only provides precise anatomical details but also allows evaluation of associated

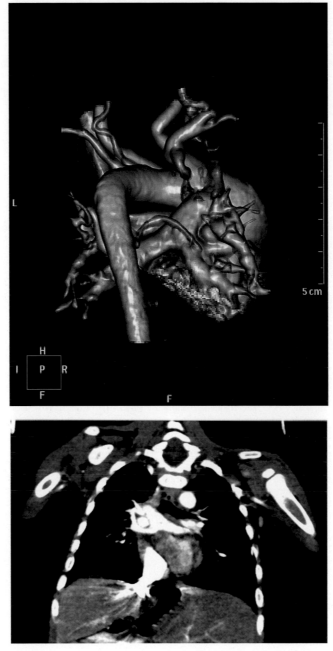

Figure 8.2 Patent foramen ovale as the only source of flow to the left heart.

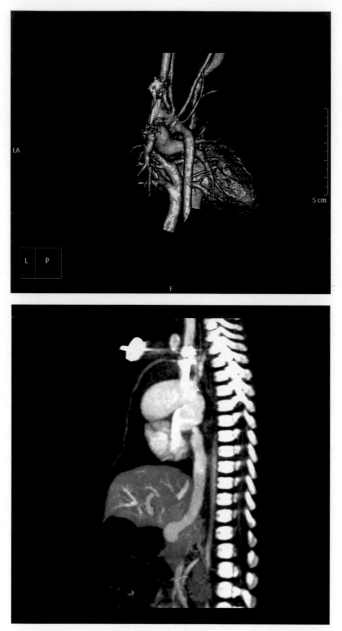

Figure 8.3 Infracardiac TAPVR. *TAPVR*, Total anomalous pulmonary venous return.

anomalies in pulmonary arteries, aortic arch, and intra-cardiac septal defects. In addition, CTA is superior to any other modalities in the assessment of bronchial anatomy
and congenital abnormalities as horseshoe lung, bi-lobed lung, and diverticulae.

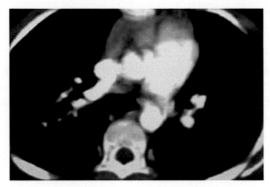

Figure 8.4 PAPVR. *PAPVR*, Partial anomalous venous return.

Preoperative evaluation of cases of TAPVR is mandatory for assessment of anatomic details such as the exact size of pulmonary veins and ostium, presence of pulmonary venous obstruction, and the exact course and site of anomalous veins. Postoperative follow-up of these cases is a very important advantage of CTA [36].

8.5 Partial anomalous pulmonary venous return

8.5.1 Partial anomalous venous return (PAPVR)

It means that one or more—but not all—pulmonary veins have abnormal drainage instead of draining into the left atrium. The right lung is more frequently affected than the left (Fig. 8.4). There are many classifications of PAPVR types.

1. Regarding the number of involved veins, PAPVR is divided into three types:
   a. Unilateral single branch
   b. Unilateral two branches
   c. Bilateral single branch
2. Regarding the site of anomalous drainage, PAPVR is divided into three types:
   a. Supracardiac
   b. Cardiac (the most common type)
   c. Infracardiac

PAPVR causes left to right shunt and becomes significant clinically if more than half of the pulmonary venous blood has anomalous drainage. The most common affected vein is the right superior pulmonary vein. The commonest sites of abnormal drainage are the right atrium and SVC on the right side and left brachiocephalic vein on the side. Right-sided PAPVR is usually associated with sinus venosus atrial septal defect. Other sites of abnormal drainage are coronary sinus, inferior vena cava azygos, and hemiazygos veins [29,30].

8.5.2 Veno-venous bridge

It means that a systemic vein acts as a bridge between the pulmonary vein and the left atrium. This is a result of abnormally persistent communication between the embryological common pulmonary vein and the cardinal veins which is similar to PAPVC. However, it differs from PAPVC in normal drainage of pulmonary veins in the left atrium. There may be an anomalous connection to SVC or less commonly to the IVC [37,38].

8.5.3 Scimitar syndrome

It is also named hypogenitic lung syndrome or congenital venolobar syndrome. It affects both the right lung and the cardiovascular system. It occurs when there is an infracardiac anomalous venous return of one or more of the right pulmonary veins associated with hypoplastic right lung, dextrocardia, hypoplastic right pulmonary artery, and abnormal arterial supply of the right lower lung lobe from descending aorta of its branches. This is called the complete form of scimitar syndrome. Other associated anomalies include bronchial or diaphragmatic anomalies, hemivertebrae, and genitourinary anomalies [1−3]. There are three types of scimitar syndrome: the infantile type, the adult type, and the third type with associated cardiac and extracardiac anomalies. The infantile type consists of a large shunt between the descending aorta and the right lower branch of the pulmonary artery. The adult type occurs when a small shunt exists between the IVC and the right pulmonary veins [4−6]. The scimitar syndrome typically appears in radiographs as a curved opacity that increases in diameter caudally seen related to the right cardiac border that passes subdiaphragmatic to the IVC which is known as scimitar sign. It is usually associated with a small right lung and dextrocardia. CTA allows accurate assessment of the anomalous drainage of the right pulmonary vein and other associated features [39,40].

8.5.4 Pseudo-Scimitar syndrome

It is characterized by an abnormal right pulmonary vein that extends through the right lung with anomalous drainage to the left atrium, not the right atrium. Pseudo-Scimitar syndrome is usually accompanied by hypoplastic right lung and dextrocardia. In many reported cases there is a simultaneous connection to the inferior vena cava as well as the left atrium [2−5].

8.5.5 Cortriatriatum sinister

It is a rare anomaly characterized by a diagonally oriented membranous diaphragm dividing the left atrium into two chambers: anterior and posterior. One of them contains the pulmonary venous return while the other contains the mitral valve and the atrial appendage. Mostly the two chambers are communicating through one or few openings in the

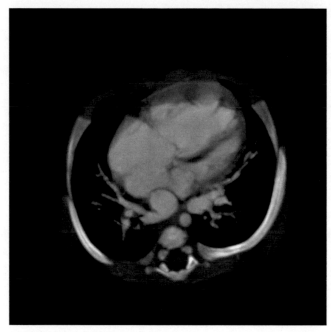

Figure 8.5 Illustrative figure for Cortriatriatum sinister.

membranous diaphragm. There are three types of Cortriatriatum anomaly: type 1 with no openings, type 2 with few small fenestrations in the membrane, and type 3 with large openings in the membrane and little or no obstruction (Fig. 8.5) [41].

8.5.6 Levoatriocardinal vein

It consists of an abnormal communication between the systemic vein and the left atrium. It is derived embryologically from the cardinal veins. This connection may be direct between the systemic vein and the left atrium or a connection between the systemic veins with one of the pulmonary veins. It is frequently accompanied by hypogenic lung syndrome [42].

8.5.7 PAPVR of left upper pulmonary vein (LUL PAPVR)

It consists of an abnormal vertical vein that conducts blood upward from the left lung into the left innominate vein then into the SVC. It is seen on CTA as a left para-aortic vascular structure where only mediastinal fat is normally present. This vertical vein should not be mistaken with a persistent left-sided SVC. Other less common drainage sites of LUL PAPVR are hemiazygos vein and coronary sinus. "Cross mediastinal" drainage has also been reported. It means that there is a PAPVR from the left lung into the inferior vena cava or venous drainage from the right lung into persistent left SVC [2−5].

8.6 Merits, limitations, and future directions

CTA is a gold standard modality in cardiac and vascular imaging as it is an easy, noninvasive technique with high spatial resolution. CTA allows accurate evaluation of cardiovascular anomalies. It is a very fast technique with a short acquisition time that helps in decreasing the time of radiation exposure and radiation dose. CTA is superior to MRA in patients with cardiac pacemakers and shorter examination time [3—9]. The main limitation is uncooperative patients of the pediatric age group especially young patients who cannot hold the breath or even breathe quietly which acquires the use of sedation. High radiation dose is still a disadvantage in CTA despite many measures for radiation dose reduction is taken into consideration. Application of intravenous route for contrast medium administration is a semiinvasive measure [5—10]. Future applications of structured reporting that has been used previously used for assessment of coronary arteries, pulmonary fibrosis, hepatic lesions, and neck after therapy [43—47] and machine learning used for the analysis of cardiac imaging to assist the radiologists with routine tasks, reducing workload, and increasing efficiency of patient care [48,49]. Future application of this reporting and machine learning for analysis of pulmonary veins will improve the results in the future. Application of advanced MR sequences will better evaluate associated incidental vascular lesions, mediastinal masses, and pericardial findings [50—57].

8.7 Conclusion

CTA is an excellent modality in evaluation of pulmonary vascular anomalies as well as other associated cardiac and extracardiac abnormalities that is very important for sitting surgical plans of treatment and postoperative follow-up of those patients.

References

[1] Abdel Razek AA, Al-Marsafawy H, Elmansy M, et al. CT angiography and MR angiography of congenital anomalies of pulmonary veins. J Comput Assist Tomogr 2019;43:399—405.

[2] Türkvatan A, Güzeltaş A, Tola HT, et al. Multidetector computed tomographic angiography imaging of congenital pulmonary venous anomalies: a pictorial review. Can Assoc Radiol J 2017;68:66—76.

[3] Bernal Garnes N, Méndez Díaz C, Soler Fernández R, et al. Magnetic resonance imaging in the assessment of anomalous pulmonary venous connections. Radiologia 2016;58:111—19.

[4] Dyer KT, Hlavacek AM, Meinel FG, et al. Imaging in congenital pulmonary vein anomalies: the role of computed tomography. Pediatr Radiol 2014;44:1158—68.

[5] Katre R, Burns SK, Murillo H, et al. Anomalous pulmonary venous connections. Semin Ultrasound CT MR 2012;33:485—99.

[6] Vyas HV, Greenberg SB, Krishnamurthy R. MR imaging and CT evaluation of congenital pulmonary vein abnormalities in neonates and infants. Radiographics 2012;32:87e98.

[7] Razek AA, Saad E, Soliman N, et al. Assessment of vascular disorders of the upper extremity with contrast-enhanced magnetic resonance angiography: pictorial review. Jpn J Radiol 2010;28:87—94.

[8] Razek AA. Vascular neurocutaneous disorders: neurospinal and craniofacial imaging findings. Jpn J Radiol 2014;32:519—28.

[9] Romberg EK, Tang ER, Chandra T, et al. Applications of pediatric body CT angiography: what radiologists need to know. Am J Roentgenol 2020;214:1019—30.

[10] Abdel Razek AAK. Imaging findings of Klippel-Trenaunay syndrome. J Comput Assist Tomogr 2019;43:786—92.

[11] Abdel Razek AAK, Al-Marsafawy H, Elmansy M. Imaging of pulmonary atresia with ventricular septal defect. J Comput Assist Tomogr 2019;43:906—11.

[12] Dong QQ, Yang WY, Sun YP, et al. Comparison of transthoracic echocardiography with computed tomography in evaluation of pulmonary veins. BMC Cardiovasc Disord 2019;19:315.

[13] Razek AA, Khalek AM, Elwakeel H, et al. Inter-observer agreement of color duplex ultrasound of central vein stenosis in hemodialysis patients. Phlebology 2019;34:636—42.

[14] Razek AA, Fouda NS, Elmetwaley N, et al. Sonography of the knee joint. J Ultrasound 2009;12:53—60.

[15] Romeih S, Al-Sheshtawy F, Salama M, et al. Comparison of contrast enhanced magnetic resonance angiography with invasive cardiac catheterization for evaluation of children with pulmonary atresia. Heart Int 2012;7:e9.

[16] Abdel Razek AAK, Albair GA, Samir S. Clinical value of classification of venous malformations with contrast-enhanced MR angiography. Phlebology 2017;32:628—33.

[17] Razek AA, Gaballa G, Megahed AS, et al. Time resolved imaging of contrast kinetics (TRICKS) MR angiography of arteriovenous malformations of head and neck. Eur J Radiol 2013;82:1885—91.

[18] Sakrana AA, Abdel Razek AAK, Yousef AM, et al. Cardiac magnetic resonance-derived indexed volumes and volume ratios of the cardiac chambers discriminating group 2 pulmonary hypertension from other World Health Organization Groups. J Comput Assist Tomogr 2020;45(1):59—64. Available from: https://doi.org/10.1097/RCT.0000000000001058.

[19] Abdel Razek AA, Denewer AT, Hegazy MA, et al. Role of computed tomography angiography in the diagnosis of vascular stenosis in head and neck microvascular free flap reconstruction. Int J Oral Maxillofac Surg 2014;43:811—15.

[20] Gamal El-Den AI, Ebeed AE, Ahmed HM, et al. Comparative study between duplex ultrasound and 160 multidetectors CT angiography in assessment of chronic lower limb ischaemia. Egypt J Radiol Nucl Med 2019;50:10.

[21] Tawfik AM, Razek AA, Kerl JM, et al. Comparison of dual-energy CT-derived iodine content and iodine overlay of normal, inflammatory and metastatic squamous cell carcinoma cervical lymph nodes. Eur Radiol 2014;24:574—80.

[22] Tawfik AM, Kerl JM, Razek AA, et al. Image quality and radiation dose of dual-energy CT of the head and neck compared with a standard 120-kVp acquisition. Am J Neuroradiol 2011;32:1994—9.

[23] Tawfik AM, Razek AA, Elhawary G, et al. Effect of increasing the sampling interval to 2 seconds on the radiation dose and accuracy of CT perfusion of the head and neck. J Comput Assist Tomogr 2014;38:469—73.

[24] Ou P, Marini D, Celermajer DS, et al. Non-invasive assessment of congenital pulmonary vein stenosis in children using cardiac-non-gated CT with 64-slice technology. Eur J Radiol 2009;70:595—9.

[25] Saha J, Roy R, Singh S, et al. Congenital pulmonary vein stenosis and pulmonary artery branch stenosis: a rare combination. J Cardiovasc Echogr 2017;27:20—2.

[26] Abe Y, Sumitomo N, Ayusawa M, et al. Congenital multiple pulmonary vein atresia and stenosis in an infant. Pediatr Int 2018;60(10):976—8.

[27] Biradar B, Sharma A, Malhi AS, et al. Unilateral pulmonary vein atresia: diagnostic dilemma unfolded on imaging. BMJ Case Rep 2018;2018.

[28] Onteddu NK, Palumbo A, Kalva SP. Pulmonary vein varix with pulmonary vein stenosis. J Vasc Interv Radiol 2017;28:147.

[29] Nasser M, Revel D, Thibault H, et al. Pulmonary vein varices are syndromic features in turner syndrome. Respiration 2017;94:70.

[30] Alam T, Hamidi H, Hoshang MM. Computed tomography features of supracardiac total anomalous pulmonary venous connection in an infant. Radiol Case Rep 2016;11:134—7.

[31] Yong MS, Zhu MZL, Konstantinov IE. Total anomalous pulmonary venous drainage repair: redefining the long-term expectations. J Thorac Dis 2018;10:S3207—10.

[32] Thummar AC, Phadke MS, Lanjewar CP, et al. Supracardiac total anomalous pulmonary venous drainage with giant superior vena cava aneurysm: a rare combination. J Am Coll Cardiol 2014;63:e51.

[33] Gopalakrishnan A, Subramanian V, Sasidharan B, et al. A rare variant of intracardiac total anomalous pulmonary venous connection. Rev Port Cardiol 2017;36(11). Available from: https://doi.org/10.1016/j.repc.2017.03.009 e1-869.e4.

[34] Aluja Jaramillo F, Hernandez C, Garzón JP, et al. Infracardiac type total anomalous pulmonary venous return with obstruction and dilatation of portal vein. Radiol Case Rep 2017;12:229—32.

[35] St Louis JD, Turk EM, Jacobs JP, et al. Type IV total anomalous pulmonary venous connection. World J Pediatr Congenit Heart Surg 2017;8:142—7.

[36] Razek AA, Tawfik AM, Elsorogy LG, et al. Perfusion CT of head and neck cancer. Eur J Radiol 2014;83:537—44.

[37] Tretter JT, Chikkabyrappa S, Spicer DE, et al. Understanding the spectrum of sinus venosus interatrial communications. Cardiol Young 2017;27:418—26.

[38] Moral S, Ballesteros E, Huguet M, et al. Differential diagnosis and clinical implications of remnants of the right valve of the sinus venosus. J Am Soc Echocardiogr 2016;29:183—94.

[39] Ngai C, Freedberg RS, Latson L, et al. Multimodality imaging of scimitar syndrome in adults: a report of four cases. Echocardiography 2018;35:1684—91.

[40] Masrani A, McWilliams S, Bhalla S, et al. Anatomical associations and radiological characteristics of Scimitar syndrome on CT and MR. J Cardiovasc Comput Tomogr 2018;12:286—9.

[41] Jha AK, Makhija N. Cor triatriatum: a review. Semin Cardiothorac Vasc Anesth 2017;21:178—85.

[42] Iida C, Muneuchi J, Watanabe M. Unique levoatriocardinal veins in neonates with hypoplastic left heart syndrome and intact atrial septum. Cardiol Young 2018;28:150—2.

[43] Abdel Razek AAK, Elrakhawy MM, Yossof MM, et al. Inter-observer agreement of the Coronary Artery Disease Reporting and Data System (CAD-RADS(TM)) in patients with stable chest pain. Pol J Radiol 2018;83:e151—9.

[44] Razek AAKA, El Badrawy MK, Alnaghy E. Interstitial lung fibrosis imaging reporting and data system: what radiologist wants to know? J Comput Assist Tomogr 2020;44:656—66.

[45] Abdel Razek AA, Ashmalla GA, Gaballa G, et al. Pilot study of ultrasound parotid imaging reporting and data system (PIRADS): inter-observer agreement. Eur J Radiol 2015;85:2533—8.

[46] Abdel Razek AAK, Abdelaziz TT. Neck imaging reporting and data system: what does radiologist want to know? J Comput Assist Tomogr 2020;44:527—32.

[47] Sabel BO, Plum JL, Kneidinger N, et al. Structured reporting of CT examinations in acute pulmonary embolism. J Cardiovasc Comput Tomogr 2017;11:188—95.

[48] Razek AAKA. Editorial for "Preoperative MRI-based radiomic machine-learning nomogram may accurately distinguish between benign and malignant soft tissue lesions: a two-center study.". J Magn Reson Imaging 2020;52:883—4.

[49] Retson TA, Besser AH, Sall S, et al. Machine learning and deep neural networks in thoracic and cardiovascular imaging. J Thorac Imaging 2019;34:192—201.

[50] Dunet V, Schwitter J, Meuli R, et al. Incidental extracardiac findings on cardiac MR: systematic review and *meta*-analysis. J Magn Reson Imaging 2016;43:929—39.

[51] Razek AA, Ashmalla GA. Prediction of venous malformations with localized intravascular coagulopathy with diffusion-weighted magnetic resonance imaging. Phlebology 2019;34:156—61.

[52] Razek AA. Diffusion magnetic resonance imaging of chest tumors. Cancer Imaging 2012;12:452—63.

[53] Abdel Razek AA, Gaballa G, Elashry R, et al. Diffusion-weighted MR imaging of mediastinal lymphadenopathy in children. Jpn J Radiol 2015;33:449—54.

[54] Abdel Razek AA, Soliman N, Elashery R. Apparent diffusion coefficient values of mediastinal masses in children. Eur J Radiol 2012;81:1311—14.

[55] Abdel Razek AA, Khairy M, Nada N. Diffusion-weighted MR imaging in thymic epithelial tumors: correlation with World Health Organization classification and clinical staging. Radiology 2014;273:268—75.

[56] Razek AAKA, Samir S. Differentiation malignant from benign pericardial effusion with diffusion-weighted MRI. Clin Radiol 2019;74(325) e19-e325.e24.
[57] Sokolowski FC, Karius P, Rodríguez A, et al. Extracardiac findings at cardiac MR imaging: a single-centre retrospective study over 14 years. Eur Radiol 2018;28:4102—10.

Further reading

Tawfik AM, Nour-Eldin NE, Naguib NN, et al. CT perfusion measurements of head and neck carcinoma from single section with largest tumor dimensions or average of multiple sections: agreement between the two methods and effect on intra- and inter-observer agreement. Eur J Radiol 2012;81:2692—6.

CHAPTER 9

Machine learning to predict mortality risk in coronary artery bypass surgery

Michael P. Rogers and Paul C. Kuo
Department of Surgery, Morsani College of Medicine, University of South Florida, Tampa, FL, United States

9.1 Introduction

Coronary artery disease is one of the leading causes of death in Western countries. First introduced in the 1960s, coronary artery bypass grafting (CABG) remains one of the most commonly performed procedures in the United States [1]. Coronary bypass grafting continues to be the mainstay treatment for patients with significant disease of the left main coronary artery, three-vessel stenosis, those undergoing valve surgery with associated coronary disease, and diffuse coronary disease not amenable to treatment with percutaneous coronary intervention (PCI) [2,3]. Outcomes have significantly improved over the last several decades with concomitant decreases in operative morbidity and mortality despite an increasingly aging population. In an effort to continue improving outcomes, various perioperative factors have been identified for optimization. Preoperative risk assessment remains crucial to identify modifiable and nonmodifiable risk factors that may contribute to patient outcome and for tailoring an individual treatment strategy. To this end, several risk calculators and scoring systems have been developed to estimate the predicted surgical risk of morbidity and mortality. The most widely used include the EuroSCORE (II) and the Society of Thoracic Surgeons (STS) risk calculator, with the latter providing granularity to include risk of renal failure, stroke, length of stay, sternal wound infection, and reoperation [4,5]. These models incorporate various patient data including demographic variables, history of prior cardiac interventions, cardiovascular-related diagnoses (including hypertension, peripheral artery disease, and COPD), number and percent stenosis of diseased coronary vessels, concurrent cardiac valvular disease or arrhythmia, preoperative hemodynamics, need for circulatory support, and functional status, among others. Comparisons between these popular models in patients undergoing isolated CABG showed similar performance [6]. All models currently in use are based on logistic regression, relying on model input to specify interactions [7]. Though these models boast comprehensive inputs, various other factors that are not accounted for including frailty index and degree of existing pulmonary hypertension, and the complex interplay between these inputs, are not included and may significantly contribute to patient

Cardiovascular and Coronary Artery Imaging
DOI: https://doi.org/10.1016/B978-0-12-822706-0.00010-X

outcomes. Some available scoring models have shown to have major limitations and tend to overestimate actual risk, potentially leading to inappropriate risk stratification and deferring of surgical intervention when it is indeed warranted, theoretically leading to unintentional confidence about center performance [8]. Because of this tendency to overestimate actual risk, especially in high-risk subgroups, they may also offer little guidance to assist surgeon judgment. The deficiencies of these current models are partly due to the models requiring user input to specify complex interactions among the variables. For example, the contributions of each feature may not be equal or constant across the coexisting comorbidities (i.e., age as it relates to the risk of mortality). Accordingly, significant interest in the usefulness of machine learning (ML) for predictive analytics in CABG surgery has increased. Consequently, various research groups have explored the application and implementation of ML techniques to this unique patient population with hopes of improving predictive models and, ultimately, patient outcomes.

ML is a burgeoning artificial intelligence subfield very much in its infancy. Computer algorithms build models based on sample data to make predictions or decisions without explicitly being programmed to do so. Originally coined in 1959 by IBM researcher Arthur Samuel, ML within medicine, and particularly within surgery, has exploded in interest and application in the last decade [9]. Given the significant increase in information collected on patients throughout the perioperative experience, ML has sought to leverage these data into meaningful metrics and predictors for morbidity and mortality. To date, numerous endeavors at characterizing an appropriate ML algorithm have been undertaken with varying levels of success. Recent *meta*-analysis suggests ML modeling for predicting CABG mortality can achieve significantly better discrimination ability compared to traditional logistic regression techniques when both models apply the same features [7]. The potential advantages in ML involve the ability to capture nonlinearity and the interactions among features without the need to manually account for all interactions. These algorithms may also manage missing variables more efficiently compared to traditional linear modeling as they do not rely on data distribution assumptions [10]. What's more, unlike traditional modeling techniques, ML is able to refine and improve prediction accuracy as it accrues more data. Combined with national cardiac surgical databases, including the STS National Database, ML is poised to have a significant impact on the future of prediction analytics for not only CABG outcomes but in all areas of medicine and its respective specialties.

In this chapter, we provide a brief introduction and overview of ML techniques and their current applications in prediction of CABG morbidity and mortality.

9.2 Principles and applications of machine learning

ML comprises the study and application of computer algorithms that improve automatically over time through experience [11]. These algorithms differ in their approach

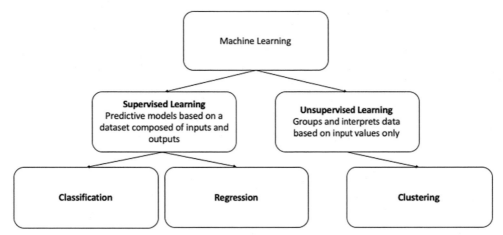

Figure 9.1 Machine learning techniques can broadly be categorized into supervised or unsupervised learning depending on their approach to solving the given problem.

in solving the defined problem, the types of data they allow for input and output, and the types of problem they seek to solve. These tools can broadly be classified as *supervised* versus *unsupervised* in their approaches to understanding data. Supervised statistical learning techniques strive to build a statistical model for novel prediction, or estimation, of an output based on defined input(s) [11]. These methods are popular and applicable to varying medical, economic, and scientific disciplines. Indeed, the majority of currently available literature for ML prediction of CABG morbidity and mortality utilizes the power of supervised techniques. In contrast, unsupervised learning uses data inputs without a corresponding output. These techniques are useful in defining the structure of data, including the grouping or clustering of data points (Fig. 9.1). Identifying the broad category of ML tools is an important first step in choosing the appropriate method for solving ML problems, with the ultimate goal of identifying a reliable algorithm capable of improving automatically through experience.

9.2.1 Data gathering

Modern healthcare applications of ML rely on large datasets of proprietary or free use data, often collected at the local, state, or national level. Previously, an investigator would approach the collection of data and analysis through a priori assumptions regarding the hypothesis to be tested to prevent collecting unnecessarily or irrelevant data. However, potentially meaningful associations may be missed by the inappropriate disregard for truly important data. With the advent of ML technology, these approaches may be applied to large existing datasets to remedy these previous pitfalls. The recent explosion of available data collected on patients has had profound significance as it relates to studying patient and hospital system outcomes. As hospital groups continue to adopt electronic medical records and collect ever-increasing amounts of patient-related data, the availability and granularity of large datasets will assuredly expand.

The STS National Database was first established in 1989 as an initiative for quality improvement and patient safety in cardiothoracic surgery [12]. The comprehensive database boasts four major components: the STS Adult Cardiac Surgery Database (ACDS), the STS Congenital Heart Surgery Database, the STS General Thoracic Surgery Database, and the STS Interagency Registry for Mechanical Circulatory Support/Pediatric Interagency Registry for Mechanical Circulatory Support (Pedimacs) Database. Recently celebrating its 30-year anniversary, the database is heralded as one of the most comprehensive and granular clinical datasets available in the world allowing for outcomes analysis, quality improvement, and research [12]. Other large datasets include those housed at individual institutions or statewide databases including the Florida Agency for Healthcare Administration. These databases comprise a wealth of clinical related data and may be combined with other datasets to infer novel predictions. Designing, collecting, maintaining, and leveraging these important data sets are a key step in healthcare analytics.

Raw, unprocessed healthcare data may be collected and entered into databases manually or automatically by downloading values from the electronic medical record or other software. In many instances, disease symptom questionnaires or objective results from diagnostic studies may be collected at the time of the patient visit and entered into a central database by a user at a later time. Because these data may contain significant outliers or obvious laboratory or data entry errors (i.e., in the case of human manual data entry), they must be corrected or "cleaned" prior to analysis. In the modern era, this data validation and processing is done via computer through a series of different tools. Large proprietary datasets often undergo this process prior to being made available to researchers.

9.2.2 Supervised learning

Supervised learning is a ML technique that seeks to build a statistical model that maps inputs to a corresponding output based on a data set containing paired inputs and outputs [11]. These techniques infer a function from a gathered *training set* of data, that is, a set of examples used to fit the parameters of interest. Training sets often contain pairs of an input variable and the corresponding output variable, where the answer is denoted as the *label* (or target). The chosen model (e.g., naïve Bayes classifier) is trained on the training set using a data optimization method and produces a result, which is then compared to the label for each of the input variables in the training set. The parameters of the model and the specific learning algorithm used are then adjusted based on the comparison outcome. Through mathematical iterative optimization of the objective function, the algorithm then learns a function that can be used to predict outputs based on new inputs [13]. The ideal function permits the algorithm to correctly ascertain new outputs from novel inputs not originally included in the training data. This requires the algorithm to generalize the training data to apply it to previously unseen data or situations. Algorithms that improve the accuracy of their predictions, or outputs, over time are considered to have learned to perform that task [13].

The general outline of solving a problem using a supervised learning technique includes the following:

1. Determine and gather the data to be used as the defined training set
2. Choose the input feature of the learned function
3. Select the structure of the learned function and the associated algorithm
4. Run the algorithm on the chosen training set
5. Evaluate the accuracy of the algorithm

Determining and choosing the appropriate training set is a key foundational step in successful implementation of a ML algorithm [11]. These training sets may be based on widely available state or national data and contain hundreds or thousands of potential inputs. In the context of healthcare data, these inputs often include various characteristics including patient factors such as age, sex, and diagnostic codes, hospital factors including staffing and certification status, surgeon factors such as time in practice, and socioeconomic factors, among others. As an example, suppose we are attempting to predict 30-day hospital readmission after undergoing coronary artery bypass surgery. Each input (i.e., age, sex, comorbidity index, etc.) will pair with a corresponding binary output (outcome) of whether or not a patient was readmitted to the hospital following CABG surgery within 30 days. Next, we wish to determine an estimator function that will allow for assessing a new patient's information (inputs) to a predicted readmission probability within 30 days. This estimator function may potentially identify factors that are able to be mitigated or eliminated to reduce possible unnecessary readmission. To achieve this, the dataset is broken into three subcategories: a training dataset, a test dataset, and a validation dataset (e.g., 70%, 15%, 15%, respectively) [14]. Each subcategory must contain a representative distribution of inputs and outputs to represent the original dataset population. The training dataset will be used to learn the estimator parameters, the validation dataset to finely adjust the parameters, and the test set to determine the generalizability of the estimator after it has been finalized [15]. Importantly, the test set is used only once in an effort to minimize the likelihood of memorizing the input—output pairs by repeatedly refining the estimator. If an estimator inappropriately "memorizes" the input—output pairs, it is less likely to fit new data with the appropriate level of accuracy. This learning of fine details rather than the larger general properties of the dataset is termed "overfitting" [15].

After appropriate selection and parsing of data, an appropriate family of estimators is then chosen. These may be broadly classified as linear and nonlinear estimators, which include traditional models such as logistic regression [15]. Each learning algorithm has its strengths and weaknesses and there is no single algorithm that will work best on all supervised learning problems. Often, the investigator chooses the best function based on intuition. We provide a brief overview of common ML techniques in the following subsections.

9.2.2.1 Linear regression

Linear regression is a common and simple approach for supervised learning in predicting a quantitative output. At its core, it predicts a linear relationship between a quantitative output (dependent variable) based on one or more input variable(s). An approach with one input variable is termed *simple* linear regression, whereas more than one is termed *multiple* (or multivariable) linear regression [16]. In this technique, the relationship between the input—output variables is modeled using linear predictor estimators to fit a linear equation to the observed data. A linear regression line has the following equation where X is the independent variable, the slope of the line is β_1, β_0 is the intercept, and the response Y is the dependent variable [Eq. (9.1)]:

$$Y = \beta_0 + \beta_1 X \tag{9.1}$$

The most common method for fitting a regression line utilizes the method of least-squares. This technique calculates the best-fitting line (regression line) for the observed data by minimizing the sum of the squares of the vertical deviations from each data point to the line of best fit (i.e., if a point lies on the line, its vertical deviation is 0) (Fig. 9.2) [16]. Of course, if the relationship between X and Y are not linear, a different shaped function would likely fit the data more appropriately.

With more than one input (multivariable linear regression) a process of optimizing the values of the coefficients by iteratively minimizing the error of the model on the training data can be employed through Gradient Descent [11]. This process works by employing random values for each coefficient. The sum of the squared errors is then calculated for each pair of input—output variables and a learning rate is used as a scale factor with the coefficients updated in the direction toward minimizing the error. This process is repeated until a minimum sum of squared error is achieved or there is no further improvement.

Extensions of the linear model called regularization methods seek to both minimize the sum of the squared error of the model on the training data (by least-squares method) and also reduce the complexity of the model by reducing the number of absolute size of the sum of all coefficients in the model. Two popular methods of regularization are known as Lasso regression and Ridge regression [11]. Lasso regression modifies the least-squares method to also minimize the absolute sum of the coefficients in the model (i.e., L1 regularization). Ridge regression modifies least squares to also

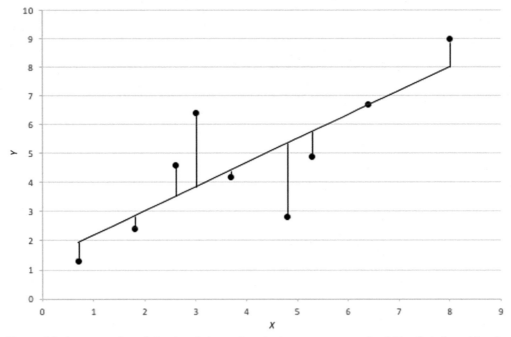

Figure 9.2 A scatter plot of simulated data using the least-squares method. The fit is found by the sum of squared errors. Each line between the data point and the regression line represents an error. The regression line minimizes the sum of the squared errors of prediction.

minimize the squared absolute sum of the coefficients (i.e., L2 regularization). These methods are effective tools when there is colinearity in the input values and least-squares would overfit the training data.

Once an appropriate linear model has been determined, making predictions using the model involves simply solving the equation using the specified inputs. For example, if we wished to predict weight from age, our linear regression model would be the following [Eq. (9.2)]:

$$\text{Weight} = \beta_0 + \beta_1 \text{Age} \qquad (9.2)$$

Once the slope and intercept are determined, this equation can then be used to make predictions on weight based on a previously unknown age. Variations of this approach have been used to determine the quality of life after CABG, post-CABG survival, and predictors of CABG cost and reimbursement [17−20]. Carr and colleagues' analysis of long-term post-CABG survival highlights the power of this technique to identify clinical variables that contribute to mortality [18]. Their multivariate analysis confirmed the previously suspected impact of preoperative renal failure on long-term patient mortality in their cohort. Similar analyses have been applied across the pre- and postoperative hospital course to identify similar factors for mitigation or optimization.

The power of linear regression remains a powerful statistical method in the armamentarium of the researcher and clinician. Moreover, it serves as an ideal starting point for learning more advanced supervised ML techniques. A proper understanding of linear regression is paramount to studying these more complex applications.

9.2.2.2 Logistic regression

Linear regression assumes the response variable Y is a quantitative value. However, in many clinical and healthcare situations, the response variable of interest is indeed qualitative. For example, eye colors (i.e., values of blue, green, hazel) are qualitative, so-called *categorical*, values. Predictions involving a qualitative response are known as classification, as the observed observation is assigned to a category. Alternatively, methods used for classification may first predict the probability of each category of the qualitative variable as the basis of its classification [11]. ML applications based on this technique encompass a wide array of options for classification problems, including logistic regression, linear discriminant analysis, and K-nearest neighbors (KNN). Indeed, more advanced computer-based classification methods such as generalized additive modeling, trees, random forests, boosting, and support vector machines (SVMs) also employ these techniques [11].

Like all regression analyses, logistic regression is a predictive analysis. How does the probability of getting lung cancer change for every pack of cigarettes smoked per day? Do bodyweight, caloric intake, and age have an effect on the probability of having a heart attack? These questions are answered utilizing the power of logistic regression. In fact, all models for prediction in coronary artery bypass surgery are currently based on logistic regression, which rely on the modeler input to manually specify interactions [7].

Logistic regression can be binomial, ordinal, or multinomial. Binomial, or binary, logistic regression is useful for situations in which the observed outcome for a dependent variable can only have two types (i.e., alive vs deceased, pass vs fail, etc.). Multinomial logistic regression is used in situations involving outcomes of three or more unordered possible types. Ordinal logistic regression involves dependent outcomes that are ordered. To solve problems where the dependent outcome is binary, we must model $p(X)$ using a function that gives outputs between 0 and 1 for all values of X. We may use the following logistic function to achieve this goal:

$$p(X) = \frac{e^{\beta_0 + \beta_1 X}}{1 + e^{\beta_0 + \beta_1 X}} \tag{9.3}$$

The STS ACDS contains patient-related demographics, baseline comorbidities, procedural details, and other clinically relevant data for >6 million procedures performed by more than 3000 surgeons, accounting for more than 90% of all adult cardiac surgeries performed in the United States [21−23]. Leveraging these data, the Duke Clinical

Research group in coordination with the Quality Measurement Task Force used the ACSD to develop calculators for predicted risk of mortality for CABG procedures [23]. This STS risk calculator is revised regularly to incorporate the most recent updates in the database. The models are constructed using the following formula:

$$\text{Predicted Risk} = \frac{e^{(\beta_0 + \beta_1 X_1 + \beta_2 X_2 + \ldots + \beta_n X_n)}}{1 + e^{(\beta_0 + \beta_1 X_1 + \beta_2 X_2 + \ldots + \beta_n X_n)}} \tag{9.4}$$

where x_1, x_2, $\ldots x_\pi$ denote patient preoperative risk factors and β_0, β_1, $\ldots \beta_\pi$ denote regression coefficients [21,24]. The preoperative risk factors are fixed in each version of the risk model and the regression coefficients are defined by the latest ACSD [21]. The regression coefficient for the time trend is updated to the specific reference period of the STS database and coincides with the time the data are collected. The robust nature of the STS dataset and the power of logistic regression have cemented the STS risk calculator among the most popular and widely used in the world.

Similarly, logistic regression has been used to define the relative contributions of the healthcare environment on 30-day hospital readmission following CABG [25]. Janjua and colleagues leveraged the Healthcare Cost and Utilization Project State Inpatient Database combined with the American Hospital Association Annual Health Survey Databases, the Healthcare Information Management Systems Society, and the Distressed Communities Index datasets to identify patient health, socioeconomic, and hospital-level data from six states over 3 years. Using logistic regression with a combination of backward elimination and forward selection to eliminate insignificant variables, specific contributors to 30-day readmission were identified with an area under the curve of 0.71, accuracy of 0.845, and sensitivity of 0.99 [25]. Moreover, the authors compared this analytic technique with a host of ML techniques to determine the best-performing predictive model. Like many recent evaluations of ML, decision tree modeling and gradient boosting, two particular ML techniques were found to have the best predictive probability compared to traditional statistical techniques.

The utility of ML in the context of predictive analytics in coronary bypass surgery is only recently being realized. These efforts highlight a novel strategy for improving on currently used risk calculators and are set to usher in a new understanding of the contributions of complex interactions between previously unrealized variables.

9.2.2.3 K-nearest neighbors

Linear regression is an example of a parametric approach as it assumes a linear functional form. In contrast, nonparametric approaches do not explicitly assume a parametric form, thereby allowing for a more flexible approach to regression [11]. KNN regression is one of the best-known nonparametric methods. Using this method, the output is the property value for the object, which is the average of the values of the k

nearest neighbors [11]. The algorithm first computes the Euclidian distance from the query example to the labeled examples. The labeled examples are next ordered by increasing distance, an optimal number of KNN is determined, and finally, an inverse distance weighted average with k-nearest multivariate neighbors is calculated [11]. The nonparametric approach will outperform the parametric approach if the nonparametric approach that is used is close to the true form of the function.

9.2.2.4 Random forest algorithm

A Random Forest is an ensemble technique that is useful for performing both classification and regression tasks with the use of multiple decision trees and a technique known as bootstrap aggregation (bagging) [11]. Decision trees involve stratifying or segmenting the predictor space into a number of regions. In order to make a prediction for a given observation, the mean or mode of the training observation is used for the region in which it typically belongs [11]. Because the set of splitting rules used to segment the predictor space can be summarized in a tree (Fig. 9.3), they are known as decision trees. Decision trees represent a flowchart-like structure in which each internal node represents a test (e.g., whether an outcome is positive or negative), each branch represents the outcome of the test, and each "leaf" node represents a class label. An ensemble method is a technique for combining the predictions from multiple ML algorithms together to make more accurate predictions than any individual model may perform alone.

Decision trees are inherently computationally expensive to train, suffer from risk overfitting of data, and have high variance. If the training dataset is split into equal halves and each is fitted with a decision tree model, the end results may be quite different due to variance. To overcome these drawbacks, a random forest algorithm

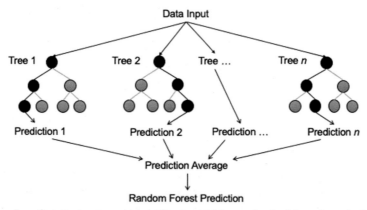

Figure 9.3 Random forest structure. Using the ensemble method of bagging, decision trees are constructed at raining time and output the class that is the mode of the classes (in classification) or mean prediction (regression) of the individual trees.

combines many decision trees into one model by employing the ensemble technique of bagging. Bagging is a general procedure for reducing the variance of a statistical learning method [11]. Bagging makes each model run independently and aggregates the outputs at the end without preference to any one model. The decision trees are run in parallel and there is no interaction between trees when building. The overall idea of Random Forest modeling is constructing a multitude of decision trees at the time of training and outputting the class that is the mode of the classes (classification method) or mean prediction (regression) of the individual trees. Random Forest is one of the most accurate learning algorithms available, runs efficiently on large datasets, and can appropriately handle thousands of input variables [11]. Moreover, it has an effective method for estimating missing data, which may be an issue in some healthcare datasets. Random Forests have been observed to overfit some noisy datasets, however. When considering whether to apply a linear model or more sophisticated technique such as Random Forest algorithm, the best approach will depend on the relationship between the features and the response of the problem attempting to be solved.

9.2.2.5 Support vector machines

SVM is an approach for discriminative classification that has continued to grow in popularity since its introduction in the 1990s [11,13]. Originally developed by AT&T Bell Laboratories by Vladimir Vapnik and colleagues, it remains one of the most robust prediction methods available [14]. Starting with a set of training examples, with each example belonging to one of two categories, an SVM training algorithm builds a model that assigns new examples to one of the two categories. An SVM model represents these examples as points in space which are mapped so that the examples of the two categories are divided by a space as large as possible. New examples to the model are then mapped onto that space and predicted to belong to either category based on the side of the space upon which they fall [14]. By finding a line (or hyperplane in situations >2 dimensions) between different classes of data such that the distance on either side of the line (or hyperplane) to the closest data points is maximized, SVMs are able to clearly separate data into two classes. If such a plane exists to maximize this space, the SVM is known as a so-called *maximum margin classifier*. The underlying mathematical details of SVMs are indeed quite technical and beyond the scope of this chapter. In addition to performing this linear classification, SVMs are also capable of performing nonlinear classification using kernels, implicitly mapping their inputs into high-dimensional feature spaces [14].

SVMs may be useful in a wide variety of applications. Previous efforts have used these techniques to classify images and satellite data, and have been implemented in a variety of healthcare applications [25,26]. Recent prediction analysis of coronary bypass graft patency by accounting for the influence of flow hemodynamics was evaluated using SVMs with improved accuracy, sensitivity, and specificity over an existing patency prediction model [27]. Other endeavors have evaluated prediction of postoperative CABG atrial fibrillation, stratification of patients at risk for needing emergency CABG following PCI to centers offering this capability, and prediction of long-term post-CABG outcomes [27−29].

9.2.3 Unsupervised learning

The previously discussed methods for ML all harnessed the power of supervised learning. Recall that in supervised learning there is an input−output pair of data from which we infer a function to make predictions. In contrast, unsupervised learning is used in settings in which the only available set of features is inputs without associated outputs [11]. Accordingly, we are not interested in prediction because there is no associated response variable Y. The goal of unsupervised learning instead is to discover interesting associations about the variables or observations. Unsupervised techniques ask the questions: is there an informative way to visualize the data? Are there subgroups among the variables or observations [11]? Because the goal is not to predict a response, unsupervised learning can often be more challenging in its overall application. There is no universally accepted method for validating results on an independent data set, for example, as there is no valid method for checking the results by seeing how well the response was predicted. However, unsupervised learning remains an important tool for evaluating data and identifying groups within large datasets. For instance, a cancer researcher evaluating groupings in the gene expression assays of 100 patients with colon cancer. Two of the most common unsupervised methods include principal component and cluster analysis, which are briefly discussed below.

Principal component analysis (PCA) is a tool used for visualizing data or in data preprocessing before applying supervised learning techniques [13]. When evaluating a large set of variables, principal components analysis allows for summarization of the dataset with a smaller number of representative variables to collectively explain most of the variability in the starting dataset, also known as dimensionality reduction. Principal components are the linear combination of the original variables and the data set and the analysis seeks to find a low-dimensional representation of data that represent as much information as possible from the original dataset. In the new coordinate system, the first axis corresponds to the first principal component that explains the greatest amount of variance in the data. The second principal component is selected that lies perpendicular to the first principal component. By finding a new set of dimensions (or basis of views) such that all the dimensions are orthogonal and ranked according to the variance of the data (in the direction of maximal variance), PCA allows for better visualization of the data of interest. This application can be applied to dimensionality reduction, exploratory data analysis, visualization of high dimensionality data, or in finding patterns [13].

Cluster analysis is an exploratory, descriptive data analysis technique that uses a process of systematically arranging data into groups [13,14]. Clustering allows similar data and dissimilar data to be grouped accordingly to expose structure within the dataset. Hierarchical clustering uses methods to split the data using some criterion into clusters which form into a tree-like structure of clusters. A *bottom-up* approach starts with a single parent cluster and builds on the child cluster until the desired criteria are met. A *top-down* approach begins with all data observations in one cluster and splits in stages to move down the hierarchy to reach the desired criteria. Nonhierarchical uses various partitions in the data observations and then evaluates them by some criteria. Finally, a model-based method can be employed to prepare each cluster to find the best model. Similarity in data can be expressed in terms of a distance function and represent a set of rules that serve as the criteria for grouping or separating data elements.

Both clustering and PCA seek to simplify the data into a smaller number of summaries through different mechanisms. The techniques have broad application in modern society and include marketing products to consumers (e.g., using median household income, occupation, residence location, etc.), and in healthcare by partitioning large datasets when looking for similarities across groups (e.g., gene expression assays). Often, small decisions in how the clustering is performed and the criteria for how the data are standardized may have large effects on the results and therefore clustering is often performed many times with different choices of parameters to evaluate the full set of results [14]. The outcome of the clustering analysis is often a starting point for hypothesis generation and further inquiry, rather than prediction alone, and can be a valuable tool in the evaluation of large datasets.

9.2.4 Discussion

ML has broad implications for the future of healthcare delivery and in predictive analytics to appropriately tailor an individual risk profile for each patient with improved accuracy and reliability. As data collected on patients continue to rise, ML applications are poised to have a significant impact and improve over previous statistical techniques for evaluating complex interactions between patient, surgeon, and hospital variables. Indeed, many contemporary evaluations of ML versus traditional techniques have shown superior accuracy, sensitivity, and specificity in prediction of 30-day hospital readmission following CABG, mortality risk, cost modeling, and long-term outcomes [7,18,25,29]. Janjua and colleagues' evaluation of various ML algorithms including random forest, decision tree, KNN, and logistic regression to determine the relative contributors of the health care environment on 30-day hospital readmission following CABG highlights the potential power of these techniques when applied to large patient datasets. Boasting respectable accuracy and sensitivity, modeling allowed for the novel identification of previously unrealized contributors which may be ripe for mitigation or elimination, leading to decreased 30-day hospital readmission, decreased cost, and improved outcomes. The STS national database, and indeed many other national and international databases are well positioned to adopt ML algorithms to elevate their predictive power [30]. As ML techniques become more widespread and more researchers are trained in their application, it will become increasingly important to understand their purpose and role in the healthcare environment.

Accurately and reproducibly predicting CABG mortality risk has been an ongoing effort with continual refinement and improvement. Algorithms that are able to automatically adjust to new data elements and incorporate variables of the entirety of the perioperative experience will be invaluable tools toward realizing this goal. Meta-analyses evaluating the power of these techniques continue to show significantly better discrimination ability compared to traditional techniques [7]. Risk stratification scoring, currently employing the STS-Predicted Risk of Mortality and EuroSCORE II, is set to undergo a transition from logistic regression to ML [4,7]. The potential to capture nonlinearity and the interactions among features without modeler input is significant potential advantages. Additionally, as previously discussed, missing variables are less detrimental when employing ML techniques over traditional logistic regression.

Drawbacks certainly exist in the current iteration of ML applications. The theory of so-called "No Free Lunch," no one ML technique works best for all problems or in all situations, often means many different ML algorithms must be performed and the best performing model chosen from the results [31]. This is due to ML algorithms making some assumptions regarding the predictor and target variable relationships, which introduces bias into the model. These assumptions will inherently fit some datasets better than others. The availability and granularity of large datasets needed to employ the true power of ML is also an existing limitation. Both traditional statistical and cutting-edge ML techniques will perform poorly when the predictor is developed on a small or nongranular dataset. For this reason, ML should only be considered in situations where very large datasets with many events are available for evaluation and learning [7].

With an expanding amount of data collected on patients, surgeons, and hospital systems, several hurdles must be addressed and overcome if new technology is to be fully embraced. These include storage capacity, computing power, and data privacy, among others. In the era of increased collection of data from everyday life, including cell phone metadata, purchasing habits, geo-tracking, banking, and web tracking, demands have been made for stronger personal data protection rights, improved transparency, and enhanced security. Because of the enormous value of individually targeted advertisements, corporations have steadily improved their ability to use large swaths of their users' data to design and deliver targeted advertising in an effort to maximize revenue. Indeed, data have recently been described as the "new oil of the digital economy" [32]. Similarly, concerns have arisen surrounding the storage and use of patient data in determining insurance policy coverage eligibility, setting premiums, and using genetic predispositions to decline certain coverage. Major hospitals across the United States have been targeted with large-scale cyberattacks and ransomware, a type of malicious software that spreads across networks to encrypt files and demands a payment to decrypt them [33]. Accordingly, calls for patient and consumer protections have come to the forefront of recent legislative sessions in the United States Congress. Novel safeguards will need to be designed and implemented to ensure patient protection with the goals of mitigating data breaches and discrimination. In 2008 the Genetic Information Nondiscrimination Act was enacted to bar the use of genetic information in health insurance coverage and employment [34]. Other similar efforts have been made to compel companies to provide adequate protection for their patients and clients. These legislative enforcements will be necessary as an ever-increasing amount of personal data is collected and used.

9.3 Conclusion

The future of predictive analytics utilizing ML algorithms is indeed bright. Prediction of CABG morbidity, mortality, 30-day hospital readmission, and the factors that contribute to each scenario will be refined and perfected as technology and algorithms improve. As these techniques become pervasive, familiarity with their advantages and pitfalls will be necessary to successfully employ them in clinical practice.

References

[1] Head SJ, et al. Current practice of state-of-the-art surgical coronary revascularization. Circulation 2017;136(14):1331–45.
[2] Hillis LD, et al. 2011 ACCF/AHA guideline for coronary artery bypass graft surgery: executive summary: a report of the American College of Cardiology Foundation/American Heart Association Task Force on Practice Guidelines. J Thorac Cardiovasc Surg 2012;143(1).4–34.
[3] Neumann FJ, et al. 2018 ESC/EACTS guidelines on myocardial revascularization. Eur Heart J 2019;40(2):87–165.
[4] Shahian DM, et al. The Society of Thoracic Surgeons 2008 cardiac surgery risk models: part 1–coronary artery bypass grafting surgery. Ann Thorac Surg 2009;88(1 Suppl):S2–22.
[5] Osnabrugge RL, et al. Performance of EuroSCORE II in a large United States database: implications for transcatheter aortic valve implantation. Eur J Cardiothorac Surg 2014;46(3):400–8 discussion 408.
[6] Wang TK, et al. Comparison of four risk scores for contemporary isolated coronary artery bypass grafting. Heart Lung Circ 2014;23(5):469–74.
[7] Benedetto U, et al. Machine learning improves mortality risk prediction after cardiac surgery: systematic review and meta-analysis. J Thorac Cardiovasc Surg 2020.
[8] Gummert JF, et al. EuroSCORE overestimates the risk of cardiac surgery: results from the national registry of the German Society of Thoracic and Cardiovascular Surgery. Clin Res Cardiol 2009; 98(6):363–9.
[9] Samuel AL. Some studies in machine learning using the game of checkers. IBM J Res Dev 1959;3:210–29.

[10] Gupta ALM. Estimating missing values using neural networks. J Oper Res Soc 1996;47:229−38.

[11] James G, et al. An introduction to statistical learning: with applications in R. Springer texts in statistics, xvi. New York: Springer; 2013. p. 426.

[12] Fernandez FG, et al. The society of thoracic surgeons national database 2019 annual report. Ann Thorac Surg 2019;108(6):1625−32.

[13] Mohri M, Rostamizadeh A, Talwalkar A. Foundations of machine learning. Adaptive computation and machine learning series, xii. Cambridge, MA: MIT Press; 2012. p. 414.

[14] Hastie T, Tibshirani R, Friedman JH. Springer series in statistics 2nd (ed.) The elements of statistical learning: data mining, inference, and prediction, xxii. New York, NY: Springer; 2009. p. 745.

[15] Doupe P, Faghmous J, Basu S. Machine learning for health services researchers. Value Health 2019;22(7):808−15.

[16] Schillow NW. Statistical models: theory and practice. Choice: Curr Rev Acad Libraries 2006; 43(8):1438.

[17] Taghipour HR, et al. Quality of life one year after coronary artery bypass graft surgery. Iran Red Crescent Med J 2011;13(3):171−7.

[18] Carr BM, et al. Long-term post-CABG survival: performance of clinical risk models versus actuarial predictions. J Card Surg 2016;31(1):23−30.

[19] Rumsfeld JS, et al. Predictors of health-related quality of life after coronary artery bypass surgery. Ann Thorac Surg 2004;77(5):1508−13.

[20] Denton TA, Luevanos J, Matloff JM. Clinical and nonclinical predictors of the cost of coronary bypass surgery: potential effects on health care delivery and reimbursement. Arch Intern Med 1998;158(8):886−91.

[21] Kumar A, et al. Current society of thoracic surgeons model reclassifies mortality risk in patients undergoing transcatheter aortic valve replacement. Circ Cardiovasc Interv 2018;11(9):e006664.

[22] Thourani VH, et al. The society of thoracic surgeons Adult Cardiac Surgery Database: 2017 update on research. Ann Thorac Surg 2017;104(1):22−8.

[23] Winkley Shroyer AL, et al. The society of thoracic surgeons Adult Cardiac Surgery Database: the driving force for improvement in cardiac surgery. Semin Thorac Cardiovasc Surg 2015;27(2):144−51.

[24] O'Brien SM, et al. The society of thoracic surgeons 2008 cardiac surgery risk models: part 2−isolated valve surgery. Ann Thorac Surg 2009;88(1 Suppl):S23−42.

[25] Janjua H, et al. Defining the relative contribution of health care environmental components to patient outcomes in the model of 30-day readmission after coronary artery bypass graft (CABG). Surgery 2020;169(3):557−66.

[26] Maity A. Supervised classification of RADARSAT-2 polarimetric data for different land features. Comput Vis Pattern Recognit 2016.

[27] Mao B, et al. The influence of hemodynamics on graft patency prediction model based on support vector machine. J Biomech 2020;98:109426.

[28] Syed Z, et al. Predicting emergency coronary artery bypass graft following PCI: application of a computational model to refer patients to hospitals with and without onsite surgical backup. Open Heart 2015;2(1):e000243.

[29] Forte JC, et al. Predicting long-term mortality with first week post-operative data after Coronary Artery Bypass Grafting using Machine Learning models. In: MLHC; 2017.

[30] Fernandez FG. The future is now: the 2020 evolution of the society of thoracic surgeons national database. Ann Thorac Surg 2020;109(1):10−13.

[31] D. Gomez AR. An empirical overview of the no free lunch theorem and its effect on real-world machine learning classification. Neural Comput 2016;28:216−28.

[32] Yonego JT. Data is the new oil of the digital economy. Wired Magazine; 2014.

[33] Cameron D. Today's massive ransomware attack was mostly preventable; here's how to avoid it; 2017.

[34] National Human Genome Research Institute. President Bush signs the genetic information nondiscrimination act of 2008; 2008.

CHAPTER 10

Computed tomography angiography of congenital anomalies of pulmonary artery

Ahmed Abdel Khalek Abdel Razek[1], Maha Elmansy[1], Mahmoud Abd El-Latif[2] and Hala Al-Marsafawy[3]
[1]Department of Diagnostic Radiology, Faculty of Medicine, Mansoura University, Mansoura, Egypt
[2]Mansoura University Hospital, Mansoura, Egypt
[3]Pediatric Cardiology Unit, Pediatrics Department, Faculty of Medicine, Mansoura University, Mansoura, Egypt

10.1 Introduction

There is a wide spectrum of congenital anomalies affecting pulmonary vessels and appears in pediatric patients due to abnormal embryonic vascular development. Those anomalies vary from small isolated lesions to large complex anomalies with multiple associated abnormalities. Accurate assessment of pulmonary vascular anomalies is very important in the treatment plans of those patients [1—5].

Different imaging modalities are used in the evaluation of vascular lesions. The gold standard modality in patients with congenital cardiac and pulmonary vascular defects is digital subtraction angiography which allows excellent vascular assessment but its invasiveness and overlapping of adjacent vascular structures are limitations for its usage in pediatric patients [6—10]. Echocardiography is usually the first line modality used for patients with congenital cardiac anomalies as it is an easy a noninvasive and safe way for cardiac assessment, but it has a small field of view that limits visualization of extracardiac structures as the pulmonary veins and it cannot provide three-dimensional views that are provided by the cross-sectional imaging modalities [8—12]. MR imaging is a very good imaging modality in the assessment of pulmonary vessels. MR angiography allows good visualization of pulmonary vessels better than white blood imaging sequences that cannot usually visualize small peripheral pulmonary veins in a sufficient spatial resolution, but MRA takes a long time and has contraindication in patients with cardiac pacemakers and prosthesis [13—15].

CT angiography (CTA) has been an ideal modality for the evaluation of pulmonary vessels in congenital cardiac anomalies as it is the noninvasive procedure with a high spatial resolution allowing rapid and accurate assessment of pulmonary vessel size, course, origin, and any abnormalities. It also allows good evaluation of associated other cardiovascular abnormalities and any other extracardiac anomalies as lung or vascular

211

Table 10.1 Classification of congenital anomalies of pulmonary artery.

Anomalies caliber of pulmonary artery
—**Congenital pulmonary artery stenosis**
—**Congenital pulmonary artery dilation**

Anomalies origin or course of central branch of pulmonary artery
  —Pulmonary artery sling
  —Crossed pulmonary arteries

Anomalous origin/development of main pulmonary artery (Conotruncal anomalies):
  —Tetralogy of Fallot (TOF)
  —Pulmonary atresia with VSD
  —Transposition of the great arteries (TGA)
  —Double-outlet right ventricle (DORV)
  —Truncus arteriosus

anomalies. So it is now better than echocardiography and catheterization in the evaluation of pediatric cardiovascular abnormalities [16,17].

The purpose of this chapter is to review the role of CTA in pulmonary arterial anomalies.

10.2 Classification

Table 10.1 shows the classification of congenital anomalies of pulmonary artery.

10.2.1 Anomalies of caliber
10.2.1.1 Congenital pulmonary artery stenosis
Pulmonary artery stenosis is mostly congenital (95%) rather than acquired. There are three types: valvular (the most common type), subvalvular, and supravalvular types. There is a congenital fusion of the pulmonary valve leaflets at the commissures which causes restriction of the opening of those leaflets in the systolic phase. The pulmonary valve is dome shaped. It may be associated with right ventricular hypertrophy and pulmonary artery dilatation [18,19] (Fig. 10.1).

10.2.1.2 Congenital pulmonary artery dilatation
It is characterized by abnormal dilatation of the main pulmonary trunk without any pulmonary and cardiac diseases (mainly pulmonary valve stenosis) and with normal right ventricular and pulmonary artery pressure. The right and left pulmonary arteries may be dilated or of normal diameter. Another point in the diagnosis of congenital pulmonary artery dilatation is a long period of observation without significant change in the diameters of the pulmonary arteries. It is usually discovered incidentally on chest radiographs or CT scans. On chest radiographs, the dilated pulmonary artery appears

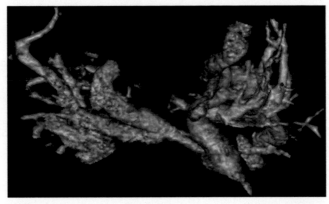

Figure 10.1 3D VR image showing hypoplastic MPA, RPA, and LPA with MAPCAs.

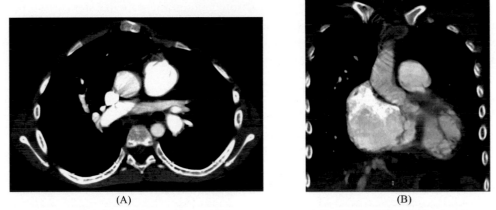

(A)   (B)

Figure 10.2 Congenital pulmonary artery dilatation. (A) Axial and (B) coronal CTA images showing abnormally dilated MPA with normal diameter of both RPA and LPA. *CTA*, CT angiography.

as a rounded bulge that mimics a mass in the left mediastinal border. A definitive diagnosis may be achieved with the use of CTA [20,21] (Fig. 10.2).

10.2.2 Anomalies origin or course of central branch of pulmonary artery

10.2.2.1 Crossed pulmonary arteries
This anomaly consists of the upward and rightward origin of the left pulmonary artery that crosses the right pulmonary artery then passes leftward to cross in front of the trachea. However, there is usually no subsequent airway compression or narrowing. It is associated usually with the stenotic origin of the LPA. There is an association with other cardiac anomalies as TOF, aortic arch anomalies, double outlet ventricle, and truncus arteriosus [22,23].

10.2.2.2 Pulmonary artery sling

It consists of anomalous origin of the left pulmonary artery arising from the right pulmonary artery and courses between trachea and esophagus at the anterior commissure compressing it and causing respiratory and swallowing difficulty. Pulmonary artery sling may be associated with tracheal anomalies including tracheal bronchus, complete tracheal ring, and tracheomalacia [24,25].

10.2.3 Anomalous origin/development of main pulmonary artery (conotruncal anomalies)

10.2.3.1 Tetralogy of Fallot

The primary abnormality in TOF is abnormal anteriorly positioned conal septum. It results in the four components of TOF which are: (1) enlarged overriding aorta, (2) ventricular septal defect (VSD), (3) right ventricular outflow tract stenosis, and (4) right ventricular hypertrophy. There is a variable degree of pulmonary obstruction ranging from mild right ventricular outflow obstruction ± pulmonic valvular stenosis to pulmonary atresia with pulmonary vascular supply from a patent ductus arteriosus or multiple aortopulmonary systemic collateral vessels. Hypoplastic or absent pulmonary valve leaflets can also occur that is usually associated with aneurysmal dilatation of central pulmonary arteries [26,27] (Fig. 10.3).

10.2.3.2 Pulmonary atresia with ventricular septal defect

Pulmonary atresia with VSD is classified into three types. Type A, the native pulmonary arteries are present and are supplied by the patent ductus arteriosus.

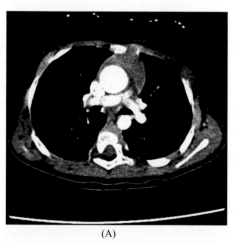 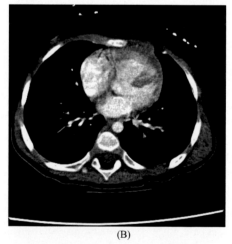

(A)   (B)

Figure 10.3 Classic case of TOF. (A) and (B) Axial CTA images showing the classic tetralogy of pulmonary stenosis, right ventricular hypertrophy, ventricular septal defect, and overriding aorta. *TOF*, Tetralogy of Fallot; *CTA*, CT angiography.

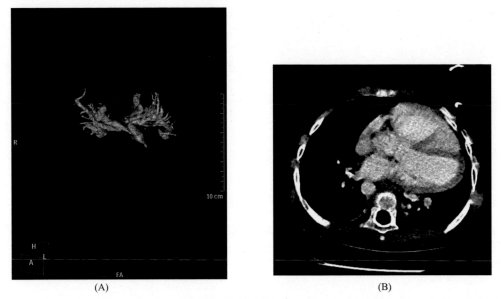

(A)   (B)

Figure 10.4 Pulmonary stenosis with VSD. (A) 3D VR image showing atretic MPA and (B) axial CTA image showing a large ventricular septal defect. *VSD*, Ventricular septal defect.

Type B, pulmonary blood flow is provided by both native pulmonary arteries and aortopulmonary collateral arteries (MAPCAs). Type C, Absent native pulmonary arteries, and the blood supply is conducted only through MAPCAs [28,29] (Fig. 10.4).

10.2.3.3 Truncus arteriosus

Truncus arteriosus consists of a single arterial trunk that supplies both systemic and pulmonary circulation as well as the coronary system. It is usually associated with a large VSD due to absent infundibular septum. There are four types of truncus arteriosus regarding the origin of pulmonary trunk. Truncus arteriosus should be differentiated from another condition named "hemi-truncus" which means that one branch of pulmonary artery is arising from the aorta while the other branch is normally originating from the main pulmonary artery [3,30] (Fig. 10.5).

10.2.3.4 Double outlet right ventricle

In double outlet right ventricle, this anomaly in both aorta and pulmonary artery are arising from the morphologically right ventricle. There are four types of double outlet right ventricle [31,32] (Fig. 10.6).

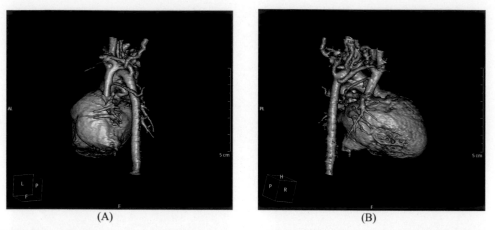

Figure 10.5 Truncus arteriosus. (A, B) 3D volume-rendered CTA images showing a single large arterial truck where the MPA arising from its posterior aspect proximal to aortic arch. *CTA*, CT angiography.

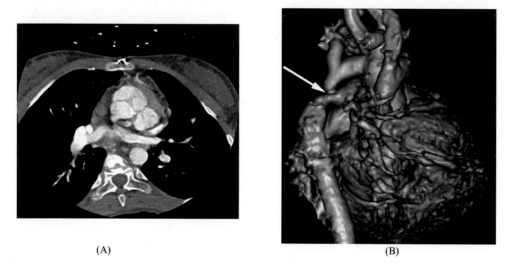

Figure 10.6 Double outlet right ventricle. (A) Coronal and (B) axial images showing that both PA (black arrow) and aorta (white arrow) are arising from the right ventricle.

10.3 Merits, limitations, and future directions

CTA is a gold standard modality in cardiac and vascular imaging as it is an easy, noninvasive technique with high spatial resolution. CTA allows accurate evaluation of cardiovascular anomalies. It is a very fast technique with a short acquisition time that helps in decreasing the time of radiation exposure and radiation dose. CTA is superior to MRA in patients with cardiac pacemakers and shorter examination time [1—5]. The main limitation is uncooperative patients of the pediatric age group especially young patients who cannot hold the breath or even breathe quietly which acquires the use of sedation. High radiation dose is still a disadvantage in CTA despite many measures for radiation dose reduction is taken into consideration [4—8]. Future application of combined advanced MR imaging may help for detection of associated lesions [33—36] and the use of artificial intelligence [37] in the future will improve the results.

10.4 Conclusion

CTA is an excellent modality in the evaluation of congenital anomalies of the pulmonary artery as well as other associated cardiac and extracardiac abnormalities that are very important for sitting surgical plans of treatment and postoperative follow-up of those patients.

References

[1] Zucker EJ. Cross-sectional imaging of congenital pulmonary artery anomalies. Int J Cardiovasc Imaging 2019;35:1535—48.
[2] Aziz M, Krishnam M, Madhuranthakam AJ, et al. Update on MR imaging of the pulmonary vasculature. Int J Cardiovasc Imaging 2019;35:1483—97.
[3] Goerne H, Chaturvedi A, Partovi S, et al. State-of-the-art pulmonary arterial imaging - Part 2. Vasa 2018;47:361—75.
[4] Carter BW, Lichtenberger 3rd JP, Wu CC. Congenital abnormalities of the pulmonary arteries in adults. Am J Roentgenol 2014;202:W308—13.
[5] Krishnan AS, Babar JL, Gopalan D. Imaging of congenital and acquired disorders of the pulmonary artery. Curr Probl Diagn Radiol 2012;41:165—78.
[6] Razek AA, Saad E, Soliman N, et al. Assessment of vascular disorders of the upper extremity with contrast-enhanced magnetic resonance angiography: pictorial review. Jpn J Radiol 2010;28:87—94.
[7] Razek AA. Vascular neurocutaneous disorders: neurospinal and craniofacial imaging findings. Jpn J Radiol 2014;32:519—28.
[8] Abdel Razek AAK. Imaging findings of Klippel-Trenaunay syndrome. J Comput Assist Tomogr 2019;43:786—92.
[9] Abdel Razek AA, Al-Marsafawy H, Elmansy M, et al. CT angiography and MR angiography of congenital anomalies of pulmonary veins. J Comput Assist Tomogr 2019;43:399—405.
[10] Razek AAKA, Samir S. Differentiation malignant from benign pericardial effusion with diffusion-weighted MRI. Clin Radiol 2019;74(325):e19—24.
[11] Razek AA, Khalek AM, Elwakeel H, et al. Inter-observer agreement of color duplex ultrasound of central vein stenosis in hemodialysis patients. Phlebology 2019;34:636—42.
[12] Razek AA, Fouda NS, Elmetwaley N, et al. Sonography of the knee joint. J Ultrasound 2009;12:53—60.
[13] Razek AA, Ashmalla GA. Prediction of venous malformations with localized intravascular coagulopathy with diffusion-weighted magnetic resonance imaging. Phlebology 2019;34:156—61.
[14] Abdel Razek AAK, Albair GA, Samir S. Clinical value of classification of venous malformations with contrast-enhanced MR angiography. Phlebology 2017;32:628—33.
[15] Razek AA, Gaballa G, Megahed AS, et al. Time resolved imaging of contrast kinetics (TRICKS) MR angiography of arteriovenous malformations of head and neck. Eur J Radiol 2013;82:1885—91.

[16] Abdel Razek AA, Denewer AT, Hegazy MA, et al. Role of computed tomography angiography in the diagnosis of vascular stenosis in head and neck microvascular free flap reconstruction. Int J Oral Maxillofac Surg 2014;43:811—15.

[17] Tawfik AM, Razek AA, Kerl JM, et al. Comparison of dual-energy CT-derived iodine content and iodine overlay of normal, inflammatory and metastatic squamous cell carcinoma cervical lymph nodes. Eur Radiol 2014;24:574—80.

[18] Rahkonen O, Chaturvedi RR, Benson L, et al. Pulmonary artery stenosis in hybrid single-ventricle palliation: high incidence of left pulmonary artery intervention. J Thorac Cardiovasc Surg 2015;149 1102—10.e2.

[19] Abdel Razek AAK, Elrakhawy MM, Yossof MM, et al. Inter-observer agreement of the Coronary Artery Disease Reporting and Data System (CAD-RADS(TM)) in patients with stable chest pain. Pol J Radiol 2018;83:e151—9.

[20] Greutmann M. Pulmonary artery dilatation in congenital heart disease: size doesn't matter. Int J Cardiol 2019;277:235—6.

[21] Sakrana AA, Abdel Razek AAK, Yousef AM, et al. Cardiac magnetic resonance-derived indexed volumes and volume ratios of the cardiac chambers discriminating group 2 pulmonary hypertension from other World Health Organization groups. J Comput Assist Tomogr 2021;45:59—64.

[22] Hernandez LE, Anderson RH, Hoggard E, et al. Crossed pulmonary arteries with hypoplasia of the transverse aortic arch. Cardiol Young 2015;25:718—24.

[23] Talwar S, Rajashekar P, Gupta SK, et al. Crossed pulmonary arteries in a patient with persistent truncus arteriosus. Ann Thorac Surg 2016;101:2377—9.

[24] Xie J, Juan YH, Wang Q, et al. Evaluation of left pulmonary artery sling, associated cardiovascular anomalies, and surgical outcomes using cardiovascular computed tomography angiography. Sci Rep 2017;7:40042.

[25] Binsalamah ZM, Fraser CD, Mery CM. A pulmonary artery sling with a vascular ring in a toddler: an uncommon combination. Cardiol Young 2018;28:783—5.

[26] Sánchez Ramírez CJ, Pérez de Isla L. Tetralogy of Fallot: cardiac imaging evaluation. Ann Transl Med 2020;8:966.

[27] Shaaban M, Tantawy S, Elkafrawy F, et al. Multi-detector computed tomography in the assessment of tetralogy of Fallot patients: is it a must? Egypt Heart J 2020;72:17.

[28] Abdel Razek AAK, Al-Marsafawy H, Elmansy M. Imaging of pulmonary atresia with ventricular septal defect. J Comput Assist Tomogr 2019;43:906—11.

[29] Romeih S, Al-Sheshtawy F, Salama M, et al. Comparison of contrast enhanced magnetic resonance angiography with invasive cardiac catheterization for evaluation of children with pulmonary atresia. Heart Int 2012;7:e9.

[30] Hong SH, Kim YM, Lee CK, et al. 3D MDCT angiography for the preoperative assessment of truncus arteriosus. Clin Imaging 2015;39:938—44.

[31] Ugurlucan M, Arslan AH, Yildiz Y, et al. Double outlet right ventricle with unilateral absence of left pulmonary artery. Cardiol Young 2013;23:466—9.

[32] Tawfik AM, Kerl JM, Razek AA, et al. Image quality and radiation dose of dual-energy CT of the head and neck compared with a standard 120-kVp acquisition. Am J Neuroradiol 2011;32:1994—9.

[33] Razek AA. Diffusion magnetic resonance imaging of chest tumors. Cancer Imaging 2012;12:452—63.

[34] Abdel Razek AA, Elkammary S, Elmorsy AS, et al. Characterization of mediastinal lymphadenopathy with diffusion-weighted imaging. Magn Reson Imaging 2011;29:167—72.

[35] Abdel Razek AA, Gaballa G, Elashry R, et al. Diffusion-weighted MR imaging of mediastinal lymphadenopathy in children. Jpn J Radiol 2015;33:449—54.

[36] Abdel Razek AA, Soliman N, Elashery R. Apparent diffusion coefficient values of mediastinal masses in children. Eur J Radiol 2012;81:1311—14.

[37] Razek AAKA. Editorial for "Preoperative MRI-based radiomic machine-learning nomogram may accurately distinguish between benign and malignant soft tissue lesions: a two-center study." J Magn Reson Imaging 2020;52:883—4.

CHAPTER 11

Obstructive coronary artery disease diagnostics: machine learning approach for an effective preselection of patients

Mateusz Krysiński[1], Małgorzata Krysińska[1] and Ewaryst Tkacz[2]
[1]Silesian Center for Heart Diseases, Zabrze, Poland
[2]Faculty of Biomedical Engineering, Department of Biosensors and Processing of Biomedical Signals, Silesian University of Technology, Zabrze, Poland

11.1 Introduction

According to World Health Organization, cardiovascular diseases are the leading cause of death globally, taking about 18 million lives annually. In the United States alone, one person dies from cardiovascular disease every 36 seconds [1], which is one in every four deaths [2]. Heart disease costs the United States more than $200 billion each year [3], including health care services, medicines, and lost productivity. The most common type of heart disease is coronary artery disease (CAD).

In the course of the atherosclerotic process, lasting for many years, lipids and blood-derived inflammatory cells accumulate in the artery, forming the so-called atherosclerotic plaques. The plaques tend to form dystrophic calcification, which in the later stages of the disease development leads to hardening of the arteries and the formation of endothelial defects above the atherosclerotic foci. The presence of atherosclerotic lesions reduces the lumen of the vessel and thus impairs normal blood flow to the heart, which may lead to cardiovascular events. In the case of significant arterial stenosis, i.e. when the vessel lumen is reduced by at least 50%, the obstruction is hemodynamically significant (obstructive coronary artery disease—oCAD), and resulting ischemia is characterized by an increased risk of death and cardiovascular events [4]. As studies show [5], atherosclerosis is closely related to the presence of risk factors. Among them are dyslipidemias, smoking, diabetes, hypertension, obesity, and low physical activity. The more risk factors, the greater the risk of CAD. Treatment of choice depends heavily on the stage of the disease and the location of atherosclerotic plaques. The key is to eliminate risk factors and use appropriate drugs. Some patients require coronary angioplasty or coronary bypass grafting.

Cardiovascular and Coronary Artery Imaging
DOI: https://doi.org/10.1016/B978-0-12-822706-0.00006-8

The basis of oCAD diagnostics is medical imaging, enabling physicians to make an appropriate decision regarding further treatment [6,7]. Hence, computed tomography (CT) is increasingly used in the diagnosis of coronary heart disease. Patients are selected for a CT scan based on the assessment of the likelihood of significant atherosclerotic stenosis. According to the American College of Cardiology and American Heart Association guidelines, this likelihood depends on the present risk factors and reported symptoms. With the help of CT, it is possible to quantify the CAD-specific calcifications in the coronary arteries and determine the severity of the atherosclerosis. For this purpose, the most commonly used marker is known as Calcium Score (CaSc), developed by Agatston [8]. The evaluation of coronary artery calcium scan (CACS) is based on the indication of calcifications in the coronary arteries, with calcifications considered as structures of more than 130 Hounsfield Units peak intensity. The CACS examination does not allow for the assessment of the functional significance of atherosclerotic lesions [9], hence the need to perform complementary coronary computed tomography angiography (CCTA), in which, thanks to the administration of a contrast agent, it is possible to assess the percentage of artery lumen obstruction caused by atherosclerotic plaque. Approximately 85% of patients referred to CCTA do not have significant ($\geq$50%) stenosis, which means that the examination is highly likely to exclude CAD but also exposes patients to the harmful effects of radiation and contrast agent, notably the prognosis of these patients is very good [10].

Negative effects of the diagnostics may be reduced by a more precise preselection of patients for CCTA testing. Currently, the threshold for further imaging is usually high CaSc, typically at least 600 Agatston units, with insufficient limitation as a result. The solution may be to improve preselection through the use of machine learning. According to Hampe et al. [11], over the last 10 years, the PubMed database has included 59 publications related to the use of artificial intelligence in the imaging of CAD. Most of the manuscripts are on automating the assessment of standard tests, such as the automatic calcium quantification in CACS or the degree of coronary stenosis in CCTA. Attempts to predict the results of the second study on the basis of the results of the first (for the purpose of effective preselection) are few and most often carried out on a small group of patients. The best examples of such an approach are the works of Al'Aref et al. [12], which appeared in the European Heart Journal, and Głowacki et al. [13] published by Academic Radiology. The first manuscript describes the use of the CACS results and clinical data to classify significant stenosis with a score of 80% sensitivity, 80% specificity, and 83% negative predictive value (NPV). For the classification, however, the authors used features that are not pathognomonic of CAD, such as chest pain or exertional dyspnea, which may add unwanted bias to the model and hamper its predictive abilities. They also emphasize the importance of CACS quantification for effective predictions, although the calcification marker used in their work is calculated jointly for the coronary arteries (total CaSc expressed in Agatston units). The second mentioned manuscript proves that CACS assessment can be extended to include the evaluation of extra-coronary calcifications (ECC) and three calcifications markers in place of singular one improve classification accuracy. In addition, the separate quantification for each of the coronary arteries leads to further improvements in algorithm performance. The final reported result was 100% sensitivity, 70% specificity, and 100% NPV.

11.2 In search for additional diagnostic information

11.2.1 Various methods of calcium quantification

The most commonly used marker of calcification is the CaSc, which is a minimally invasive assessment of patient's risk of cardiovascular events that also allows to estimate the total burden of atherosclerotic plaques in coronary arteries [14]. However, it has its limitations, hence the attempts to develop other markers based on volumetric measurements, such as the mass equivalent (Eq) or the volume of a single atherosclerotic lesion (Vol). These methods yield values closely correlated with CaSc, however, literature shows some differences, for example, in the reproducibility of obtained measurements [15]. For this reason, calcium quantification performed with three separate markers may provide more diagnostic information than the routine evaluation of calcification using the Agatston method alone.

11.2.2 Extracoronary atherosclerosis assessment

Extracoronary atherosclerosis is associated with the same risk factors as the development of CAD: advanced age, smoking or diabetes [16]. The disease often progresses unnoticed for many years, usually starting in the lower limbs. Approximately 20%—25% of patients require revascularization, i.e. invasive restoration of circulation, while in the case of about 5% of patients advanced pathologies of blood supply require limb removal, with mortality in the first 24 months after amputation reaching 40% [17]. Atherosclerotic lesions can also develop in the abdominal arteries. Therefore, extracoronary calcifications often precede the process of atherosclerotic plaque formation in the vessels supplying the heart muscle with blood. There is a correlation between severity, dispersion, and the burden of calcified changes in extracoronary areas with corresponding factors within the coronary arteries [18]. On this basis, it can be concluded that assessment of extracoronary disease may provide additional diagnostic information in diagnostics and treatment of oCAD.

Calcified atherosclerotic lesions are preceded by atherosclerotic plaques composed of lipids, proteins, and foam cells. Calcification occurs in the later stages of the disease development. Noncalcified lesions, usually refferd to as "soft", are not imaged in standard noncontrast tomography and in their case the result of a typical marker in the form of CaSc is "zero." Soft lesions are found in 73% of such patients [19]. In most cases, these lesions are not associated with oCAD, although in 5%–7% of cases [20,21] artery lumen narrowing is hemodynamically significant. Thus the CaSc alone, calculated for the coronary arteries, cannot exclude the presence of oCAD as soft plaques are detectable only after contrast agent administration. For these patients, the assessment of extracoronary calcifications may prove useful due to the progressive nature of CAD.

11.2.3 The development of CAD in coronary arteries is not uniform

Atherosclerotic lesions develop within the coronary arteries in a heterogeneous manner. Plaques most frequently emerge in the proximal sections [22], especially at vascular bifurcations. In the left anterior descending (LAD) artery, the lesions are most often located right next to the exit of the first diagonal branch and in the proximal segment of this branch [23]. Most often LAD is also the vessel of first CAD appearance [24]. This is also true in the case of noncalcified lesions, as they usually affect LAD first [25]. Moreover, with disease development and involvement of other coronary vessels in advanced stages, LAD remains the artery with the highest calcification burden [22]. Increased CaSc is associated with moderate or severe ischemia in LAD, its branches, or in the left circumferential branch (Cx) [26]. Right coronary artery (RCA) atherosclerosis is less common than LAD but more common than Cx. It is associated with the greater number of ramifications in these vessels, which makes them susceptible to the so-called milking effect [27,28]. It is caused by the formation of myocardial bridge that compresses the coronary vessel during the heart's work, which causes a backflow of blood and reduces shear stress within the compressed areas. These areas are then particularly prone to the development of atherosclerosis. Therefore, the assessment of the CACS examination while taking into consideration the distribution of atherosclerotic lesions may improve clinical reasoning.

11.3 Materials and methods

11.3.1 Supervised machine learning

As indicated in the publication [21] summarizing the works using machine learning in CAD diagnostics published in the years 1992–2019, as many as 90% of them are based on the supervised learning process. This algorithm development methodology is based on previously identified solutions for a given group of cases. Thanks to the appropriate labeling, apart from the input data, the final results are also sent to the model. This way, the program finds the relationship between the initial parameters and the results to which they lead. Then after being presented with the input vector of unlabeled and previously unknown cases, the model is able to predict the expected result. This means, for example, predicting the results of a given test based on the available assessment of another diagnostic procedure. In cardiological diagnostics, these are often tests such as coronary angiography, electrocardiography, single-photon emission tomography, optical tomography, or intravascular measurement with an ultrasound probe.

11.3.2 CCTA examination as a reference

In our work, the main diagnostic procedure is the aforementioned CCTA test. This tomography has already been the subject of studies using machine learning techniques, for example, for the classification of hemodynamically significant atherosclerotic lesions [29] or for automatic recognition of calcium and lipid-protein accumulation areas [30]. These works describe the use of convolutional and recursive networks with deep learning approach, using the CCTA as the basis for algorithm inference. The points of reference, and at the same time the desired indications of the algorithm, are the results of other studies. The methodology used in our study is different—CCTA was a basis for assessing the degree of stenosis in coronary arteries and the desired outcome is differentiation between lesions indicating oCAD and less significant ones.

11.3.3 Extended CACS evaluation

The parameters used for our machine learning model development were derived from noncontrast CACS tomography. In comparison to standard diagnostics, the examination was extended to include the quantification of ECC. There are reports [31] that the ECC assessment in the thoracic area is associated with main risk factors of cardiovascular disease development. This is not true for atherosclerotic lesions present in the coronary arteries. Moreover, quantifications of extracoronary and coronary calcifications are correlated with each other, but it is not completely collinear, which may suggest an additional information from the ECC assessment for the diagnosis of oCAD. Therefore the assessments of calcifications in the aortic valve (AoV) and the aorta (Ao) in the thoracic segment: the ascending and descending aorta, without the aortic arch (which is generally excluded from the field of view of the tomograph) were obtained. In addition to the aorta, routinely examined coronary arteries were evaluated separately, which means an individual evaluation of the LAD, RCA, Cx, and left main artery (LM). For each of the anatomical structures, three calcification markers were determined: CaSc, Eq, and Vol. Additional parameters were the age and sex, indicated [32] as important risk factors for the development of CAD, while being one of the most basic patient data.

11.3.4 Classifier and optimization methods

Classifier of choice was extreme gradient boosting (XGB) algorithm. Model parameters were optimized with the Bayesian method and the commonly used grid search method. The Bayesian algorithm was tree-structured Parzen estimator (TPE). This is the method that proved to be the best among all tested [33] in the optimization of the XGB model for the credit risk assessment. Due to the supervised learning process, the data were divided into a training set and a test set. The training set was used to validate the algorithm with the 10-fold cross-validation method, and then it was used as a whole to develop the final version of the classifier. Separated test group was the final evaluation of the algorithm. This part of the data included individual patients whose diagnostic results were not used in any way to develop the algorithm. Such an approach allows for simulation of the classifier's performance in a real clinical environment.

11.3.5 Study population

The study included patients who were at low to moderate risk of CAD (assessed at the time of admission by a cardiologist), who were referred in 2017—2019 for CT scans for coronary artery imaging at the Computed Tomography and X-ray Diagnostics Laboratory, Silesian Center for Heart Diseases in Zabrze. The inclusion criteria for this study was performed examination of both CACS and CCTA. The exclusion criteria were as follows: a result of at least 600 Agatston units in CACS, previously diagnosed CAD, history of arterial bypass surgery, stent implantation in coronary vessels, or contraindications for CCTA, such as chronic kidney disease (determined on the basis of high creatinine levels in blood) or previous allergic reactions to iodine contrast administration. Ultimately, 764 patients were enrolled in the study.

11.3.6 Acquisition and diagnostic evaluation of CCTA scans

All coronary artery scans were collected using a dual-source tomograph (SOMATON Definition Flash, Siemens Healthineers, Forchheim, Germany). Non-contrast-enhanced tomographies were performed in the longitudinal scanning field from the level of tracheal carina to the diaphragm. Image reconstruction was carried out assuming a layer thickness of 3 mm, with an increment of 1.5 mm, using B35f kernel type. The voltage on X-ray tube was 120 kV and the amperage was 75 mA.

After CACS, ECG-gated CCTA tests were performed on stable patients without arrhythmias. Images were reconstructed using protocol with a layer thickness of 0.75 mm and an increment of 0.5 mm (which caused an overlapping effect), using B26f kernel type. The X-ray tube voltage was 100—120 kV (depending on patient's mass index) and the amperage was 300—450 mA. We used $2 \times 64 \times 0.6$ mm collimation. Patients received a nonionic low osmolar contrast Omnipaque (Iohexol) 350 mg/mL (GE Healthcare); average dose was 55 mL per patient, administered at a flow rate of 5—5.5 mL/s. Each patient also received 0.8 mg nitroglycerin. In cases where heart rate was 75—80 beats per minute, metoprolol was administered in the amount of 2.5—7.5 mg.

Diagnostic interpretation of collected data was performed by an experienced radiologist and cardiologist specialized in the assessment of atherosclerotic lesions, employed at the Silesian Center for Heart Diseases in Zabrze. Calcifications were quantified using dedicated, semiautomatic software (Volume Wizard, Siemens). Evaluation included visible calcifications of at least 1 mm^2 and a peak intensity greater than 130 Hounsfield units. These changes were automatically recognized and color marked by the software. The values of three types of calcification markers were determined for each of the lesions: CaSc expressed in Agatston units, Vol expressed in mm^3, and Eq expressed in mg.

11.4 Results

11.4.1 Tools used

We performed all statistical calculations in the Python environment and open-source computing libraries available in this language, in particular NumPy and SciPy. To optimize model hyperparameters, we used the scikit-learn library and grid search method. Bayesian optimization was performed with the hyperopt library. We created a classifier model using the available XGBoost library, containing the Gradient Boosting model, with a base algorithm in a form of decision tree. Statistical comparisons, depending on distribution and type of data, were conducted using Student's t-test, Mann–Whitney U test, or chi-square test (when the data were in contingency tables form). Comparisons involving more than two groups were performed with the following tests: ANOVA, Kruskal–Wallis test, or multidimensional chi-square test. For the statistical inference, we assumed a significance level of 5%.

11.4.2 Study population characteristics

Results collected from 764 patients were divided into two groups: 560 people were qualified to training group and 204 to test group, to simulate a clinical trial and final evaluation of developed classifier. Statistical comparison of the groups is presented in Table 11.1.

Groups did not differ in mean age, percentage of men, and percentage of oCAD. However, statistically significant differences were found in mean calcification of coronary arteries, aorta, and AoV. Results indicate that on average patients in the test group had more severe CAD.

11.4.3 Calcific burden

An important aspect of this study is a conclusion that burden of calcified lesions in each of the coronary arteries is different, and these differences are important for the diagnosis of oCAD. Therefore, we conducted a series of statistical analyzes to showcase contrasts in the development of atherosclerotic lesions in coronary vessels. As the main goal of our research is to identify patients who do not require further diagnostic procedures in their current stage of CAD, the initial phase of atherosclerosis is the most important. For this reason, in our analyzes we emphasized single-vessel CAD, i.e. when only one of the coronary vessels is diseased. However, with the progress of CAD, usually more arteries are involved. A more detailed illustration of this process is presented in Fig. 11.1.

Table 11.1 Statistical comparison of training group of 560 patients and test group of 204 patients.

		Training group N = 560	Test group N = 204	P
Age		60.3 ± 10.2	60.2 ± 11.1	.49
Male (%)		25	28	.31
oCAD		81	19	.06
Calcium score:		65 ± 114	245 ± 111	< .00001
	LAD	38 ± 74	68 ± 83	< .00001
	LM	3.9 ± 17.7	26.1 ± 28.4	< .00001
	RCA	15 ± 44	39 ± 55	< .00001
	Cx	8.2 ± 24.6	27 ± 31	< .00001
	Ao	200 ± 664	719 ± 1517	< .00001
	AoV	10.4 ± 68.7	465 ± 812	< .00001

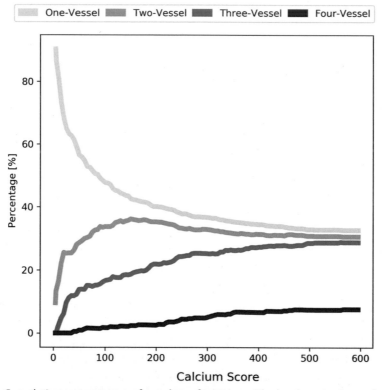

Figure 11.1 Cumulative percentages of number of arteries with developed atherosclerotic lesions in relation to Calcium Score expressed in Agatston units.

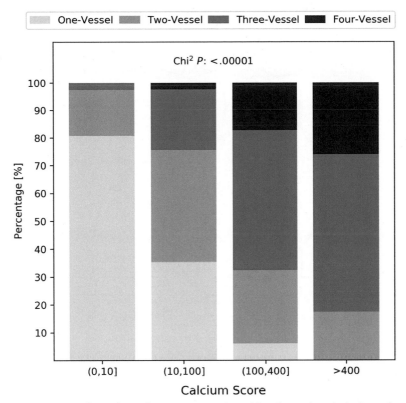

Figure 11.2 Percentage of number of coronary arteries with atherosclerotic lesions depending on the risk category of coronary artery disease, identified by Calcium Score value.

The graph shows cumulative percentage of up to 600 CaSc, because exceeding this value was one of the exclusion criteria from the study. There is a clearly visible trend of decreasing proportion of single vessel disease and increasing proportion of multi-vessel disease. The results are consistent with our presuppositions: they confirm dynamic development of atherosclerosis, which, as plaques in coronary vessels continue to grow, takes up subsequent coronary arteries due to blood flow disturbance in these areas. We made a similar comparison after prior division into subgroups depending on the value of the CaSc. The comparison is shown in Fig. 11.2.

Ranges of CaSc values presented in the figure are the most commonly used ranges that categorize this calcification marker, equated with an increasing risk of coronary heart disease. These are:

- [0, 10)—minimal risk of CAD
- (10, 100]—mild risk of CAD
- (100, 400]—moderate risk of CAD
- > 400—severe risk of CAD

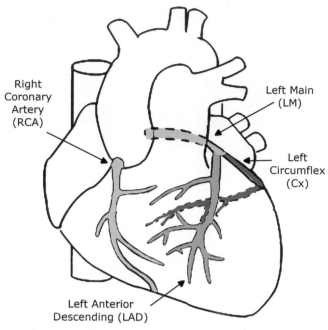

Figure 11.3 Schema of myocardial blood supply with color markings of coronary arteries analogous to those used in further analyzes. *RCA*, Right coronary artery; *LM*, left main; *Cx*, left circumflex artery; *LAD*, left anterior descending.

We compared categorical data with chi-square test, which confirmed statistically significant differences between the groups in indicated ranges. Again, there is an evident decreasing proportion of single-vessel atherosclerosis with increasing risk of CAD. The greater the risk of CAD, the more common is multivessel atherosclerosis.

Apart from number of diseased vessels, localization of lesions is also an important information. Therefore, for further analyzes coronary arteries were considered separately. In order to facilitate the understanding of the results, colors corresponding to analyzed arteries were drawn on a coronary vessels schema (Fig. 11.3).

The comparison of single-vessel disease prevalence in particular vessels is presented in Fig. 11.4. Similar to the analysis of number of diseased vessels, we divided data into groups with the same risk of CAD, determined with CaSc values.

There was not a single case of one-vessel CAD in the highest risk range. This is in line with previous results showing dynamic pace of atherosclerotic lesions development when one vessel is involved and atherosclerotic plaques are forming in subsequent vessels. The most frequently involved coronary artery in one-vessel disease is LAD artery (for our analysis treated jointly with its septal branches). In patients at moderately high risk of CAD (100—400 CaSc), it is the only artery in which atherosclerosis is of single-vessel type. This means that LAD is a vessel in which CAD can

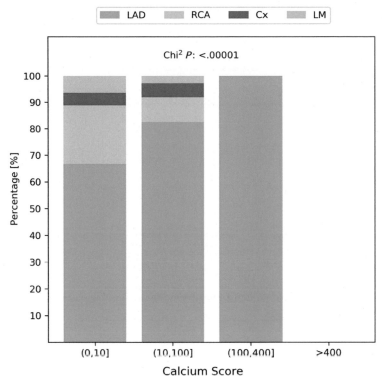

Figure 11.4 Percentage of single-vessel disease in each coronary artery, based on typical risk ranges for CAD. *CAD*, Coronary artery disease.

develop for the longest time without affecting other arteries. The reverse trend is visible for other coronary arteries, particularly RCA. In the lowest risk category, RCA percentage is more than twice as large as in the next category. We also presented percentage changes in each artery as a cumulative percentage curve, in the CaSc 0−100 range (Fig. 11.5), i.e. the two lowest risk categories. In our population increased risk of CAD is related to the lack of single-vessel CAD cases, other than LAD.

There is a trend of decreasing RCA percentage in single-vessel CAD cases with an increase in total heart burden due to calcified atherosclerotic lesions. This indicates that after the involvement of RCA, atherosclerosis tends to develop in subsequent vessels of left coronary artery. The proportion of Cx and LM is approximately constant and in both cases does not exceed 10% of all of the patients.

In the next step we analyzed the average calcium burden of each artery. We made a comparison taking into consideration all cases, and also after separating cases of single-vessel CAD. Obtained results in the form of mean values (histogram bars height) with standard deviations (marked with a dashed line) are shown in Fig. 11.6.

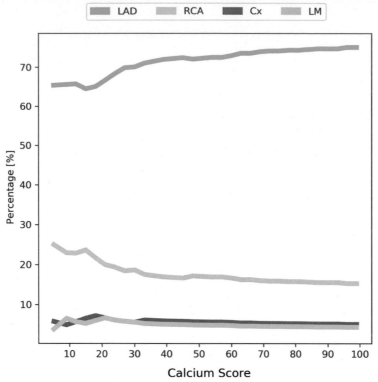

Figure 11.5 Cumulative percentage of single-vessel CAD among coronary arteries, in relation to calcium score. *CAD*, Coronary artery disease.

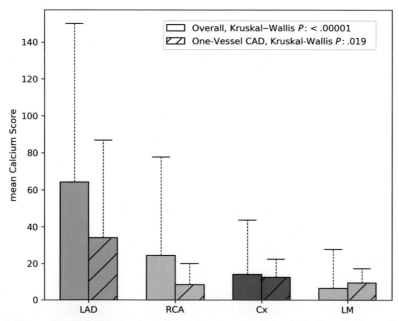

Figure 11.6 Mean values of Calcium Score in each coronary artery, including single- and multivessel CAD. *CAD*, Coronary artery disease.

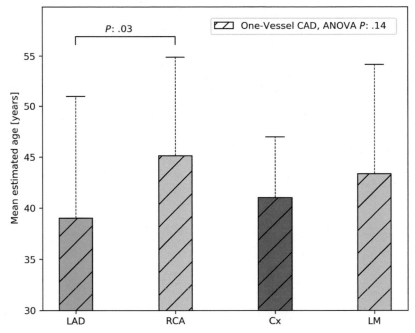

Figure 11.7 Estimated average initial age of coronary artery disease.

Due to inconsistency of data distributions with the normal distribution (determined using Shapiro—Wilk test) and heteroscedasticity of groups (Levene's test), the comparison between groups was performed using the Kruskal—Wallis test. Tests showed statistically significant differences in mean calcium burden of coronary arteries in both comparisons. This confirms the initial assumptions about heterogeneous distribution of atherosclerotic plaques in patients, regardless of the stage of CAD development.

Next analysis was based on estimation of the initial age of CAD, using only data from patients with single-vessel CAD. There are reports indicating an annual increase of CaSc by 20%—30% [34], 24% [35], or 26% [36]. On this basis, we assumed an average annual increase of this marker of 25%. Using this value, we calculated at what age patient's CaSc was less than 0.1 Agatston units. The mean values are presented in Fig. 11.7.

Due to a large variance in estimated age, the ANOVA test did not show any significant differences in mean values. We made an additional comparison between the mean age in LAD and RCA using the Student's Tukey HSD test. In this case, comparison proved a statistically significant difference. The graph shows that the earliest atherosclerotic lesions can be expected in LAD, significantly more often than in RCA.

Obtained results confirm not only the initial assumptions about heterogeneity of atherosclerotic lesions occurrence in coronary vessels but also a differentiation of their

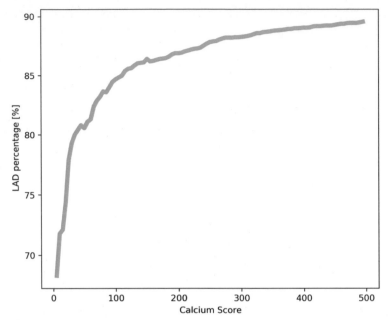

Figure 11.8 Percentage of LAD among vessels with atherosclerotic plaques, in relation to Calcium Score value. *LAD*, Left anterior descending.

total calcification burden or estimated initial age of disease. Consequently, throughout all analyzes, the most prone artery seems to be LAD. It may be related to previously discussed milking effect. Therefore, our next analyzes regarded only this one artery. We examined how LAD percentage changes depending on the severity of CAD. Fig. 11.8 shows changes in LAD percentage with an increase in CaSc value in all patients.

The graph shows that with the increase in total calcification of coronary arteries, the percentage of LAD among diseased vessels increases. This is related to a tendency of CAD to spread and invade subsequent coronary arteries, but also to already confirmed increased susceptibility of LAD to atherosclerotic plaques formation. This is illustrated in Fig. 11.9.

Combined with the previous results, we can conclude that the susceptibility of LAD to development of atherosclerotic lesions is the main reason for the highest rates of CAD in this artery. As the number of calcified arteries increases, percentage of LAD increases significantly. On average, CAD develops the earliest and the most often in LAD. Even if the development of atherosclerosis begins in a different vessel, probability of calcified lesions formation in LAD increases with development of the disease. In the case of two-vessel disease, it is over 90%, and in three-vessel disease—nearly 100%.

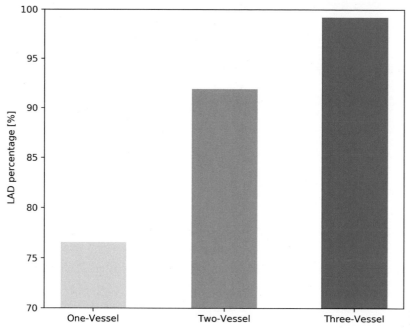

Figure 11.9 Percentage of LAD among diseased vessels depending on number of arteries affected by atherosclerosis. *LAD*, Left anterior descending.

Performed analysis of coronary artery calcific burden provides evidence for the thesis that development of atherosclerosis in vessels supplying heart muscle with blood is not heterogeneous. Differences are observed in the susceptibility of vessels to CAD, the average initial age of atheroslerotic process, or total accumulated calcific burden. This suggests that the individual assessment of calcifications in each of the coronary vessels separately may allow for a more accurate inference about the stage of CAD in every patient. This information is important not only for the purpose of oCAD diagnostics but also for the development of a classifier which was the main goal of this work.

11.4.4 Model development

11.4.4.1 Number of base models

As an ensemble algorithm, XGB models are put together by combining selected number of lower-order algorithms into one model. In this work, we used a decision tree as the basic model. Number of decision trees that make up the final model is one of the optimized hyperparameters, named "boosting rounds". An important issue in this process is optimization of error made by the algorithm and variance of this error between the training set and the test set. It is necessary to follow simultaneous minimalization of both these parameters, which always takes place on the basis of a

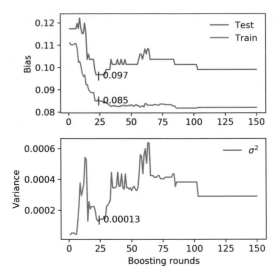

Figure 11.10 First step of hyperparameters tuning is based on test and training error, and their variance.

compromise named bias–variance tradeoff. It is not possible to decrease classification or regression error limitlessly because it will lead to model overfitting. It is a situation in which the model perfectly recognizes dependencies in training set, but cannot cope with the problem in the case of test data. An algorithm highly specialized in guessing known results loses on generalization of the problem and is not applicable to unknown cases. Results of number of basic models selection in terms of bias–variance tradeoff are presented in Fig. 11.10. The graph shows the optimization of one of the prepared models, but the best result is the same for all other analyzes.

The graph shows that the best conditions for the above-mentioned compromise occur after assembling the classifier from 23 basic models. Despite the fact that in subsequent iterations training error decreases, test error and variance show the opposite trend. Results were obtained by dividing the training set (560 patients) by randomization into a temporary test set (20% of data) and a temporary training set (80% of data). We used the same division in all other operations during development and validation of the classifier.

11.4.4.2 Optimization of hyperparameters

In addition to the number of base models, the algorithm is regulated by a number of other hyperparameters. Their names and briefly described functions are described in Table 11.2.

We optimized parameters using the grid search and TPE methods, which lead to two separate sets (Table 11.3) used to train the algorithm.

Table 11.2 Hyperparameters optimized during a machine learning model development process.

Name	Function
Alpha	Lasso regression regularization parameter
colsample_bytree	Fraction of randomly selected parameters among all parameters used to develop a single model
Eta	An algorithm's speed of learning, responsible for the change of weights in each iteration
Gamma	The minimum increment of cost function required to split a tree "leaf"
Lambda	Ridge regression regularization parameter
max_depth	The maximum size of a single decision tree; necessary to control overfitting
min_child_weight	The minimum sum of weights in each decision tree "leaf" required to create it. This parameter is used to prevent the model from absorbing very specialized and niche data dependencies
scale_pos_weight	The scaling value of weight, helpful for significant disproportions in class representativeness
Subsample	A randomly selected fraction of all observations used to create a single model

Table 11.3 Sets of hyperparameters corresponding to both methods of their optimization.

Parameter	Grid search	TPE
Alpha	0.000	6.158
colsample_bytree	1.000	0.532
Eta	0.25	0.149
Gamma	4.5	0.363
Lambda	3	6.814
max_depth	6	12
min_child_weight	15	3
scale_pos_weight	1	2.265
Subsample	1	0.709

11.4.4.3 Classifier training and validation

Using both sets of parameters, we developed two versions of the classifier. For this purpose, we used a previously separated training set. The classification results as receiver operating characteristic (ROC) curve are presented in Fig. 11.11.

As our main goal is an effective preselection of patients, it is particularly important to maintain the highest possible sensitivity, i.e. True Positive Rate, as it translates directly into NPV. The graph shows that with 100% sensitivity, the highest specificity was achieved by the model using coronary and ECC evaluation with TPE

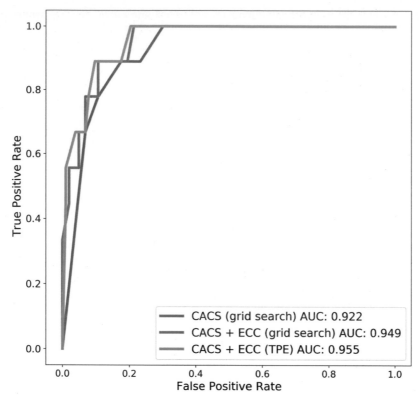

Figure 11.11 Receiver operating characteristic curve created from classification results. *CACS,* Coronary artery calcium scan; *ECC,* extra-coronary calcifications; *TPE,* tree-structured Parzen estimator.

optimization parameters. In addition, we also calculated the area under curve (AUC) for each of the models and again the TPE-based model turned out to be the best. The most important conclusion provided by the graph, however, is that the use of ECC evaluation leads to better results. AoV leaflet calcifications, which have a different etiopathology from that of coronary calcifications [37], were also one of the parameters. To evaluate the significance of this parameter, we developed two additional models based on previously determined sets of hyperparameters, but without taking into account the assessment of AoV calcifications in training data. The classification results on the reduced data set are presented with the ROC curves in Fig. 11.12.

In this case, the best model was created with a set of parameters from grid search optimization. Results of the TPE optimization model deteriorated compared to the full data set. However, this is still a clearly more accurate classification than if the data were limited to the assessment of coronary calcifications only. Since plotted curves do not provide a clear answer whether limiting the size of data improves or

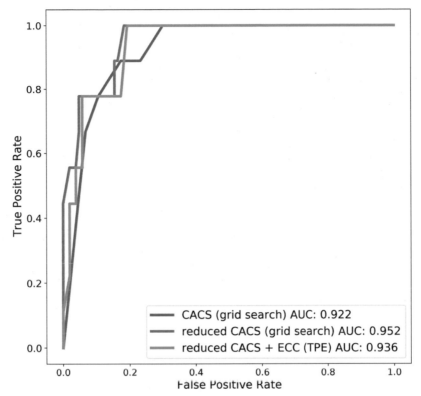

Figure 11.12 Receiver operating characteristic curve created from classification results based on the reduced (without aortic valve examination) data set. *CACS*, Coronary artery calcium scan; *ECC*, extra-coronary calcifications; *TPE*, tree-structured Parzen estimator.

worsens classification results, we conducted further analysis of each of the four models showing the best results. The assessment was performed using the 10 fold cross validation method. It is a method in which the entire training set is divided into 10 subsets, each of which is a test set in one of the 10 draws, and in the remaining ones, it is part of the training set consisting of nine subsets. We have plotted mean error curves within the training set in Fig. 11.13.

Results do not correspond to previously plotted ROC curves, i.e. in the case of grid search optimization, the classification results did not improve with dataset reduction. The most effective models (characterized by 18%−20% lower error than others) were based on a full set of data. For further analysis of models, we also plotted the mean error on the test set (Fig. 11.14).

The situation is identical to the training error: best two models use a complete data set. In the case of models developed on a limited data set, the mean test error increased by about 10% compared to the mean training error. Plotted characteristics

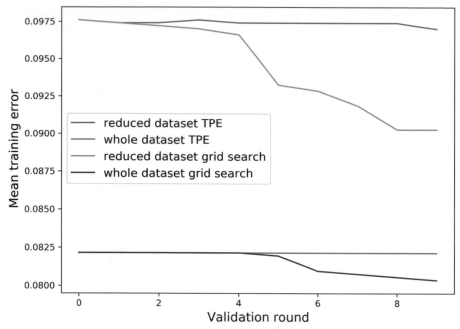

Figure 11.13 An average training error in each of the 10 iterations of 10-fold cross-validation. *TPE*, Tree-structured Parzen estimator.

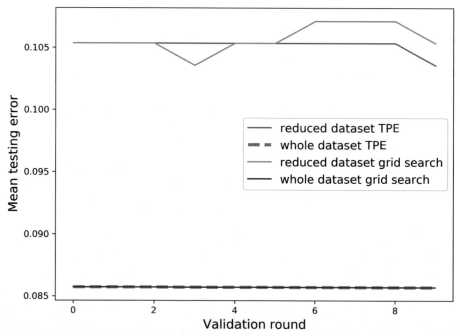

Figure 11.14 Mean test error in each of the 10 iterations of 10-fold cross-validation. *TPE*, Tree-structured Parzen estimator.

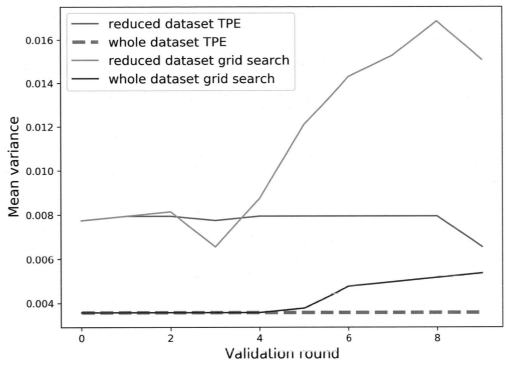

Figure 11.15 Mean variance in each of the 10 iterations of 10-fold cross-validation. *TPF*, Tree-structured Parzen estimator.

are complemented by a curve showing an average variance of tested models over cross-validation iterations, presented in Fig. 11.15.

A variance of models developed on reduced data set, regardless of hyperparameter optimization method, is 2—4 times greater than a variance of both models based on full data set. In the last stage of evaluation of prepared models, we developed each of them based on the entire training set, i.e. 560 patients. We conducted their evaluation on results of remaining 204 patients, which we had not used at all in any of the previous processes. Classification results in the form of ROC curve are presented in Fig. 11.16.

Results indicate that limiting the data set and excluding AoV observations ultimately improve classifier performance. Models based on full data set showcased smaller errors and variance during validation probably due to too high specialization for specific cases. However, the area under the ROC curve alone is not sufficient to assess suitability of each model for the purposes of this study. Therefore, we also determined values of the highest possible classification specificity while maintaining 100% NPV. The results are presented in Table 11.4.

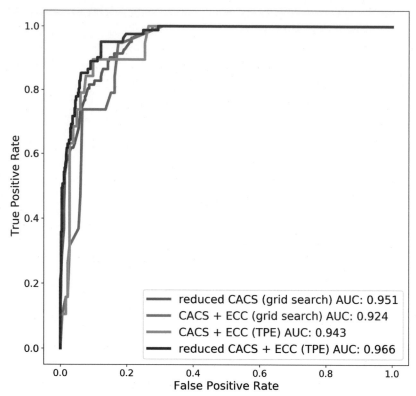

Figure 11.16 Final classification results on the test set plotted as ROC curves. *CACS,* Coronary artery calcium scan; *ECC,* extra-coronary calcifications; *TPE,* tree-structured Parzen estimator; *ROC,* receiver operating characteristic.

Table 11.4 Sensitivity and specificity values achieved in classification on the test set by each of the developed models.

Model	Sensitivity (%)	Specificity (%)
Grid search all data	100	61
Grid search limited data	100	74
TPE all data	100	61
TPE limited data	100	66

11.5 Conclusions

11.5.1 Heterogeneity of coronary arteries atherosclerotic plaque burden

Results show that in the lowest ranges of CaSc values, the most common are cases of single-vessel disease. As CAD progresses, more coronary vessels are involved.

The most burdened is LAD artery. Atherosclerosis in LAD occurs most often, and it is commonly transferred to LAD when the process of atherosclerotic plaque formation already started in another coronary artery. These results are in line with the reports in the literature [38], which also indicate that calcifications in LAD lead to myocardial infarction with ST-segment elevation significantly more often than in other arteries. The aspect of coronary calcifications localization is therefore important not only from the point of view of this study and the use of such information for predictive purposes, but it is also an important factor in the prognosis of patients suffering from CAD.

11.5.2 Machine learning model validation

An extremely important element in the process of creating a machine learning model is focus on the appropriate generalization of the problem. It is very easy to overtrain the algorithm, which hampers the usefulness of the obtained tool. While results appear to be encouraging, in subsequent operations care and appropriate methodology should be taken. In this study, better results of models obtained on full data set in the validation process are a typical sign of overfitting. This phenomenon becomes apparent only after the attempt to generalize the problem and predict results for previously unknown data. These models were specialized in a very specific group of patients, for whom observation of AoV calcifications allowed for a slight improvement in classification results. It leads, however, to a worse model performance in the clinical trial simulation. These results are consistent with the literature [37], which indicates that the assessment of AoV leaflet calcification is of low significance for prediction of oCAD.

11.5.3 Effectiveness of developed tool

The best of obtained models was characterized by a 74% specificity at 100% sensitivity. This is a much better result than in a similar study [12] in the same area. Al'Aref et al. described an algorithm achieving 80% specificity at 80% sensitivity. In their work, however, they used parameters that are not pathognomonic for CAD, such as exertional dyspnea or chest pain, which may introduce an unnecessary bias into the machine learning model and hamper its predictive abilities. In addition, quantitative assessments of CACS scans were carried out in a standard, cumulative way. On the other hand, Głowacki et al. described a model that uses the extended assessment of CACS test to develop a classifier characterized by 70% specificity at 100% sensitivity [13]. Compared to these results, the classifier obtained in this study, to the authors' knowledge, is the best tool currently described in the literature for selecting patients in whom it is possible to refrain from further diagnostics due to the low risk of oCAD.

References

[1] Centers for Disease Control and Prevention. Underlying Cause of Death, 1999−2018. CDC WONDER Online Database. Atlanta, GA: Centers for Disease Control and Prevention; 2018 [Accessed 12 March 2020].

[2] Virani SS, et al. Heart disease and stroke statistics—2020 update: a report from the American Heart Association. Circulation 2020;141(9). Available from: https://doi.org/10.1161/cir.0000000000000757.

[3] Fryar CD, Chen T-C, Li X. Prevalence of uncontrolled risk factors for cardiovascular disease: United States, 1999−2010 pdf icon[PDF-494K]. NCHS data brief, 103. Hyattsville, MD: National Center for Health Statistics; 2012 [Accessed 9 May 2019].

[4] Pizzi C, et al. Nonobstructive versus obstructive coronary artery disease in acute coronary syndrome: a meta-analysis. JAHA 2016;5:12. Available from: https://doi.org/10.1161/jaha.116.004185.

[5] De Backer G, et al. European guidelines on cardiovascular disease and prevention in clinical practice. Atherosclerosis 2003;171:145−55.

[6] Libby P, Theroux P. Pathophysiology of coronary artery disease. Circulation 2005;111(25):3481−8. Available from: https://doi.org/10.1161/circulationaha.105.537878.

[7] Bielak LF, Rumberger JA, Sheedy II PF, Schwartz RS, Peyser PA. Probabilistic model for prediction of angiographically defined obstructive coronary artery disease using electron beam computed tomography calcium score strata. Circulation 2000;102(4):380−5. Available from: https://doi.org/10.1161/01.cir.102.4.380.

[8] Agatston AS, Janowitz WR, Hildner FJ, Zusmer NR, Viamonte Jr. M, Detrano R. Quantification of coronary artery calcium using ultrafast computed tomography. J Am Coll Cardiol 1990;15 (4):827−32. Available from: https://doi.org/10.1016/0735-1097(90)90282-t.

[9] Moradi M, Nouri S, Nourozi A, Golbidi D. Prognostic value of coronary artery calcium score for determination of presence and severity of coronary artery disease. Pol J Radiol 2017;82:165−9. Available from: https://doi.org/10.12659/pjr.900643.

[10] Thomas DM, et al. Management of coronary artery calcium and coronary CTA findings. Curr Cardiovasc Imaging Rep 2015;8:6. Available from: https://doi.org/10.1007/s12410-015-9334-0.

[11] Hampe N, Wolterink JM, van Velzen SGM, Leiner T, Išgum I. Machine learning for assessment of coronary artery disease in cardiac CT: a survey. Front Cardiovasc Med 2019;6:172. Available from: https://doi.org/10.3389/fcvm.2019.00172.

[12] Al'Aref SJ, et al. Machine learning of clinical variables and coronary artery calcium scoring for the prediction of obstructive coronary artery disease on coronary computed tomography angiography: analysis from the CONFIRM registry. Eur Heart J 2019;41(3):359−67. Available from: https://doi.org/10.1093/eurheartj/ehz565.

[13] Głowacki J, Krysiński M, Czaja-Ziółkowska M, Wasilewski J. Machine learning-based algorithm enables the exclusion of obstructive coronary artery disease in the patients who underwent coronary artery calcium scoring. Acad Radiol 2020;27(10):1416−21. Available from: https://doi.org/10.1016/j.acra.2019.11.016.

[14] Alluri K, Joshi PH, Henry TS, Blumenthal RS, Nasir K, Blaha MJ. Scoring of coronary artery calcium scans: history, assumptions, current limitations, and future directions. Atherosclerosis 2015; 239(1):109−17. Available from: https://doi.org/10.1016/j.atherosclerosis.2014.12.040.

[15] Detrano RC, et al. Coronary calcium measurements: effect of CT scanner type and calcium measure on rescan reproducibility—MESA study. Radiology 2005;236(2):477−84. Available from: https://doi.org/10.1148/radiol.2362040513.

[16] Bartholomew JR, Olin JW. Pathophysiology of peripheral arterial disease and risk factors for its development. Clevel Clin J Med 2006;73(4):S8. Available from: https://doi.org/10.3949/ccjm.73.suppl_4.s8.

[17] Garcia LA. Epidemiology and pathophysiology of lower extremity peripheral arterial disease. J Endovasc Ther 2006;13(2). Available from: https://doi.org/10.1583/05-1751.1 II-3-II−9.

[18] Hodara M, Bonithon-Kopp C, Courbon D, Guérin F, Richard. J. Extra-coronary atherosclerosis in documented coronary patients. Arch des Maladies du Coeur et des Vaisseaux 1998;91(2):201−7.

[19] Uretsky S, et al. The presence, characterization and prognosis of coronary plaques among patients with zero coronary calcium scores. Int J Cardiovasc Imaging 2010;27(6):805−12. Available from: https://doi.org/10.1007/s10554-010-9730-0.

[20] Sosnowski M, Pysz P, Szymański L, Gola A, Tendera M. Negative calcium score and the presence of obstructive coronary lesions in patients with intermediate CAD probability. Int J Cardiol 2011;148(1):e16−18. Available from: https://doi.org/10.1016/j.ijcard.2009.01.077.

[21] Rubinshtein R, Gaspar T, Halon DA, Goldstein J, Peled N, Lewis BS. Prevalence and extent of obstructive coronary artery disease in patients with zero or low calcium score undergoing 64-slice cardiac multidetector computed tomography for evaluation of a chest pain syndrome. Am J Cardiol 2007;99(4):472−5. Available from: https://doi.org/10.1016/j.amjcard.2006.08.060.

[22] Amanuma M, et al. Segmental distributions of calcifications and non-assessable lesions on coronary computed tomographic angiography: evaluation in symptomatic patients. Jpn J Radiol 2015;33 (3):122−30. Available from: https://doi.org/10.1007/s11604-015-0389-2.

[23] Halon DA, Sapoznikov D, Lewis BS, Gotsman MS. Localization of lesions in the coronary circulation. Am J Cardiol 1983;52(8):921−6. Available from: https://doi.org/10.1016/0002-9149(83) 90506-4.

[24] Alluri K, et al. Distribution and burden of newly detected coronary artery calcium: results from the multi-ethnic study of atherosclerosis. J Cardiovasc Comput Tomogr 2015;9(4):337−44. Available from: https://doi.org/10.1016/j.jcct.2015.03.015.

[25] Liu Y-C, et al. Significance of coronary calcification for prediction of coronary artery disease and cardiac events based on 64-slice coronary computed tomography angiography. BioMed Res Int 2013;2013:1−9. Available from: https://doi.org/10.1155/2013/472347.

[26] Lai HM, et al. Association of coronary artery calcium with severity of myocardial ischemia in left anterior descending, left circumflex, and right coronary artery territories. Clin Cardiol 2011;35 (1):61−3. Available from: https://doi.org/10.1002/clc.20997.

[27] Wasilewski J, et al. Predominant location of coronary artery atherosclerosis in the left anterior descending artery. The impact of septal perforators and the myocardial bridging effect. KITP 2015;4:379−85. Available from: https://doi.org/10.5114/kitp.2015.56795.

[28] Poloński L. The role of septal perforators and 'myocardial bridging effect' in atherosclerotic plaque distribution in the coronary artery disease. Pol J Radiol 2015;80:195−201. Available from: https://doi.org/10.12659/pjr.893227.

[29] van Hamersvelt RW, Zreik M, Voskuil M, Viergever MA, Išgum I, Leiner T. Deep learning analysis of left ventricular myocardium in CT angiographic intermediate-degree coronary stenosis improves the diagnostic accuracy for identification of functionally significant stenosis. Eur Radiol 2018;29(5):2350−9. Available from: https://doi.org/10.1007/s00330-018-5822-3.

[30] Zreik M, van Hamersvelt RW, Wolterink JM, Leiner T, Viergever MA, Isgum I. A recurrent CNN for automatic detection and classification of coronary artery plaque and stenosis in coronary CT angiography. IEEE Trans Med Imaging 2019;38(7):1588−98. Available from: https://doi.org/10.1109/tmi.2018.2883807.

[31] Dirrichs T, Penzkofer T, Reinartz SD, Kraus T, Mahnken AH, Kuhl CK. Extracoronary thoracic and coronary artery calcifications on chest CT for lung cancer screening. Acad Radiol 2015;22 (7):880−9. Available from: https://doi.org/10.1016/j.acra.2015.03.005.

[32] Jousilahti P, Vartiainen E, Tuomilehto J, Puska P. Sex, age, cardiovascular risk factors, and coronary heart disease. Circulation 1999;99(9):1165−72. Available from: https://doi.org/10.1161/01.cir.99.9.1165.

[33] Xia Y, Liu C, Li Y, Liu N. A boosted decision tree approach using Bayesian hyper-parameter optimization for credit scoring. Expert Syst Appl 2017;78:225−41. Available from: https://doi.org/10.1016/j.eswa.2017.02.017.

[34] McEvoy JW, et al. Coronary artery calcium progression: an important clinical measurement. J Am Coll Cardiol 2010;56(20):1613−22. Available from: https://doi.org/10.1016/j.jacc.2010.06.038.

[35] Maher JE, Bielak LF, Raz JA, Sheedy II PF, Schwartz RS, Peyser PA. "Progression of coronary artery calcification: a pilot study. Mayo Clin Proc 1999;74(4):347−55. Available from: https://doi.org/10.4065/74.4.347.

[36] Raggi P, et al. Progression of coronary calcium on serial electron beam tomographic scanning is greater in patients with future myocardial infarction. Am J Cardiol 2003;92(7):827—9. Available from: https://doi.org/10.1016/s0002-9149(03)00892-0.

[37] Henein M, et al. Aortic root, not valve, calcification correlates with coronary artery calcification in patients with severe aortic stenosis: a two-center study. Atherosclerosis 2015;243(2):631—7. Available from: https://doi.org/10.1016/j.atherosclerosis.2015.10.014.

[38] Deora S, Kumar T, Ramalingam R, Nanjappa Manjunath C. Demographic and angiographic profile in premature cases of acute coronary syndrome: analysis of 820 young patients from South India. Cardiovasc Diagn Ther 2016;6(3):193—8. Available from: https://doi.org/10.21037/cdt.2016.03.05.

CHAPTER 12

Heart disease prediction using convolutional neural network

Ajay Sharma[1,2], Tarun Pal[3] and Varun Jaiswal[4,5]
[1]Department of Biotechnology and Bioinformatics, Jaypee University of Information Technology (JUIT), Solan, India
[2]Department of Computer Science, Shoolini University, Solan, India
[3]Department of Biotechnology (Bioinformatics), Vignan's Foundation for Science, Technology and Research, Guntur, India
[4]National Centre for Disease Control (NCDC), New Delhi, India
[5]Department of Food and Nutrition, College of Bio-Nano Technology, Gachon University, Seongnam, South Korea

12.1 Introduction

Hyperkinesia (or hyperkinesis movement disorder) is a term derived from the ancient Greek language, which describes the abnormal or restless state, excessive movement of the heart, or combination of both. In the western medical history, the concept of hyperkinesia was introduced by Paracelsus in the 16th century. Heart disease, a range of conditions that could affect one's heart, is one of the most prevalent diseases worldwide. Nearly half of the Americans—Africans are suffering from cardiological disorder, out of which 46% are men and other are women [1]. Coronary heart disease is the chief cause of death in the United States and more than 370,000 people annually succumb to the same. In the United States, every year almost 735,000 people suffer from a heart attack [2]. In terms of productivity and morality, it would cost about $351.2 billion. A survey of nearly 14,000 individuals with diabetes or other threat influences for diseases of heart revealed that doctors regularly miss chances to classify heart difficulties early. Just one in five measured patients having heart disease supposed they were diagnosed correctly as an outcome of routine screening. More than half of patients containing type 2 diabetes (55%) and a little less than half of patients having no diabetes (48%) described having their disease diagnosed after they developed symptoms. A number of individuals confirmed that there were being analyzed because of screening, indicating that they missed their chances to avoid coronary disease.

The danger of having heart problems and the associated investigation were accompanied by a determination to measure whether supported screening guiding principle are important in an earlier diagnosis of cardiac disease. The learning includes a nationally demonstrative example of patients having diabetes or other major hazardous influences for heart disease. Heart patients identified after American Heart Association (AHA) and the American College of Cardiology (ACC) studied their screening guidelines were somewhat similar to those identified during regular screening as patients identified before this time.

Cardiovascular and Coronary Artery Imaging
DOI: https://doi.org/10.1016/B978-0-12-822706-0.00012-3

This study was published in the May–June 2017 issue of The International Journal of Clinical Practice. The AHA and ACC now assert that all grown-ups should get themselves tested for cardiovascular threat factors at a young age of 20 years itself. The past cardiac records of people affected with the disease in question should be updated on a regular basis.

Physicians have an obligation to recurrently enquire from their patients about the latter's liquor consumption, smoking habits, diet, and physical development level. Timely estimation of fasting serum lipoprotein profile, or aggregate and high-density lipoprotein cholesterol, and fasting blood glucose can help control the patient's risk for diabetes and elevated cholesterol. All adults 40 years or older should identify their complete threat of emerging cardiovascular disease. This is mainly important for people belonging to this age group and those with two or extra threat influences for heart disease.

Global hypokinesia means poor functioning of the heart. Heart failure, or congestive heart failure (CHF), is a disorder of small heart, which gives rise to increased rapidity in inhalation and inflammation in the boundaries [4]. The most general source of heart failure is ischemic (secondary to obstructions in blood vessel). Other reasons include hypertensive (high blood pressure), viral, valvar, and idiopathic. The analysis of CHF is made by symptoms and testing of heart. An echocardiogram or cardiac catheterization is mainly done to diagnose working of the pumping chamber. Other investigations can be done to identify conditions that can cause CHF [3,5,6].

Medical or surgical are two forms of treatments for heart failure. The surgery is typically suggested if the reasons behind failure are blockages or valve problems. Medical administration includes digoxin, angiotensin-converting enzyme (ACE) inhibitors and diuretics. Recent studies have demonstrated that low-dose beta blockers increase symptoms and survival in patients having CHF. Heart transplantation is generally used during the final stage of CHF. As CHF is a highly prevalent problem, new treatments are being developed.

12.1.1 Causes

Certain reasons of global hypokinesia that can lead to heart outbreak underlie occurrence of different disorders that can damage cardiac muscle. These causes are as follows:

1. Overload of the cardiac scheme
2. Coronary artery disease
3. Heart attack
4. Cardiomyopathy

12.1.2 Overload of the cardiac scheme

Having different health conditions, such as hypertension, congenital heart defects, thyroid disorder, valve abnormalities, kidney ailments, and diabetes, can increase pressure on heart, and such pressure on cardiovascular framework can lead to global hypokinesia—related heart attack. Patients suffering from such a disorder will effects one these numerous issues, increasingly expected and to experience such cardiovascular anomalies like as the overloading of the cardiovascular system.

12.1.3 Coronary artery disease

In coronary artery disease, the arteries, which provide oxygen and blood for cardiac system get semiblocked with protein, which leads to a low level of oxygen having blood resource to the heart muscles. This blockage can also decrease flow of vital nutrients to heart, which damage can in turn it and cause global hypokinesia—associated heart failure. This is an important cause of global hypokinesia disease.

12.1.4 Heart attack

In this condition, a cardiac capture is caused because of obstruction in a coronary artery. Such clogging can stop flow of blood to the muscles of heart, thereby damaging it. Some parts of heart muscle system, or in several instances all parts, may not receive the requisite amount of oxygen-rich blood. Such parts of heart may then get damaged, resulting in its dysfunction.

12.1.5 Cardiomyopathy

In this condition, injury to the heart occurs because of a wide array of causes other than blood supply or artery anomalies, which are drug or liquor abuse or underlying infections.

12.1.6 Treatment

Global hypokinesia can be preserved on the basis of its different stages. There are four stages of this disease which are described as follows:

12.1.7 Stage A

Global hypokinesia patients include those individuals who have high susceptibility toward emerging heart failure risk, in addition to those having diabetes, hypertension, metabolic syndrome, and coronary artery disease, a history of alcohol misuse, cardiotoxic drug treatment, rheumatic fever, and a family history of cardiomyopathy. The treatment procedure typically used for this includes leaving smoking and prohibited drug and liquor misuse, regular physical exercise, treating fat anomalies and hypertension, and the use of instructed medications ACE inhibitors.

12.1.8 Stage B

Stage B includes systolic left ventricular dysfunction patients with no previous symptoms that could lead to heart failure, along with those having cardiomyopathy, valve disease, and prior heart attack. The treatment typically used under this stage in addition to that with Stage A treatments includes doctors endorsing aldosterone inhibitor drugs, surgical patchup, or replacement of the damaged artery or valve.

12.1.9 Stage C

Stage C patients experience symptoms of Stage A and Stage B along with symptoms such as fatigue, breathlessness, and decreased stamina for exercising. The treatment typically used under this stage in addition to Stage A treatments includes doctors endorsing aldosterone inhibitors for chronic symptoms digoxin and diuretics, a nitrate/hydralazine gathering to African—American patients with decided pointers; utilization of Implantable Cardioverter Defibrillator (ICD) as well as cardiovascular resynchronization treatment, that is, biventricular pacemaker, monitoring weight, regulated consumption of liquids and salt, and discontinuation of medications that amplify global hyperkinesia—related heart failure.

12.1.10 Stage D

Systolic heart failure patients who have progressive symptoms even upon receiving the best medical care fall under this category. The treatment typically used under this stage is that in addition to that for Stage A, B, and C, doctors go with the recommendation such as ventricular-assisting devices, continuous administration of intravenous inotropic drugs, research treatments, heart transplant, other surgical mediations, and hospital or palliative care.

12.1.11 Different imaging test

Different types of imaging tests that are used for examining heart include echocardiography, chest X-ray, computed tomography (CT), and magnetic resonance imaging (MRI).

12.1.12 Echocardiography

Echocardiography, generally known as an echo or cardiac echo, is a sonogram of cardiac system. Echocardiography uses normal 2D, 3D, and Doppler ultrasound to generate pictures of heart. The Swedish physician Inge Edler (1911—2001) also known as the "Father of Echocardiography," was the first person in his field to identify cardiac infection using ultrasonic pulse echo imaging method. Echocardiography has grown for characteristically use in analysis, organization, and continuation of patients with apparent or well-known cardiac diseases [3]. It is broadly used in analytical tests in cardiology. It can offer highly valuable data with size and outline of the heart with

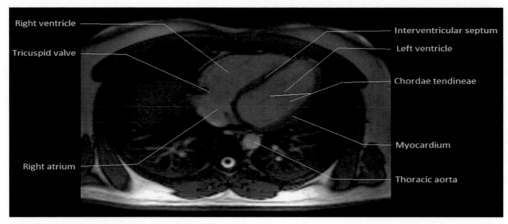

Figure 12.1 Image of electrocardiography [3].

interior chamber size quantification, pumping function and site, and extent of the tissue damage. An echocardiogram also provides doctors with other estimations of cardiac function such as a calculation of the cardiac results, ejection fraction, and diastolic function (Fig. 12.1).

The procedure of stress echocardiography can help understand whether chest ache or accompanying symptoms are indications to heart disease or not. Echocardiogram produces ultrasound pictures of heart's configuration and produces an accurate evaluation of blood flowing from one side to another side in heart using Doppler echocardiography, with vibrated or consistent wave Doppler ultrasound. This enables calculation of both normal and abnormal blood flow from one side to another side of the heart. Both color Doppler and spectral Doppler can be used to visualize any irregular communications between the left and rights side of the heart, any dripping of blood through the valves, which leads to valvular regurgitation, and to evaluate in what way, the valves open or do not open in the case of valvular stenosis.

12.1.13 Chest X-ray

In medical imaging, X-ray imaging is a form of test that uses small amounts of radiation to take photos of the bones, organs, and tissues of the body. When the part under consideration is chest, this imaging identifies abnormalities from the norm or sicknesses of the airways, heart, veins, lungs, and bones. A chest X-ray is needed if a patient is in emergency room because of chest pain or had an accident that included impact on the chest area [6].

The doctor can also recommend a chest X-ray if there is a plausibility of CHF symptoms having a connection to the problems in chest. Such symptoms include chest pain, fever, persistent cough, and smallness of breath. These symptoms could lead to

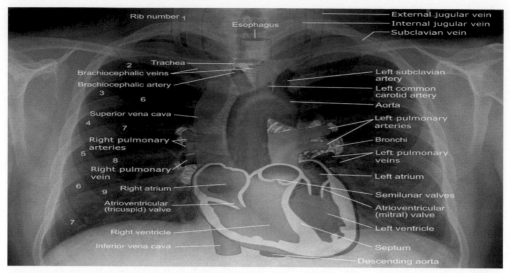

Figure 12.2 Image of chest X-ray (The Anatomy Project, 1997).

further conditions, which chest X-ray can detect, for example, broken ribs, heart failure, lung cancer, pneumonia. The other use for a chest X-ray is to see the size and shape of heart. Abnormalities in the size and shape of heart can lead to issues with the functioning of the heart. Doctors often use chest X-rays to monitor the progress after surgery in the chest area. A lab typically generates pictures from a chest X-ray on large sheets of film. When viewed against a lit background, the doctor can look for an array of glitches, from tumors to damaged bones and heart problem. When the part under focus is chest, X-ray helps detect abnormalities or diseases of the airways, heart, blood vessels, lungs, and bones [7,8] (Fig. 12.2).

A chest X-ray is a simple, fast, and effective test that has been used for decades to help doctors view some of the most important body organs. If a patient moves during X-ray imaging, pictures might turn out blurry as the radiation passes through the body and onto the plate, and denser organs, such as bone and the muscles of heart, will appear white.

12.1.14 Computed tomography

A CT scan or CAT scan is a test that uses X-rays to view specific areas of body. These scans use safe quantities of radiation to produce detailed pictures of the body. A cardiac CT scan is used to check heart and blood vessels. During this test, a specialized dye is injected into patients' bloodstream. The dye is then viewed under a special camera in a hospital or testing facility [9]. A heart CT scan, also known as coronary CT angiogram, is used to view the arteries that bring blood to heart. The test is known as coronary calcium scan if they are used to diagnose whether there is accumulation of

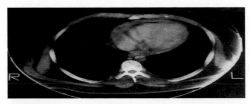

Figure 12.3 Image of cardiac CT.

calcium in heart. Doctors may recommend a heart CT scan to view some conditions such as birth defects in the heart like congenital heart disease, buildup of a hard substance called lipid plaque, which can block coronary arteries deficiencies, or wounds to the heart's four primary valves where blood clots within the heart's chambers tumors in or on the heart. A heart CT scan is a general test for people having heart problems, since it allows doctor to explore structure of the heart and the head-to-head blood vessels without making any cut or wound or insertion of any device into body. A heart CT scan has very few risks involved. Most dyes used for CT scans contain iodine, which is later flushed by kidneys from the body. While characteristically harmless, this is an important issue for pregnant women. The levels of radiation are well-thought-out safe for adults, and there have been no documented side effects from low levels of radiation but not for a developing fetus [10–12] (Fig. 12.3).

A heart CT scan procedure is accomplished in a hospital's radiology department or a clinic that specializes in diagnostic methods. This medication (Metoprolol (Lopressor), propanolol (Inderal), and atenolol (Tenormin)) slows down heart so that clearer images can be taken. At the start of the scan, patient lies down for rests on a seat or bed. In addition, there is a need to hold breath during brief individual sweeps, which last just 10–20 seconds. To start the scan, the radiologist moves the table via a remote from a separate room into the CT machine. In most cases, patients go through the machine several times. The whole test should take no longer than 10 minutes.

12.1.15 Magnetic resonance imaging

MRI uses magnets and radio waves to generate an image of body's internal organs without making a surgical cut or a wound. It allows doctor to view the soft tissues in body, along with bones. An MRI can be done on any part of body, although a heart or cardiac MRI exactly shows the heart and nearby blood vessels. Distinct from a CT scan, an MRI does not use radiation. It is considered a safer alternative for pregnant women. If possible, it is the best to wait until after the first trimester [13].

MRI is a noninvasive procedure, which means it does not involve the introduction of any instruments into the body. MRI involves a commanding magnetic field, radio frequency pulses, and a computer system to yield thorough images of organs, soft tissues, bone, and almost all other internal body parts. Detailed MRI allows physicians to

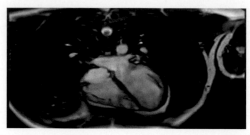

Figure 12.4 Image of MRI.

diagnose numerous parts of body and define occurrence of definite diseases. The images generated by machine can be used to examine on a computer monitor printed or copied to a CD and transmitted electronically. Cardiac MRI uses a powerful magnetic field, radio waves, and a computer system to produce whole images of the structures inside the heart. MRI is used to diagnose cardiac disease and estimate the heart's structure and role in patients through congenital heart disease. Cardiac MRI does not use ionizing radiation as normal MRI, and it provides pictures of the heart that are better than other imaging methods. The magnetic field is not dangerous, but it may cause some medical devices to breakdown.

Cardiac MRI is used to help doctor in diagnosing cardiac disease by:

1. Calculating the structure and work of the heart chambers, valves, size, and blood flow through main vessels and surrounding structures such as the pericardium.
2. Calculating influence of coronary artery disease such as limited blood flow to the heart muscle and scarring within the heart muscle after a heart attack.
3. Scheduling a patient's action for cardiovascular disorders.
4. Monitoring the progression of certain disorders over time.
5. Calculating the anatomy of the heart and blood vessels in children and adults with congenital heart disease (Fig. 12.4).

The MR scanner captures this energy and produces output in the form of images of the tissues scanned on the basis of this information. By passing electric current through wire coils, the magnetic field is generated in most MRI components. Other coils, placed in the machine or positioned around the part of the body being imaged, send and receive radio waves, generating signals that are sensed by the coils. A computer then routes the signals and creates a series of images, each of which demonstrates a thin slice of the body. The images can then be considered from different angles by radiologist [14−16].

12.1.16 Benefits of magnetic resonance imaging

1. MRI does not involve an insertion of instruments into the body, and this technique does not include contact with ionizing radiation.

2. MRI images of the heart are better than other imaging methods for certain conditions. This advantage makes MRI a precious tool in premature analysis and estimation of certain cardiac abnormalities, particularly those including the heart muscle.
3. MRI has proven reliable in analyzing a wide variety of conditions, involving cardiovascular anatomical anomalies such as congenital heart defects, functional abnormalities like valve failure, tumors, and conditions associated with coronary artery disease and cardiomyopathy.
4. This imaging can be taken in account during certain interventional procedures, such as catheter-based ablation procedures to diagnose irregular heart rhythms, involving atrial fibrillation. The use of MRI imaging can significantly shorten the time required to accomplish these procedures, resulting in enhanced accuracy.
5. MRI allows the detection of abnormalities that might be covered by bone when using other imaging methods.

12.1.16.1 Risks associated with the use of magnetic resonance imaging

1. MRI test does not pose much hazard to an ordinary patient when adequate guidelines are adopted.
2. If a sedative is used to induce a state of calm or sleep, there are risks associated with excessive consumption of the same.
3. While a durable magnetic field is not harmful in the situation, entrenched medical devices that have metal that can malfunction or cause problems during an MRI exam.
4. Nephrogenic systemic fibrosis is presently a familiar, rare, and tricky situation of MRI supposed to begin when the injection of high doses of gadolinium-based contrast material is introduced in patients with very poor kidney functioning.
5. There is a very minor threat of an allergic effect if contrast material is injected. These effects are generally minor and simply controlled via medication.

12.1.17 Limitations for cardiac magnetic resonance imaging

1. High-quality images are generated only if the procedure is conducted properly, following breath-holding guidelines while the images are recorded. If patients are nervous, confused, or in severe pain, they may find it hard to lie still during imaging.
2. A person with weight on higher side may not fit into certain types of MRI machines. The existence of a graft or other metallic object occasionally makes it hard to get clear images.
3. A very uneven heartbeat can affect the quality of images acquired using techniques that time the imaging on the basis of the electrical action of the heart, such as electrocardiography. An uneven heartbeat or atrial fibrillation can cause ancient rarities in cardiovascular MR pictures.

4. The continuous gesture of the heart introduces difficulties in acquiring clear pictures. These challenges can be overcome by numerous approaches such as synchronizing the imaging with ECG outlining, carrying into line the imaging with breathing, or repetitive short breath holds during imaging.
5. Obtaining detailed images of the coronary arteries and their subdivisions is harder with MRI and hence is frequently done instead with cardiac CT or a more offensive process using a catheter placed into the blood vessels via the groin or arm.

12.1.18 Heart disease classification using convolutional neural network

In the above section, we described the different imaging tests that are available. The heart disease classification is done on an MRI image. Implementation was done by using some open-source software. We will now discuss the technology used with regard to establishing a system that can predict global hyperkinesis heart disease on the basis of MRI datasets. Heart disease prediction involves various steps such as data collection, labeling, and development of architecture for the classification, and the training and testing of the developed model. Details of the methodologies are given below.

12.2 Materials

For the completion of this research, Operating System (OS) Window 10/Ubuntu18 was used. MicroDicome Viewer [17] was installed to view images. Anaconda was installed as a virtual machine for the requirement of Jupyter Notebook. Python 3.6 was installed as a platform for Notebook. NumPy 1.11.2, TensorFlow [18], and Keras, were installed as per requirement of Jupyter Notebook. The method was developed on system having OS of 64 bit with RAM 16 GB, and the capacity of hard disk was 500 GB. In this research, MRI images were collected from the different sources and labeled with the help of a radiologist.

12.3 Methods

The current work involves a number of steps to reach the conclusion. For each step, a research plan was created that was customized to our needs; these steps involved MRI data collection, processing of the collected data, extracting features from images, training and testing of data, and in the final step, there was development of model (Fig. 12.5) [19].

12.3.1 Data collection

The data related to cardiac MRI images was collected. There were 30 patients of each set with 900−1200 images depending upon cases. The images Were in Digital Imaging and Communications in Medicine (DICOM) format with different folders of

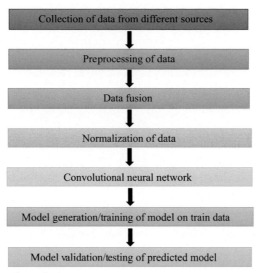

Figure 12.5 Methodology flow chart.

images for categorization of them. These folders had names in medical terms with the number of the folders with each name:

1. trufi_loc_multi having two folders of this name.
2. trufi_loc_multi@isocenter having a single folder.
3. haste_16-sl_tra-db-pace having two folders of this name.
4. haste_16-sl_tra-db-pace-RESP having a single folder.
5. tf2d18_retro_iPAT_12s.SA having 13 folders of this name according to the beat.
6. tf2d18_retro_p2_2CH(VLA) having 13 folders of this name according to the beat (Figs. 12.5 and 12.6).

12.3.2 Direct DICOM images

In this method, images used for feature extraction were first processed by the software. DICOM viewer software was used for DICOM images. This software read all the images and displayed them so that there was as less as possible loss of information when features were extracted from images. The images were taken from the patient's folder image set of each folder named [20].

12.3.3 Merge DICOM images

In this work, AMIDE software was used to merge DICOM images. The group of all patients were made on the basis of their categorization of MRI. The 30 patients

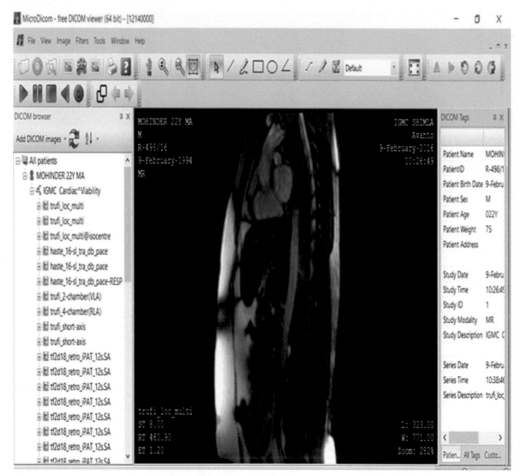

Figure 12.6 Image sets view on microdicom.

having disease with their merged image was compared with the single merged image of a healthy patient. Further processing on image was then performed (Fig. 12.7).

Steps used for Jupyter Notebook [21]:

1. Step 1: After installation of Jupyter Notebook, we need one Integrated Development Environment named Anaconda.
2. Step 2: Install the libraries and the other repository to work on the system for running the convolutional neural network (CNN) on the images.
3. Step 3: Install the libraries, namely, NumPy, TensorFlow, Keras, Matplotlib, OS, and CV2, for making the pipeline.
4. Step 4: Develop pipeline for the prediction of heart disease from the image dataset.
5. Step 5: Measure the accuracies in different sample size split between training and testing dataset.

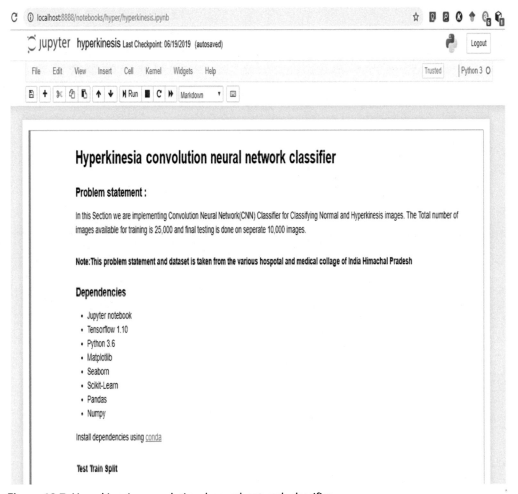

Figure 12.7 Hyperkinesia convolutional neural network classifier.

12.3.4 Preprocessing of the images form the data set

The dataset has been described in the previous segment. The complete dataset is available for the further studies and other computational research. In this method, images were used for running the CNN. We divided the images into two categories: normal ($-$ve) and hyper ($+$ve).

Data collection and preprocessing of data includes:
1. Involves the labeling of data
2. Correction of data
3. Removal of noisy, corrupted, and distorted images form the data set (Figs. 12.8 and 12.9, Table 12.1).

Figure 12.8 Data preprocessing.

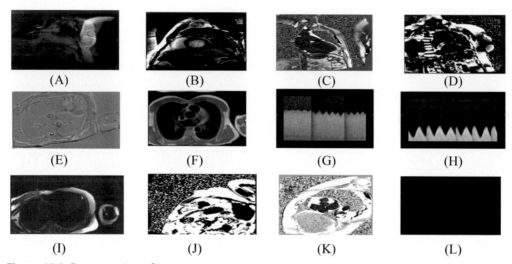

Figure 12.9 Preprocessing of image.

Table 12.1 Table showing the original dataset.

S. no.	Type	RAW image dataset	Processed image
1	Normal image	13,540	12,596
2	Hyperkinesis image	22,855	20,554
3	Total	36,395	33,150

12.3.5 Data fusion

Data fusion or assembling is the process of integrating the information about the preprocessed data to obtain comprehensive and specific results. Generally, data fusion is divided into three parts, namely low level image, feature level, and decision-level. After preprocessing the images

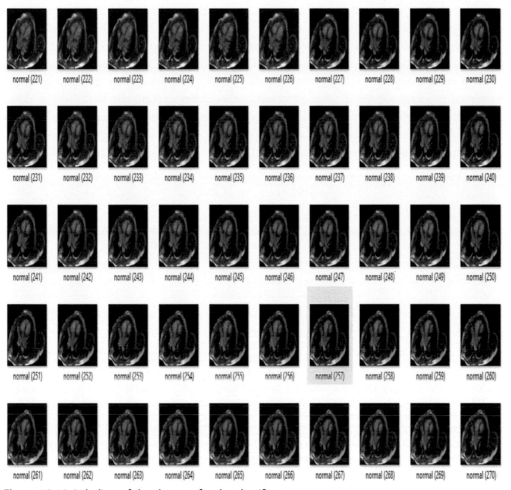

Figure 12.10 Labeling of the data set for the classifier.

of different patients, we had the images in different folder labeled according to medical termi-nology. Next step involved the fusion of all the images on the basis of the normal images, which showed the negative sign and the positive image of patients with the disease. The dataset was labeled with the normal and hyper for the training the model with CNN, on which further classification was done and the model predicted the results (Fig. 12.10).

12.3.6 Data normalization and randomization

Data normalization is the process applied for the data preparation for the deep learning models. The objective of data normalization is to change the estimations of numeric segments in a dataset to utilize a typical scale, without misshaping contrasts in the images, scopes of qualities, or losing information within the dataset. Normalization is likewise required for certain calculations to display the preprocessed data correctly. In our dataset, we have the images of different patients ranging from different image size. Thus everything in the dataset should be normalized. For normalization, we used the inbuilt function via batch normalization and every image in the dataset was set up to minimal image size for running through the CNN. The images in the dataset were converted to grayscale for the binary classification. After getting the heart image data, we needed to randomize the dataset so that our model could simultaneously learn both the features. The shuffling of the entire dataset was done through the randomizing function available in the Python library (Fig. 12.11).

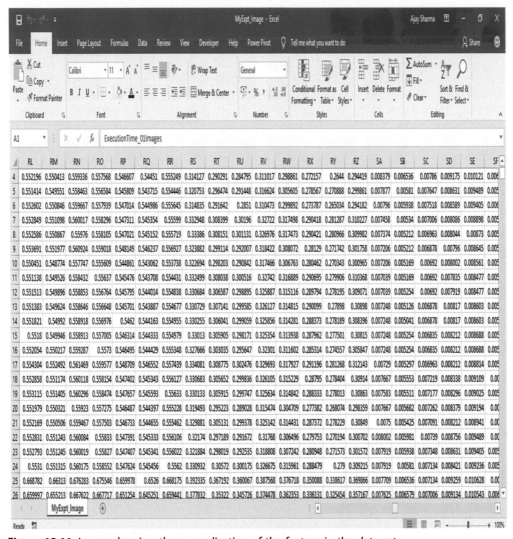

Figure 12.11 Image showing the normalization of the feature in the data set.

12.3.7 Model generation

CNN pipeline written in Python was used for training and testing the model on the heart image dataset. The dataset is labeled as positive and negative in the TensorFlow pipeline. The training dataset was run with the input feature labels in the classifier. In the classifier, for the prediction form the preferences used the binary cross entropy for the loss function, Adam optimization, accuracy, batch size, validation splits and cross validation folds for the training and testing rounds (Fig. 12.13). The Fig. 12.13 displays the accuracies on different epochs with accuracy on the validation set and validation loss. (Figs. 12.12 and 12.13). The Tables 12.21−12.24 shows the accurcies along with the time stamp when the dataset is splitted into different rations for traing and testing purpose. After when the training and testing validation we can use one of the model or a hybrid based approch for make a GUI (Graphical User Interface) to make a computation based prediction on the real time data sets.

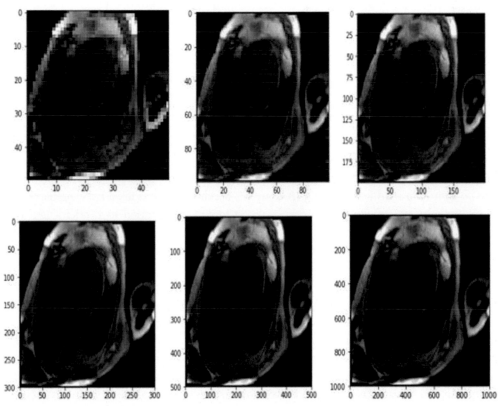

Figure 12.12 Different size of the data for training and testing the model.

Figure 12.13 Figure showing the running CNN architecture on the data set use binary_crossentropy for loss, optimizer as Adam, and accuracy matrices to test and validation results.

12.3.8 Convolutional neural network

In this section we will discuss CNN and the related concepts. CNNs have a long history starting with the perceptron algorithm in 1958 [22]. Although they can be explained intuitively as models that learn visual filters to recognize high-level image features, understanding the functionality of neural networks first can facilitate understanding how CNNs work. In the following, the perceptron, its extension to the multilayer perceptron, feed-forward neural networks and the basics of CNNs are explained. The work below shows the different layers used in the CNN based architecture.

12.3.9 The perceptron

Rosenblatt designed the first learning neural computer, the perceptron, in 1958 in an effort to mimic human learning [22]. A neuron's dendrites are modeled by weights, which are multiplied with input values. Additionally, a bias value is added to model a neuron's required activation potential. Afterward, the multiplied values and bias are summed up in the cell body and passed through an activation function to produce an output representing the firing rate in the neuron. This architecture is shown in Fig. 12.14.

The perceptron is a linear classifier defined by weights w^j, and bias b and an activation function $f_{(x)}$ according to Fig. 12.14. It is possible to merge the bias with the weights by using homogeneous coordinates, that is, putting the bias at the bottom of the weight vector and adding a constant 1 to the input vector x. Different activation functions, which are discussed in the next section, can be used, but the original perceptron uses the heavy-side step function, resulting in a binary output. Therefore the perceptron is a linear classifier, and its weights define a hyperplane as a linear decision boundary between classes. Thus its representational power is limited; it is not possible

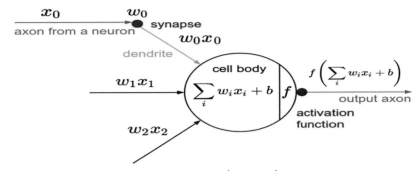

Figure 12.14 The perceptron model with weights w^j, inputs x^j and bias b [23].

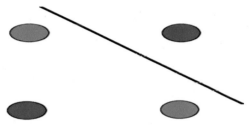

Figure 12.15 The XOR function creates a not linearly separable set. The two classes red and blue cannot be separated by a single straight line.

to model, for example, an XOR function using a perceptron, since no line can be drawn to separate the classes as shown in Fig. 12.15.

12.3.10 Neural network

To overcome the limited representational capabilities of a single perceptron, neural networks were developed. In a neural network, or artificial neural network, multiple perceptrons, also commonly referred to as units or neurons, are connected in acyclic graphs, although one of the most common architectures is that of the multilayer perceptron in which the neurons are organized in layers. There are input and output layers and additional hidden layers that increase network size and complexity. Fig. 12.16 shows an example of this layered architecture.

Multilayer perceptrons are universal approximators, that is, they can approximate any continuous function and thus do not suffer the same limitations as a single perceptron [23].

Typically, the layers are fully connected, meaning that every neuron is connected to each neuron of the previous and next layers. However, neurons of the same layer are not connected to each other. The number of units in each layer and the number of layers have to be chosen and result in networks that approximate functions of

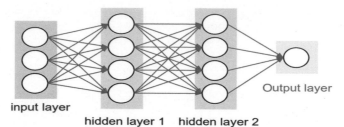

Figure 12.16 A multilayer perceptron with two hidden layers [24].

varying complexity. It can be difficult to find a good architecture, as using too many units and layers may result in a complex function that overfits training data, and choosing too few units can produce a biased function that is too simple to adequately represent the data distribution (Fig. 12.16).

Historically, the sigmoid function has been used as activation function for neurons, as it can be easily interpreted as firing rate of a neuron. The hyperbolic tangent function has a similar form but is zero-centered. Since 2010, the rectified linear unit (ReLu) has become the de-facto standard, as it improves training speed and does not suffer from gradient vanishing [24,25]. Output units do not have any activation function, so that they can produce arbitrarily valued output.

Neural networks can be trained, that is, the network can learn weights, by defining a loss function (also called cost or objective function) and using the backpropagation algorithm to adapt weights. An example of a loss function is the sum-of-squared-distances. The backpropagation algorithm works by calculating the loss from the current network output and a ground truth and computing a weight update from it by passing the error backward through the network [26] This is straightforward for the output layer, as the error can be used directly. For hidden layers, however, a sensitivity for the unit has to be calculated using the activation function's gradients. The sensitivity is then used to distribute the error backward through the network.

12.3.11 Convolutional neural network

Standard neural networks do not handle shifts and distortions in images, which occur frequently in image datasets, since objects are usually not perfectly aligned or appear multiple times in the same image. However, despite these drawbacks, neural networks should still be able to learn robust features. Therefore LeCun et al. developed CNNs, which are designed specifically for computer vision applications introducing shift and distortion invariance [26]. A sample network is shown in (Fig. 12.17).

Using convolutional layers, the networks are able to learn to recognize local features, such as edges or corners, by restricting the receptive fields of hidden units to local connectivity and to add shift invariance by enforcing spatially shared weights.

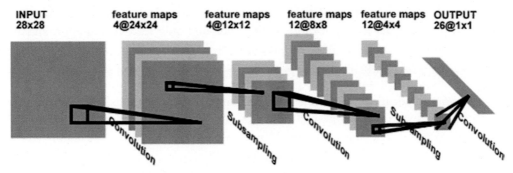

Figure 12.17 The Lenet convolutional neural network architecture with convolutional and pooling layers [26].

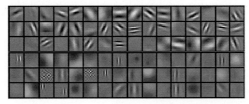

Figure 12.18 Filter weights learned by the first convolutional layer in AlexNet [29,30].

Furthermore, spatial or temporal subsampling in the form of pooling layers reduces sensitivity to shifts and distortion (Fig. 12.17).

The architecture of CNNs is made up of distinct layers that are usually arranged in multiple stages [27,28]. The basic layers include convolutional layers, nonlinearities, pooling layers, and fully connected layers. One stage may comprise a convolutional layer to learn filter banks a nonlinearity identical to the activation function in standard neural networks and a feature-pooling layer. In the first level, such a stage typically learns simple visual features such as edges or color blobs. The second stage then combines the previous level's features, for example, learning corners as combinations of edges. Adding more stages results in more complex high-level features, such as faces, depending on data and application.

Convolutional layers consist of multiple filters that are defined by their weights. The layer defines the number of filters and their kernel size, the stride in which they are applied, and the amount of padding to handle image borders. Examples of filters learned in the first convolutional layer are shown in Fig. 12.18 [29]. The convolved output of a filter is called a feature map and a convolutional layer with n filters creates n feature maps, which are the input for the next layer. For backpropagation, the gradient of the convolution is required, which is the forward-pass convolution with weights flipped along each axis (Fig. 12.18).

Pooling layers reduce feature map resolutions and thereby the sensitivity to shift and distortions, as exact feature location is discarded and only relative and approximate location information remains. Max-pooling selects the maximum output from a local receptive field and is applied in a sliding-window fashion similar to convolutions. Fig. 12.19 shows the result of max-pooling. To obtain the gradient, it is necessary to store the original location of the selected maximum value, since maximum operations act as a routing mechanism in neural networks. An additional benefit of pooling layers is reduced memory cost. For example, 22 max-pooling results in output feature maps with half the input's width and height (Fig. 12.19).

One method that is applicable to CNNs is transfer learning, where a network is pretrained with a dataset and subsequently fine-tuned to another dataset. In this case, a network is pretrained ideally on a large dataset to learn robust filters and features that are generalizable to new data and then trained with application-specific data benefiting from features identical or similar to the pretrained ones [31] (Fig. 12.20).

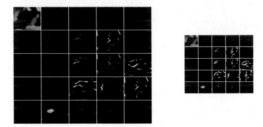

Figure 12.19 Max-pooling of 25 feature maps. Fully convolutional layers work identically to hidden layers of a standard neural network. They can be used at the end of a convolutional neural network after several stages to compute arbitrary features and output scores (cf. universal approximators) [29].

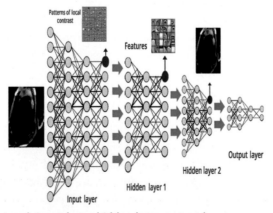

Figure 12.20 Neural network input layer, hidden layer, output layer.

Since 2010, CNNs have been applied to various computer vision tasks and have been developed further [32]. Various architectures have been published and open-source frameworks have been developed, creating large user bases [32,33]. Furthermore, several important robustness-increasing techniques have been developed, such as dropout and batch normalization, which allow higher learning rates for faster training while minimizing the degree of overfitting [34,35]. These and other improvements are discussed in the related work.

12.3.12 Results of heart disease prediction using convolutional neural network

As stated earlier, MRI datasets were taken. The steps were followed to obtain the maximum accuracy of input MRI images. First, training of the system was accomplished by using different dataset or sample, and then the system was tested for few of the given samples, and accuracy was measured. The image set was partitioned into two portions. The first portion was used for trainingstem and the second was used for testing purpose. Sixty percent of the image set was used as training, and th the sye remainder 40% was used for the testing set. For each image set, features were figured out and stored for training the of data. The result summary is shown in Figures. The table given below display the results obtained from the program. The variance is very small, but it is there. Following are main results of MRI images (Figs. 12.21–12.24, Tables 12.2–12.4).

12.4 Conclusion/summary

This chapter entitled "Heart Disease Prediction Using Convolutional Neural Network" was carried out in Department of Biotechnology and Bioinformatics at Jaypee University of Information Technology Waknaghat Solan. The summary of the findings is as follows:

THREE EPOCHS					
Training set (23205)				Validation set(9945)	
Epochs	Timestamp	Loss	Accuracy	Val loss	Val accuracy
1	854s 37ms	0.1862	0.9241	0.1378	0.9507
2	868s 37ms	0.1285	0.9434	0.1237	0.9454
3	858s 37ms	0.1217	0.9468	0.1297	0.9350

Figure 12.21 Training and test accuracies the given data set three epocs.

TEN EPOCHS					
Training set (23205)				Validation set(9945)	
Epocs	Timestamp	Loss	Accuracy	Val loss	Val accuracy
1	854s 37ms	0.1800	0.9264	0.1334	0.9439
2	898s 39ms	0.1264	0.9458	0.1350	0.9501
3	855s 37ms	0.1157	0.9484	0.1315	0.9422
4	809s 35ms	0.1117	0.9500	0.1222	0.9451
5	802s 35ms	0.1072	0.9507	0.1264	0.9517
6	850s 37ms	0.1065	0.9510	0.1188	0.9483
7	855s 37ms	0.1048	0.9515	0.1149	0.9513
8	868s 37ms	0.1030	0.9532	0.1159	0.1159
9	856s 37ms	0.1022	0.9519	0.1192	0.9432
10	858s 37ms	0.0999	0.9539	0.1166	0.9459

Figure 12.22 Training and testing accuracy on the ten epocs with decreasing loss in the data set.

TEN EPOCHS					
Training set (16575)				Validation set(16575)	
Epocs	Timestamp	Loss	Accuracy	Val Loss	Val Accuracy
1	719s 43ms	0.2112	0.9116	0.1437	0.9441
2	750s 45ms	0.1311	0.9440	0.1655	0.9319
3	669s 40ms	0.1248	0.9463	0.1367	0.9484
4	667s 40ms	0.1156	0.9482	0.1300	0.9383
5	712s 43ms	0.1138	0.9498	0.1331	0.9406
6	701s 43ms	0.1115	0.9509	0.1225	0.9485
7	725s 44ms	0.1090	0.9511	0.1888	0.9481
8	715s 43ms	0.1063	0.9527	0.1232	0.9517
9	725s 44ms	0.1044	0.9525	0.1159	0.9459
10	695s 42ms	0.1035	0.9531	0.1257	0.9440

Figure 12.23 Training and testing accuracy on the ten epocs with equal data for training and testing.

1. Hyperkinesia (i.e., hyperkinesis moment disorder), term derived from the ancient Greek language, describes the abnormal or restless state and excessive movement of the heart or combination of both. These image prediction methods typically rely on machine learning/DL here in the current author has devleoped a computational based prediction method for the cardiovascular heart diease (Hypokinesia).

| FIFTEEN EPOCHS | | | | | |
| Training Set (26520) | | | | Validation Set(6630) | |
Epocs	Timestamp	Loss	Accuracy	Val Loss	Val Accuracy
1	895s 34ms	0.1776	0.9282	0.1270	0.9477
2	879s 33ms	0.1273	0.9454	0.1168	0.9446
3	923s 35ms	0.1197	0.9473	0.1137	0.9495
4	989s 37ms	0.1135	0.9494	0.1107	0.9525
5	950s 36ms	0.1099	0.9510	0.1125	0.9498
6	965s 36ms	0.1077	0.9510	0.1093	0.9446
7	955s 36ms	0.1055	0.9522	0.1176	0.9373
8	958s 36ms	0.1044	0.9516	0.1106	0.9495
9	943s 36ms	0.1030	0.9523	0.1062	0.9511
10	953s 36ms	0.1020	0.9523	0.1108	0.9523
11	986s 37ms	0.1004	0.9535	0.1065	0.9516
12	997s 38ms	0.1011	0.9534	0.1085	0.9501
13	934s 35ms	0.1001	0.9541	0.1113	0.9404
14	950s 40ms	0.0982	0.9534	0.1110	0.9516
15	940s 25ms	0.0980	0.9530	0.1102	0.9510

Figure 12.24 Training and testing accuracy on the fifteen epocs data for training and testing.

Table 12.2 Table showing the dataset split into 70%   30% ratio for the training and testing purpose.

S. no.	Type	Training set	Validation set
1	Normal image	8817	3778
2	Hyperkinesis image	14,387	6116
3	Total	23,204	9894

Table 12.3 Table showing the dataset split into 90%−10% ratio for the training and testing purpose.

S. no.	Type	Training set	Validation set
1	Normal image	11,336	1259
2	Hyperkinesis image	18,498	2283
3	Total	29,843	3542

Table 12.4 Table showing the dataset split into 50%—50% ratio for the training and testing purpose.

S. no.	Type	Training set	Validation set
1	Normal image	6298	6298
2	Hyperkinesis image	10,227	10,227
3	Total	16,525	16,525

2. Area number of different imaging tests exist for heart. With the help of artificial intelligence, machine learning, and deep learning method, we have implemented an architecture for the prediction of this disease and used the Python TensorFlow, NumPy, and other libraries for the training and testing of the model.

3. Accuracies were measured in different sample size and the data was split into different ranging into 70/30, 50/50,90/10 for the training and testing purposes.

4. Although over the years, a large number of prediction tools have been presented, there is no such tool that works on cardiac diseases. There are some working in area of MRI brain prediction, and yet, to date, to our knowledge, there is no resource available that provides prediction tools for heart diseases.

5. It is expected that the availability of such a method would save time and effort of specialists involved in this field and will help doctors and clinicians in diagnosis, treatment, and prevention of heart diseases.

6. CNN and most powerful architectures are used in the field of machine learning and deep learning. The technique is available online and in open-source form for doctors, radiologists, medical practitioners, and researchers across globe

Acknowledgments

Great things emerge through collaborative efforts. A number of people were sincerely involved directly as well as indirectly in drafting this book chapter. So would like to honor Mr. Rohit Shukla, my lab member, for helping in the rewriting the literature of the manuscript of this chapter (Ph.D. Scholar Dept. of Bioinformatics, JUIT), Mr. Sameer (Ph.D. Scholar Dept. of Mathematics JUIT), for rewriting the mathematical part of the CNN, and my grandfather for the moral support. I would like to thank Dr. Gaurav Gupta, Assistant Professor, School of Electrical and Computer Science Engineering, Shoolini University, Bajhol, Solan, for providing me some of the valuable computational resources to process the data.

Author contribution

COVID-19 has made a huge impact on everyone's life; during this period, we decided to write a book chapter in order to utilize the lockdown time. During this period, Mr. Ajay Sharma (Ph.D. Scholar Dept. of Bioinformatics JUIT) drafted the manuscript of this chapter and searched out some of the literature review on that particular topic, as some of the work was done in the field of image processing and biomedical image processing; we collected and compiled all the existing literature in the form of this chapter. Dr. Varun Jaiswal, my Bachelor and Master's supervisor (Ex. Assist Director, National Centre for Disease Control NCDC New Delhi, Current Assist Prof. Gachon University Dept. of Biotechnology, revised the prepared manuscript and identified the areas of rectification.

This book chapter contains some of the novel work, which makes it different form the existing available literature from all the available resources. As in today's world, interdisciplinary approach is prevalent, and as a result, the author took into the consideration that this chapter should be understood by a common person or a beginner in the field of image processing, deep learning, and medical field has and thus divided this chapter into different segments. Therefore a reader with an intermediate level of expertise in the field of deep learning or biomedical image processing can better understand the concept of Deep learning in biomedical image processing.

Conflict of interest

There is no conflict of interest. The book chapter entitled "Heart Disease Prediction Using CNN" has completely authentic work. The literature for this book chapter was mined form the various internet resources and journals. The author has taken care that the credit is given to the contributors in terms of authorship or referencing and citation of their research paper articles or book chapter written by the contributors.

References

[1] Members WG, et al. Heart disease and stroke statistics 2012 update: a report from the American Heart Association. Circulation 2012;125(1):e2.
[2] Quezada A. Examining the association between acculturation indicators and metabolic syndrome among Hispanic adults. Dec 2019.
[3] Edler I, Lindström K. The history of echocardiography. Ultrasound Med Biol 2004;30(12):1565−644.
[4] Ghali JK, et al. Precipitating factors leading to decompensation of heart failure: traits among urban blacks. Arch Intern Med 1988;148(9):2013−16.
[5] Whitehurst T, et al. Treatment of congestive heart failure, Google Patents; 2004.
[6] Webb AG. Introduction to biomedical imaging. John Wiley & Sons; 2017.
[7] de Groot MR, et al. Value of chest X-ray combined with perfusion scan vs ventilation/perfusion scan in acute pulmonary embolism. Thrombosis Haemost 2000;83(03):412−15.
[8] Johansson SA, Johansson TB. Analytical application of particle induced X-ray emission. Nucl Instrum Methods 1976;137(3):473−516.
[9] Hu H. Multi-slice helical CT: scan and reconstruction. Med Phys 1999;26(1):5−18.
[10] Isner JM, et al. Computed tomography in the diagnosis of pericardial heart disease. Ann Intern Med 1982;97(4):473−9.
[11] Goo HW, et al. CT of congenital heart disease: normal anatomy and typical pathologic conditions. Radiographics 2003;23(1):S147−65.
[12] Goo HW. State-of-the-art CT imaging techniques for congenital heart disease. Korean J Radiol 2010;11(1):4−18.

[13] Schenck JF. The role of magnetic susceptibility in magnetic resonance imaging: MRI magnetic compatibility of the first and second kinds. Med Phys 1996;23(6):815—50.

[14] Higgins CB, et al. Magnetic resonance imaging in patients with congenital heart disease. Circulation 1984;70(5):851—60.

[15] Prakash A, et al. Magnetic resonance imaging evaluation of myocardial perfusion and viability in congenital and acquired pediatric heart disease. Am J Cardiol 2004;93(5):657—61.

[16] Manganaro L, et al. Assessment of congenital heart disease (CHD): is there a role for fetal magnetic resonance imaging (MRI)? Eur J Radiol 2009;72(1):172—80.

[17] Kapoor C, et al. A what, when and where guide on open source DICOM viewers for radiologists. European Congress of Radiology 2020; 2020.

[18] Abadi M, et al. Tensorflow: a system for large-scale machine learning. In: Proceedings of the twelvth {USENIX} symposium on operating systems design and implementation ({OSDI} 16); 2016.

[19] Foster KR, Koprowski R, Skufca JD. Machine learning, medical diagnosis, and biomedical engineering research-commentary. Biomed Eng Online 2014;13(1):94.

[20] Rosset A, Spadola L, Ratib O. OsiriX: an open-source software for navigating in multidimensional DICOM images. J Digital Imaging 2004;17(3):205—16.

[21] Kluyver T, et al. Jupyter notebooks—a publishing format for reproducible computational workflows. In: ELPUB; 2016.

[22] Rosenblatt F. The perceptron: a probabilistic model for information storage and organization in the brain. Psychol Rev 1958;65(6):386.

[23] Karpathy A, Fei-Fei L. Deep visual-semantic alignments for generating image descriptions. In: Proceedings of the IEEE conference on computer vision and pattern recognition; 2015.

[24] Dahl GE, Sainath TN, Hinton GE. Improving deep neural networks for LVCSR using rectified linear units and dropout. In Proceedings of the IEEE international conference on acoustics, speech and signal processing. IEEE; 2013.

[25] Nair V, Hinton GE. Rectified linear units improve restricted boltzmann machines. In: Proceedings of the twenty-seventh international conference on machine learning (ICML-10); 2010.

[26] Rumelhart DE, Hinton GE, Williams RJ. Learning representations by back-propagating errors cognitive modeling. Nature 1986;1988:533—6.

[27] LeCun Y, Kavukcuoglu K, Farabet C. Convolutional networks and applications in vision. In: Proceedings of IEEE international symposium on circuits and systems. IEEE; 2010.

[28] LeCun Y, Bengio Y, Hinton G. Deep learning. Nature 2015;521:436—44.

[29] Canziani A, Paszke A, Culurciello E. An analysis of deep neural network models for practical applications. *arXiv:1605.07678*; 2016.

[30] Ballester P, Araujo RM. On the performance of GoogLeNet and AlexNet applied to sketches. In: Proceedings of the thirteenth AAAI conference on artificial intelligence; 2016.

[31] Goodfellow I, et al. Generative adversarial nets. In: Advances in neural information processing systems; 2014.

[32] Russakovsky O, et al. Imagenet large scale visual recognition challenge. Int J Comput Vis 2015;115 (3):211—52.

[33] Jia Y, et al. Caffe: Convolutional architecture for fast feature embedding. In Proceedings of the twenty-second ACM international conference on Multimedia; 2014.

[34] Srivastava N, et al. Dropout: a simple way to prevent neural networks from overfitting. J Mach Learn Res 2014;15(1):1929—58.

[35] Ioffe S, Szegedy C. Batch normalization: accelerating deep network training by reducing internal covariate shift. *arXiv:1502.03167*; 2015.

CHAPTER 13

Gene polymorphism and the risk of coronary artery disease

Gowtham Kumar Subbaraj[1], Sindhu Varghese[1], Langeswaran Kulanthaivel[2], Lakshmi Alagarsamy[3], Sangeetha Rajaram[3] and Sangeetha Ramanathan[4]

[1]Faculty of Allied Health Sciences, Chettinad Academy of Research and Education, Kelambakkam, India
[2]Cancer Genetics & Molecular Biology Laboratory, Department of Bioinformatics, Science Campus, Alagappa University, Karaikudi, India
[3]Department of Physics, Mannar Thirumalai Naicker College, Pasumalai, Madurai, India
[4]Department of Physics, Madurai Kamaraj University, Madurai, India

13.1 Introduction

Coronary artery disorder is a common kind of coronary heart disease that is otherwise called coronary heart sickness or ischemic coronary heart disease. Coronary artery disease (CAD) is the contracting or obstruction of the coronary arteries, typically occur as a result of atherosclerosis. Atherosclerosis is correspondingly known to occur because of "toughening" or "blockage" of the arteries and the result of build-up of LDL-cholesterol and fat accumulation referred to as plaque present on the internal artery walls. These plaque causes restriction blood glide into the heart muscle by means of obstructing the artery or by instigating unusual artery tone and activity deprived of an enough delivery of blood, the heart will become ravenous of oxygen as well as without critical nutriment it wishes to work appropriately which deliberately causes chest pain also known as angina [1].

With this condition in which the supply of blood to a part of the coronary heart muscle reduces completely, or otherwise the energy requirements of coronary heart turn out to be much more than the blood supply, a coronary heart attack (injuries to the muscle) might also happen. It is seen that the calcium phosphate hydroxyapatite deposition inside the muscular coating of the blood vessel appears to have an important role in the hardening of the arteries and also induce the initial segment of coronary arteriosclerosis. This is also observed in a metastatic medium of calciphylaxis as it is known to occur in hemodialysis as well as chronic kidney disease [2].

Gradually, the interior of the artery progress in the formation of plaques of various dimensions. Several plaque deposits are smooth on the interior side having a tough stringy cap that covers the skin. If in case the surface crashes, the fatty and soft interior is visible. The platelets (disc-shaped elements in the blood which assist coagulation) arrive to the area, and blood clotting appears around the plaques. Epithelial tissue may similarly develop irritation and further fails to function accurately, inflicting the muscular arteries to restrain at irrelevant periods [3].

13.1.1 Symptoms of coronary artery disease

If the coronary arteries are constricted, they cannot offer enough oxygen-rich blood to the heart—particularly once it's beating exhaust, like throughout the exercise. At first, the shrunken blood flow might not cause any arterial sickness symptoms. As plaque continues to make up in your coronary arteries, however, you will develop arterial sickness signs and symptoms of chest ache (angina) [4]. It may also sense strain or tightness in the chest as if people have been standing on your chest. This pain, is referred to as angina, commonly takes place on the center or left side of the chest. Angina is typically induced with the aid of bodily or emotional stress. The ache typically declines inside after stopping the severe activity. In some people, particularly women, this ache can also be fleeting or sharp and can also be felt in the neck, arm, or back [5].

Shortness of breath: If your coronary heart cannot pump ample blood to meet your body's needs, you may also enhance shortness of breath or excessive fatigue with exertion. *Heart attack*: A definitely blocked coronary artery will be the reason for a coronary heart attack. The basic signs and symptoms of a coronary heart attack include severe strain in your chest and ache in your shoulder or arm, on occasion with dyspnea and sweating [4]. Women are extremely probable than guys to display less traditional symptoms and signs of a coronary heart attack [3].

13.1.2 Risk factors associated with coronary artery disease

13.1.2.1 Age and gender

Getting older increases the risk of CAD by damaging and contracting the arteries. For men and women between the ages 45–55 there are many risk factors to get CAD. When compared to women, men are vulnerable to get cardiac complications easily. Developing heart muscle weakening and arteries damage is the common problem in aged people. Ethnicity is also a major risk factor for developing cardiac complications. People who are older than 50 years may experience angina as well as dyspnea due to abnormal function of heart. Physical inactivity can lead to fat and cholesterol deposition in major blood vessels [6].

13.1.2.2 Diet factors

Taking more amount of saturated fat, trans-fat, sugar, and salt is the risk of getting CAD. These fats increase the blood cholesterol level and heart attack rate. Obesity may result from an intake of saturated fat which causes various kinds of cardiac complications [7]. The people who are obese will experience shortness of breathing while walking and exercising. Increased level of cholesterol is the main risk factor to get cardiac arrest. Abnormal cholesterol will destroy the normal metabolic function.

Thus, the excess amount of cholesterol will get deposit in arteries through which blood flows to the heart.

The cholesterol amount is maintained by several genes. If they get mutated, it will elevate the risk of CAD. Low-density lipoprotein cholesterol leads to the formation of plaque in the blood vessels. LDL cholesterol may increase by two major problems causing fats (i.e., saturated fat and trans fat) that are present in beef and chicken skin, butter, and some other dairy products. In healthy people, blood sugar level is maintained by insulin. In the case of diabetic conditions, they will have abnormal level of blood sugar levels. Type 2 diabetes may disrupt the arteries and leads to various kinds of heart disease [8] (Fig. 13.1).

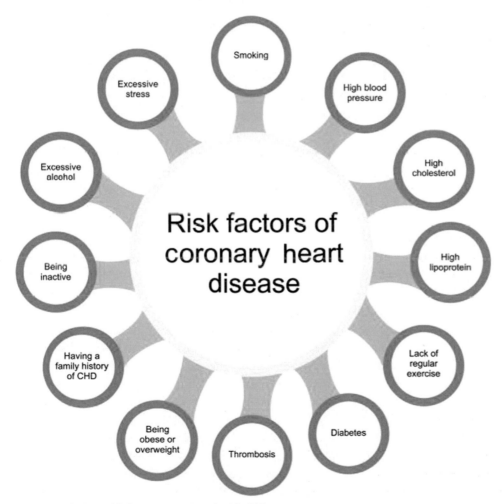

Figure 13.1 Various risk factors associated with CAD.

13.1.2.3 Lifestyle factors

Lifestyle factors like cigarette smoking, alcohol consumption, stress, and hypertension may lead to severe level of CAD. Many studies reported that cigarette smoking is strongly associated with CAD, myocardial infraction, and some other cardiac complications. Both active and passive smokers have equal chance to get cardiac vascular diseases [9]. Drinking excess amount of alcohol can cause dangerous health complications. Intake of alcohol increases the level of triglycerides in blood which are strongly associated with CAD. Similarly, the alcohol consumption will affect the level of blood coagulator factors as well as blood pressure. Because of this alteration, the blood supply to the heart will disrupt. Long-term stress, hypertension, blood cholesterol, blood sugar, and triglycerides can cause changes in the normal metabolic function and promote the accumulation of cholesterol in the major blood vessel. Mild stress can also trigger heart problems by abnormal blood flow, gradual plaque formation in the arteries [10].

13.1.3 Coronary artery disease detection and diagnostics

13.1.3.1 Electrocardiogram

Electrocardiogram records the electrical signals which travel through the heart. It provides the information and evidence about previous heart attacks and also reveals the problems at present. ECG records electric impulses from the patient for the diagnostic purpose by placing electrodes on the skin. The recorded information will be monitored and resulted as a graph of voltage versus time of electrical activity of the heart. Through this graph, physician can diagnose the abnormal activity of the heart. Changes in the normal ECG pattern on the graph represent cardiac complications such as inadequate blood flow to the heart, irregular cardiac rhythm, murmuring sound of heart, abnormal rate of heartbeat, presence of damage in heart's conduction system, blockage in arteries, and size of the chambers [11].

13.1.3.2 Echocardiogram

Echocardiogram is the diagnostic test that makes use of high frequency of sound waves to generate view of the heart's wall, blood vessels, valves as well as chambers. It is also known as cardiac ultrasound diagnostic technique. In this procedure, a probe called transducer is allowed to bypass over chest region. This transducer assembles sound waves that resile on the heart and resonate backward to the probe. These ultrasound waves are transformed into images to monitor and diagnose the appropriate and exact complications. Through this picture, tumor growth around valves, narrowing of blood vessels, size of the heart, shape of the heart, position of the heart, thickness of the heart's wall, infectious growth in the arteries, functioning of heart's valve, pumping strength, blood clots in the chamber, presence of a hole in the middle of the two chambers and problems with pericardium layer can be detected [11].

13.1.3.3 Exercise stress test

It is also known as thread mill test which helps to identify the level of heart functioning. This test shows if there is a reduced blood supply to the heart. By the exercise stress test, CAD can be diagnosed by physician at an early stage. It helps to determine a safe level of exercise for the diseased patient and predict the risk of cardiac complications such as myocardial infarction and heart attack. Exercise stress test examines the heart during times when it is working its hardest [12].

13.1.3.4 Nuclear stress test

Nuclear stress test gives the information about flow of blood to the heart by using radioactive dye and an imaging machine. By performing this test, the reduced blood pass to the heart and damage in the blood vessels can be identified. The procedure starts with injection of radioactive dye, then taking images of the heart; first one while the person is at rest and the other one will be taken after exertion. Nuclear stress test provides more and clear picture of CAD and some other cardiac complications. To know how the treatment works in the heart diseased person, the nuclear stress test can be used [13].

13.1.3.5 Cardiac catheterization and angiogram

Cardiac catheterization is the procedure that provides information about the blood pressure and patterns of blood flow to the heart, whereas angiogram is the diagnostic test in which a special fluid is injected into the major blood vessel, and the X-ray image will be taken. This specialized dye will be visible under X-ray. Sometimes some cardiac defects can be treated during this procedure called cardiac catheterization. This treatment procedure followed by diagnostic procedure is known as therapeutic catheterization. Angiogram is the commonly used diagnostic process to identify the blockage of valves, abnormal activity of heart, and presence of hole between two chambers [11,13].

13.1.4 Prevention

Modification of behavior, blood pressure-lowering, lipid-lowering, antihypertensive and statin therapy are the precaution measures taken to prevent the CAD. Arterial hypertension and diabetes mellitus are the main reasons for CAD. Controlling blood strain maintains sugar level in the blood as it primarily prevents CAD. Guidance is made for the control of foremost cardiovascular hazard elements through moderate lifestyle and prophylactic drug therapies. Lowering the tobacco use, building healthy food choices, living energetically active, decreasing body mass index (too much less than 25 kg/m^2) and waist—hip ratio, lowering blood strain (too much less than 140/90 mmHg), reducing blood cholesterol (too much less than 5 mmol/L or 190 mg/dL), lowering LDL cholesterol (too much less than 3.0 mmol/L or a 115 mg/dL), regulating glycemia levels, particularly in those with damage fasting glycemia and reduce glucose tolerance or diabetes, taking aspirin (75 mg daily), as soon as blood pressure has been controlled are ways to avoid CAD [14].

The above figure shows the minimum that needs to attain in more or less sub-groups of elevated vulnerable people, especially people with inherited cardiovascular disorder or diabetes, a case can be made for lower goals for blood strain (130/80 mmHg), avoiding stress, general LDL cholesterol and LDL cholesterol, which might also need additional rigorous treatment, aspirin therapy, and hormone remedy additionally have a great impact of lowering the chance of CAD, even though it is the distinctive preventing system [15].

13.1.4.1 Modification of behavior
A variation of the way of life moderation takes to lessen blood pressure. These involve weight loss in case of obesity, exercise activities, reducing alcohol intake, multiplied sparkling fruit and veggies and less saturated fat diet, sodium intake, and high potassium intake, changing the day-to-day activities, circular calorie balanced diet, and so on.

13.1.4.2 Physical activity
Lifestyle is linked with an elevated chance of cardiovascular disease. Physical activity is related to decreased probability of CAD in both men and women; over body weight is related to CAD. Consistent physical activity significantly reduces the chance of CAD. Regular exercise strengthens the cardiac muscle. It lowering LDL cholesterol, blood pressure, then elevates high-density lipoproteins levels [16].

13.1.4.3 Diet
Dietary consumption of fat, fruits, vegetables, fish, and sodium are linked with CAD. Omega-3 fatty acid plays a role in a modified lipid profile, lowering thrombotic tendency, antihypertensive and antiinflammatory effects. Improving the intake of vegetables and fruits reduces trans-fat in the body; trans-fatty acids increase the chance of CAD. Foods that are rich in vitamin E and beta-carotene help to reduce the risk of CAD, more than a teaspoon of sodium (per day) can raise blood pressure [15].

13.1.4.4 Alcohol and tobacco
Nicotine elevates blood pressure resulting in CAD. Tobacco can limit down the arteries and injured heart valves alcohol consumption increases the levels of an alternative type of fat in the blood the triglycerides, which are related to a high chance of coronary heart diseases, alcohol has a miscellaneous consequence on coronary risk element by elevating high-density lipoproteins-Cholesterol and triglyceride levels [16].

13.1.4.5 Blood pressure lowering
Arterial hypertension can form the destruction of arteries and make them more likely to progress to atherosclerosis. Angiotensin-transmute enzyme suppression and

angiotensin II receptor blockers help modify blood vessels to allow additional blood flow (e.g., valsartan). Calcium channel blockers modify blood vessels by reduced calcium from moving into muscle cells in the heart and blood vessels such as amlodipine (Norvasc), bepridil (Vascor), and diltiazem [17].

13.1.4.6 Lipid lowering
Fibrates are mainly used for lowering triglycerides and raising low HDL levels. Nicotinic acid is an effective HDL raising agent. These lipid-lowering drugs reduce the risk of CAD. Cholesterol-lowering drugs can help lower your LDL cholesterol and increase your HDL cholesterol such as atorvastatin (Lipitor) and fluvastatin (Lescol XL). Bile acid and calcium chloride help to reduce cholesterol in the blood. Examples include cholestyramine (Prevalite), colesevelam (Welchol), and colestipol (Colestid). Fabric acid derivatives (fibrates) increase HDL cholesterol and lower triglycerides such as clofibrate (Atromid-S) [16].

Drugs for clot prevention
Plaque build-up in arteries makes additional clot formation. A clot could partially or completely block the blood flow to the heart. These capsules together prevent blood clots: Apixaban (Eliquis), clopidogrel (Plavix), dabigatran (Pradaxa), enoxaparin (Lovenox), rivaroxaban (Xarelto), ticagrelor (Brilinta), ticlopidine (Ticlid), and warfarin (Coumadin) [17].

13.1.4.7 Antihypertensive and stain therapy
Cholesterol-decreasing agents mixed with antihypertensive therapy prevent cardiovascular activities and also a pill carry the complex of the antihypertensive amlodipine desolate, lipid lowering remedy atorvastatin calcium (SPAA) it increase adherence to lipid-reducing and decrease cardiovascular occasions [16].

13.1.5 Genetic factor
Genetic predisposition is the main risk factor of developing CAD and vascular disease. The genetic variations are highly associated with hypertension, inflammation, cholesterol maintenance, triglyceride—metabolism and various metabolic pathway. LDLR and PCSK-9 genes help to regulate the cholesterol in the blood in maintaining the LDL receptors. When those genes get mutated, it will cause increased level of LDL receptors and accumulates in the blood vessels. Variations at NOS3 and GUCY1A3 are highly related to CAD by gradually increasing blood pressure. Genetic variants in chromosome 9 are associated with irregular lipid levels and abnormal metabolic functions [18].

CAD is known to be caused by multiple factors [19]. Together with the risk factors such as hypertension, age, gender, family history, diabetes mellitus, and smoking the most recent research studies have proved the involvement of environmental and genetic factors in the progression of CAD [20,21]. Remarkably, the RAS which regulates the blood pressure is evidenced to have a critical role in the pathophysiology of CAD. The renin—angiotensin system is found to be a main regulatory entity in the physiology of the cardiovascular system. This involves the remodeling of cardiovascular system, sustainment of the vascular tone as well as homeostasis of sodium [22]. Numerous findings have indicated major verdicts about the involvement of the single-nucleotide polymorphisms (SNPs) of RAS which further leads to the development and advancement of CAD in some susceptible individuals.

13.1.5.1 Angiotensin converting enzyme gene

ACE determines the vasoactive peptide called Angiotensin II which is involved in the RAS pathway [23]. The ACE is very common in the renin—angiotensin—aldosterone system as well as in the kinin—kallikrein system. It is known to be a zinc metalloproteinase that splits the terminal of histidine—leucine dipeptide of Ang I and thus turns it into Ang II which is an extremely constricting component. Because of the intrusion of these two systems, the ACE thereby deactivates the bradykinin which is a vasodilating component. Through these roles, the ACE is known to maintain the vascular tone as well as the sodium homeostasis [24,25].

The ACE gene is situated at the chromosomal location 17q23 which is known to have a size of 21 kb and also comprises 25 introns and 26 exons [26]. The polymorphism of ACE involves several insertions and deletions specifically present in the intron 16. Therefore, from the polymorphism present in the intron 16 there are known to be three main genotypes such as insertional homozygote (II), heterozygote (DI), and teletional homozygote (DD). The serum levels of ACE are resolved by the genetic polymorphism in the order DD > ID > II [27]. The aforementioned SNP is proved by several studies to have a link with the interpersonal inconsistency of the ACE levels found in the blood which circulates in the body [28]. The allele which gets deleted at the gene location of ACE is linked with amplified activity of the plasma ACE [29].

An additional polymorphism seen in the ACE gene is known to be silent as well as synonymous coding SNP with an rsid 4343 (2350A > G) present in the exon 17. Various research findings have proved the link between ACE I/D rs4340 and 2350A > G SNPs which progress to several ailments such that systemic lupus erythematous, increase in blood pressure, Alzheimer's disease, CAD, renal disease, and diabetic nephropathy [30,31].

13.1.5.2 IL-10 gene polymorphism

It is known that inflammation has a pivotal role in the development and progression of atherosclerotic-related vascular ailments [32]. Interleukins are identified as a group of cytokines, which were initially documented as vital agents that participate in the inflammatory responses by the host [33]. The interleukin 10 (IL-10) is produced by the TH2 cells and the macrophages. IL-10 is identified to be a notable antiinflammatory cytokine with the presence of potential neutralizing properties on both T cells as well as macrophages. IL-10 is known to be manifested in the human atherosclerotic plaques which plays a role as a defensive factor in atherosclerosis by stabilizing the pro-inflammatory cytokine movement and thereby also decreases the plaque variability and improves the diagnosis [34,35].

It is being evidenced that decrease in the serum levels of IL-10 is linked with a more adverse diagnosis in the patients having acute coronary syndrome [36,37]. The IL-10 gene is situated in chromosome 1, and it is also known to have five exons and is also mapped between the intersection amongst 1q31 and 1q32 [38]. Various SNPs found in the promoter region of the interleukin-10 gene like IL-10–819 C/T, IL-10–1082G/A, and IL-10–592C/A are evidenced to be intricated in the regulation and expression of IL-10 gene that can also impact the predisposition of CAD [39]. IL-10 gene is identified to have various sites such as microsatellites and SNPs which affect the IL-10 expression levels. Thus, it might be directly or indirectly linked in the progression of CAD [40] (Fig. 13.2).

13.1.5.3 Angiotensinogen gene

The AGT is known to be formed by the liver cells, which is altered to angiotensin through renin. After this the angiotensin I is altered to angiotensin II, further leading to fibrosis, vasoconstriction, and myocardial hypertrophy. The AGT gene comprises five exons. It is located in the chromosomal location 1q12–13 position [41]. A replacement of threonine to methionine at the amino acid 174th position is a frequently occurring polymorphism which is also called rs699 or T174M terming the T and M alleles separately [42]. Over the last several decades, the AGT SNP T174M has been studied to find its link in the progression of CAD.

The T174M polymorphism was initially investigated to find out the relationship between the aforementioned polymorphism and myocardial infarction (MI) [43]. The outcome exhibited that the genotype distribution of T174M had no difference amongst the cases and control groups and no substantial link leading to CAD was found. Afterward, few studies on the same topic were carried out but none of the studies established the association between AGT T174M SNP and risk of developing CAD [44]. The inconsistency in the literature search might be because of varied factors comprising of the genetic framework in the diverse ethnicity. In view of the important role exhibited by these three genetic polymorphisms in the development and progression of coronary artery disease a meta–analysis study was conducted inorder to find out the susceptibility of these polymorphisms and the risk of developing CAD at an early phase.

Aim

The current *meta*-analysis was performed to attain a more specific investigation on the link between the polymorphisms ACE (rs4340), IL-10(rs1800896), and AGT (rs699) and the risk of developing CAD.

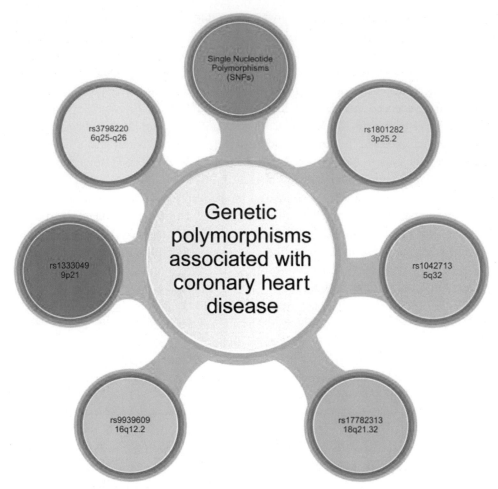

Figure 13.2 Genetic polymorphisms associated with CAD.

13.2 Methodology

13.2.1 Literature search

The previous investigations which displayed the link between ACE, IL-10, and AGT polymorphisms with the increased risk of developing CAD were scrutinized from various electronic databases such as Embase, Web of Science, Google Scholar, and PubMed from 2000 to 2021. Different Mesh terms were used for the extensive search like "CAD" or "Coronary Artery Disease," "SNP" and "Polymorphisms" and "ACE or angiotensin-converting enzyme" and IL-10" or "Interleukin 10" and "AGT" or "Angiotensinogen" and "rs699" and "rs4340" and "rs1800896." All the selected studies were human-related case—control studies. The outcome was compared with each other and thereby resolved.

13.2.2 Selection criteria

The studies suitable for this *meta*-analysis had to satisfy some of the detailed inclusion standards such as CAD-related case—control study, evaluation between the association among ACE, IL-10, and AGT genetic polymorphisms and progression to CAD, presence of allelic and genotypic frequencies of the polymorphisms, full-text articles, only English articles will be selected for further study, *meta*-analysis papers will be included. The odds ratio (OR) and its corresponding confidence interval (CI) were also taken into account for the study. The articles that were excluded are other language articles, review articles, abstracts, and animal studies.

13.2.3 Extraction of data

The data were retrieved from each study based on the first author name, journal name and year of publication, population, and PMID. The extracted articles were properly checked for the following information such as allelic and genotypic frequencies of patients and control participants. The frequencies were derived from each genetic polymorphism separately and were compared with the cases and controls of the study. The OR along with its CI, *P*-value, distribution of genes, method of genotyping, and the HWE values were extracted from the selected articles for further calculations.

13.2.4 Statistical analysis

The derived allelic and genotypic data from the previous studies were carefully pooled. From these data, the minor allelic frequencies were calculated and compared among the case and control group. All the derived data were correctly entered into a software called RevMan 5.3 and the statistical analysis was executed. The OR and CI were also taken in order to investigate the statistical relationship of the ACE, IL-10, and AGT genetic polymorphisms in the development of CAD. Any deviance in the Hardy—Weinberg Equilibrium (HWE) was checked properly for all the selected studies. *P*-value $<.05$ were taken as statistically significant with the disease. The OR was analyzed by using a fixed-effect model. Revman version 5.3 was used for further plotting the forest plots and the funnel plots needed for the study.

13.3 Results

13.3.1 Literature search

The literature search and data arrangement processes executed in the *meta*-analysis were as per the PRISMA guidelines. There were four main steps, identification, screening, eligibility, and inclusion conditions, which were carried out in order to select the eligible studies for this particular *meta*-analysis study. Initially, 530 articles were derived from various databases. Out of which only 460 articles were recovered after the removal of 70 articles due to the duplicate records. Subsequently, as soon as the screening process was over, 298 articles were retrieved after the deletion of 162 articles based on the exclusion criteria like abstracts, review articles, articles not applicable for CAD. A total of 156 articles were removed because of the absence of the allelic and genotypic frequency distribution as well as due to the lack of statistical data. Full-text articles were sorted out and evaluated based on the inclusion criteria. Lastly, 41 articles were retrieved after the removal of 101 articles. The full-text articles were selected on the basis of the qualitative analysis used to evaluate the link between the ACE, IL-10, and AGT genetic polymorphisms and its risk in the development of CAD. Fig. 13.3 illustrates the selection process of the *meta*-analysis.

Broadly, the information of the genetic polymorphisms was retrieved from two different populations such as Asian and Caucasian. On the whole, the studies were

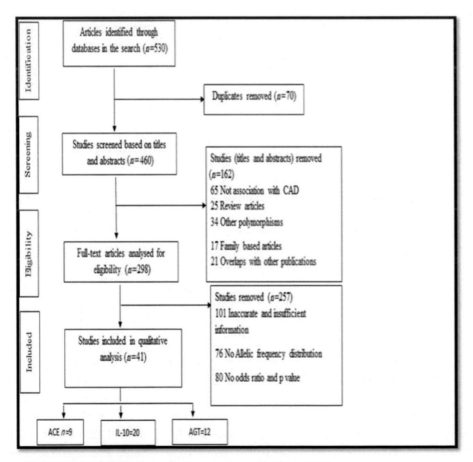

Figure 13.3 Flowchart illustrating selection process of meta-analysis.

evaluated for ethnicity and 18 studies were found to be Asian studies, whereas 23 studies came under the Caucasian population. The information extracted about the three genetic polymorphisms is shown in Tables 13.1—13.3.

Table 13.1 *Meta*-analysis of ACE (rs4340) gene polymorphism and the risk of coronary artery disease.

S. no.	Reference	Ethnicity	Odds ratio	95% CI	*P*-value
1	Acarturk et al. [45]	Caucasian	1.48	1.01—2.18	<0.05
2	Niemiec et al. [46]	Caucasian	1.88	1.13—3.15	0.01
3	Freitas et al. [47]	Caucasian	1.41	1.15—1.74	<.0001
4	Jamil et al. [48]	Asian	0.58	0.37—0.90	<0.01
5	Ramakrishnan et al. [49]	Asian	1.22	0.50—2.94	0.65
6	Poorgholi et al. [50]	Asian	0.61	0.35—1.07	0.49
7	Firouzabadi et al. [31]	Asian	1.49	0.96—2.28	0.06
8	Heidari et al. [51]	Asian	1.07	0.66—1.75	0.80
9	Vladeanu et al. [27]	Caucasian	5.25	2.02—13.5	0.006

Table 13.2 *Meta*-analysis of IL-10 (rs1800896) gene polymorphism and the risk of coronary artery disease.

S. no.	Reference	Ethnicity	Odds ratio	95% CI	*P*-value
1	Koch et al. [37]	Caucasian	0.97	0.76—1.24	0.84
2	Donger et al. [52]	Caucasian	1.02	0.83—1.24	0.81
3	Lio et al. [53]	Caucasian	2.15	1.31—3.53	0.002
4	O'Halloran et al. [54]	Caucasian	0.86	0.66—1.12	0.27
5	Chen et al. [55]	Asian	1.33	0.74—2.41	0.33
6	Lorenzova et al. [56]	Caucasian	0.86	0.65—1.15	0.34
7	Ben-Hadj-Khalifa et al. [57]	Caucasian	1.46	0.99—2.15	0.05
8	Fragoso et al. [38]	Caucasian	0.99	0.77—1.28	0.99
9	Karaca et al. [58]	Caucasian	0.97	0.49—1.92	0.94
10	Yu et al. [59]	Asian	0.98	0.75—1.29	0.92
11	Babu et al. [60]	Asian	1.24	0.99—1.55	0.05
12	Afzal et al. [61]	Asian	1.59	0.43—5.83	0.47
13	Ianni et al. [62]	Caucasian	1.04	0.72—1.50	0.80
14	Cruz et al. [63]	Caucasian	0.73	0.50—1.06	0.10
15	Elsaid et al. [64]	Caucasian	0.33	0.06—1.59	0.16
16	Qian et al. [65]	Asian	1.03	0.81—1.33	0.76
17	Ren and She [66]	Asian	2.21	1.32—3.43	0.001
18	Xu and Liu [67]	Asian	2.31	1.29—4.19	0.003
19	Mousavi et al. [68]	Asian	1.79	1.12—2.87	0.01
20	Menshed et al. [69]	Asian	0.88	0.40—1.93	0.76

Table 13.3 *Meta*-analysis of AGT (rs699) gene polymorphism and the risk of coronary artery disease.

S. no.	Reference	Ethnicity	Odds ratio	95% CI	*P*-value
1	Fatini et al. [70]	Caucasian	1.69	0.40−7.20	0.47
2	Spiridonova et al. [71]	Caucasian	9.07	0.46−17.8	0.14
3	Babunova et al. [72]	Caucasian	2.75	0.33−22.6	0.34
4	Nair et al. [73]	Asian	0.19	0.009−4.05	0.28
5	Zhang et al. [74]	Asian	5.10	1.32−19.6	0.01
6	Renner et al. [75]	Caucasian	0.08	0.04−0.14	<0.0001
7	Tsai et al. [76]	Asian	2.11	0.76−5.86	0.14
8	Frritas et al. [77]	Caucasian	2.28	0.50−10.2	0.28
9	Abboud et al. [78]	Caucasian	6.48	2.25−18.7	0.0005
10	Konopka et al. [79]	Caucasian	4.75	0.54−41.4	0.15
11	Khatami et al. [80]	Asian	0.52	0.22−1.24	0.14
12	Azova et al. [81]	Caucasian	0.57	0.29−1.12	0.10

13.3.2 Quantitative data analysis

A total of 15,666 CAD cases and 10,908 controls were retrieved from a total of 41 studies, which exhibited a link between ACE, IL-10, and AGT genetic polymorphisms and an increased risk of developing CAD in Caucasian and Asian populations. The ACE (rs4340) polymorphism associated with risk of CAD comprised of 1889 CAD cases and 1710 controls which was retrieved from four Caucasian and five Asian population evidence. The association test of ACE rs4340 genetic polymorphism was assessed as pooled OR in allelic model OR 0.83; 95% CI 0.74−0.92, Recessive model OR 0.90; 95% CI 0.76−1.06, Dominant model OR 0.69; 95% CI 0.58−0.82 and Over dominant model OR 0.83; 95% CI 0.72−0.96. The association data of ACE genetic polymorphism with risk of developing CAD condition in various genetic models are shown in Figs. 13.4−13.7.

The forest plots exhibit the result of the estimated outcome by means of fixed-effect model. The HWE values of ACE genetic polymorphism are shown in Table 13.4.

The IL-10 genetic polymorphism rs1800896 comprising of nine Asian and 11 Caucasian studies exhibited a total of 8690 CAD cases and 6075 controls. The association test of IL-10 rs1800896 genetic polymorphism was evaluated as pooled OR in allelic model OR 1.03; 95% CI 0.97−1.08, Recessive model OR 1.01; 95% CI 0.93−1.10, Dominant model OR 1.07; 95% CI 0.97−1.18, and Over dominant model OR 1.03; 95% CI 0.95−1.11. The association between IL-10 genetic polymorphism and progression into CAD shown in various genetic models is illustrated in Figs. 13.8−13.11.

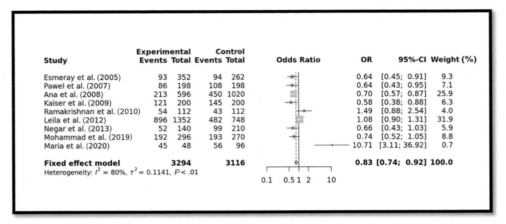

Figure 13.4 The link between ACE rs4340 genetic polymorphism and risk of CAD illustrated by allelic contrast model.

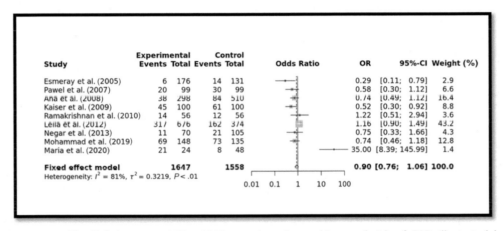

Figure 13.5 The link between ACE rs4340 genetic polymorphism and risk of CAD illustrated by recessive model.

The forest plots exhibit the result of the estimated outcome by means of fixed-effect model. The HWE values of IL-10 genetic polymorphism are shown in Table 13.5.

The AGT genetic polymorphism rs688 is comprised of 5087 CAD cases and 3123 controls. The association test of IL-10 rs1800896 genetic polymorphism was evaluated as pooled OR in allelic model OR 1.19; 95% CI 1.08−1.32; Recessive model OR 1.27; 95% CI 0.92−1.74; Dominant model OR 1.20; 95% CI 1.20−1.34, Over dominant OR 1.1; 95% CI 1.02−1.28. The association between AGT genetic polymorphism and progression into CAD shown in various genetic models are illustrated in Figs. 13.12−13.15.

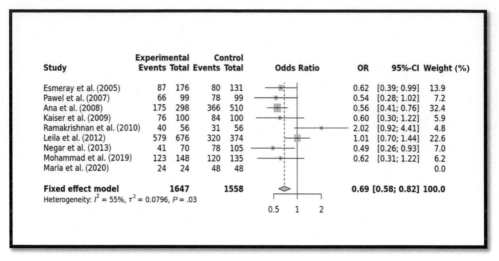

Figure 13.6 The link between ACE rs4340 genetic polymorphism and risk of CAD illustrated by dominant model.

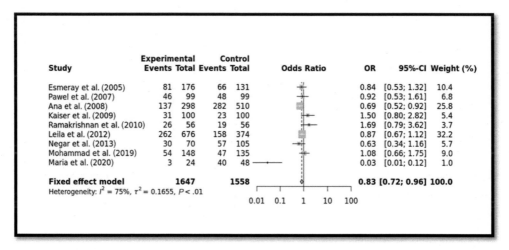

Figure 13.7 The link between ACE rs4340 genetic polymorphism and risk of CAD illustrated by over-dominant model.

The forest plots exhibit the result of the estimated outcome by means of fixed–effect model. The HWE values of AGT genetic polymorphism are shown in Table 13.6.

13.3.3 Publication bias

The Egger's test was conducted to assess the possible publication bias amongst the overall investigation. In order to carry out this method, a minimum of four studies

Table 13.4 HWE results of ACE (rs4340) polymorphism involved in coronary artery disease.

S. no.	Reference	Ethnicity	Case\control				HWE
			II	ID	DD	Total	
1	Acarturk et al. [45]	Caucasian	6/14	81/66	89/51	176/131	0.35
2	Niemiec et al. [46]	Caucasian	20.3/30.2	46/48.5	33.7/21.3	100/100	0.8
3	Freitas et al. [47]	Caucasian	38/84	137/282	123/144	298/510	0.01
4	Jamil et al. [48]	Asian	45/61	31/23	24/16	100/100	0
5	Ramakrishnan et al. [49]	Asian	14/12	26/19	16/25	56/56	0.07
6	Poorgholi et al. [50]	Asian	317/162	262/158	97/54	676/374	0.19
7	Firouzabadi et al. [31]	Asian	11/21	30/57	29/27	70/105	0.40
8	Heidari et al. [51]	Asian	69/73	54/47	25/15	148/135	0.16
9	Vladeanu et al. [27]	Caucasian	21/8	3/40	0/0	24/48	0

HWE, Hardy—Weinberg equilibrium; *ACE*, angiotensin-converting enzyme.

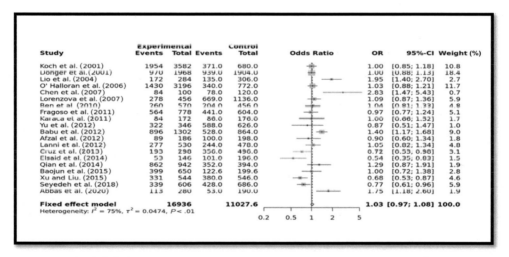

Figure 13.8 The link between IL-10 (rs1800896) genetic polymorphism and risk of CAD illustrated by allelic contrast model.

were essential. The funnel plot displayed the effect size on the *x*-axis and the sample size is plotted on the *y*-axis. This was further used to check the presence or absence of probable publication bias where *P*-value $>.05$. In the present study, the Egger's test did not display any considerable publication bias by the ACE genetic polymorphism (rs4340) specifically amongst the genetic models ($P>.05$). The genetic models of

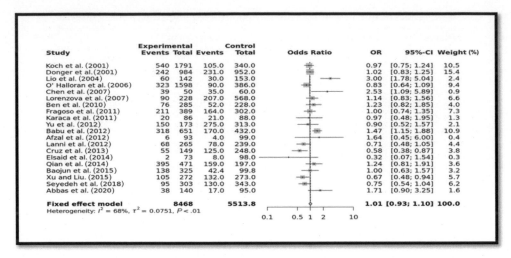

Figure 13.9 The link between IL-10 (rs1800896) genetic polymorphism and risk of CAD illustrated by recessive model.

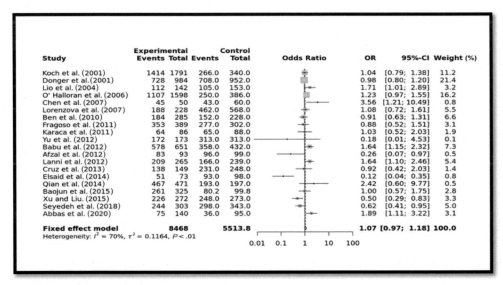

Figure 13.10 The link between IL-10 (rs1800896) genetic polymorphism and risk of CAD illustrated by dominant model.

IL-10 genetic polymorphism (rs1800896) also have not displayed any significant difference in the results ($P > 0.05$). No publication bias was seen in the various genetic models of the AGT genetic polymorphism (rs699) also. The funnel plots retrieved for all the three genetic polymorphisms are displayed in Figs. 13.16–13.18.

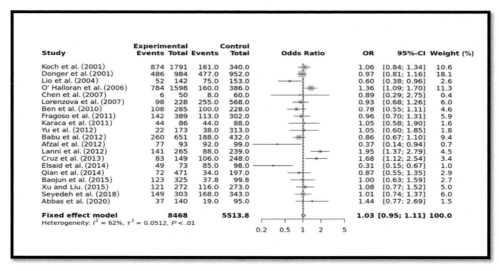

Study	Experimental Events	Total	Control Events	Total	Odds Ratio	OR	95%-CI	Weight (%)
Koch et al. (2001)	874	1791	161.0	340.0		1.06	[0.84; 1.34]	10.6
Donger et al.(2001)	486	984	477.0	952.0		0.97	[0.81; 1.16]	18.1
Lio et al. (2004)	52	142	75.0	153.0		0.60	[0.38; 0.96]	2.6
O' Halloran et al. (2006)	784	1598	160.0	386.0		1.36	[1.09; 1.70]	11.3
Chen et al. (2007)	6	50	8.0	60.0		0.89	[0.29; 2.75]	0.4
Lorenzova et al. (2007)	98	228	255.0	568.0		0.93	[0.68; 1.26]	6.0
Ben et al. (2010)	108	285	100.0	228.0		0.78	[0.55; 1.11]	4.6
Fragoso et al. (2011)	142	389	113.0	302.0		0.96	[0.70; 1.31]	5.9
Karaca et al. (2011)	44	86	44.0	88.0		1.05	[0.58; 1.90]	1.6
Yu et al. (2012)	22	173	38.0	313.0		1.05	[0.60; 1.85]	1.8
Babu et al. (2012)	260	651	188.0	432.0		0.86	[0.67; 1.10]	9.4
Afzal et al. (2012)	77	93	92.0	99.0		0.37	[0.14; 0.94]	0.7
Lanni et al. (2012)	141	265	88.0	239.0		1.95	[1.37; 2.79]	4.5
Cruz et al. (2013)	83	149	106.0	248.0		1.68	[1.12; 2.54]	3.4
Elsaid et al. (2014)	49	73	85.0	98.0		0.31	[0.15; 0.67]	1.0
Qian et al. (2014)	72	471	34.0	197.0		0.87	[0.55; 1.35]	2.9
Baojun et al. (2015)	123	325	37.8	99.8		1.00	[0.63; 1.59]	2.7
Xu and Liu. (2015)	121	272	116.0	273.0		1.08	[0.77; 1.52]	5.0
Seyedeh et al. (2018)	149	303	168.0	343.0		1.01	[0.74; 1.37]	6.0
Abbas et al. (2020)	37	140	19.0	95.0		1.44	[0.77; 2.69]	1.5
Fixed effect model		**8468**		**5513.8**		**1.03**	**[0.95; 1.11]**	**100.0**

Heterogeneity: $I^2 = 62\%$, $\tau^2 = 0.0512$, $P < .01$

0.2 0.5 1 2 5

Figure 13.11 The link between IL-10 (rs1800896) genetic polymorphism and risk of CAD illustrated by over-dominant model.

13.4 Discussion

The current meta-analysis study presents the association of ACE (rs4340), IL-10 (rs1800896), and AGT (rs699) genetic polymorphisms with an increased risk of developing CAD, especially amongst Caucasian and Asian populations. In order to carry out the meta-analysis, a sum total of 15,666 CAD cases and 10,908 controls were taken into account derived from various populations. The outcome of this study shows statistically substantial link between the ACE, IL-10, and AGT genetic polymorphisms and risk of developing CAD in an early stage.

Several genetic linked studies were performed in order to prove the impact of certain genetic polymorphisms in the progression of diseases. These genetic association findings can be a boon for the early diagnosis of subjects who are more vulnerable to certain ailments. One of the recently published articles by Arthiya et al. [43] has proved the involvement of genetic polymorphisms of LDLR, MTHFR, and KLOTHO and the risk of developing CAD [82]. *Meta*-analysis investigations are used to compare the outcomes of the previously done studies with the new studies. It also increases the statistical power of the information collected from various findings [83]. These studies are used to forecast the susceptibility of ailments by using genetic polymorphisms as a biomarker amongst different ethnicity and can predict the progression of diseases by studying the genetic framework of various populations.

It is known that CAD can thereby increase the progression of other heart-related ailments such as cardiovascular disease as well as a comprehensive block leading to a

Table 13.5 HWE results of IL-10 (rs1800896) polymorphism involved in coronary artery disease.

S. no.	Reference	Ethnicity	Case/control				HWE
			AA	CA	CC	Total	
1	Koch et al. [37]	Caucasian	540/105	874/161	377/74	1791/340	0.52
2	Donger et al. [52]	Caucasian	242/231	486/477	256/244	984/952	0.99
3	Lio et al. [53]	Caucasian	60/30	52/75	30/48	142/153	0.10
4	O'Halloran et al. [54]	Caucasian	323/90	784/160	491/136	1598/386	0.006
5	Chen et al. [55]	Asian	39/35	6/8	5/17	50/60	0
6	Lorenzova et al. [56]	Caucasian	90/207	98/255	40/106	228/568	0.17
7	Ben-Hadj-Khalifa et al. [57]	Caucasian	76/52	108/100	101/76	285/228	0.18
8	Fragoso et al. [38]	Caucasian	211/164	142/113	36/25	389/302	0.52
9	Karaca et al. [58]	Caucasian	20/21	44/44	22/23	86/88	0.10
10	Yu et al. [59]	Asian	150/275	22/38	1/0	173/313	0.42
11	Babu et al. [60]	Asian	318/170	260/188	73/74	651/432	0.17
12	Afzal et al. [61]	Asian	6/4	77/92	10/3	93/99	0
13	Ianni et al. [62]	Caucasian	68/78	141/88	56/73	265/239	0
14	Cruz et al. [63]	Caucasian	55/125	83/106	11/17	149/248	0.52
15	Elsaid et al. [64]	Caucasian	2/8	49/85	22/5	73/98	0
16	Qian et al. [65]	Asian	395/159	72/34	4/4	471/197	0.34
17	Ren and She [66]	Asian	138/42.46	123/37.85	64/19.69	325/100	0.12
18	Xu and Liu [67]	Asian	105/132	121/116	46/25	272/273	0.99
19	Mousavi et al. [68]	Asian	95/130	149/168	59/45	303/343	0.52
20	Menshed et al. [69]	Asian	38/17	37/19	65/59	140/95	0

HWE, Hardy–Weinberg equilibrium.

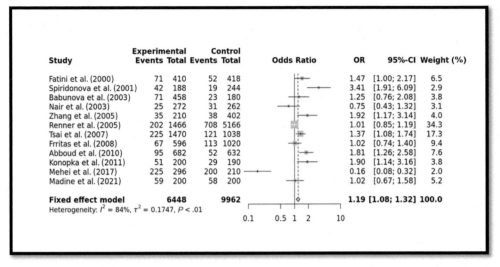

Figure 13.12 The link between AGT (rs699) genetic polymorphism and risk of CAD illustrated by allelic contrast model.

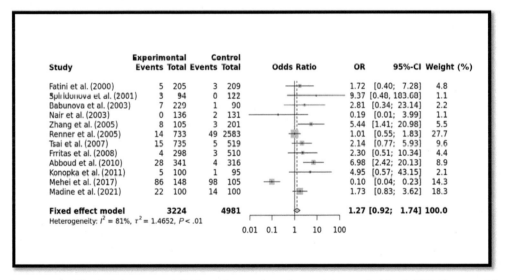

Figure 13.13 The link between AGT (rs699) genetic polymorphism and risk of CAD illustrated by recessive model.

cardiac arrest or heart failure [84]. CAD is known to begin at an early phase and there are evidence to support that this has a major link to genetic factors. Various former studies have proposed that genetic aspects are more likely to be seen in younger generation rather than elderly people [85]. The current investigation has pointed out the

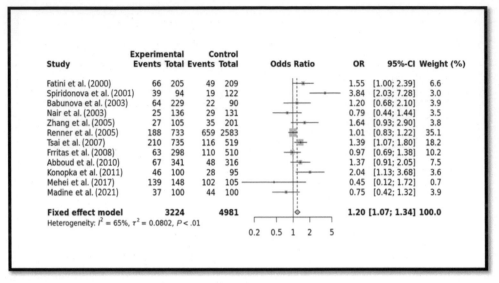

Figure 13.14 The link between AGT (rs699) genetic polymorphism and risk of CAD illustrated by dominant model.

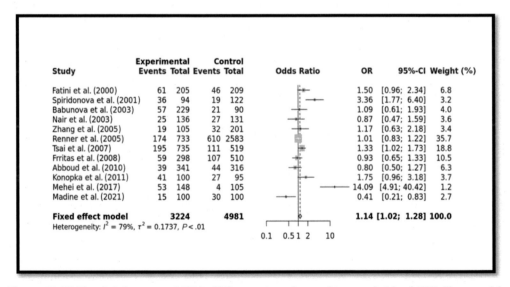

Figure 13.15 The link between AGT (rs699) genetic polymorphism and risk of CAD illustrated by over- dominant model.

outcomes of the link between genetic polymorphisms of ACE, IL-10, and AGT in the progression of CAD by using certain genetic models like allele contrast, recessive model, over dominant model, and dominant model. This genetic association study has

Table 13.6 HWE results of AGT (rs699) polymorphism involved in coronary artery disease.

S. no.	Reference	Ethnicity	Case/control				HWE
			MM	MT	TT	Total	
1	Fatini et al. [70]	Caucasian	5/3	61/46	139/160	205/209	0.93
2	Spiridonova et al. [71]	Caucasian	3/0	36/19	55/103	94/122	0.57
3	Babunova et al. [72]	Caucasian	7/1	57/21	165/68	229/90	0.87
4	Nair et al. [73]	Asian	0/2	25/27	111/102	136/131	0.93
5	Zhang et al. [74]	Asian	8/3	19/32	78/166	105/201	0.58
6	Renner et al. [75]	Caucasian	14/49	174/610	545/1924	733/2583	0.94
7	Tsai et al. [76]	Asian	15/5	195/111	525/403	735/519	0.57
8	Freitas et al. [77]	Caucasian	4/3	59/107	235/400	298/510	0.50
9	Abboud et al. [78]	Caucasian	28/4	39/44	274/268	341/316	0.49
10	Konopka et al. [79]	Caucasian	5/1	41/27	54/67	100/95	0.57
11	Khatami et al. [80]	Asian	86/98	53/4	9/3	148/105	0
12	Azova et al. [81]	Caucasian	22/14	15/30	63/56	100/100	0.03

HWE, Hardy–Weinberg equilibrium, *AGT*, Angiotensinogen.

shown a significant association between ACE (rs4340), IL-10 (rs1800896), AGT (rs699) genetic polymorphisms with an increased risk of developing CAD.

The studies on ACE genetic polymorphisms are known to be used as genetic biomarkers for the early detection of certain heart-related ailments like MI, ischemic heart disease, ischemic cerebrovascular disease, and coronary artery stenosis [85,86]. The genetic link of the polymorphisms such as rs4343 and rs4340 with CAD has been found to be beneficial by previous findings. The difference in the populations might be due to some discrepancies in the environment as well as in the genetic framework. The pathophysiological mechanism of CAD is atherosclerosis, and IL-10 is known to present a crucial impact on the development and advancement of atherosclerotic plaque [87]. In a previous study IL-10 (rs1800896) polymorphism was reported to be linked with an increased risk of CAD and the same polymorphism was also found to be linked with tobacco smoking and advancement of CAD [88]. Renin—angiotensin system is reported to be one among other factors which regulate the blood pressure and cardiovascular homeostasis. Angiotensin is a major component of

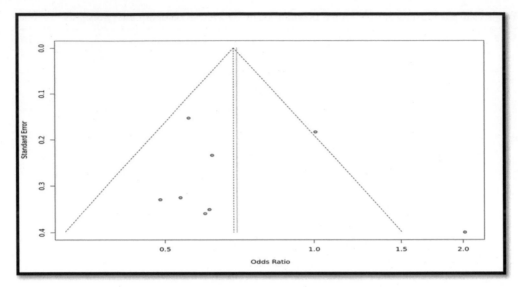

Figure 13.16 Funnel plot illustrating dominant model of the ACE (rs4340) genetic polymorphism.

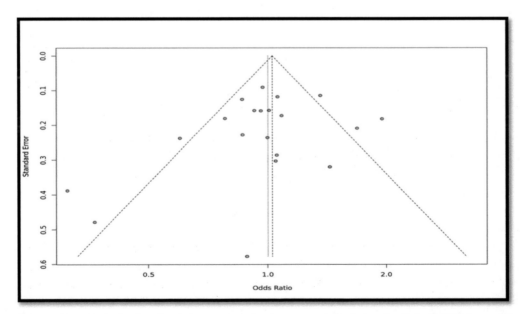

Figure 13.17 Funnel plot illustrating over- dominant model of the IL-10 (rs1800896) genetic polymorphism.

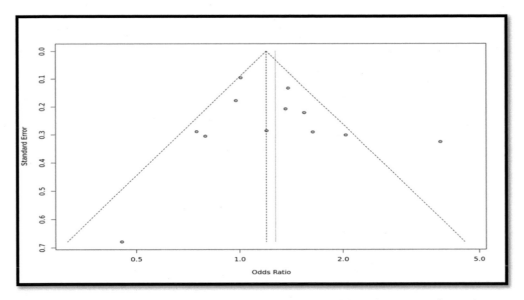

Figure 13.18 Funnel plot illustrating dominant model of the AGT (rs699) genetic polymorphism.

renin—angiotensin system [89]. Amongst the AGT genetic variants, rs699 have been widely investigated. The CC homozygotes of rs699 polymorphism are found to have 10%—20% elevated AGT plasma levels which might be due to the linkage equilibrium with the G-6A loci present in the gene's promoter region [90].

To summarize, the present *meta*-analysis has specified the link between three different genetic polymorphisms with the progression of CAD. It has showed that ACE (rs4340), IL-10 (rs1800896), and AGT (rs699) have been studied to have elevated risk of CAD more frequently in the Asian population when compared to the Caucasian population. This piece of work might be useful to understand the importance of SNPs in the progression of ailments such as CAD in this case. This article has listed three main polymorphisms which could be used as a genetic marker to detect CAD. Further studies with larger sample sizes in diverse populations are required to come to a consistent result.

13.5 Conclusion

SNPs are known to be a very frequently occurring genetic variation among human beings because of its plethora presence throughout the human genome [91]. The SNPs are very useful to map human diseases and can also be used as biomarkers, in the field of population genetics as well as in evolutionarily related investigations. These genetic polymorphisms have been potentially significant ever since the usage of high-throughput techniques such as DNA sequencing have become accessible and readily available [91,92]. The advancement and usage of these genetic biomarkers have a solitary substantial role in the field of genetics which aid in the early diagnostics of diseases. It has a paramount significance in personalized diagnostics and personalized medicine which differs from person to person. SNPs are powerful and consistent biomarkers having indicative value and might be also a guide to identify the ultimate disease causative factors. Genetic biomarkers are able to associate the development of any devastation leading to clinical or preclinical problems. It can also qualify in better decision-making during drug discovery as well as in the management of diseases among patients [93].

The current meta-analysis study has publicized enough information collected from larger sample size studies mainly on the impact of the investigated genetic polymorphisms and its progression to CAD. Larger sample-sized patient-involved findings are useful in order to validate these genetic biomarkers in the blood and serum samples. Along with this, it is also important to study the other factors such as gene—gene interaction, ethnicity, and environmental factors which alter the genetic framework and predispose to CAD in an early phase.

References

[1] Squeri A. Coronary artery disease: new insights and novel approaches. BoD—Books on Demand; 2012. Available from: http://doi.org/10.5772/1168.
[2] McCullough PA. Coronary artery disease. Clin J Am Soc Nephrol 2007;2(3):611—16. Available from: https://doi.org/10.2215/CJN.03871106.
[3] Parmet S, Glass TJ, Glass RM. Coronary artery disease. JAMA 2004;292(20):2540. Available from: https://doi.org/10.1001/jama.292.20.2540.
[4] Hravnak M, Whittle J, Kelley ME, Sereika S, Good CB, Ibrahim SA, et al. Symptom expression in coronary heart disease and revascularization recommendations for black and white patients. Am J Public Health 2007;97(9):1701—8. Available from: https://doi.org/10.2105/AJPH.2005.084103.
[5] MÖlzer G, Stollberger C, Finsterer J, Krugluger W, Stanek G. Possible causes of symptoms in suspected coronary heart disease but normal angiograms. Clin Cardiol 2001;24(4):307—12. Available from: https://doi.org/10.1002/clc.4960240410.
[6] Hajar R. Risk factors for coronary artery disease: historical perspectives. Heart Views Off J Gulf Heart Assoc 2017;18(3):109. Available from: https://doi.org/10.4103/HEARTVIEWS.HEARTVIEWS_106_17.
[7] Mayen AL, Marques-Vidal P, Paccaud F, Bovet P, Stringhini S. Socioeconomic determinants of dietary patterns in low- and middle-income countries: a systematic review. Am J Clin Nutr 2014;100(6):1520—31. Available from: https://doi.org/10.3945/ajcn.114.089029.
[8] Jang Y, Lee JH, Kim OY, Park HY, Lee SY. Consumption of whole grain and legume powder reduces insulin demand, lipid peroxidation, and plasma homocysteine concentrations in patients with coronary artery disease: randomized controlled clinical trial. Arterioscler Thromb Vasc Biol 2001;21(12):2065—71. Available from: https://doi.org/10.1161/hq1201.100258.
[9] Shi L, Morrison JA, Wiecha J, Horton M, Hayman LL. Healthy lifestyle factors associated with reduced cardiometabolic risk. Br J Nutr 2011;105(5):747—54. Available from: https://doi.org/10.1017/S0007114510004307.
[10] Freund KM, Belanger AJ, D'Agostino RB, Kannel WB. The health risks of smoking. The Framingham study: 34 years of follow-up. Ann Epidemiol 1993;3(4):417—24. Available from: https://doi.org/10.1016/1047-2797(93)90070-k.
[11] Wah TY, Gopal Raj R, Iqbal U. Automated diagnosis of coronary artery disease: a review and workflow. Cardiol Res Pract 2018;2016282. Available from: https://doi.org/10.1155/2018/2016282.

[12] Shu T, Zhang B, Tang YY. Effective heart disease detection based on quantitative computerized traditional chinese medicine using representation based classifiers. Evidence-Based Compl Altern Med 2017;7483639. Available from: https://doi.org/10.1155/2017/7483639.

[13] Stangl V, Witzel V, Baumann G, Stangl K. Current diagnostic concepts to detect coronary artery disease in women. Eur Heart J 2008;29(6):707−17. Available from: https://doi.org/10.1093/eur-heartj/ehn047.

[14] Bullock-Palmer RP. Prevention, detection and management of coronary artery disease in minority females. Ethnicity Dis 2015;25(4):499. Available from: https://doi.org/10.18865/ed.25.4.499.

[15] Grundy SM, Balady GJ, Criqui MH, American Heart Association, et al. Primary prevention of coronary heart disease: guidance from Framingham: a statement for healthcare professionals from the AHA Task Force on Risk Reduction. Circulation 1998;97(18):1876−87. Available from: https://doi.org/10.1161/01.cir.97.18.1876.

[16] Bakris GL, Williams M, Dworkin L, National Kidney Foundation Hypertension and Diabetes Executive Committees Working Group, et al. Preserving renal function in adults with hypertension and diabetes: a consensus approach. Am J Kidney Dis 2000;36(3):646−61. Available from: https://doi.org/10.1053/ajkd.2000.16225.

[17] Stone NJ, Robinson J, Lichtenstein AH, et al. ACC/AHA guideline on the treatment of blood cholesterol to reduce atherosclerotic cardiovascular risk in adults: a report of the American College of Cardiology/American Heart Association Task Force on Practice Guidelines. J Am Coll Cardiol 2013;63(25 Pt B):2889−934. Available from: https://doi.org/10.1016/j.jacc.2013.11.002.

[18] Achari V, Thakur AK. Association of major modifiable risk factors among patients with coronary artery disease – a retrospective analysis. JAPI. 2004;52:103−8.

[19] Yakovleva L, Matuzok O, Kuznetsov I, et al. Factors associated with atherosclerosis expansion in patients with coronary artery disease. Int J Mol Med Sci 2014;4(3):27−32. Available from: https://doi.org/10.5376/ijmms.2014.04.0003.

[20] Sahin S, Ceyhan K, Benli I, et al. Traditional risk factors and angiotensin-converting enzyme insertion/deletion gene polymorphism in coronary artery disease. Genet Mol Res 2015;14(1).2063−8. Available from: https://doi.org/10.4238/2015.March.20.16.

[21] Liu D, Jiang Z, Dai L, Zhang X, Yan C, Han Y. Association between the−786T > C 1polymorphism in the promoter region of endothelial nitric oxide synthase (eNOS) and risk of coronary artery disease: a systematic review and meta-analysis. Gene 2014;545(1):175−83. Available from: https://doi.org/10.1016/j.gene.2013.09.099.

[22] Moradzadegan A, Vaisi-Raygani A, Nikzamir A, Rahimi Z. Angiotensin converting enzyme insertion/deletion (I/D) (rs4646994) and Vegf polymorphism (þ405G/C; rs2010963) in type II diabetic patients. association with the risk of coronary artery disease. J Renin Angiotensin Aldosterone Syst 2015;16(3):672−80. Available from: https://doi.org/10.1177/1470320313497819.

[23] Zhu X, Bouzekri N, Southam L, Cooper RS, Adeyemo A, McKenzie CA, et al. Linkage and association analysis of angiotensin I-converting enzyme (ACE)-gene polymorphisms with ACE concentration and blood pressure. Am J Hum Genet 2001;68(5):1139−48. Available from: https://doi.org/10.1086/320104.

[24] Sayed-Tabatabaei FA, Oostra BA, Isaacs A, van Duijn CM, Witteman JCM. ACE polymorphisms. Circ Res 2006;98:1123−33. Available from: https://doi.org/10.1161/01.RES.0000223145.74217.e7.

[25] Pfohl M, Koch M, Prescod S, Haase KK, Häring HU, Karsch KR. Angiotensin I-converting enzyme gene polymorphism, coronary artery disease and myocardial infarction. An angiographically controlled study. Eur Heart J 1999;20:1318−25. Available from: https://doi.org/10.1053/euhj.1999.1543.

[26] Hubert C, Houot AM, Corvol P, Soubrier F. Structure of the angiotensin I-converting enzyme gene. Two alternate promoters correspond to evolutionary steps of a duplicated gene. J Biol Chem 1991;266:15377−83. Available from: https://doi.org/10.1016/S0021-9258(18)98626-6.

[27] Vladeanu MC, Bojan IB, Bojan A, Iliescu D, Badescu MC, Badulescu OV, et al. Angiotensin-converting enzyme gene D-allele and the severity of coronary artery disease. Exp Therap Med 2020;20(4):3407−11. Available from: https://doi.org/10.3892/etm.2020.8978.

[28] Tiret L, Rigat B, Visvikis S, Breda C, Corvol P, Cambien F. Evidence, from combined segregation and linkage analysis, that a variant of the angiotensin I-converting enzyme (ACE) gene

controls plasma ACE levels. Am J Hum Genet 1992;51:197−205 PMID: 1319114; PMCID: PMC1682892.

[29] Mayer B, Schunkert H. ACE gene polymorphism and cardiovascular diseases. Herz 2000;25:1−6. Available from: https://doi.org/10.1007/bf03044118.

[30] Wollinger LM, Dal Bosco SM, Rempe C, Almeida SE, Berlese DB, Castoldi RP, et al. Role of ACE and AGT gene polymorphisms in genetic susceptibility to diabetes mellitus type 2 in a Brazilian sample. Genet Mol Res 2015;14(4):19110−16. Available from: https://doi.org/10.4238/2015.December.29.20.

[31] Firouzabadi N, Tajik N, Bahramali E, Bakhshandeh H, Maadani M, Shafiei M. Gender specificity of a genetic variant of angiotensin-converting enzyme and risk of coronary artery disease. Mol Biol Rep 2013;40(8):4959−65. Available from: https://doi.org/10.1007/s11033-013-2596-1.

[32] Meuwissen M, van der Wal AC, Siebes M, Koch KT, Chamuleau SA, van der Loos CM, et al. Role of plaque inflammation in acute and recurrent coronary syndromes. Neth Heart J 2004;12:106−9 PMID: 25696307; PMCID: PMC2497049.

[33] Slattery ML, Herrick JS, Torres-Mejia G, John EM, Giuliano AR, Hines LM, et al. Genetic variants in interleukin genes are associated with breast cancer risk and survival in a genetically admixed population: the Breast Cancer Health Disparities Study. Carcinogenesis 2014;35:1750−9. Available from: https://doi.org/10.1093/carcin/bgu078.

[34] Mallat Z, Besnard S, Duriez M, Deleuze V, Emmanuel F, Bureau MF, et al. Protective role of interleukin-10 in atherosclerosis. Circ Res 1999;85:e17−24. Available from: https://doi.org/10.1161/01.res.85.8.e17.

[35] Anguera I, Miranda-Guardiola F, Bosch X, Filella X, Sitges M, Marin JL, et al. Elevation of serum levels of the anti-inflam-matory cytokine interleukin-10 and decreased risk of coronary events in patients with unstable angina. Am Heart J 2002;144:811−17. Available from: https://doi.org/10.1067/mhj.2002.124831.

[36] Heeschen C, Dimmeler S, Hamm CW, Fichtlscherer S, Boersma E, Simoons ML, et al. Serum level of the antiinflammatory cytokine interleukin-10 is an important prognostic determinant in patients with acute coronary syndromes. Circulation 2003;107:2109−14. Available from: https://doi.org/10.1161/01.CIR.0000065232.57371.25.

[37] Koch W, Kastrati A, Bottiger C, Mehilli J, von Beckerath N, Schomig A. Interleukin-10 and tumor necrosis factor gene polymorphis-ms and risk of coronary artery disease and myocardial infarction. Atherosclerosis 2001;159:137−44. Available from: https://doi.org/10.1016/s0021-9150(01)00467-1.

[38] Fragoso JM, Vallejo M, Alvarez-Leon E, Delgadillo H, Pena-Duque MA, Cardoso-Saldana G, et al. Alleles and haplotypes of the interleukin 10 gene polymorphisms are associated with risk of developing acute coronary syndrome in Mexican patients. Cytokine 2011;55:29−33. Available from: https://doi.org/10.1016/j.cyto.2011.03.021.

[39] Rezayani S, Farazmandfar T, shahbazi M. Association assessment of platelet derived growth factor B gene polymorphism and its expression status with susceptibility to coronary artery disease. Egypt J Med Hum Genet 2017;18:359−63. Available from: https://doi.org/10.1016/j.ejmhg.2017.03.004.

[40] Benigni A, Cassis P, Remuzzi G. Angiotensin II revisited: new roles in inflammation, immunology and aging. EMBO Mol Med 2010;2:247−57. Available from: https://doi.org/10.1002/emmm.201000080.

[41] Sivitskaia LN, Kushnerevich EI, Danilenko NG, et al. Gene polymorphism of the renin-angiotensin system in six ethnic/geographic regions of Belarus. Genetika 2008;44:702−9. Available from: https://doi.org/10.1134/S1022795408050141.

[42] Tiret L, Ricard S, Poirier O, et al. Genetic variation at the angiotensinogen locus in relation to high blood pressure and myocardial infarction: the ECTIM Study. J Hypertens 1995;13:311−17 PMID: 7622852.

[43] Arthiya M, Bhavani S, Jenisha J, Sharmila D, Varghese S, Kulanthaivel L, et al. LDLR, MTHFR and KLOTHO gene polymorphisms as an early predictor in the risk of coronary artery disease: a *Meta*-analysis. Gene Rep 2021;23:101120. Available from: https://doi.org/10.1016/j.genrep.2021.101120.

[44] Ye H, Zhao Q, Huang Y, et al. *Meta*-analysis of low density lipoprotein receptor (LDLR) rs2228671 polymorphism and coronary heart disease. Biomed Res Int 2014;564940. Available from: https://doi.org/10.1155/2014/564940.

[45] Acarturk E, Attila G, Bozkurt A, Akpinar O, Matyar S, Seydaoglu G. Insertion/deletion polymorphism of the angiotensin converting enzyme gene in coronary artery disease in southern Turkey. BMB Rep 2005;38(4):486—90. Available from: https://doi.org/10.5483/bmbrep.2005.38.4.486.

[46] Niemiec P, Zak I, Wita K. Modification of the coronary artery disease risk associated with the presence of traditional risk factors by insertion/deletion polymorphism of the ACE gene. Genet Test 2007;11(4):353—60. Available from: https://doi.org/10.1089/gte.2007.0005.

[47] Freitas AI, Mendonça I, Brión M, Sequeira MM, Reis RP, Carracedo A, et al. RAS gene polymorphisms, classical risk factors and the advent of coronary artery disease in the Portuguese population. BMC Cardiovasc Disord 2008;8(1):1—2. Available from: https://doi.org/10.1186/1471-2261-8-15.

[48] Jamil K, Syed R, Rao H. Implications of I/D (rs4340) polymorphism in CAD among South Indian population. Int J Med Med Sci 2009;1(5):151—7. Available from: https://doi.org/10.5897/IJMMS.9000133.

[49] Ramakrishnan V, Jaikumar V, Kumar SG, Thiyagarajan G, Vincent S. Angiotensin-converting enzyme gene polymorphism in patients with coronary artery disease. J Adv Lab Res Biol 2010; 1(1):35—40.

[50] Poorgholi L, Saffar H, Fathollahi MS, Davoodi G, Anvari MS, Goodarzynejad H, et al. Angiotensin-converting enzyme insertion/deletion polymorphism and its association with coronary artery disease in an Iranian population. J Tehran Univ Heart Cent 2013;2:89 PMC3740114.

[51] Heidari MM, Hadadzadeh M, Fallahzadeh H. Development of one-step tetra-primer ARMS-PCR for simultaneous detection of the angiotensin converting enzyme (ACE) I/D and rs4343 gene polymorphisms and the correlation with CAD patients. Avicenna J Med Biotechnol 2019;11(1):118 PMCID: PMC6359703.

[52] Donger C, Georges JL, Nicaud V, Morrison C, Evans A, Kee F, et al. New polymorphisms in the interleukin-10 gene—relationships to myocardial infarction. Eur J Clin Invest 2001;31:9—14. Available from: https://doi.org/10.1046/j.1365-2362.2001.00754.x.

[53] Lio D, Candore G, Crivello A, Scola L, Colonna-Romano G, Cavallone L, et al. Opposite effects of inter leukin 10 common gene polymorphisms in car-diovascular diseases and in successful ageing: genetic background of male centenarians is protective against coronary heart disease. J Med Genet 2004;41:790—4. Available from: https://doi.org/10.1136/jmg.2004.019885.

[54] O'Halloran AM, Stanton A, O'Brien E, Sh-ields DC. The impact on coronary artery disease of common polymorphisms known to modulate responses to pathogens. Ann Hum Genet 2006;70:934—45. Available from: https://doi.org/10.1111/j.1469-1809.2006.00281.x.

[55] Chen J, Sun ZQ, Xia JH, Xu L. Relationship between polymorphism of IL-10—1082 gene and coronary atherosclerotic heart diseases. Acta Med Univ Sci Technol Huazhong 2007;36:614 16.

[56] Lorenzova A, Stanek V, Gebauerova M, Bohuslavova R, Stavek P, Hubacek JA, et al. High-sensitivity C-reactive protein concentration in patients with myocardial infarction-environmental factors, and polymorphisms in interleukin-10 and CD14 genes. Clin Chem Lab Med 2007;45:855—61. Available from: https://doi.org/10.1515/CCLM.2007.157.

[57] Ben-Hadj-Khalifa S, Ghazouani L, Abboud N, Ben-Khalfallah A, Annabi F, Addad F, et al. Functional interleukin-10 promoter variants in coronary artery disease patients in Tunisia. Eur Cytokine Netw 2010;21:136—41. Available from: https://doi.org/10.1684/ecn.2010.0194.

[58] Karaca E, Kayikcioglu M, Onay H, Gunduz C, Ozkinay F. The effect of interleukin-10 gene promoter polymorphisms on early-onset coronary artery disease. Anadolu Kardiyol Derg 2011;11:285—9. Available from: https://doi.org/10.5152/akd.2011.077.

[59] Yu GI, Cho HC, Cho YK, Park HS, Yoon HJ, Kim HS, et al. Association of promoter region single nucleotide polymorphisms at positions -819C/T and -592C/A of interleukin 10 gene with ischemic heart disease. Inflamm Res 2012;61:899—905. Available from: https://doi.org/10.1007/s00011-012-0482-2.

[60] Babu B, Reddy BP, Priya VHS, Munshi A, Rani HS, Latha GS, et al. Cytokine gene polymorphisms in the susceptibility to acute coronary syndrome. Genet Test Mol Biomarkers 2012;16:359—65. Available from: https://doi.org/10.1089/gtmb.2011.0182.

[61] Afzal MS, Anjum S, Farooqi ZUR, Noreen M, Safi SZ, Ashraf M, et al. Influence of IL-10 polymorphism on the development of coronary artery disease in Pakistan. Asian Biomed. 2012;6:159—65. Available from: https://doi.org/10.5372/1905-7415.0602.042.

[62] Ianni M, Callegari S, Rizzo A, Pastori P, Moruzzi P, Corradi D, et al. Pro-inflammatory genetic profile and familiarity of acute myocardial infarction. Immun Ageing 2012;9:14. Available from: https://doi.org/10.1186/1742-4933-9-14.

[63] Cruz M, Fragoso JM, Alvarez-Leon E, Escobedo-de-la-Pena J, Valladares A, Juarez-Cedillo T, et al. The TGF-B1 and IL-10 gene polymorphisms are associated with risk of developing silent myocardial ischemia in the diabetic patients. Immunol Lett 2013;156:18—22. Available from: https://doi.org/10.1016/j.imlet.2013.09.007.

[64] Elsaid A, Abdel-Aziz AF, Elmougy R, Elwaseef AM. Association of polymorphisms G(-174)C in IL-6 gene and G(-1082)A in IL-10 gene with traditional cardiovascular risk factors in patients with coronary artery disease. Indian J Biochem Biophys 2014;51:282—92 PMID: 25296499.

[65] Qian ZH, Ni Y, Li YF, Shi LZ, Jiang J, Yan LL. Association between interleukin-10 gene 1082G/A polymorphism and acute coronary syndrome. Chin Heart J 2014;26:693—6.

[66] Ren B, She Q. Study on the association between IL-1β, IL-8 and IL-10 gene polymorphisms and risk of coronary artery disease. Int J Clin Exp Med 2015;8(5):7937 PMCID: PMC4509296.

[67] Xu HM, Liu YR. Role of interleukin-10 gene polymorphisms in the development of coronary artery disease in Chinese population. Genet Mol Res 2015;14(4):15869—75. Available from: https://doi.org/10.4238/2015.December.1.38.

[68] Mousavi SZ, Salehi A, Jorjani E, Manzari RS, Farazmandfar T, Shahbazi M. Association assessment of Interleukine-10 gene polymorphism and its expression status with susceptibility to coronary artery disease in Iran. Egypt J Med Hum Genet 2018;19(1):31—5. Available from: https://doi.org/10.1016/j.ejmhg.2017.06.005.

[69] Menshed AA, Hasan RK, Ali LH. Determination of the gene polymorphisms of tumor necrosis factor-alpha and interleukin-10 in coronary artery disease patients in Iraq. Nano Biomed Eng 2020;12(2):178—83. Available from: https://doi.org/10.5101/nbe.v12i2.p178-183.

[70] Fatini C, Abbate R, Pepe G, et al. Searching for a better as-sessment of the individual coronary risk profile: the role of angiotensin-converting enzyme, angiotensin II type 1 receptor and angiotensinogen gene polymorphisms. Eur Heart J 2000;21:633—8. Available from: https://doi.org/10.1053/euhj.1999.1738.

[71] Spiridonova MG, Stepanov VA, Puzyrev VP, et al. Associa-tion between polymorphism T174M of the angiotensinogen gene and coronary atherosclerosis in the Tomsk population. Mol Biol 2001;35:11—14. Available from: https://doi.org/10.1023/A:1004838431446.

[72] Babunova NB, Minushkina LO, Zateishchikov DA, et al. Association of the T174M and M235T polymorphisms of the angiotensinogen gene with coronary heart disease in ethnic Russians from Moscow. Mol Biol 2003;37:52—5. Available from: https://doi.org/10.1023/A:1022328712292.

[73] Nair KG, Shalia KK, Ashavaid TF, et al. Coronary heart disease, hypertension, and angiotensinogen gene variants in In-dian population. J Clin Lab Anal 2003;17:141—6. Available from: https://doi.org/10.1002/jcla.10084.

[74] Zhang AP, Ning SC, Li ZQ, et al. Polymorphism of angio-tensinogen gene is associated with myocardial infarction in Chinese Han population. J Fourth Mil Med Univ 2005;26:729—31.

[75] Renner W, Nauck M, Winkelmann BR, et al. Association of angiotensinogen haplotypes with angiotensinogen levels but not with blood pressure or coronary artery disease: the Ludwigshafen Risk and Cardiovascular Health Study. J Mol Med (Berl) 2005;83:235—9. Available from: https://doi.org/10.1007/s00109-004-0618-0.

[76] Tsai CT, Hwang JJ, Ritchie MD, et al. Renin-angiotensin system gene polymorphisms and coronary artery disease in a large angiographic cohort: detection of high order gene-gene interaction. Atherosclerosis 2007;195:172—80. Available from: https://doi.org/10.1016/j.atherosclerosis.2006.09.014.

[77] Freitas AI, Mendonça I, Brión M, et al. RAS gene polymor-phisms, classical risk factors and the advent of coronary artery disease in the Portuguese population. BMC Cardiovasc Dis-ord 2008;8:15. Available from: https://doi.org/10.1186/1471-2261-8-15.

[78] Abboud N, Ghazouani L, Kaabi B, et al. Evaluation of the contribution of renin angiotensin system polymorphisms to the risk of coronary artery disease among Tunisians. Genet Test Mol Biomarkers 2010;14:661—6. Available from: https://doi.org/10.1089/gtmb.2010.0070.

[79] Konopka A, Szperl M, Piotrowski W, et al. Influence of renin-angiotensin system gene polymorphisms on the risk of ST-segment-elevation myocardial infarction and association with coronary artery

disease risk factors. Mol Diagn Ther 2011;15:167—76. Available from: https://doi.org/10.1007/BF03256407.

[80] Khatami M, Heidari MM, Hadadzadeh M, Scheiber-Mojdehkar B, Sani MB, Houshmand M. Simultaneous genotyping of the rs4762 and rs699 polymorphisms in angiotensinogen gene and correlation with Iranian CAD patients with novel Hexa-primer ARMS-PCR. Iran J Public Health 2017;46(6):811 PMCID: PMC5558075.

[81] Azova M, Timizheva K, Ait Aissa A, Blagonravov M, Gigani O, Aghajanyan A, et al. Gene polymorphisms of the renin-angiotensin-aldosterone system as risk factors for the development of instent restenosis in patients with stable coronary artery disease. Biomolecules 2021;11(5):763. Available from: https://doi.org/10.3390/biom11050763.

[82] Garg A. Low prevalence of mutations in known loci for autosomal dominant hypercholesterolemia in a multi-ethnic patient cohort. Circ Cardiovasc Genet 2012;5(6):666—75. Available from: https://doi.org/10.1161/CIRCGENETICS.112.963587.

[83] Roncaglioni MC, Santoro L, D'Avanzo B, Negri E, Nobili A, Ledda A, et al. Role of family history in patients with myocardial infarction: an Italian case-control study. GISSIEFRIM Investigators. Circulation 1992;85:2065—72. Available from: https://doi.org/10.1161/01.cir.85.6.2065.

[84] Vargas-Alarcon G, Zamora J, Sanchez-Garcia S, Rodriguez-Perez JM, Cardoso G, Posadas-Romero C. Angiotensin-I-converting enzyme (ACE) insertion/deletion polymorphism in Mexican patients with coronary artery disease. Association with the disease but not with lipid levels. Exp Mol Pathol 2006;81(2):131—5. Available from: https://doi.org/10.1016/j.yexmp.2006.04.001.

[85] Bouzekri N, Zhu X, Jiang Y, McKenzie CA, Luke A, Forrester T, et al. Angiotensin I-converting enzyme polymorphisms, ACE level and blood pressure among Nigerians, Jamaicans and African-Americans. Eur J Hum Genet 2004;12(6):460—8. Available from: https://doi.org/10.1038/sj.ejhg.5201166.

[86] Wang BJ, Liu J, Geng J, Zhang Q, Hu TT, Xu B. Association between three interleukin-10 gene polymorphisms and coronary artery disease risk: a *meta*-analysis. Int J Clin Exp Med 2015;8(10):17842 PMC4694279.

[87] Xu HM, Liu YR. Role of interleukin-10 gene polymorphisms in the development of coronary artery disease in Chinese population. Genet Mol Res 2015;14(4):15869—75. Available from: https://doi.org/10.4238/2015.December.1.38.

[88] Wang WZ. Association between T174M polymorphism in the angiotensinogen gene and risk of coronary artery disease: a *meta*-analysis. J Geriatric Cardiol 2013;10(1):59. Available from: https://doi.org/10.3969/j.issn.1671-5411.2013.01.010.

[89] Jeunemaitre X. Genetics of the human renin angiotensin system. J Mol Med 2008;86:637—41. Available from: https://doi.org/10.1007/s00109-008-0344-0.

[90] Nakajima T, Inoue I, Cheng T, Lalouel JM. Molecular cloning and functional analysis of a factor that binds to the proximal promoter of human angiotensinogen. J Hum Genet 2002;47:7—13. Available from: https://doi.org/10.1007/s10038-002-8649-2.

[91] Ismail S, Essawi M. Genetic polymorphism studies in humans. Middle East J Med Genet 2012;1(2):57—63. Available from: https://doi.org/10.5772/intechopen.79517.

[92] Rothberg JM, Hinz W, Rearick TM, Schultz J, Mileski W, Davey M, et al. An integrated semiconductor device enabling non-optical genome sequencing. Nature 2011;475(7356):348—52. Available from: https://doi.org/10.1038/nature10242.

[93] Rao SR, Trivedi S, Emmanuel D, Merita K, Hynniewta M. DNA repetitive sequences-types, distribution and function: a review. J Cell Mol Biol 2010;7(2):1 ISSN 1303—3646.

CHAPTER 14

Role of optical coherence tomography in borderline coronary lesions

Jit Brahmbhatt, Roopesh Singhal and Zeeshan Mansuri
Department of Cardiology, SBKS Medical College & Research Center, Piparia, India

14.1 Introduction

Although coronary angiography is the mainstay imaging modality to assess the presence, extent, and severity of CAD, and to guide PCI procedures, intravascular imaging has played a fundamental role during PCI maturation and evolution. Visual estimation of the two-dimensional silhouette of the contrast-filled luminogram may be insufficient for accurate diagnosis of CAD severity and extension. By providing higher-resolution tomographic images of the entire circumference of the vessel wall, intracoronary imaging may overcome these limitations. In the mid-1990s Colombo et al. [1] demonstrated after intravascular ultrasound (IVUS)-guided high-pressure balloon post dilatation, full expansion and complete stent apposition were achieved in 96% of the patients. This strategy resulted in very low rates of acute (0.6%) and subacute (0.3%) stent thrombosis, eliminating the need for systemic anticoagulants, and consolidating the widespread use of coronary stents for the percutaneous treatment of CAD in the years to come.

More recently introduced optical coherence tomography (OCT) uses near-infrared light to generate cross-sectional images of the coronary arteries. Near-infrared light has a shorter wavelength and higher frequency than ultrasound, thus providing images with 10-fold higher resolution than those provided by IVUS. The faster and safe acquisition of longitudinal sequences of sharp and detailed images, along with ease of use and interpretation, leverages OCT as an attractive imaging modality with the potential to guide and optimize PCI, which ultimately may translate into improved clinical outcomes.

14.2 Physics of optical coherence tomography

The science behind OCT is analogous to pulse-echo ultrasound imaging, but light is used rather than sound to create the image [2]. Although ultrasound produces images from backscattered (reflected) sound "echoes," OCT uses infrared light waves (approximately 1300 nm wavelength) that reflect off the internal microstructure within the biological tissues. Time delay between emission and receipt of the light is used to generate spatial image information, the intensity of the received (reflected or backscattered) light is translated into a color scale. As the speed of light is much faster than that of sound, an interferometer is required to measure the backscattered light. The interferometer splits the light source into two "arms," a reference arm and a sample arm, which is directed into the tissue. The light from both arms is recombined at a detector, which registers the so-called interferogram, the sum of reference and sample arm fields. This interferogram is then processed to result into an image.

Time-domain OCT—First-generation OCT used for intracoronary imaging employed "time-domain" technology. Relatively slow data acquisition and the need to clear the artery from blood during image acquisition resulted in a complex imaging procedure, which limited its use.

Fourier-domain OCT—Since 2008, a new generation of OCT systems (also called Fourier domain OCT systems) have been available for widespread clinical use. With these systems, the interferogram is detected as a function of wavelength, either by using a broadband source as in the time domain systems, and spectrally resolved detection, or by incorporating a novel wavelength-swept laser source. This latter technique is also called "swept-source OCT," or optical frequency domain imaging [3,4]. From the signal received in one wavelength sweep, the depth profile can be constructed by the Fourier transform operation. Most signals can be thought of as a summation of sine waves with different frequencies. The Fourier transform extracts those frequencies, and their relative weights, from the signal. The source wavelength in Fourier-domain OCT can be swept at a much higher rate than the position scan of the reference arm mirror in a time-domain OCT system. This development has led to faster image acquisition speeds, with greater penetration depth, without loss of vital detail or resolution, and represents a great advancement on current conventional OCT systems. Coronary arteries can be imaged with high OCT catheter pullback speeds within seconds, which allows for widespread clinical use in a broad range of patients and lesions [5].

Since both the bandwidth of infrared light used and wave velocity are orders of magnitude higher than in medical ultrasound, the resulting resolution is one order of magnitude larger than that of IVUS: The axial resolution of OCT is about 15 μm; the lateral resolution is approximately 25 μm. However, the imaging depth of approximately 1−1.5 mm within the coronary artery wall is less than that of IVUS.

14.3 Imaging technique

OCT imaging catheters contain an OCT imaging core at their distal tip (Fig. 14.1). Similar to IVUS, the imaging core is oriented at a 90-degree angle to the length of the catheter; and is rotated during imaging. As a result, OCT images are displayed similar to IVUS as cross-sectional views of the coronary artery. Automated pullback of the OCT imaging core allows the user to scan through the coronary artery.

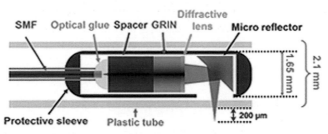

Figure 14.1 Schema showing mechanical details of OCT catheter tip. *OCT*, Optical coherence tomography.

Intracoronary OCT is performed by introducing the small imaging catheter over a guide wire distally into the coronary artery using standard guide catheters (6 F or larger). A motorized pullback is performed to scan the coronary artery segment. The pullback speed is typically 20 mm/s with a frame rate of 100 frames per second or higher. Since blood scatters the OCT signal, it is temporarily cleared by an injection of radiograph contrast medium during the duration of the OCT pullback (typical flush rate 3.0 mL/s). A variety of solutions, warmed to 37°C have been used alternatively as flush medium, including ringer's lactate, viscous isoosmolar contrast media, and low-molecular-weight dextrose. The time needed to image a 50 mm artery segment is typically 3 seconds with a total volume of radiograph contrast of 10−12 mL, which is comparable to the amount of radiograph contrast needed for a single angiographic run.

All epicardial coronary arteries and venous or arterial grafts that are accessible by a guiding catheter are eligible for OCT imaging. OCT should not be performed in patients with severely impaired left ventricular function or those presenting with severe hemodynamic compromise, as the imaging procedure might induce brief ischemia. Furthermore, OCT should be used with caution in patients with single remaining vessel, as any guide wire or catheter insertion carries a small risk of dissection or arterial spasm, or those with markedly impaired renal function. In these clinical circumstances, the gain in diagnostic accuracy must be balanced against potential adverse effects in individual patients.

A technical drawback is that plaques located at the very ostium of the left or right coronaries cannot be accurately addressed by OCT, as it is difficult to clear the artery from blood during a nonselective guide catheter position, required for the visualization of the ostium.

The principle safety considerations relate to the possible induction of ischemia due to the need of blood displacement for image acquisition. Current OCT systems allow for very fast data within a few seconds and therefore are unlikely to lead to significant ischemia. In a report of 114 OCT acquisitions in 90 patients, the procedure was successful in 89 [6]. No patients suffered contrast-induced nephropathy and no major complications were recorded. One patient had a transient vessel spasm that was resolved with intracoronary administration of nitrates. During frequency-domain OCT images acquisition no ischemic electrocardiographic changes were occurred. Ventricular ectopic beats were found only in three patients while other major arrhythmias (ventricular tachycardia or fibrillation) were not observed.

14.4 Optical coherence tomography image

OCT creates cross-sectional images of the coronary artery wall, as a result, the normal coronary artery wall appears as a circular structure with three concentric layers at OCT images (Fig. 14.2). The innermost signal-rich layer reflects the internal elastic membrane, the middle dark layer represents the media, and the outer, signal-rich layer represents the external elastic lamina [7,8].

A normal three-layer appearance by OCT is not synonymous to three-layer appearance by IVUS. While OCT (resolution approximately 15 μm) is able to visualize a normal, nondiseased coronary artery, the resolution of IVUS (approximately 120 μm) is not able to visualize truly nondiseased vessels. Thus, OCT can confirm the absence of significant atherosclerosis or indicate the degree of subclinical atherosclerotic lesion formation. Serial measurements can be performed to monitor the structural changes that occur in the vessel wall over time.

Atherosclerotic plaques—OCT has the ability to characterize the structure and extent of coronary artery disease in greater detail than IVUS or angioscopy (Fig. 14.3). Compared to IVUS, OCT has a higher accuracy to detect early atherosclerosis, necrotic core or lipid-rich tissues, thrombi, and allows for visualization of calcifications

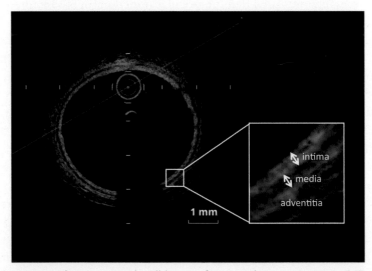

Figure 14.2 OCT image showing vessel wall layers of a normal coronary artery. *OCT*, Optical coherence tomography.

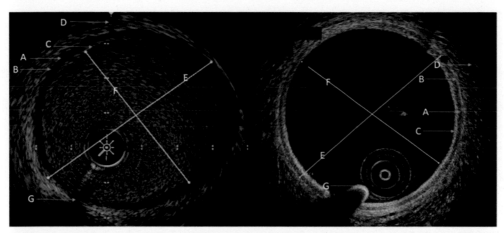

Figure 14.3 Intracoronary image comparison of IVUS and OCT. *OCT*, Optical coherence tomography; *IVUS*, intravascular ultrasound.

without blooming artifact, which typically causes overestimation of the calcium extent by IVUS [9,10].

When atherosclerotic lesions are present, OCT can provide details on the tissue composition. The following classifications have been used and validated:

- Fibrous plaques are typically rich in collagen or muscle cells and have a homogeneous OCT signal. Calcifications within plaques are identified by the presence of well-delineated, low backscattering, signal-poor heterogeneous regions (Fig. 14.4).
- Necrotic cores or lipid-rich tissues are less well-delineated than calcifications, appearing as diffusely bordered, signal-poor regions with overlying signal-rich bands, corresponding to fibrous caps. The superiority of OCT for lipid rich plaque detection has been confirmed in other studies comparing OCT, IVUS and IVUS-derived techniques for plaque composition analysis. A specific type of plaque is called thin-cap fibroatheroma (TCFA). Thin fibrous cap atheroma is considered the most important morphologic substrate for a plaque at high risk of rupture and causing acute coronary syndrome. OCT allows the diagnosis of thin fibrous cap atheroma with a sensitivity of 90% and a specificity of 79% when compared to histopathology [11] and for accurate measurement of the fibrous cap thickness with low variability [12,13]. Ongoing research suggests that the ability of OCT to measure changes in the fibrous cap thickness could be used to monitor the effect of therapeutic agents aiming at plaque stabilization. Exploratory registries evaluating the fibrous cap thickness in patients on statin therapy suggest a trend toward an increased cap thickness [14] and lower incidence of plaque rupture under statin therapy [15]. Such data, however, need to be confirmed by adequately powered, prospective studies.

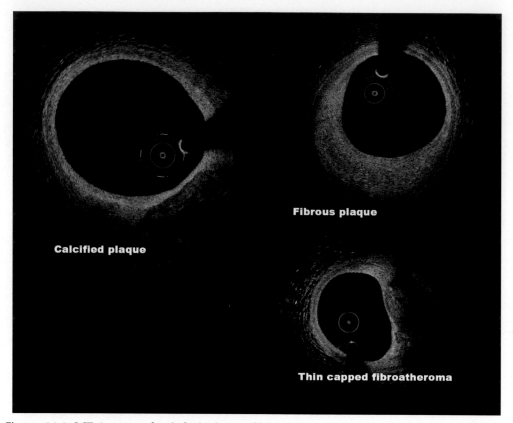

Figure 14.4 OCT images of calcified plaque, fibrous plague, and thin capped fibroatheroma, respectively. *OCT*, Optical coherence tomography.

- Thrombi are identified as masses protruding into the vessel lumen discontinuous from the surface of the vessel wall. Red thrombi (Fig. 14.5) consist mainly of red blood cells; relevant OCT images are characterized as high-backscattering protrusions with signal-free shadowing. White thrombi (Fig. 14.6) consist mainly of platelets and white blood cells and are characterized by a signal-rich, low-backscattering billowing projection protruding into the lumen [12]. OCT is highly sensitive in diagnosing intracoronary thrombi, as the high contrast between the lumen and the surrounding structures facilitates the diagnosis. This is in contrast to IVUS where it is often difficult to differentiate thrombi from the blood-filled lumen.
- Neoatherosclerosis (Fig. 14.7): Less well-validated entities are local macrophage accumulations and neovascularization. Macrophages can be seen by OCT as signal-rich, distinct, or confluent punctate dots that exceed the intensity of background speckle noise [16]. They may be seen at the boundary between the bottom of the cap and the top of a necrotic core. Likewise, experts believe that the visualization

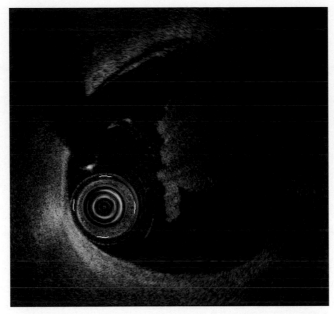

Figure 14.5 OCT acquisition of red thrombus. *OCT*, Optical coherence tomography.

Figure 14.6 OCT acquisition of white thrombus. *OCT*, Optical coherence tomography.

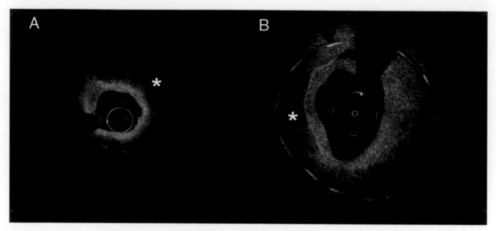

Figure 14.7 Classic visualization of lipid-rich neoatherosclerosis in a restenotic tissue.

of vasa vasorum and neovascularization is possible; however, no substantial validation studies have been published. Neovascularization within the intima appears as
signal poor voids that are sharply delineated and usually contiguous and seen on
multiple frames [17].

14.5 Optical coherence tomography versus intravascular ultrasound

An attempt was made to understand the role of OCT in patients undergoing PCI in
the ILUMIEN III: OPTIMIZE PCI trial [18], which randomly assigned patients with
native coronary artery lesions to OCT guidance, IVUS guidance, or coronary
angiography-guided stent implantations. The primary efficacy endpoint was post–PCI
minimum stent area (measured by OCT at a masked independent core laboratory at
the completion of enrollment) in all patients and the primary safety endpoint was procedural major adverse procedural complications. The study demonstrated that post–
PCI minimum stent area by OCT guidance was noninferior to IVUS. Neither IVUS
nor OCT was superior to angiography-guided PCI. Major complications were 3% or
less in the three groups.

14.6 Optical coherence tomography in borderline lesions
14.6.1 ACS with unclear culprit

The optimal management of acute coronary syndromes usually relies on rapid treatment of the culprit vessel. The culprit vessel is sometimes indicated by the localization
of the pathognomonic electrocardiographic changes or by the finding of a thrombotic,
hazy lesion by angiography. However, the identification of the culprit lesion can be

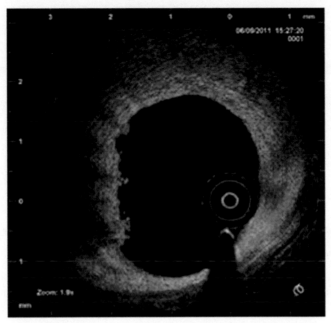

Figure 14.8 OCT image depicting a ruptured vulnerable plaque. *OCT*, Optical coherence tomography.

challenging in some individuals, especially when multivessel disease is present. Similarly, in 15% of the patients undergoing primary PCI for ST elevation myocardial infarction, angiography shows a patent infarct-related vessel with TIMI 3 flow [19]. OCT can provide accurate information on the superficial composition of the plaque, can identify ruptured plaques, and most importantly can reveal thrombosed lesions, and thus identify the culprit lesion (Fig. 14.8).

14.6.2 Functional significance of stenosis

The first step in the planning strategy starts with identifying the stenosis that will benefit from revascularization. Having in mind the measurement differences between IVUS and OCT, clinicians should refrain from applying IVUS-derived parameters to define coronary stenosis severity to OCT studies.

Over the years, it became common practice to use anatomic parameters derived from IVUS to estimate the functional significance of angiographically intermediate (40%—70%) coronary stenoses. A variety of observational studies validated IVUS-derived parameters against invasive and noninvasive tests for the assessment of lesion severity. However, low sensitivities (66.3%—92%), specificities (56%—92%), and positive predictive values (27%—67%), as well as poor accuracy (64%—72%) limit the clinical application of such parameters for predicting the physiological significance of coronary stenoses.

Due to more accurate and reproducible lumen quantification, it was expected that OCT could provide better diagnostic efficiency in identifying hemodynamically severe coronary stenoses. Following six studies have compared OCT-derived parameters with fractional flow reserve (FFR) for intermediate lesion assessment [10,20–24].

	N	FFR cutoff	MLA cutoff	AUC	Sensitivity (%)	Specificity (%)	PPV (%)	NPV (%)	Accuracy (%)
Gonzalo et al. [10]	61	0.80	1.95	0.74	82	63	66	80	72
Shiono et al. [23]	62	0.75	1.91	0.90	93.5	77.4	80.6	92.3	85.4
Reith et al. [20]	62	0.80	1.59	0.81	75.8	79.3	80.6	74.2	77.4
Pawlowski et al. [24]	71	0.80	2.05	0.91	75	90	70.6	92.6	87
Pyxaras et al. [22]	55	0.80	2.88	0.78	73	71	N/A	N/A	72
Reith et al. [20]	142 (all lesions)	0.80	1.64	0.83	78.8	75.8	80.8	73.4	N/A
	80 (diabetics)	0.80	1.59	0.84	76.6	78.8	83.7	70.3	N/A
	62 (nondiabetics)	0.80	1.64	0.83	78.8	75.9	78.8	75.9	N/A

As expected, the MLA cutoff values that better predicted an FFR of <0.80 were significantly smaller than those traditionally used for IVUS, ranging from 1.59 to $2.88\,mm^2$. Although OCT slightly improved sensitivity (75%–93.5%), specificity (63%–90%), and positive predictive value (66%–80.6%) in comparison with previous IVUS data, this intravascular imaging showed only moderate efficiency to determine functionally significant lesions, with accuracy ranging from 72% to 87%. These data reinforce the low specificities of intravascular anatomic metrics to predict functionally significant stenosis, precluding the routine use of intravascular imaging tools as substitutes for functional evaluation for decision making of intermediate angiographic stenoses.

14.6.3 Vulnerable plaque

OCT also allows precise identification and quantification of high-risk features associated with plaque instability and vulnerability, such as the presence of lipid and its longitudinal and circumferential distribution, the quantification of fibrous cap thickness (an important predictor of plaque rupture) [12,13], and macrophage infiltration (a marker of intraplaque inflammation) [16,25] (Fig. 14.9). OCT studies have shown that patients presenting with ST-elevation myocardial infarction (STEMI) had significantly thinner fibrous caps protecting the lipid or necrotic core than patients presenting with non- ST-elevation myocardial infarction (NSTEMI) or stable angina [26,27]. Fibrous cap thickness was thinner in patients presenting with resting angina in comparison with those presenting with exercise-induced angina [14]. TCFA, plaque rupture, and red thrombus are more

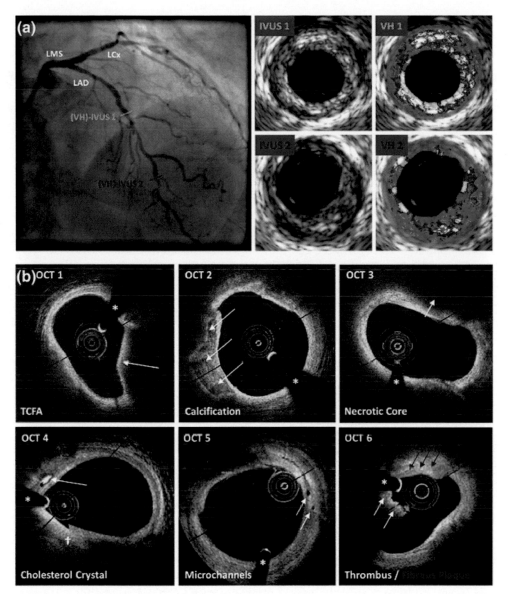

Figure 14.9 Image comparison of IVUS, radiofrequency IVUS, and OCT in various lesion-like TCFA, calcific lesion, necrotic core, lipid-rich plaque. *OCT*, Optical coherence tomography; *IVUS*, intravascular ultrasound; *TCFA*, thin-cap fibroatheroma.

frequent in STEMI patients than in NSTEMI and stable CAD patients [27]. ACS patients presenting with preserved protective fibrous caps were shown to have better prognoses than those presenting with plaque rupture [36]. When plaque rupture is present, it has been shown that a "proximal-type" rupture of the fibrous cap is more often seen in STEMI patients, while "distal-type" apertures are more frequent in patients with NSTEMI [27]. Detailed qualitative and morphometric assessments of atherosclerotic plaques, in combination with quantitative measures, provide important pathophysiological and prognostic information that may be of value during the clinical decision-making process and may assist physicians in individualizing management. TCFA, as determined by OCT, has been identified as a predictor for periprocedural complications. In a study by Tanaka et al. [14], the presence of lipid-rich plaques with an overlying fibrous cap thickness of ≤ 65 μm was identified as an independent predictor of no reflow after successful stenting in patients with NSTE ACS. The frequency of no reflow increased significantly, and the final thrombolysis in myocardial infarction myocardial blush grade deteriorated according to the amplitude of the lipid arc in the culprit plaque [28]. In a study of 115 ACS patients successfully treated with stenting, culprit lesions were classified into three groups according to the pre-PCI findings: (1) ruptured plaque ($n = 59$), (2) nonruptured TCFA ($n = 21$), and (3) nonruptured, non-TCFA ($n = 35$). Nonruptured TCFAs (43%) were significantly more often associated with microvascular obstruction as determined by cardiac contrast-enhanced magnetic resonance imaging than ruptured plaques (27%) and nonruptured, non-TCFA plaques (9%). Interestingly, the prevalence of microvascular obstruction increased as the fibrous cap thickness decreased [29]. Following the same pathophysiological principles, TCFA was also identified as an independent predictor for type IVa (periprocedural) MI [30,31]. Lastly, the presence of TCFA at the stent landing zone is responsible for a sixfold increase in the risk of having a stent edge dissection [32].

14.6.4 MI with no obstructive coronary atherosclerosis

MI with no obstructive coronary atherosclerosis (MINOCA) is a distinct clinical syndrome characterized by evidence of MI with normal or near-normal coronary arteries on angiography (stenosis severity $\leq 50\%$) in the absence of obvious noncoronary causes of MI like a severe hemorrhage or severe respiratory failure [33]. Aside from coronary angiography and assessment of LV wall motion, the following tests may be useful for elucidating the cause of MINOCA: OCT or IVUS; acetylcholine (Ach) or ergonovine challenge; cardiac magnetic resonance imaging with contrast material (CMR/CM); endomyocardial biopsy; contrast-enhanced echocardiography and transesophageal echocardiography; and testing for markers of thrombophilia (e.g., protein C and S deficiency, as well as enhanced Factor VII activity). The sequence in which these tests are performed depends on the likelihood of the cause based on the history and evaluation of LV wall motion (Fig. 14.10).

If coronary angiography is abnormal but reveals less than 50% luminal obstruction and/or nonocclusive thrombus, we often perform IVUS or OCT to identify subcritical plaque fissure or erosion and thrombus or spontaneous coronary artery dissection

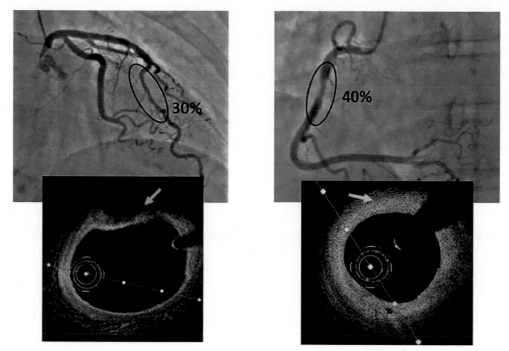

Figure 14.10 Relevance of OCT in strategy making of borderline coronary lesions. *OCT*, Optical coherence tomography.

(SCAD). These studies are performed before the patient is discharged from the catheterization laboratory.

14.6.5 Spontaneous coronary artery dissection

SCAD is a nontraumatic and noniatrogenic separation of the coronary arterial wall and is an infrequent cause of acute myocardial infarction. It is more common in younger patients and in women. Criteria for the angiographic definition include the presence of a noniatrogenic dissection plane in the absence of coronary atherosclerosis, with typical changes of radiolucent intimal flap and contrast staining [34,35]. However, a contemporary angiographic series has shown that such stereotypical changes were seen in only <30% of nonatherosclerotic SCAD cases. The majority of SCAD had long and diffuse narrowing on angiography due to intramural hematoma, and this appearance was frequently unrecognized on angiography leading to under-diagnosis of this condition. Imaging with OCT or IVUS may be helpful (Fig. 14.11). With these imaging modalities, SCAD diagnosis is made with the presence of intramural hematoma and/or a double lumen. Alternatively, repeat coronary angiography may be pursued 4—6 weeks later to evaluate for spontaneous angiographic healing of the dissected segment, if the diagnosis is uncertain.

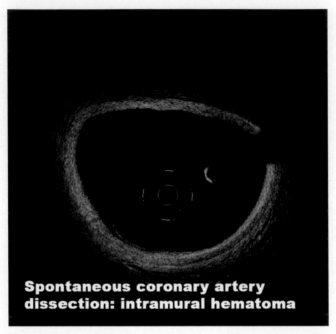

Figure 14.11 Classical OCT image of SCAD. *OCT*, Optical coherence tomography; *SCAD*, spontaneous coronary artery dissection.

14.6.6 Transplant vasculopathy

Although coronary angiography is the clinical gold standard for the diagnosis of nontransplant coronary artery disease, it is less sensitive in detecting transplant vasculopathy, as acknowledged in the ISHLT consensus document [36–39]. The lower sensitivity of angiography for CAV is due to the often diffuse, longitudinal, and concentric nature of the disease, as opposed to the focal and eccentric pattern of nontransplant atherosclerosis. IVUS is suggested when angiographic findings seem insufficient to explain left ventricular dysfunction. IVUS is used mainly in two settings: Some centers perform an IVUS exam early after transplantation (typically at the 1-year mark) and risk-stratify patients based on the findings. Other centers perform IVUS both a few weeks after transplantation and after 1 year, thus enabling discrimination between donor-transmitted disease and true transplant vasculopathy.

IVUS is performed in patients with graft failure when endomyocardial biopsy lacks clear signs of rejection and conventional angiography does not show evidence of CAV. In these cases, demonstration of significant intimal thickening on IVUS is required to confirm a diagnosis of CAV.

Clear consensus on the diagnostic criteria for CAV using IVUS has not been reached. However, most apply the criterion used in clinical trials, which is an increase

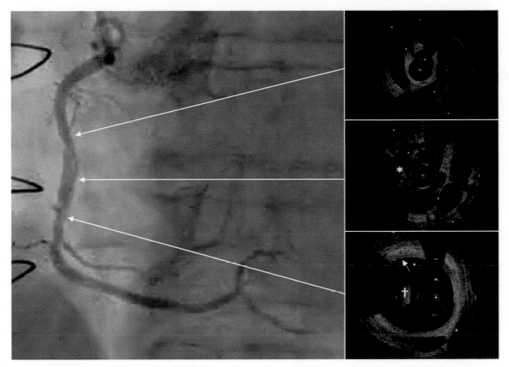

Figure 14.12 OCT images in transplant vasculopathy. *OCT*, Optical coherence tomography.

in maximal intimal thickness ≥ 0.5 mm in the left ascending anterior branch from the time of transplantation to one year after transplantation. OCT (Fig. 14.12) is not yet used for clinical decision making but is predicted to replace or supplement IVUS in some patients, especially if differentiation between donor-transmitted disease and transplant vasculopathy is important [40]. A greater understanding of CAV has emerged from studies using OCT angiography, allowing for high-resolution evaluation of the coronary artery wall structure and composition. It appears to be particularly well suited to detect very early CAV and evaluate plaque stability in these patients. More research is needed before a definite role for OCT in cardiac transplantation can be defined.

14.6.7 Clinical evidence of optical coherence tomography

The clear, detailed, and accurate information provided by OCT is easier to interpret, with a shorter learning curve than other intravascular imaging modalities. As a consequence, an elevated rate of interaction of operators in response to the data provided by the OCT has been reported.

In the prospective series by Stefano et al. [41], 100 OCT was used pre-PCI, post-PCI, or both pre- and post-PCI in 150 consecutive patients enrolled during a 2-month period aiming to assess the safety, success, and impact of FD-OCT on patient management in the cardiac catheterization laboratory. Notably, operators changed the initial angiographic-based strategy in 81.8% of the cases after performing pre-PCI OCT. The most frequent changes were in the predicted stent length (48.5%) and diameter (27.3%). Most of the changes in stent length (30.3%) were for longer stent lengths, as is frequently the case with any invasive imaging modality, which allows visualization of more diseased segments than angiography. Of note, it is important to observe that pre-PCI OCT shortened the predicted stent length in 18.2% of the cases. When OCT was used post stenting, further interventions were performed in an additional 54.8% of the treated target vessels. Post stenting, mal-apposition was detected in 39.2% of the cases (89.4% of which underwent further balloon dilatation), and stent edge dissection in 32.5% (21.1% treated with additional stents).

In the largest and more recent ILUMIEN II study [42,43], OCT and documentary FFR were performed pre- and post-PCI in 418 patients. Based on pre-PCI OCT, the initial strategy was altered in 55% of patients (57% of all stenoses). Once again, longer stents were selected (43%), but a nonnegligible proportion of lesions had their predicted stent lengths shortened (25%). After clinically successful stent implantation, post-PCI OCT and FFR were repeated. Suboptimal results as per the operator's interpretation of OCT findings were frequent (14.5% mal-apposition, 7.6% under-expansion, and 2.7% edge dissection) and prompted further optimization in 25% of patients (27% of all stenoses), by either additional balloon dilatation (81%) or placement of additional stents (12%). Interestingly, the final FFR (~ 0.89) was not significantly different with respect to the timing of OCT use to plan or optimize the PCI. Of note, in the subset of cases with paired final FFR and OCT measurements following optimization, FFR values improved from 0.86 ± 0.07 to 0.90 ± 0.10 following correction of OCT findings that were deemed unsatisfactory by the operator [42].

These reports reaffirm the importance of pre-PCI imaging for strategy planning, as demonstrated by the elevated change and refinement of the initially predicted strategy. Post-PCI OCT also offered additional opportunities for optimization of the PCI results. However, other than correcting small minimal in-stent lumen areas and regions of under-expansion (strong predictors of late stent failure), exaggerated stent mal-apposition, and extensive and deep edge dissections with lumen compromise, overreaction to other smaller abnormalities (although frequently detected by post-PCI OCT) may not be of clinical relevance.

Currently, there is a paucity of data on OCT predictors of stent failure, as well as prospectively validated protocols for stent sizing and optimization.

In the CLI-OPCI observational study, Prati et al. [44] compared the clinical outcomes of PCI guided by angiography alone with those of PCI guided by angiography plus OCT in a matched population of 670 patients (335 for each group). A pragmatic protocol was used at the involved centers to make practices uniform and enforce similar criteria for intervention when OCT use was considered to guide PCI. No quantitative criteria were proposed for stent sizing or positioning, which were left to the operator's discretion. The protocol recommended the following actions to specific OCT disclosed issues: (1) edge dissection (linear rim of tissue with a width of ≥ 200 μm and a clear separation from the vessel wall) and reference lumen narrowing (lumen area of <4.0 mm^2) required implantation of an additional stent; (2) stent under-expansion (MLA of $\leq 90\%$ of the average reference lumen area or $\geq 100\%$ of the lumen area of the smallest reference) required further dilatation with a noncompliant balloon the same diameter of the stent inflated ≥ 18 atm, or with a semicompliant balloon ≥ 0.25 mm larger than the stent inflated at ≥ 14 atm; (3) stent malapposition (strut-to-lumen distance of >200 μm) required further dilatation with a noncompliant or semicompliant balloon with a diameter ≥ 0.25 larger than that of the previously used balloon, at ≥ 14 atm; (4) thrombus required further dilatation with a noncompliant or semicompliant balloon of the same diameter as the stent at 8–16 atm for 60 seconds. Features disclosed by OCT, and not detected by angiography, represented edge dissections in 14.2%, lumen narrowing in 2.8%, stent malapposition in 29.7%, stent under-expansion in 11.4%, and intracoronary thrombus in 22.0%. These findings led to additional interventions in 34% of the cases (additional stents in 12.6% and additional balloon dilatations in 22.1%). At the end of 1 year, patients submitted to PCI with angiography plus OCT guidance experienced significantly lower rates of cardiac death (1.2% vs 4.5%, $P = .01$), cardiac death or MI (6.6% vs 13%, $P = .006$), and the composite of cardiac death, MI, and repeat revascularization (9.6% vs 14.8%, $p = .044$). These favorable clinical outcomes persisted after extensive multivariable regression analysis (OR 0.49, 95% CI 0.25–0.96, $P = .037$), propensity score–adjusted analysis with bootstrap resampling (OR 0.37, 95% CI 0.10–0.90, $P = .050$), and CoX proportional hazards analysis (hazard ratio 0.51, 95% CI 0.28–0.93, $P = .028$).

The currently ongoing DOCTORS study [15] is a prospective, randomized, multicenter, open-label clinical trial that evaluates the utility of OCT to optimize results of angioplasty of a lesion responsible for a non–ST-elevation ACS. Patients ($n = 250$) are randomized to OCT-guided PCI or angiography-guided PCI. A protocol for stent sizing and deployment is not enforced, but guidelines for procedural optimization are applied as follows: (1) additional balloon inflations should be performed in the case of stent under-expansion, defined as a minimal stent area of $\leq 80\%$ of the reference lumen area; (2) additional stent implantation should be performed to rectify incomplete lesion coverage (including edge dissection); (3) use of glycoprotein IIb/IIIa inhibitors and/or thrombus aspiration should be systematically considered in the case of thrombus presence; and (4) rotational atherectomy should be considered in the case of circumferential calcification. The primary endpoint is the functional result of PCI as assessed by FFR measured at the end of the procedure.

14.7 Conclusion

OCT is an imaging tool that provides real-time intravascular data in high resolution. It gives intricate details of superficial intracoronary structures including type and nature of plaques and position of stents. In patients with borderline coronary lesions, OCT helps delineating treatment strategies where angiographic dilemma of whether to stent the lesion or not exists. With rapidly evolving technology and advent of three-dimensional imaging, OCT has a potential of regular and guideline-directed usage in coronary interventions. Especially while dealing with complex lesions, stent thrombosis, and borderline coronary lesions.

References

[1] Colombo A, Hall P, Nakamura S, Almagor Y, Maiello L, Martini G, et al. Intracoronary stenting without anticoagulation accomplished with intravascular ultrasound guidance. Circulation. 1995; 91(6):1676−88.

[2] Huang D, Swanson EA, Lin CP, Schuman JS, Stinson WG, Chang W, et al. Optical coherence tomography. Science 1991;254(5035):1178−81.

[3] Yun S, Tearney G, Bouma B, Park B, de Boer J. High-speed spectral-domain optical coherence tomography at 1.3 mum wavelength. Opt Express 2003;11(26):3598−604.

[4] Chinn SR, Swanson EA, Fujimoto JG. Optical coherence tomography using a frequency-tunable optical source. Opt Lett 1997;22(5):340−2.

[5] Tearney GJ, Waxman S, Shishkov M, Vakoc BJ, Suter MJ, Freilich MI, et al. Three-dimensional coronary artery microscopy by intracoronary optical frequency domain imaging. JACC Cardiovasc Imaging 2008;1(6):752−61.

[6] Imola F, Mallus MT, Ramazzotti V, Manzoli A, Pappalardo A, Di Giorgio A, et al. Safety and feasibility of frequency domain optical coherence tomography to guide decision making in percutaneous coronary intervention. EuroIntervention J Eur Collab Work Group Interv Cardiol Eur Soc Cardiol 2010;6(5):575−81.

[7] Kawasaki M, Bouma BE, Bressner J, Houser SL, Nadkarni SK, MacNeill BD, et al. Diagnostic accuracy of optical coherence tomography and integrated backscatter intravascular ultrasound images for tissue characterization of human coronary plaques. J Am Coll Cardiol 2006; 48(1):81−8.

[8] Kume T, Akasaka T, Kawamoto T, Watanabe N, Toyota E, Neishi Y, et al. Assessment of coronary intima−media thickness by optical coherence tomography: comparison with intravascular ultrasound. Circ J J Jpn Circ Soc 2005;69(8):903−7.

[9] Yabushita H, Bouma BE, Houser SL, Aretz HT, Jang I-K, Schlendorf KH, et al. Characterization of human atherosclerosis by optical coherence tomography. Circulation. 2002;106(13):1640−5.

[10] Gonzalo N, Tearney GJ, Serruys PW, van Soest G, Okamura T, García-García HM, et al. Second-generation optical coherence tomography in clinical practice. High-speed data acquisition is highly reproducible in patients undergoing percutaneous coronary intervention. Rev Esp Cardiol 2010;63 (8):893−903.

[11] Kume T, Okura H, Yamada R, Kawamoto T, Watanabe N, Neishi Y, et al. Frequency and spatial distribution of thin-cap fibroatheroma assessed by 3-vessel intravascular ultrasound and optical coherence tomography: an ex vivo validation and an initial in vivo feasibility study. Circ J J Jpn Circ Soc 2009;73(6):1086−91.

[12] Kume T, Akasaka T, Kawamoto T, Ogasawara Y, Watanabe N, Toyota E, et al. Assessment of coronary arterial thrombus by optical coherence tomography. Am J Cardiol 2006;97 (12):1713−17.

[13] Cilingiroglu M, Oh JH, Sugunan B, Kemp NJ, Kim J, Lee S, et al. Detection of vulnerable plaque in a murine model of atherosclerosis with optical coherence tomography. Catheter Cardiovasc Interv J Soc Card Angiogr Interv 2006;67(6):915—23.

[14] Tanaka A, Imanishi T, Kitabata H, Kubo T, Takarada S, Kataiwa H, et al. Distribution and frequency of thin-capped fibroatheromas and ruptured plaques in the entire culprit coronary artery in patients with acute coronary syndrome as determined by optical coherence tomography. Am J Cardiol 2008;102(8):975—9.

[15] Chia S, Raffel OC, Takano M, Tearney GJ, Bouma BE, Jang I-K. Association of statin therapy with reduced coronary plaque rupture: an optical coherence tomography study. Coron Artery Dis 2008;19(4):237—42.

[16] Tearney GJ, Yabushita H, Houser SL, Aretz HT, Jang I-K, Schlendorf KH, et al. Quantification of macrophage content in atherosclerotic plaques by optical coherence tomography. Circulation 2003;107(1):113—19.

[17] Regar E, van Beusekom HMM, van der Giessen WJ, Serruys PW. Images in cardiovascular medicine. Optical coherence tomography findings at 5-year follow-up after coronary stent implantation. Circulation 2005;112(23):e345—6.

[18] Ali ZA, Maehara A, Généreux P, Shlofmitz RA, Fabbiocchi F, Nazif TM, et al. Optical coherence tomography compared with intravascular ultrasound and with angiography to guide coronary stent implantation (ILUMIEN III: OPTIMIZE PCI): a randomised controlled trial. Lancet Lond Engl 2016;388(10060):2618—28.

[19] Van de Werf F, Bax J, Betriu A, Blomstrom-Lundqvist C, Crea F, Falk V, et al. Management of acute myocardial infarction in patients presenting with persistent ST-segment elevation: the Task Force on the Management of ST-Segment Elevation Acute Myocardial Infarction of the European Society of Cardiology. Eur Heart J 2008;29(23):2909—45.

[20] Reith S, Battermann S, Jaskolka A, Lehmacher W, Hoffmann R, Marx N, et al. Relationship between optical coherence tomography derived intraluminal and intramural criteria and haemodynamic relevance as determined by fractional flow reserve in intermediate coronary stenoses of patients with type 2 diabetes. Heart Br Card Soc 2013;99(10):700—7.

[21] Reith S, Battermann S, Hellmich M, Marx N, Burgmaier M. Correlation between optical coherence tomography-derived intraluminal parameters and fractional flow reserve measurements in intermediate grade coronary lesions: a comparison between diabetic and non-diabetic patients. Clin Res Cardiol J Ger Card Soc 2015;104(1):59—70.

[22] Pyxaras SA, Tu S, Barbato E, Barbati G, Di Serafino L, De, et al. Quantitative angiography and optical coherence tomography for the functional assessment of nonobstructive coronary stenoses: comparison with fractional flow reserve. Am Heart J 2013;166(6).1010—18 e1.

[23] Shiono Y, Kitabata H, Kubo T, Masuno T, Ohta S, Ozaki Y, et al. Optical coherence tomography-derived anatomical criteria for functionally significant coronary stenosis assessed by fractional flow reserve. Circ J J Jpn Circ Soc 2012;76(9):2218—25.

[24] Pawlowski T, Prati F, Kulawik T, Ficarra E, Bil J, Gil R. Optical coherence tomography criteria for defining functional severity of intermediate lesions: a comparative study with FFR. Int J Cardiovasc Imaging 2013;29(8):1685—91.

[25] MacNeill BD, Jang I-K, Bouma BE, Iftimia N, Takano M, Yabushita H, et al. Focal and multifocal plaque macrophage distributions in patients with acute and stable presentations of coronary artery disease. J Am Coll Cardiol 2004;44(5):972—9.

[26] Jang I-K, Tearney GJ, MacNeill B, Takano M, Moselewski F, Iftima N, et al. In vivo characterization of coronary atherosclerotic plaque by use of optical coherence tomography. Circulation 2005;111(12):1551—5.

[27] Ino Y, Kubo T, Tanaka A, Kuroi A, Tsujioka H, Ikejima H, et al. Difference of culprit lesion morphologies between ST-segment elevation myocardial infarction and non-ST-segment elevation acute coronary syndrome: an optical coherence tomography study. JACC Cardiovasc Interv 2011; 4(1):76—82.

[28] Tanaka A, Imanishi T, Kitabata H, Kubo T, Takarada S, Tanimoto T, et al. Lipid-rich plaque and myocardial perfusion after successful stenting in patients with non-ST-segment elevation

acute coronary syndrome: an optical coherence tomography study. Eur Heart J 2009; 30(11):1348−55.

[29] Ozaki Y, Tanaka A, Tanimoto T, Kitabata H, Kashiwagi M, Kubo T, et al. Thin-cap fibroatheroma as high-risk plaque for microvascular obstruction in patients with acute coronary syndrome. Circ Cardiovasc Imaging 2011;4(6):620−7.

[30] Porto I, Di Vito L, Burzotta F, Niccoli G, Trani C, Leone AM, et al. Predictors of periprocedural (type IVa) myocardial infarction, as assessed by frequency-domain optical coherence tomography. Circ Cardiovasc Interv 2012;5(1):89−96 S1−6.

[31] Lee T, Yonetsu T, Koura K, Hishikari K, Murai T, Iwai T, et al. Impact of coronary plaque morphology assessed by optical coherence tomography on cardiac troponin elevation in patients with elective stent implantation. Circ Cardiovasc Interv 2011;4(4):378−86.

[32] Chamié D, Bezerra HG, Attizzani GF, Yamamoto H, Kanaya T, Stefano GT, et al. Incidence, predictors, morphological characteristics, and clinical outcomes of stent edge dissections detected by optical coherence tomography. JACC Cardiovasc Interv 2013;6(8):800−13.

[33] G N, G S, F C. Acute myocardial infarction with no obstructive coronary atherosclerosis: mechanisms and management. Eur Heart J 2015;36(8):475−81. Available from: https://pubmed.ncbi.nlm.nih.gov/25526726/.

[34] Saw J, Aymong E, Sedlak T, Buller CE, Starovoytov A, Ricci D, et al. Spontaneous coronary artery dissection: association with predisposing arteriopathies and precipitating stressors and cardiovascular outcomes. Circ Cardiovasc Interv 2014;7(5):645−55.

[35] Saw J, Humphries K, Aymong E, Sedlak T, Prakash R, Starovoytov A, et al. Spontaneous coronary artery dissection: clinical outcomes and risk of recurrence. J Am Coll Cardiol 2017; 70(9):1148−58.

[36] Gao SZ, Alderman EL, Schroeder JS, Hunt SA, Wiederhold V, Stinson EB. Progressive coronary luminal narrowing after cardiac transplantation. Circulation 1990;82(5 Suppl):IV269−75.

[37] Kofoed KF, Czernin J, Johnson J, Kobashigawa J, Phelps ME, Laks H, et al. Effects of cardiac allograft vasculopathy on myocardial blood flow, vasodilatory capacity, and coronary vasomotion. Circulation. 1997;95(3):600−6.

[38] Uretsky BF, Murali S, Reddy PS, Rabin B, Lee A, Griffith BP, et al. Development of coronary artery disease in cardiac transplant patients receiving immunosuppressive therapy with cyclosporine and prednisone. Circulation 1987;76(4):827−34.

[39] Mehra MR, Crespo-Leiro MG, Dipchand A, Ensminger SM, Hiemann NE, Kobashigawa JA, et al. International Society for Heart and Lung Transplantation working formulation of a standardized nomenclature for cardiac allograft vasculopathy-2010. J Heart Lung Transpl Off Publ Int Soc Heart Transpl 2010;29(7):717−27.

[40] Shan P, Dong L, Maehara A, Nazif TM, Ali ZA, Rabbani LE, et al. Comparison between cardiac allograft vasculopathy and native coronary atherosclerosis by optical coherence tomography. Am J Cardiol 2016;117(8):1361−8.

[41] Stefano GT, Bezerra HG, Mehanna E, Yamamoto H, Fujino Y, Wang W, et al. Unrestricted utilization of frequency domain optical coherence tomography in coronary interventions. Int J Cardiovasc Imaging 2013;29(4):741−52.

[42] Wijns W, Shite J, Jones MR, Lee SWL, Price MJ, Fabbiocchi F, et al. Optical coherence tomography imaging during percutaneous coronary intervention impacts physician decision-making: ILUMIEN I study. Eur Heart J 2015;36(47):3346−55.

[43] Maehara A, Ben-Yehuda O, Ali Z, Wijns W, Bezerra HG, Shite J, et al. Comparison of stent expansion guided by optical coherence tomography vs intravascular ultrasound: the ILUMIEN II study (observational study of optical coherence tomography [OCT] in patients undergoing fractional flow reserve [FFR] and percutaneous coronary intervention). JACC Cardiovasc Interv 2015; 8(13):1704−14.

[44] Prati F, Di Vito L, Biondi-Zoccai G, Occhipinti M, La Manna A, Tamburino C, et al. Angiography alone vs angiography plus optical coherence tomography to guide decision-making

during percutaneous coronary intervention: the Centro per la Lotta contro l'Infarto-Optimisation of Percutaneous Coronary Intervention (CLI-OPCI) study. EuroIntervention J Eur Collab Work Group Interv Cardiol Eur Soc Cardiol 2012;8(7):823—9.

[45] Meneveau N, Ecarnot F, Souteyrand G, Motreff P, Caussin C, Van Belle E, Ohlmann P, Morel O, Grentzinger A, Angioi M, Chopard R, Schiele F. Does optical coherence tomography optimize results of stenting? Rationale and study design Am Heart J 2014;168(2):175—81e1-2. Available from: https://pubmed.ncbi.nlm.nih.gov/25066556/.

Index

Note: Page numbers followed by "*f*" and "*t*" refer to figures and tables, respectively.

Printed in the United States
by Baker & Taylor Publisher Services